"WE ARE HERE"

"WE ARE HERE"

New Approaches to Jewish Displaced Persons in Postwar Germany

---

Edited by Avinoam J. Patt and Michael Berkowitz

Wayne State University Press Detroit

© 2010 by Wayne State University Press, Detroit, Michigan 48201. All rights reserved. No part of this book may be reproduced without formal permission. Manufactured in the United States of America.

14 13 12 11 10   5 4 3 2 1

Library of Congress Cataloging-in-Publication Data

We are here : new approaches to Jewish displaced persons in postwar Germany / edited by Avinoam J. Patt and Michael Berkowitz.
p. cm.
Includes bibliographical references and index.
ISBN 978-0-8143-3350-1 (pbk. : alk. paper)
 1. Jews—Germany—History—1945–1990. 2. Holocaust survivors—Germany—History—20th century. 3. Holocaust survivors—Germany—Social conditions—20th century 4. Jewish refugees—Germany—History—20th century. 5. Germany—Ethnic relations—History—20th century.
I. Patt, Avinoam J. II. Berkowitz, Michael.
DS134.26.W4 2010
940.53'1814—dc22
2009031168

The opinions expressed in this book and the context in which images provided by the United States Holocaust Memorial Museum (USHMM) are used do not necessarily reflect the views or policy of, nor imply approval or endorsement by, the USHMM.

Typeset by Maya Rhodes
Composed in Scala and Meta

In honor and memory of John D. Klier (1946–2007),
esteemed colleague and dear friend

In honor and memory of Officer Stephen Tyrone Johns (1969–2009),
killed on duty at the United States Holocaust Memorial Museum

CONTENTS

Acknowledgments

This book originated with the thought that an intensive, collaborative effort should be undertaken to nurture and coordinate the burgeoning scholarship on the immediate post–World War II period in Europe, centering on the history of Jewish displaced persons (DPs). One of the major fruits of this initiative was a two-week workshop hosted in July 2005 by the Center for Advanced Holocaust Studies of the United States Holocaust Memorial Museum (USHMM). The chapters in this volume largely evolved from that stimulating forum, for which critical support was provided by our colleagues Paul Shapiro, Robert Ehrenreich, Ann Millin, Suzanne Brown-Fleming, Jürgen Matthaus, Lisa Yavnai, and Martin Dean, as well as many others on the dedicated staff of CAHS and the USHMM. We are grateful for their dedication and advice. We also would like to thank David Weinberg, an original participant in the workshop, for his insightful contributions and assistance in the publication of this volume.

The archival staffs of numerous institutions in the United States, Europe, and Israel assisted the authors of these contributions. Among the treasures utilized in the writing of these articles are materials found in the archives of the USHMM in Washington, DC; the YIVO Institute for Jewish Research Archives and the American Jewish Joint Distribution Committee Archives in New York City; the CDJC Archives in Paris; the Yad Vashem Archives in Jerusalem, as well as the Haganah Archives, the Central Zionist Archives, and the archives of Beit Lochamei HaGetaot in Israel; and various other archives around the world. Warm thanks are due to Judith Cohen, Caroline Waddell, and Michlean Amir for research assistance in the archives and photo archives of the USHMM. We are especially grateful to the phenomenal staff at Wayne State University Press, including Kathy Wildfong, Carrie Downes Teefey, Maya Rhodes, and M. Yvonne Ramsey. And of course, to our friends and colleagues at the University of Hartford and University College London—our most sincere appreciation.

A number of individuals who personally experienced the events described in these chapters have generously shared memories of their lives in Europe, America, and Israel after the Holocaust. To them—as well as all of the members of the Surviving Remnant discussed in this volume—we extend our thanks and appreciation. Their resilience and dedication in reconstructing their lives in the wake of tragedy is truly a testament to the strength of the human spirit.

To our wives, Ivy Patt and Debby Rozansky: your love and support continue to make our research and writing possible.

And to our children, Maya Rose and Alexander Simon Patt, and Rachel and Stephen Berkowitz: You serve as a constant reminder of the importance of learning from the past to teach for the future.

Acknowledgments

INTRODUCTION

Avinoam J. Patt and Michael Berkowitz

> The Jews suddenly faced themselves. Where now? Where to? They
> saw that they were different from all the other inmates of the camp.
> For them things were not so simple. To go back to Poland? To Hun-
> gary? To streets empty of Jews, towns empty of Jews, a world wit-
> hout Jews? To wander in those lands, lonely, homeless, always with
> the tragedy before one's eyes . . . and to meet, again, a former Gentile
> neighbor who would open his eyes wide and smile, remarking with
> double meaning, "What! Yankel! You're still alive!" Yes, the Jews faced
> themselves. Was our tragedy only beginning?
>
> —Hayim-Meir Gottlieb, from the diary of Kibbutz Buchenwald

In the first days and weeks following the liberation of Germany by the
Allied forces, the country was inundated with the liberated captives of
the Nazi regime who sought to make sense of the new situation, for
which they had long hoped. With the conclusion of the war on May
8, 1945, up to ten million forced laborers, prisoners of war, and other
displaced persons (DPs) flooded the roads of Germany in the desire to
return home. While most refugees made the decision to return home
with ease, the fifty thousand or so Jewish DPs did not face such a clear
decision. Unsure of what awaited them in their former communities
and often fairly certain that their families had been destroyed during
the war, those who decided to stay in a DP camp also had to face the
fact that this meant continuing to live with collaborators who also refused to return home. As a number of Jewish survivors of Buchenwald
wrote soon after liberation, in the wake of tremendous destruction,
the future was uncertain. And yet despite this disorder and confusion,
the surviving Jewish population quickly organized itself, asserting its
presence, vitality, and resilience.

Major Jewish DP Camps and Assembly Centers, 1945–46

Principal Source: Summary of DP Population: UNRRA Assembly
Centers in United States Zone (Washington, D.C.: United Nations
Relief and Rehabilitation Administration, 1946)

0   100
MILES

ZONES OF OCCUPATION

British   Soviet
French   American

Map courtesy of *Life Reborn: Jewish Displaced Persons 1945–1951,* Conference Proceedings,
Washington, DC, January 14–17, 2000 (Menachem Z. Rosensaft, 2001), 146.

By the spring of 1947, less than two years after Nazi Germany's defeat, the surviving Jewish population in continental Europe numbered some 250,000 in the DP camps of Germany, Italy, and Austria. Furthermore, Jewish refugees continued to return to Poland from the far reaches of the Soviet Union following the repatriation agreement of 1946. The future of the surviving Jewish population was by no means secure, however, and the creation of the State of Israel was far from guaranteed. Many Jews were uncertain as to where they would make their future lives, be it in their former homes in Eastern, Western, or Central Europe or in Palestine, the Americas, or Australia. For this reason, the supposedly transitional space created for the stateless individuals in the recently defeated Reich became an important location of political, cultural, social, and biological rebirth but one tempered by the complications of overcoming recent trauma on both the individual level and the collective level.

The chapters in this volume seek to illuminate facets of this rich history and reflect on questions such as what were the first reactions of survivors to liberation? To search for lost family? To document the past? To build new families? To mourn and memorialize the dead? How might the DPs' initial responses to these questions have changed over time? "Mir zaynen doh," the stark assertion "We are here" from Hirsch Glik's partisan theme, appears frequently in the literature by and about the Jewish DPs living in Europe after the Holocaust.[1] But what exactly did "We are here" signify in the context of postwar Germany and Europe generally? Who was included within this "we"? How did the Jewish DPs understand the fact that "here" referred mainly to Germany, the land of the murderers?

Over the last decade scholarly and commemorative meetings as well as a provocative vein of historiography on Jewish DPs and Jews in postwar Europe generally have shed light on the remarkable accomplishments of the She'erit Hapletah (Surviving Remnant) in the wake of the Holocaust.[2] Popular and historical attention has focused as well on the roles of numerous outside groups who encountered and were themselves affected by the Jewish DPs. A few of the contributors to the present volume have in fact been among the chief progenitors of these trends. Given the increased interest, significant studies, and voluminous source material recently made accessible, it is an opportune moment to present a diverse selection of scholarship on this crucial period that often has been treated as merely an interregnum between the Holocaust and the creation of the State of Israel. Furthermore, there is a growing desire on the part of some Jews born in DP camps who have little or no memory of these places to learn about the experience of their parents and their respective milieu. For scholars confronting the postwar period in general and the Jewish DPs in particular, there is no shortage of documentation on the subject. Jewish DPs constituted a particularly active community that generated copious historical, sociological, cultural, visual, musical, and literary records of their experiences. Out of these sources and those emanating from agencies and individuals who worked with and observed the DPs have emerged contradictory depictions and even stereotypes of the DPs. They have been cast as lazy, broken, dispirited, and demoralized, often occupied in nefarious activities and beyond hope of rehabilitation, and in contrast they have been rendered as remarkably creative, resilient, enthusiastic, politically savvy, and well aware of their significance on the postwar stage.[3] Thus, in this volume we are responding to a need to coordinate work on the DP experience that utilizes disparate sources and in so doing attempt to reconcile, but not necessarily harmonize, these contradictory impressions and emerge with a more complete and nuanced interpretation of the DPs' experiences.

A number of the contributions in this volume challenge prior assumptions about the Jewish DPs and Holocaust survivors generally, including the supposedly unified background of the DP population, the notion of a general reluctance to confront the past, the idea of Zionism as an inevitable success after the war, and the suggestion that Jews, despite their presence in Germany, strenuously avoided contact with Germans. Far from constituting a monolithic whole as might seem to derive from a shared identity implied in the term "She'erit Hapletah," the DPs were composed of diverse groups with disparate wartime experiences. This book highlights the differences among the DP population as well as the myriad activities that comprised a vibrant Jewish DP society overall. The contributions by Laura Jockusch on Jewish historical commissions in Europe, Tamar Lewinsky on the Yiddish journalism and literature of the DP population, Shirli Gilbert on the music performed and produced among the DPs, and Boaz Cohen concerning early efforts to collect and analyze children's testimony, along with complementary scholarship by themselves and others, show evidence of the silence that never was: the fact that elements of the surviving population were prepared to confront their wartime trauma while focusing on the future in the immediate aftermath of the Holocaust. Avinoam Patt, focusing on the organizational activity for youths, demonstrates that the ardent Zionism of the Jewish DPs was not merely an automatic reaction to the experience of the Holocaust; it filled a number of key functions for various groups in postwar Europe that enabled it to flourish. Even so, the overwhelming Zionist enthusiasm of the DPs did not mean that the entire population made it to the shores of Palestine or even aspired to do so. Beth Cohen's

Avinoam J. Patt and Michael Berkowitz

analysis of Holocaust survivors from 1946 to 1954 highlights the experiences of the large number of DPs who came to the United States. While entering and acclimating to the United States was a success story for many, indicating both the degree to which they were accepted in their new homes and the tremendous effort and goodwill they dedicated to reestablishing themselves, there were others for whom the transition to a better life was burdened by difficulties and unresolved tensions. Another aspect of the history of Jewish DPs that is often lost in mythologized retellings is that on the most basic level thousands of Jews migrated to Germany, especially the American zone in Bavaria, and even remained there for periods of weeks, months, and even years and that this time spent in the ruins of the Third Reich may have been extremely significant, conceived from numerous vantage points.[4] Furthermore, as Atina Grossmann relates in this book and elsewhere, Jews did have numerous encounters with Germans, forming relations that were loaded with symbolic meaning and that met everyday needs.

Taken as a whole, a number of common themes emerge in this collective work. These unite many of the questions with which these scholars have struggled, and the ways in which the chapters connect to the larger postwar context and historiographic debates about the Holocaust, World War II, the establishment of the State of Israel, postwar European displacement, and reconstruction. We have attempted to be sensitive to the relationship between the scholarly literature (and other retrospective analyses of the DPs) and the primary sources upon which these works have been based. This volume, then, arises from the self-conscious use of novel sources as well as fresh approaches to previously discussed material.

The first of these themes is the diversity of the Jewish DPs in terms of their lives before 1945 as well as their postwar experiences. The population that came to be known as the She'erit Hapletah might have survived World War II in ghettos or concentration camps, by hiding with non-Jews or the partisans in forests, or, most importantly for a large percentage of those who would come to Germany in 1946–47, by being in the Soviet Union. The fate of deported or evacuated Jews in the Soviet Union defies generalization as well. Hagit Lavsky's examination of DPs in the British zone of occupation reveals both similarities and differences compared with the much larger number who either found themselves in or migrated into the American zone. Laura Hilton's study of the DP communities of Frankfurt and the Zeilsheim camp is distinctive in setting these cases in a comparative framework along with non-Jewish Polish, Baltic, Ukrainian, and Russian DPs. The chapters by Atina Grossmann, recounting Jewish German social relations in general, and Suzanne Brown-Fleming and Michael

Berkowitz, about the lingering stigma of criminality attached to Jews, deal particularly with Jewish DPs' encounter with surrounding populations in what had been the very crucible of National Socialism. In fact, most Jews and Germans got along decently, but the ways that both parties thought about their erstwhile tormentors or victims were manifested at times as distrust, hostility, and open conflict.

Another significant question involves identity and self-identification. Jews after the war were able to represent themselves in numerous ways and present multiple identities to themselves and the outside world. In this way some DPs could be ardently Zionist while intending to live in a place other than Palestine/Israel. A great many, in fact, assumed a multiplicity of roles. In a sense, a division of labor emerged in the DP camps that allowed Jews to do the work of documenting the recent past, to create a DP Yiddish literature, to farm German soil on kibbutzim to prepare for a future in Palestine, to have babies, to study the Talmud and preserve religious observance, to write and make music, to work the black market, or to participate in an active and contentious internal political life, in other words, to create order and restore a sort of normality. Perhaps this is most apparent in Margarete Myers Feinstein's survey of rites surrounding mourning, marriage, and birth in the German DP camps, where the domains of these typically distinct realms were often intermingled, as there could scarcely be a birth that did not invoke the memory of recently murdered loved ones or marriages that could only be consecrated amid the memory of all those who could not share in the *simcha* (festive or joyous occasion). This diversity of means of affirming roles and histories served to create a community out of chaotic conditions and despair and allowed DPs to strike a balance between individual and collective needs.

Jewish DPs articulated a rhetoric of responsibility and obligation to the past and to the Jewish future, which was marshaled by forces among as well as outside of the DP communities in order to encourage DPs to perform various tasks. For example, DPs attached special significance to youths and babies as exemplified in film and photo images as well as in written, oral, and visual testimonies. At the same time, the contradictory obligations of aliyah and creating new families pulled young people in different directions. The particular place they inhabited and their sense of time also weighed heavily on the Jewish DPs living in Germany. The collective understanding that their stay in Germany was temporary made certain forms of behavior possible, whether as symbolic or even actual revenge or in the more mundane tasks of everyday life that required interactions with Germans. Much of the current historiographic debate over the origins of DP Zionist enthusiasm revolves around another major theme: the notion of agency. A number of the chapters in the present volume also seek to address to what extent the Jewish DPs, in their interactions with many other groups including the U.S. Army, United Nations Relief and Rehabilitation Administration (UNRRA), the American Jewish Joint Distribution Committee (JDC), emissaries from Palestine, and the surrounding German population, acted on their own volition as opposed to fulfilling objectives of greater powers. Studies using sources created by the DPs, which demonstrate a high degree of DP autonomy, often challenge depictions of DPs as tools and subjects of outside powers in much of the secondary literature.

The statelessness of the DPs must be understood on several levels. The category of statelessness was important to the DPs, to the U.S. and British administrations, and to UNRRA representatives. Zionism was able to fill a perceived gap in national identity by providing notions of citizenship for DPs themselves and to present Zionism to the international community as the de facto nationality of stateless Jews. Statelessness as well as numerous other aspects of the Jewish DPs experience and interpretations thereof are relevant to current discussions on human rights, recovery from trauma, the situation of refugees, the challenge of rebuilding community after devastation, and the often dueling imperatives of remembering the past while planning for the future and coping with the present.

Any study of Jewish DPs must examine continuities and discontinuities with the prewar and wartime experiences of the survivors. Leading historians of the Holocaust, such as Gerhard Weinberg, Saul Friedlaender, Christopher Browning, and Omer Bartov, have encouraged fellow scholars to adopt perspectives that acknowledge and fully engage the context of World War II. As evinced by the work of these historians and others, the yield from this advice has been penetrating. Likewise, we have attempted to operate from a larger methodological concern: to attempt to interpret and illuminate the lives of Jewish DPs by consistently exploring the extent to which their existence in post-Holocaust Germany—albeit distinctive and often bizarre—was comparable to their lives before as well as during World War II. Just as it is imperative to understand the pre-Holocaust spectrum of Jewish politics in order to appreciate Jewish political behavior in settings such as ghettos, it is crucial, we maintain, to see the Jewish DPs as part of a continuum of modern Jewish history. To be sure, it is crucial to avoid back shadowing from a Zionist vantage point, yet Jewish history up to 1945 need not be given short shrift. The lives of Jewish DPs in Germany were indeed an unmistakable break from what had occurred both before and after the war. Yet in reconstructing and further analyzing their lives, it remains important—as so many of the DPs themselves wished—to restore them to Jewish and world history not simply as a postscript to the Holocaust or as a prelude to the establishment of the state of Israel but as creators of a significant period of history in their own right.

This volume is organized around the themes of the contributions, which center on the crucial components of the social history of the Jewish DPs. However, as Atina Grossmann suggests in her chapter, despite an overwhelming amount of source material to document the experiences of DPs, the writing of this history has only just begun following a disproportionate focus on the political and diplomatic history of the postwar period. The vast amount of often contradictory sources, written in a transitional time and space about a highly mobile and fluid population, makes the writing of this history quite complicated but essential. Several of the contributions in the volume address the issue of transition as the surviving population sought to memorialize the dead and document the past while planning for the future. As Laura Jockusch notes, Jews throughout Europe formed historical commissions soon after liberation, often drawing on both prewar and wartime documentation projects. While some observers fretted that DPs would become obsessed with their past, it became clear that the documentation projects relied on a number of dedicated amateur historians who worked to ensure that DPs would "Remember what Amalek" had done to them. The initiators of the documentation projects wished to preserve the voices of those who had suffered. Boaz Cohen details the focus on the children, a specific portion of the surviving population. As he suggests, however, Israel Kaplan's commitment to publishing the experiences of the children in the journal *Fun Letsten Hurbn* highlighted the survivors' focus on the future of the Jewish people and importantly on his own personal relationship with his son.

As survivors sought to come to terms with the immediate past they also faced the question of where to continue their lives, which for most would not be the accursed soil of Germany. While much has been written on the Zionist enthusiasm of the surviving population, Avinoam Patt notes the importance of paying attention to the youthful nature of the surviving population and the success of the Zionist youth movements in addressing the most pressing practical needs of youths after the Holocaust. By providing warmth, camaraderie, and a sense of home that was lost in the war, the kibbutzim appealed to young survivors and instilled an ardent Zionist belief that would indeed play a crucial role in the ultimate creation of the State of Israel.

As Beth Cohen notes, however, Zionist enthusiasm among the DPs was perhaps contingent upon the availability of other immigration options. A sizable portion of the surviving population did eventually make its way to the United States, where they faced a difficult adjustment to life in the so-called Goldene Medinah. While contemporary reports depicted a triumphant arrival in America, DPs often were disappointed and frustrated with their American coreligionists who were reluctant to acknowledge what they had just experienced.

Nonetheless, this volume also points to the importance of the months and years that DPs were indeed forced to spend in Germany. In rebuilding lives in this transitional space, survivors encountered continued anti-Semitism, administration authorities often more concerned with the reconstruction of Germany and the emergent Cold War, and the frustrations of a traumatic past, an uncertain future, and a demoralizing present. Michael Berkowitz and Suzanne Brown-Fleming detail the pervasive nature of German stereotypes of Jewish DPs as morally lax, natural criminals and black marketers, leftist agitators, and communists. As Berkowitz and Brown-Fleming suggest, attention to the topic is especially important in the context of any study on black market activity, postwar reconstruction, and the triangle of German-Allied-Jewish relations in postwar Germany. Within this context as well, Laura Hilton examines the complexities of identity formation among Jews in the immediate postwar period with a focus on the Jewish community of Frankfurt and the DP camp of Zeilsheim. She details living conditions, the creation of community organizations, and the interaction among Jewish DPs, Germans, occupation forces, UNRRA, and voluntary agency workers in both the relative sanctuary of the DP camp and within Frankfurt in the crucial six-month period after liberation. Hagit Lavsky also notes an important but often overlooked site in postwar Germany, the British zone of occupation and the largest DP camp in postwar Germany, Bergen-Belsen. The survivors there played a crucial role in the struggle against the British blockade of Palestine while working to create an active political, social, and cultural life in the camp.

The final three chapters in the volume pay attention to central components of the renascent DP society: religion, music, and literature. Margarete Myers Feinstein notes that while much has been written about theological responses to the Holocaust, little research has focused on the role of religion among the wider Jewish DP community. The study of religious practices among the DPs can in turn illuminate how survivors mourned and commemorated their dead while sanctifying marriages and births in the continuation of life and tradition. Shirli Gilbert turns to another overlooked chapter of the postwar period, the diverse musical life that thrived among Jewish DPs. As she suggests, music provides a lens for examining how surviving victims shaped their understanding of what had happened to them and their relationship to the individual and collective future. Last but certainly not least, Tamar Lewinsky examines the emergence of a multifaceted Yiddish literary scene in postwar Germany that, she argues, effectively replaced the prewar East European context and created a new cultural landscape. Like the survivors around them, the writers reflected their need to continue the life of a destroyed world while creating a new one in the midst of their tenuous present.

NOTES

1. Hirsch Glik's partisan anthem "Zog nit keyn mol" (Never Say), arguably the best known of all Holocaust songs, was composed in the forests of Lithuania and became a symbol of Jewish resistance against the Nazi persecution during the Holocaust.
2. In 1985 Yad Vashem convened the first scholarly conference dedicated to the topic of the She'erit Hapletah, the proceedings of which were published in Yisrael Gutman and Avital Saf, eds., *She'erit Hapletah, 1944–1948: Rehabilitation and Political Struggle* (Jerusalem: Yad Vashem, 1990). In January 2000 the United States Holocaust Memorial Museum organized and hosted "Life Reborn: Jewish Displaced Persons, 1945–1951," a conference that brought together scholars, survivors, and participants involved in the administration and operation of the DP camps.
3. The historiography has also presented these divergent depictions of the DPs, often reflecting the perspectives of the available source material. Contemporaneous depictions written by those working with the DPs, including JDC member Leo Schwarz, *The Redeemers: A Saga of the Years 1945–1952* (New York: Farrar, Straus and Young, 1953), and *The Root and the Bough: The Epic of an Enduring People* (New York: Rinehart, 1949), and President Dwight Eisenhower's adviser on Jewish affairs Rabbi Judah Nadich, *Eisenhower and the Jews* (New York: Twayne, 1953), tended to present triumphal presentations of the DPs as overcoming numerous obstacles to rebuild their lives but dependent nonetheless on the assistance of outsiders to do so. Yehuda Bauer's *Flight and Rescue: Bricha* (New York: Random House, 1970), a study on the Bricha, was among the first works to treat the postwar period as a distinct subject of inquiry independent of the study of the Holocaust and sought to account for the role of Holocaust survivors in the formation of the postwar movement of departure from Poland. Studies of the Bricha (including memoirs written by Bricha activists such as Shlomo Kless and Efrayim Dekel) have often sought to assess, either explicitly or implicitly, the connec-

Avinoam J. Patt and Michael Berkowitz

tions between the aftermath of the Holocaust and the rise of Israel. And nowhere do these contradictory depictions emerge more clearly than in the debate over the role of Holocaust survivors in the creation of the State of Israel. Many of the sources created by Zionist emissaries from Palestine reflected a view of survivors based on assessments of their ability to help create a Jewish state. See, for example, Zeev Tzahor, "Holocaust Survivors as a Political Factor," *Middle Eastern Studies* 24, no. 4 (1988): 432–44, or the debate between Yechiam Weitz, "Sheelat HaPlitim HaYehudim BaMediniut HaTzionit," and Hagit Lavsky, "Sheerit HaPletah veHakamat HaMedinah: Hizdamnut asher Nutzlah," *Cathedra* 55 (1990): 162–74. See also Dalia Ofer, "The Dilemma of Rescue and Redemption: Mass Immigration to Israel in the First Year of Statehood," *YIVO Annual* 20 (1991): 185–210. Hanna Yablonka also addresses the role of Holocaust survivors in the conscription program in Europe and its impact on the Israeli War of Independence in *Achim Zarim: Nitzulei HaShoah BeMedinat Yisrael, 1948–1952 (Foreign Brethren: Holocaust Survivors in Israel, 1948–1952)* (Jerusalem: Yad Yitzchak ben Tzvi, 1994). Yehoyakim Cochavi, *Shoresh le-'Akurim: Tnu' ot ha-No'ar be-Mahanot ha-'Akurim be-Germanyah, 1945–1949* (Giv'at Havivah: Yad Ya'ari, 1999), examines the development of youth movements in the DP camps in Germany, while Irit Keynan, *Lo nirga ha-ra'av: Nitzolei ha-sho'ah u-shelihei Eretz-Yisrael, Germaniyah 1945-1948* [Holocaust Survivors and the Emissaries from Eretz Israel: Germany, 1945–1948] (Tel Aviv: Am Oved, 1996), focuses on the activities of Zionist emissaries from the Yishuv in Palestine among the Jewish DPs. Two works have examined the *Exodus* Affair in this regard and have come to differing conclusions on the role of survivors in its ultimate successes and failures: Aviva Halamish, *The Exodus Affair: Holocaust Survivors and the Struggle for Palestine* (Syracuse, NY: Syracuse University Press, 1998), and Idith Zertal, *From Catastrophe to Power: Holocaust Survivors and the Emergence of Israel* (Berkeley: University of California Press, 1998).

This is also true in those works that focus on the Jewish DP situation in light of other outside influences and use sources created by such groups as the JDC, the U.S. Army, UNRRA, and others. For the influence of American Jewry, particularly the JDC on the Jewish DP situation, see Yehuda Bauer, *Out of the Ashes: The Impact of American Jews on Post-Holocaust European Jewry* (New York: Pergamon, 1989). Leonard Dinnerstein, *America and the Survivors of the Holocaust* (New York: Columbia University Press, 1982), focused on the American military and the Jewish DPs. For a more general perspective on the postwar situation of DPs in Europe, see Mark Wyman, *DPs: Europe's Displaced Persons, 1945–1951* (Ithaca, NY: Cornell University Press, 1998). Alexander Grobman, *Rekindling the Flame: American Jewish Chaplains and the Survivors of European Jewry, 1944–1948* (Detroit: Wayne State University Press, 1993), looks at American Jewish chaplains and the Jewish DPs. Arieh Kochavi, in several works, places the postwar experiences of Jewish DPs in the context of international diplomacy after the Holocaust: "Anglo-American Discord: Jewish Refugees and United Nations Relief and Rehabilitation Administration Policy, 1945–1947," *Diplomatic History* 14 (Fall 1990): 529–551; *Akurim ve-Politikah Beinleumit: Britaniah ve-HaAkurim HaYehudim Le-Achar Milchemet HaOlam HaShniah* [*Refugees and International Politics: Britain and the Jewish Displaced Persons after the Second World War*] (Tel Aviv: Tel Aviv University, Am Oved, 1992); and *Post-Holocaust Politics: Britain, the United States, and Jewish Refugees, 1945–1948* (Chapel Hill: University of North Carolina Press, 2001).

In recent years, a number of works have been published that have sought to cover the postwar DP period more generally with a focus on the experiences of the Jewish DPs themselves using sources created by the DPs. One of the first works to focus on a particular group of survivors was Judith Tydor Baumel, *Kibbutz Buchenwald: Survivors and Pioneers* (New Brunswick, NJ: Rutgers University Press, 1997). Zeev Mankowitz focuses on the organization of the DP community, politically and culturally, in *Life between Memory and Hope: The Survivors of the Holocaust in Occupied Germany* (Cambridge: Cambridge University Press, 2002). Hagit Lavsky examines Jewish DP life in the British zone in *New Beginnings: Holocaust Survivors in Bergen-Belsen and the British Zone in Germany, 1945–1950* (Detroit: Wayne State University Press, 2002). A number of dissertations have also examined the development of educational and cultural organizations in the DP camps, including Ada Schein, "Ma'arehet ha-hinukh be-mahanot ha-'akurim ha-yehudiyim be-Germanyah ube-Austryah, 1945–1951" [The Educational System in the Jewish Displaced Persons Camps in Germany and in Austria, 1945–1951] (PhD dissertation, Hebrew University, 2001). Angelika Königseder and Juliane Wetzel, *Waiting for Hope: Jewish Displaced Persons in Post–World War II Germany* (Evanston, IL: Northwestern University Press, 2001), is representative of the work of German scholars who have turned to this subject.

Recently, several scholars have begun to focus on the relationship between the Jewish survivors and the surrounding German society. Among the first works to examine the period in this regard is Michael Brenner's *After the Holocaust: Rebuilding Jewish Lives in Postwar Germany* (Princeton, NJ: Princeton University Press, 1997). Jay Howard Geller, *Jews in Post-Holocaust Germany, 1945–1953* (Cambridge: Cambridge University Press, 2005), also studies the reorganization of Jewish life in postwar Germany. Most recently, Atina Grossmann has focused on this relationship in *Jews, Germans, and Allies: Close Encounters in Occupied Germany* (Princeton, NJ: Princeton University Press, 2007)

4. See Anthony D. Kauders, *Unmegliche Heimat: Eine deutsch-jüdische Geschichte der Bundesrepublik* [Impossible Homeland: A German-Jewish History of the Federal Republic] (München: Deutsche Verlags-Anstalt, 2007), for the most recent analysis of the postwar German Jewish community. Although the boundaries between DPs and those who imag-

ined themselves as the harbingers of a permanent reinstated German Jewry are occasionally blurred, Kauders offers a number of insights for understanding the attitudes toward Jewish DPs in Germany by Jews and non-Jews outside of the community as well as among the DPs, international Jewish bodies, and the developing political order of the Bundesrepublik.

Entangled Histories and Lost Memories

Jewish Survivors in Occupied Germany, 1945–49

A TINA G ROSSMANN

In 1933 at the beginning of the National Socialist regime, Germany counted approximately five hundred thousand Jews. In 1946-47, more than a quarter of a million Jews were gathered in Germany, most of them in the American zone. About fifteen thousand were German Jews, of whom almost half were in Berlin. The majority were East European Jewish displaced persons (DPs) of whom only a minority were survivors of Nazi camps. The largest cohort by a substantial margin, and the least studied, comprised perhaps two hundred thousand Jews who had been repatriated to Poland from their difficult but lifesaving refuge in the Soviet Union and then had fled again from postwar Polish anti-Semitism. Moreover, and absolutely central to this story, by 1946 and into 1947, occupied Germany, far from being *judenrein* (cleansed of Jews), counted a Jewish birth rate estimated to be "higher than that of any other population" in the world.[1]

The story of these survivors, while huge, multifarious, and confusing, in many ways still remains quite underresearched. I want to insist on the importance of telling complex, entangled histories and recuperating lost memories of the highly diverse population that came to constitute the She'erit Hapletah, the surviving remnant of European Jewry, in occupied Germany (as well as in Austria and Italy, although my focus is on the American zone in Germany where most gathered). This chapter flags research questions that have been neglected both in historiography and in public memory. Despite the enormous amount of sources and significant prior scholarship, historians are just beginning to focus on the social and gender history of the Jewish DPs. Two areas deserve particular attention. First, we need to analyze more closely the many encounters among Jews and Germans as well as with Allied occupiers, international aid workers (Jewish and not), and other DPs, predominantly from Poland, Ukraine, and the Baltic states, who were after all in the majority. These interactions were as commonplace as they were complicated and were simultaneously loaded with symbolic meaning and part of everyday life. Second, we urgently require further research on the impact of the Soviet experience on definitions and memories of being a survivor.

Throughout the liminal occupation years 1945–1949, defeated Germans and surviving Jews lived, as is often remarked, in different worlds on the same terrain, divided by memory and experience.[2] But so much of everyday life and political discourse in the years immediately after the war and the Holocaust was conceptualized and negotiated in the interactions among Germans, Jews (both German and DP), and DPs. Even as they claimed to live in entirely separate antagonistic worlds, Germans and Jews—always regulated and observed by the occupiers—also encountered each other in political contests over memories, definitions, and calibrations of victimization and over entitlement to victim status and the material as well as moral consequences of that designation. They continually interacted in uneasy, sometimes cordial, and always pragmatic ways in black market enterprises and the general messy stuff—the nitty gritty—of everyday life: feeding people, taking care of children and the sick, establishing local businesses, administering the refugee camps, and engaging in sports, education, and entertainment as well as sexual relations and even marriage. DPs insisted that "My world was divided into two parts, those who had lived outside the camp and those who lived inside. Outside the camp were enemies."[3] But in reality, as archival evidence makes abundantly clear, the so-called enemies—the people of Amalek, referring to the biblical people who had tried to exterminate the Jews—were part of everyday life within as well as outside the camps. And it was precisely in the basic and intimate arenas of food, reproduction, and sexuality that relations were both most fraught and most close.

Jews gave birth in German hospitals where they were attended by German physicians, midwives, and nurses.[4] Jewish marriages and births were registered in German town halls. Local German women, hired, paid for, and regulated by camp welfare authorities, cared for the babies, did the DPs' laundry, and cleaned the Jewish homes and barracks. German doctors wrote the medical affidavits (*Atteste*) certifying that Jewish women needed help with babies and housework. Germans with permits (*Lagerausweise*) and duly medically inspected entered DP camps daily not only as baby nurses but also as cleaning women and men and as skilled workers such as plumbers, mechanics, tradesmen, teachers, and doctors. DP camp functionaries employed German secretaries, virtually a necessity at a time when all official communiqués had to be in German and often translated into English as well for the United States Military Government.

Jews, for whom survival had so often depended on their ability to work, could now use their very lack of that ability as a lever for gaining German assistance and labor power. DPs demanded that Germans be hired to help them perform their daily chores and meet the incessant demands by camp and United Nations Relief and Rehabilitation Administration (UNRRA) administrators as well as occupation officials for levels of hygiene and cleanliness set unrealistically high for a refugee population housed in overcrowded and temporary quarters. Jewish survivors were often of the opinion that this was a kind of restitution: "We have worked so much for the Germans, it is about time the Germans now worked for us."[5] If you want us to be so tidy, the message often seemed to be, send us some Germans—the generally acknowledged cleanliness mavens—to clean up after us. The head of the tailor shop in the Feldafing DP camp near Munich coolly informed the Camp Sanitation Department that since his workshop had been deemed too messy, he had engaged a German woman, "*sie soll sauber halten.*"[6] A German *Pflegerin* or *Bedienerin* (caregiver or servant) was one of the odd privileges of survivor status in postwar Germany.

Jews and Germans met in the village cafés, bars, and cheap dance halls run by Jewish DPs; on the soccer field and at boxing matches; and of course in the thriving bazaars of the black market on Berlin's *Hermannplatz,* in Munich's famous *Möhlstrasse* (the site of numerous DP offices and a good deal of black market trade as well), and anywhere in the German landscape dotted with DP camps. The thriving Yiddish-language press relied on the equipment, facilities, and skills of German printers. More than 20 percent, probably as many as one-quarter, of Jewish DPs lived outside the camps in German cities and villages with Germans as their neighbors. More than five hundred young DPs attended German universities, especially but not only in technical fields such as medicine, dentistry, and engineering; in Bavaria, at least, their tuition was paid for by German state restitution funds, and their food rations were provided by the DP camps. German farmers sold their cows and equipment to young Jewish DPs preparing for aliyah to Palestine on kibbutzim and hakhsharot. Some 20 percent of these settlements had German managers, farmhands, and agricultural instructors.[7]

Of course there were also violent confrontations, some of them murderous, between Germans and Jews including encounters between German police and Jewish DPs defined as criminals and black marketers; sometimes there were acts of calculated vengeance, such as an only minimally successful plan to taint the bread supply of an American camp for prisoners of war near Nuremberg in 1946 or efforts by American Counter Intelligence Corps agents to dump particularly egregious Nazi war criminals at the gates of DP camps where they knew they would be subjected to proper rough justice.[8] The point is that so many of these encounters, both hateful and cooperative, have been shelved and forgotten, deemed insignificant and discomforting, by both Jews and Germans. We have only partial and fragmented information fitting into neither collective memory, much of it absent from the written secondary history. If we read archival files, memoirs, and oral histories carefully—sometimes even against the grain of received memory—we can, however, tease out a sense of those relationships.

The problem is certainly not one of meager sources. As with any administered group subject to large bureaucracies such as armies and relief organizations, DP life was methodically and voluminously documented in a huge variety of venues. The existence of DPs and the so-called DP problem are certainly not new topics for historians. Yet it has been particularly difficult for historians to chronicle or understand adequately the East European and German Jewish experience in occupied Germany during the DP years from 1945 to 1949. For both scholars and survivors, these transitional years have generally been bracketed and overshadowed by the preceding tragic drama of war and Holocaust and the subsequent establishment of new communities and the State of Israel. Since the mid-1990s there has finally been a proliferation of publications, conferences, films, and exhibitions on Jewish DPs, pushed in large part by the efforts of second-generation DPs, those born in DP camps or communities.[9] Yet despite the truly overwhelming amount of source material (historical, sociological, visual, and literary) and a substantial and ever-growing secondary literature, we are just beginning to think about the social rather than the political history of Jewish DPs and to examine seriously how and where they endured the war.[10] Historians are faced with a dizzying array of actors and agencies (sponsored by four Allied military occupations and a plethora of nongovernmental humanitarian aid groups) all dealing with a highly mobile, transient, stateless, and traumatized population and operating on a territory that lacked central or universally legitimate authorities and record keepers. Despite—or perhaps because of—the vast amount of lists, charts, indexes, surveys, and studies produced at the time, statistical evidence is notoriously inaccurate, at times wildly so, reflecting the chaos of the time as well as the interest of both authorities and DPs to fudge numbers for the most advantageous allocation of resources. Statistics therefore depend very much on who is counting whom when and where and for what purpose (numbers range from 160,000 to 300,000 DPs at various points). Given the status of DPs as a stateless client population, their official record has been mostly constructed out of reports by those who managed them rather than the substantial documentation that was created by the DPs themselves, which scholars are only beginning to mine. And the stories they themselves tell—of trade and the black market (or, more appropriately, gray market); of bickering, idleness, and resourceful wheeling and dealing; and of multiple encounters of all sorts with Germans—do not correspond to either the dominant contemporary view of DPs as human debris mainly concerned, as the American Jewish Joint Distribution Committee (JDC) put it, with "How many Joint packages and cigarettes are we entitled to?" or with our own present-day valorization of survivors.[11]

My prior research has focused especially on gendered experiences of the body, of sexuality and reproduction. I have looked particularly at the role of German nannies and domestics who worked for Jews both within and outside the DP camps. Paradoxically, the vaunted Jewish baby boom of 1946-47 was the occasion for pragmatic and yet intimate encounters among Germans and Jews. A strange dance of distance and intimacy defined the relationship between Jewish mothers—generally very young, newly married to men they barely knew, and desperately alone, bereft of mothers, sisters, or aunts and cousins who would traditionally have supported them—and the Germans who often delivered and cared for their babies. One could say the same of the sexual relationships between Jewish men and German women, which are even harder, though not impossible, to document.

On both sides it seems, the immediate larger past, while its shadow was always hovering, was silenced in favor of an explicitly temporary but mutually advantageous interaction.[12] When, for example, not wanting to offend, I carefully asked one of my interview partners, an Auschwitz survivor and Feldafinger, to tell me what she remembered about Jewish men going out with German women, she looked at me indignantly and burst out, "Jewish men did not *go out* with German women, they *slept* with them!"[13] German women, often themselves refugees, lonely and eager to have some fun, provided an easy and relatively carefree introduction to sex, unburdened by the obliga-

Atina Grossmann

tions and associations attached to Jewish women. Another interview partner, a seventeen-year-old survivor of the Vilna Ghetto, forced labor, Auschwitz, and Stutthof, recalled of his time at the Schlachtensee DP camp in Berlin, "The Kurfurstendamm was a good place to start having sex." And there was perhaps some added satisfaction in the knowledge that they were engaging in a bit of "*Rassenschande*," that "Hitler would not have agreed with it, he had other things in mind for me."[14]

Another male DP explained in retrospect, "It is hard to believe—and even harder to understand—how that happened . . . many German women were attractive and knew how to handle their love affairs." He meant perhaps that toughened and scarred by war, they were not only savvy about sex and birth control but also knew not to make too many unrealistic demands on men highly unlikely to remain with them.[15] Jewish men did marry German women although in a stigmatized minority of cases. By 1950 more than one thousand such marriages had been registered. Of course there were many more relationships, both fleeting and more permanent, driven in part by the surplus of men resulting from the approximately 60:40 skewed gender ratio among Jewish survivors, DPs' possession of scarce goods provided by UNRRA and the JDC, and the easy access afforded by German women's employment as nurses or domestic servants. The tensions aroused by these connections are evident in the records of bitter debates within the camps, in the Yiddish press, and even in prosecutions by DP tribunals (*Ehrengerichte,* or honor courts) leading to, in particularly nasty cases, banishment from the camps.[16] But as another male survivor ruefully acknowledged, while most such relationships were motivated by "a mixture of revenge and the desire to taste the forbidden fruit," there were also "singular cases" of "deep reciprocal feelings" in which "the answer would simply have to be that a man and woman met and fell in love."[17]

It is important to stress that faced with these fraught questions of closeness and distance—everyday interaction as well as revenge and its impossibility—Jews were acutely aware that they had an obligation to the murdered, to find justice in the name of the millions of victims and in the name of humanity. In order to understand what that meant to the surviving Jews of Europe, however, much more research is needed and is possible. Already during the Holocaust and immediately afterward, survivors constructed memorials, published eyewitness accounts, set up exhibits, and created a Historical Commission, headquartered in Munich, that gathered about thirty-five hundred testimonies and more than one thousand photographs (none of them, however, about life in the Soviet Union). Theater, music, and cabaret (on the first Purim, for example, one could find Haman dressed up as Adolf Hitler) addressed the horrors of the war years so directly that relief workers were both shocked by the matter-of-fact treatment of extreme horror in DP culture and irritated by what they deemed obsessive remembering. DPs also denounced perpetrators to Allied authorities and even at personal risk, both physical and psychological, provided evidence in war crimes investigations and prosecutions. They also, especially in the early years, brought collaborators in their midst to trial before internal honor courts.

Justice, revenge, memorialization, and imaginings of a future also operated on a more personal everyday level. For people without a permanent home or even a clear destination who had just faced extinction, children seemed to promise not only a "guarantee of a future"[18] but also a measure of what was, however problematically, identified as revenge in a situation where the possibilities (and indeed the motivation) for direct vengeance were extremely limited. Historians need to take seriously and interrogate further what we are actually doing and representing when we choose for our exhibit posters and book covers the ubiquitous photos of children or women pushing baby carriages on the dusty streets of DP camps or at the head of Zionist demonstrations in German towns and then circumscribe the DP years under the rubric of "Life Reborn." There are at least five such publications; none make gender, sexuality, or reproduction central to their analysis.[19] Yet the written, visual, and oral evidence, produced at different points in time since 1945 until today, underlines the obvious but still underanalyzed point that lives and identities, both individual and collective, were reconstructed, and that process has been represented in gendered and embodied ways. Precisely because gender roles and sexed bodies had been so catastrophically unsettled by the persecution and extermination of European Jewry and specifically by a Nazi Final Solution that aimed to produce desexed *musselmen* and that prioritized the annihilation of mothers, children, and those deemed unfit, life was reborn and identity remade, for both women and men, through the rehabilitation and reimagining of gendered roles and sexed healthy bodies.

In films, newsreels, newspapers, political propaganda, and marches, women appear as young mothers in the ubiquitous and by now iconic processions pushing baby carriages, cradling newborns, holding toddlers by the hand, and caring for children in DP camp kindergartens. Men appear strong and well muscled, bare chested or in T-shirts, as athletes on the soccer or track fields or in boxing tournaments or strutting in the marching formations of the DP camp police. These are specific notions of masculinity and femininity that underline the attempted return to life and human normality. And always, we

Atina Grossmann

"We are here": Young DPs on bench at Wannsee Railway Station, Berlin. (United States Holocaust Memorial Museum, courtesy of Lucy Gliklich Breitbart)

need to ask about the actors who generally are not in the picture (except sometimes in private photo albums) or even in public memory: the Germans who were always present.

The ideology of the She'erit Hapletah turned away from Germany and from the Europe that had betrayed the faith invested in it by modern Jewry. But in fact, in the years right after the war, Germans and Jews did encounter each other and come face to face in daily life. As a German Jewish émigré British Army officer reported back to friends in Palestine in 1946, "'I hate the Germans" is a common expression. 'I can't stand to look at them, I could kill them all in cold blood.' But when the conversation continues, it becomes evident that one is speaking about 'my friend Schmidt' and 'our dear neighbors, the Müllers,' because, after all, even the biggest hater cannot live in total loneliness if he is compelled to continue to live at the sites of his tortures (*Orte der Qual*)."[20] Indeed, the desperate desire to escape Germany for Palestine or that other Goldene Medinah, the United States, may have had to do not only with fear or revulsion at living in the land of the murderers but also with an entirely realistic anxiety that duration and proximity would breed more contacts and perhaps even—against all memory and judgment—personal and economic attachments. The birth of children and the creation of families as well as daily life in occupied

Germany inevitably produced not only a sense of historical irony— of memory and revenge, of desire for compensation and satisfaction at wresting goods or privileges or money from Germans—but also a kind of quotidian normalization and commitment to building new lives.[21] That this *Leben aufs neu,* this novel proto Jewish nation of the She'erit Hapletah, should develop on German territory, surrounded by and in interaction with defeated and occupied Germans, was seen by the DP survivors as not only a great irony, a cruel joke played by history, but somehow also as just and appropriate.

Yet the designation of "She'erit Hapletah" encompassed a highly diverse group of survivors. Many of them the last remaining members of their large prewar families, they spoke different languages, came from various nations, subscribed to different political beliefs and levels of religious observance, and had endured quite varied experiences during the war. Remarkably, researchers have barely addressed the momentous fact—and its significance for Jewish DP perceptions of their German surroundings and German perceptions of the Jewish DPs—that by 1947 the majority of Jewish survivors in Germany had actually spent a good part of the war years as refugees in the Soviet Union and not under Nazi occupation. Starting in late 1945, most Jewish DPs (175,000 to 200,000) were infiltrees from Poland (and later also from Romania and to some degree Hungary) who had returned to their hometowns after liberation hoping against hope, and generally in vain, to find loved ones or retrieve property. They had survived in hiding, passing as gentiles, with partisans, but mostly in the Soviet Union. After the war, they fled west when it became clear that Poland was one vast graveyard and that they again faced anti-Semitic violence. In fact, the remarkable—and much remarked upon—DP baby boom reflected not only the high post-1945 birth rate but also the influx of Jews from Eastern Europe who had survived in the Soviet Union in relatively intact families.

It is yet another irony of DP history (the first being the presence of Jewish survivors on the *verfluchte deutsche Erde,* or "accursed German soil") that the Stalinist Soviet Union, which was engaged in its own purges and persecution of Russian Jews, also proved to be a crucial if difficult haven for East European Jewry. Some had fled the advancing *Wehrmacht* into Russia and western Ukraine in 1939 and had been pushed farther into the Russian interior as forced labor. Others had been deported as "capitalists" (or as otherwise suspect "foreigners") from parts of (then) Poland occupied by the Soviets as a result of the Nazi-Soviet Pact in 1939 and then had also evacuated farther into the Soviet interior with the onset of war. The German invasion in June 1941 prompted their release and a rush south to the Central Asian

Atina Grossmann

republics "on [distorted] rumors of warm climates and abundance of fruits and other food products."[22] Here too statistics are vague and problematic. Some sources have estimated that in 1942 the JDC was supporting five hundred thousand to six hundred thousand refugee Jews in remote communities in Siberia and Central Asia; most agree that somewhere around two hundred thousand Jews returned to Poland after the war, of whom many quickly fled again.[23]

During the war, Jewish aid groups credited the Soviet Union with having "not only admitted those refugees, but sought to help them by providing them with food and sending many of them as workers to the interior of the country." That "work" in the interior—"wood cutters in the taiga forests; as laborers at coal and timber-loading stations of trains and ships; or as miners in lead and coal mines"—generally took place under catastrophic conditions, but it also provided the main chance for East European Jewry's survival and the numerical, if not visible, core of the She'erit Hapletah.[24] As one young survivor recalled, when thinking about the uncle who had managed to escape the Soviets and remain in Vilna, it would have been "better to have been deported with them as a capitalist and enemy of the people than to fall into the hands of the Nazis as a Jew." In the end, "we were alive. Our exile had saved our lives. Now we felt ourselves supremely lucky to have been deported to Siberia. Hunger, cold, and misery were nothing; life had been granted us."[25]

Political and ideological factors, most importantly the pressures of the Cold War and the dominance of a narrative that subsumed all Jewish DPs under the rubric of the She'erit Hapletah, have shaped and distorted history and memory. An overarching and often undifferentiated story of the Holocaust, its victims and survivors, has effaced the role of the Soviet Union as the site where—with substantial financial support from American Jewish aid organizations, especially the JDC (for which, interestingly, they have not taken credit)—the great majority of Jewish DPs had in fact survived the war, as well as the great differences among and within the She'erit Hapletah. What are we saying when we say "survivor(s)"? What does it mean for our understanding of those complex encounters among Jews and Germans that for many Jewish DPs, their most recent experiences of persecution (as well as assistance) had been at the hands of Poles and Soviets, not Germans? The Soviet experience of so many survivors constitutes a gaping hole in both historiography and public memory that urgently requires further research.

While the many everyday encounters were to some extent an inevitable result of close working and living relationships, they were also facilitated by several particular historical circumstances. By 1947, in keeping with the focus on the Zionist future, much of official Jewish wrath had been transferred from the Germans to the British, who refused to open the gates of Palestine. If Hitler had been the stand-in for Haman at the first Purim celebrations, the hard-line Labour Party minister Ernest Bevin was now burned in effigy and excoriated as a hangman on Zionist banners. Moreover, many of the infiltrees from Eastern Europe had more direct or at least recent memories of mistreatment by Poles and Soviets than by Germans. Finally, when considering the center of DP life around Munich, there was the peculiar fact that many Bavarians—blithely ignoring their status as incubator and center of the National Socialist movement—insisted on their regional rather than German identity. They emphasized, as Minister President Wilhelm Hoegner had in his address to the January 1946 DP Congress, that the evil brought upon the world by Germany had been perpetrated by "Prussians."[26] At the same time, however, the fact that within a year of war's end Jewish DP camps were crowded with infiltrees from newly communist Poland and could therefore be labeled as victims of communism and Polish anti-Semitism rather than National Socialism only made Germans even less likely than they already were to express sympathy or accept responsibility for the fate and plight of the survivors.

Paradoxically, despite their very different backgrounds and wartime experiences, from this ragged and exhausted group of stateless DPs there emerged over several years a new and self-conscious Jewish collectivity, which named itself the She'erit Hapletah (or in the Yiddish vernacular, *sheyres hapleyte*).[27] They publicly identified as survivors of Nazi extermination plans (even if, as was the case for many of them, they had escaped because they had landed, either by choice or by force, in the Soviet Union). They committed to Zionism and Jewish identity (even if they were not religious and did not go to Palestine/Israel or left again after having gone). For many, Palestine surely was, as one U.S. reporter astutely observed, "a kind of magic word . . . which means not so much Palestine as some never-never Utopia of which they dream. It might be anywhere they could live freely," the dream of a home where they would be peaceful, safe, and above all among themselves.[28] For most DPs, Zionism was not a deeply held ideological or religious belief but rather, as various Israeli scholars have suggested, a catastrophic and also functional Zionism born of the conviction that there could be no viable future in a blood-soaked Europe, which gave meaning to transient and traumatized lives and some sense of future possibility, both individual and collective.[29]

In many ways this Jewish collective of the She'erit Hapletah was only invented, not in the crucible of the Holocaust but later in the

Atina Grossmann

transitional protected and highly ideologized life of the DP camps. That this remnant of Jews gathered and constituted itself among, in exchange with, and surrounded by the Germans who had tried to exterminate them after having survived, in many cases in Stalinist Russia, is the counterintuitive historical fact that we are only beginning to address.

The subject then is a fast-moving and bewildering target. Despite the increasing number of relevant publications, many of us researching DP history feel as though we are just beginning, virtually inventing and experimenting with a historiography that will surely be substantially expanded and revised in the next years.[30] Just as there is still so much history—as well as history of memory—to be uncovered, so too do we still need to understand much better the experiences, perceptions, and memories of those who survived the Final Solution.

NOTES

1. See, among many sources, Kurt R. Grossmann, *The Jewish DP Problem: Its Origin, Scope, and Liquidation*, with an Introduction by Abraham S. Hyman (New York: Institute of Jewish Affairs, World Jewish Congress, 1951), 19.
2. See, for example, Frank Stern, "Antagonistic Memories: The Post-War Survival and Alienation of Jews and Germans," in *Memory and Totalitarianism*, Vol. 1, *International Yearbook of Oral History and Life Stories*, edited by Luisa Passerini, 21–43 (New York: Oxford University Press, 1992).
3. Bert Lewyn and Bev Saltzman Lewyn, *On the Run in Nazi Berlin: Holocaust Memoirs* (Bloomington, IN: Xlibris, 2001), 315.
4. At the height of the baby boom, Elisabeth Hospital in Feldafing had twelve hundred beds, twenty-eight German doctors, and seventy-one German nurses; with time more DP staff was added. Cited in Haia Karni, "Life at the Feldafing Displaced Persons Camp, 1945–1952" (Master's thesis, Baltimore Hebrew University, May 1997), 49.
5. Letter to Moe(ses) Leavitt from Joseph Schwartz, JDC Paris, November 9, 1946, file 390, JDC Archives, New York.
6. To Sanitätsamt Feldafing, May 7, 1947, Record group (hereafter RG) 294.2, microfilm MK 483, reel 33, folder 402, frame 435, Displaced Persons Camps, Germany Collection, YIVO Archives, New York.
7. See Zeev Mankowitz, *Life between Memory and Hope: The Survivors of the Holocaust in Occupied Germany* (Cambridge: Cambridge University Press, 2002), 147. In regard to sports, officially the Central Committee of Liberated Jews banned Jewish sports teams from engaging German players, trainers, and referees, but it is clear from the bitter disputes recorded about such matters that Germans were sometimes recruited for DP teams. Moreover, as Philipp Grammes points out in the most

recent examination of sports in the DP camps, "it was the associations that prohibited such competitions and imposed drastic sanctions for violations of the ban, while the 'simple' athletes did not seem to consider contact with the Germans to be such a bad thing." See "Sports in the DP Camps, 1945-1948," in *Emancipation through Muscles: Jews and Sports in Europe*, edited by Michael Brenner and Gideon Reuveni, 187–212 (Lincoln: University of Nebraska Press, 2006).

8. On plans for (and limited actions of) revenge, see, for example, Jim G. Tobias and Peter Zinke, *Nakam: Jüdische Rache an NS-Tätern* (Berlin: Aufbau Taschenbuch, 2003).

9. Popular and historical interest in the Jewish DP experience since the political and memory shifts after 1989 is reflected in several exhibitions, conferences, and publications. A conference in Munich in 1995, convened in part by scholars and writers who had been born or raised in Föhrenwald or other DP camps near Munich, launched the German exhibit, titled "Ein Leben aufs neu: Das Robinson Album, Jüdische 'Displaced Persons' auf deutschem Boden 1945–1948." See also the exhibit titled "Rebirth after the Holocaust: The Bergen-Belsen Displaced Persons Camp, 1945–1950" at the B'nai B'rith Klutnick National Jewish Museum, Washington, DC, 2000, and on a larger scale Menachem Z. Rosensaft, ed., *Life Reborn: Jewish Displaced Persons, 1945–1951; Conference Proceedings* (Washington, DC: United States Holocaust Memorial Museum, 2000), accompanying the exhibit "Life Reborn: Jewish Displaced Persons, 1945–1951" at the United States Holocaust Memorial Museum, and the museum's 2001 calendar with photographs and text from that exhibit as well as the documentary film *The Long Journey Home*, Simon Wiesenthal Center, Los Angeles, 1997.

10. General histories of DPs in postwar Europe include Malcolm Proudfoot, *European Refugees: 1939–1952. A Study in Forced Population Movement* (London: Faber and Faber, 1957); Jacques Vernant, *The Refugee in the Postwar World* (New Haven, CT: Yale University Press, 1953); John George Stoessinger, *The Refugee and the World Community* (Minneapolis: Minnesota University Press, 1956); and Mark Wyman, *DPs: Europe's Displaced Persons, 1945–1951* (Ithaca, NY: Cornell University Press, 1998). Basic political histories of Jewish DPs include Yehuda Bauer, *Out of the Ashes: The Impact of American Jews on Post-Holocaust European Jewry* (New York: Pergamon, 1989); Michael Marrus, *The Unwanted* (New York: Oxford University, 1985); and Abram L. Sachar, *Redemption of the Unwanted* (New York: St. Martin's, 1983). For a detailed study of Jewish life in the DP camps, see Mankowitz, *Life between Memory and Hope*.

11. Letter to Leo Schwarz from Dr. Maurice Kaplan on meeting of Jewish Physicians Association at Berchtesgaden, January 13-14, 1947, Leo W. Schwarz Collection (LWS), RG 294.1, microfilm MK 488, reel 23, folder 272, frames 79-80, YIVO.

12. Frau U. Jaschinski, town clerk in Feldafing, recalled that the past was

"wrapped in deathly silence" (*völlig totgeschwiegen*). Interview, February 12, 2002.

13. Helen (Zippi) Tichauer, interview, New York City, October 2004.

14. Phone interview, Arnold K., August 5, 2004.

15. Meyer Kron, *Through the Eye of a Needle*, chap. 10, "Stopover in Germany," in Memoir Collection, Concordia University Chair in Jewish Studies, Montreal Institute for Genocide and Human Rights Studies, 2001, http://migs.Concordia.ca/survivor.html.

16. Figure from Nicholas Yantian, "Studien zum Selbstverständnis, der jüdischen 'Displaced Persons' in Deutschland nach dem Zweiten Weltkrieg" (Master's thesis, Technical University of Berlin, 1994), 43. Angelika Königseder, *Flucht nach Berlin: Jüdische Displaced Persons, 1945-1948* (Berlin: Metropol, 1998), 145 (citing *Undser Lebn*, December 27, 1946, p. 34), describes the case of two DPs in Berlin accused of relations with German women. The two DPs had allegedly gotten drunk in local bars, dishonored their Jewish wives, and endangered the community through the possible transmission of venereal disease. Punishment ranged from a warning for a first offense to six months banishment from camp.

17. Simon Schochet, *Feldafing* (Vancouver, British Columbia: November House, 1983), 161–62. For descriptions of such love affairs, see Jack Eisner, *Die Happy Boys: Eine jüdische Band in Deutshcland 1945 bis 1949*, translated from his English text (Berlin: Aufbau, 2004), 118–20, 163–78. Ruth Kluger describes her complicated relationship with fellow student Christoph (a fictionalized version of German writer Martin Walser), in *Still Alive: A Holocaust Girlhood Remembered* (New York: Feminist Press, 2001), 165-166.

18. Judah Nadich, *Eisenhower and the Jews* (New York: Twayne, 1953), 67.

19. The volumes all feature the same or very similar images. See the poster for the U.S. Holocaust Memorial Museum exhibit "Life Reborn: Jewish Displaced Persons 1945–1951" as well as the covers of books by Ruth Gay, *Safe among the Germans: Liberated Jews after World War II* (New Haven, CT: Yale University Press, 2002); Hagit Lavsky, *New Beginnings: Holocaust Survivors in Bergen-Belsen and the British Zone in Germany* (Detroit: Wayne State University Press, 2002); Mankowitz, *Life between Memory and Hope;* and David Bankier, ed., *The Jews Are Coming Back: The Return of the Jews to Their Countries of Origin after WWII* (New York: Berghahn, 2005). See also the presentation in the American documentary film *The Long Journey Home* (Simon Wiesenthal Center, Los Angeles, 1997); *Ein Leben Aufs Neu: Das Robinson Album. DP- Lager: Juden auf deutschem Boden 1945–1948* (Vienna: Verlag Christian Brandstätter, 1995); and the photographs in the 2001 calendar of the U.S. Holocaust Memorial Museum, culled from the exhibition "Life Reborn: Jewish Displaced Persons 1945–1951," and Rosensaft, *Life Reborn,* the accompanying volume to the exhibit.

20. Julius Posener, *In Deutschland 1945 bis 1946,* edited and with an after-

word by Alan Posener (Berlin: Siedler, 2001), 144. Also cited in Michael Brenner, *After the Holocaust: Rebuilding Jewish Lives in Postwar Germany* (Princeton, NJ: Princeton University Press, 1997), 52.

21. As Richard Bessel and Dirk Schumann point out in the introduction to their edited collection *Life after Death: Approaches to a Cultural and Social History of Europe during the 1940s and 1950s* (Cambridge: Cambridge University Press, 2003), historians have invested a great deal of effort in understanding how the crises of the 1930s and 1940s developed and unfolded but less in comprehending their aftermath. Studying the voices of the survivors and those who observed them in the early postwar years is one way of getting at questions about how people emerged from these horrors and about the return to a normality afterward that was entirely shadowed by the extreme horror of what had come before.

22. Susan T. Pettiss, *After the Shooting Stopped: The Story of an UNRRA Welfare Worker in Germany, 1945-1947* (Victoria, British Columbia: Trafford, 2004), 146, diary entries for December 11 and 13, 1945.

23. Although the postwar situation in Poland is well covered, there is to my knowledge remarkably little published material on the Soviet period, at least in English. See Yosef Litvak, "Polish-Jewish Refugees Repatriated from the Soviet Union to Poland at the End of the Second World War and Afterwards," in *Jews in Eastern Poland and the USSR, 1939–46*, edited by Norman Davies and Antony Polansky, 227–39 (New York: St. Martin's, 1991); L. Dobroszycki, "Restoring Jewish Life in Post-War Poland," *Soviet Jewish Affairs* 3, no. 2 (1973): 58–72; the Dr. Jerzy Glicksman Collection at the YIVO Archives in New York; and (in Hebrew) Benjamin Pinkus, *Yahadut Mizrah Eropah ben Sho'ah li-tekumah, 1944–1948* [East European Jewry from Holocaust to Redemption, 1944–1948] (Kiryat Sedeh Boker: Ben-Gurion University, 1987). See also Jan T. Gross, "A Tangled Web: Confronting Stereotypes Concerning Relations between Poles, Germans, Jews, and Communists," in *The Poltics of Retribution in Europe: World War II and Its Aftermath*, edited by Istvan Deak, Jan T. Gross, and Tony Judt, 107–16 (Princeton, NJ: Princeton University Press, 2000); Jan T. Gross, *Fear: Anti-Semitism in Poland after Auschwitz; An Essay in Historical Interpretation* (New York: Random House, 2006), on Kielce and postwar Polish anti-Semitism; and David Engel, "Patterns of Anti-Jewish Violence in Poland, 1944–1956," *Yad Vashem Studies* 26 (1998): 43–85. Joseph Berger, *Displaced Persons: Growing Up American after the Holocaust* (New York: Scribner, 2001), conveys very well how murky this history still is; see especially the compelling segments from his mother Rachel Berger's account of her experiences in the Soviet Union, postwar Poland, and German DP camps (135–39). According to UNRRA statistics, of 14,689 Jewish DPs registered in Baden-Württenberg on December 7, 1946, only about 10 percent were concentration camp survivors. Ulrich Müller, *Fremde in der Nachkriegszeit: Displaced Persons—zwangsverschleppte Personen in Stuttgart und Württemberg-Baden, 1945–1951* (Stuttgart: Klett-Cotta,

1990), 57. On the "Asiatics," as the Jews who arrived from the Soviet Union were called, see also Leo Schwarz, *The Redeemers: A Saga of the Years 1945–1952* (New York: Farrar, Straus and Young, 1953), 164; König-seder, *Flucht nach Berlin*, 38.

24. See the important text, written during the war, that calls the Soviet Union, "after France and Great Britain, the most important haven . . . for refugees." Arieh Tartakower and Kurt R. Grossmann, *The Jewish Refugee* (New York: Institute of Jewish Affairs of the American Jewish Congress and World Jewish Congress, 1944), 264. For a very different view of Soviet treatment of Soviet Jews, see Amir Weiner, *Making Sense of War: The Second World War and the Fate of the Bolshevik Revolution* (Princeton, NJ: Princeton University Press, 2001). Indeed, during the war, the Institute of Jewish Affairs believed that the only substantial group of Polish and other East European survivors were those who had fled to Russia. See also Pettiss, *After the Shooting Stopped*, 146–50, for a helpful analysis and population breakdown of the Jewish refugees pouring into Munich.

25. Esther Hautzig, *The Endless Steppe: Growing Up in Siberia* (New York: HarperCollins, 1968), 226.

26. See Anthony Kauders, *Democratization and the Jews: Munich, 1945–1965* (Lincoln: University of Nebraska Press, 2004). When informed that a DP child born in Feldafing was chagrined by having his birthplace stamped as Germany in his U.S. passport, my interview partner who had registered those births spontaneously exclaimed, "But he wasn't born in Germany, he was born in Bavaria." Interview, Jaschinski, February 2001. Rebecca Boehling, *A Question of Priorities: Democratic Reform and Economic Recovery in Postwar Germany* (Providence, RI: Berghahn, 1996), 106–7, notes that ironically, Munich, the center of the Nazi movement, prided itself on its self-liberation by anti-Nazis who successfully averted severe last-minute bombing.

27. On the biblical references from Genesis, 1 Chronicles, and Jeremiah driving the use of the term "She'erit Hapletah" (or its spoken Yiddish variant, *sheyres hayplete*), see among many other discussions Mankowitz, *Life between Memory and Hope*, 2.

28. Bud Hutton and Andy Rooney, *Conquerors Peace: Report to the American Stockholders* (New York: Doubleday, 1947), 86. For a nuanced discussion of Zionism among the survivors both in the DP camps and in international politics from 1945 to 1947, see Mankowitz, *Life between Memory and Hope*, esp. 52–100.

29. On catastrophic Zionism, see Anita Shapira, "The Holocaust and World War II as Elements of the Yishuv Psyche until 1948," in *Thinking about the Holocaust: After Half a Century*, edited by Alvin H. Rosenfeld, 61–82 (Bloomington: Indiana University Press, 1997); on the notion of functional Zionism, see Lavsky, *New Beginnings*.

30. My thoughts on the newness of the field and how surprisingly much we still do not know and how much of what we think we know needs to be

revised has been substantially influenced by the productive discussions at the July 2005 Scholars' Workshop on Jewish DPs at the United States Holocaust Memorial Museum, Washington, D.C., convened by Avi Patt and Michael Berkowitz, with the participation of Boaz Cohen, Laura Hilton, Laura Jockusch, Tamar Lewinsky, and David Weinberg.

A Folk Monument to Our Destruction and Heroism

Jewish Historical Commissions in the Displaced Persons Camps of Germany, Austria, and Italy

Laura Jockusch

Introduction

Jewish historical commissions constituted a central feature in the life of the She'erit Hapletah (Surviving Remnant) in the Jewish displaced persons (DPs) camps in Germany, Austria, and Italy. Founded by Holocaust survivors in the immediate wake of World War II, they had the purpose of systematically documenting the cataclysm of European Jews by collecting eyewitness testimonies from the survivors and data left behind by the Nazi regime and its collaborating governments. As ephemeral, transitional, and improvised as other DP institutions, these commissions embodied the earliest attempts of survivors to chronicle and research the Holocaust from a Jewish perspective. They not only laid the basis for later Holocaust research but also showed the agency of the Jewish DPs in the ways in which they encountered their traumatic past and integrated its lessons in their present and future lives.[1]

Several studies on the social and cultural lives of the Jewish DPs in postwar Germany have acknowledged the centrality of the historical commissions, and some also dedicated particular attention to their pioneering work of Holocaust documentation.[2] An analysis of the phenomenon of Holocaust documentation among Jewish DPs considering not only Germany but also Austria and Italy is still missing.[3] The present chapter is a first attempt to fill this void in the literature by uncovering the history of the Jewish historical commissions in the DP camps of Germany, Austria, and Italy and exploring the following questions: Why did the survivors in the DP camps establish historical commissions, and which motivations guided their work? Who were the people involved, and what did they expect to gain from documenting their traumatic pasts? How did they interact with the larger Jewish population on the one hand and the non-Jewish population on the other? What kind of methodology did they develop to research the almost complete destruction of Jewish life on the European continent, a tragedy that had exceeded all previous Jewish catastrophes in terms of intent, method, and geographic scope? What impact and larger significance did this early Jewish documentation work have after the DP camps closed down?

While this chapter explores the cases of Germany, Austria, and Italy, it nevertheless places the main focus on the U.S. zone of Germany whose historical commissions had been most active and had left behind the largest quantity of archival records in the archives of Yad Vashem and the YIVO Institute for Jewish Research in New York.

Documenting the Catastrophe Now and Here: The Foundation of the Historical Commissions

The first historical commission founded by Jewish DPs emerged in the British zone of occupied Germany. On October 10, 1945, members of the cultural office of the Central Committee of Liberated Jews in the British zone in the DP Camp Belsen established an archival department for the purpose of documenting the recent cataclysm of European Jews.[4] The initiators of the archive, which soon became the Central Jewish Historical Commission (Tsentrale Yidishe Historishe Komisye), included the Polish-born journalists Paul Trepman, Dovid Rosental, and Rafael Olewski—the leading personalities of the cultural office and the editors of *Undzer Shtime,* the central organ of the She'erit Hapletah in the British zone—along with the Polish-born actor Sami Feder.[5] The first announcement of the newly founded commission stated: "Every single fact of Jewish life under German occupation, of the time of the ghettos, concentration camps and crematoria is of infinite importance for us. We must fulfill this holy task with all our means."[6] To that end, the commission sought to collect "pictures, photographs, all kinds of publications . . . , songs and stories in all languages, clothing and uniforms, urns of the dead and burnt, lists of people resettled, murdered, witnesses, inmates; books and To-rah scrolls—everything, everything relating to the Hitler era."[7] The commission in Belsen supervised a few correspondents in Celle and Bremen and later a subcommission in Göttingen. The latter, named the Jewish Historical Commission for Lower-Saxonia (Jüdische Histo-rische Kommission für Niedersachsen), began its work in May 1947 under the leadership of the Polish-born Cwi Horowic.[8]

Shortly after the documentation work had begun in the British zone, survivors in the U.S. zone of Germany followed suit. On Novem-ber 28, 1945, a group of Jewish DPs founded a historical commission (*historishe komisye*) in Munich as a subdivision of the cultural office of the Central Committee of Liberated Jews in Bavaria. Key figures in this initiative included the Polish-born accountant Moyshe Yoysef Feigenbaum,[9] who had been active in the Central Jewish Historical Commission in Łódź before he left Poland for Germany in the sum-mer of 1945, and the Byelorussian-born journalist and history teacher Israel Kaplan.[10] This commission planned to "prepare material for the future historian helping him [*sic*] to fathom the reason why liberal-ism turned into Hitlerism in Germany."[11] The documentation material was to cover the years before 1939, "the Hitler epoch and our blood balance [*blut-bilans*]"[12] as well as the time since the liberation, and in-clude both German documents and eyewitness accounts and folklor-istic materials from the victims.[13] The group envisioned a network of coworkers in the entire U.S. zone, while the historical commission in Munich would consist of a team of scholars who would supervise the work, catalogue the collection, and prepare publications. The ultimate goal was to place the documentation material at the disposal of the Jewish Agency for Palestine so that it would serve "the fight for our rights in an international forum."[14] In the ensuing months, the com-mission became the Central Historical Commission (Tsentrale Histo-rishe Komisye), headquartered in Munich, and supervised a network of more than fifty departments in the entire U.S. zone.[15]

In the U.S. zone of Austria, the Polish-born Mejlech Bakalczuk, another former affiliate of the Central Jewish Historical Commission in Łódź, founded the Jewish Historical Commission (Jüdische His-torische Kommission) in Linz in early 1946.[16] In the summer of that year, the Jewish Central Committee for the American zone of Aus-tria in Linz incorporated the commission into its cultural office and placed it under the leadership of Bakalczuk and the Polish-born en-gineer Simon Wiesenthal.[17] In early 1947, Wiesenthal took the lead and renamed the commission the Jewish Historical Documentation (Jüdische Historische Dokumentation). Its goals included "collecting documents of the Jewish past in Austria, especially of the time of Nazi occupation, as well as collecting testimonies of the decline of the Jews in other occupied countries [and] publishing a scholarly journal."[18] Moreover, the initiative endeavored to fight "for Jewish rights in the world . . . and . . . for the expiation of the crimes of the war years, as well as to secure historical material for future generations."[19] In the international zone in Vienna, Polish-born Towia (Tadek) Frydman took a parallel initiative in July 1946 aiming to collect evidence among the Jewish DPs against war criminals in Austria.[20] The commissions in Vienna and Linz closely collaborated, establishing a network of correspondents in the DP camps of Austria. While gathering evidence for the prosecution of war criminals became the primary concern of both commissions, historiography remained but a secondary goal.

In Italy, the movement of former Jewish partisans, known as Pakhakh (acronym for the Yiddish *partizaner, khayalim un khalutsim,* or Partisans, Soldiers, and Pioneers), established historical commissions in Milan and Rome in the autumn of 1945 under the leadership of the Lithuanian-born journalist Moyshe Kaganowicz.[21] The Pakhakh movement had originated in Poland at the beginning of that year when former Jewish partisans maintained their organizational structures for the purpose of mutual aid and preparation for immigration to Palestine.[22] Already in Poland, a "bunch of enthusiasts" had established a small historical commission with the goal of "collecting autobiographic tales and documents of surviving partisans, their comrades in arms, their way of life in the woods and steppes, their battles and methods of fight against the Nazis."[23] Because of the difficulties of accessing Palestine even by means of illegal immigration, the majority of the Pakhakh members stayed in the DP camps of Austria, Germany, and Italy. Since many Pakhakh members regarded Italy as the "last station on our way to our homeland,"[24] it became the center of the movement, and the historical commission in Rome developed into Pakhakh's Central Historical Commission (Tsentale Historishe Komisye Bay Pakhakh) under the leadership of Moyshe Kaganowicz.

The historical commissions in the DP camps thus slightly differed in the emphasis they gave to documentation as a precondition for historical scholarship on the one hand and gathering data for the fight for justice on the other. While those in Germany were most committed to preparing the grounds for historical scholarship and to a lesser degree also hoped that their documentation would serve the fight for Jewish rights in the postwar era, those in Austria saw their principal goal in bringing the perpetrators to justice through collecting evidence against them, which in the long run would also serve the writing of Jewish history. The commissions of Pakhakh were primarily interested in documenting the struggle of Jewish partisans against the

Nazi regime and thus writing the history of their own movement. Nevertheless, despite their differences of focus, the Jewish DPs active in the historical commissions shared similar motivations for their work.

THE DUTY OF BEARING WITNESS:
THE MOTIVATIONS BEHIND THE HISTORICAL COMMISSIONS

From the outset of their work, the commission activists in the DP camps used a rhetoric of duty that expressed a rationalization process in which they began to understand their survival as not merely accidental but as having bestowed upon them a moral imperative to bear witness, document, and testify. Consequently, they related to historical documentation as holy work (*heylike arbet*), and as survivors they saw themselves called upon to fulfill a holy duty (*heyliker khoyv*), a moral obligation toward past, present, and future.

Documenting the traumatic events appeared as an obligation toward the past because the commission activists deemed historical documentation as a means to mourn and commemorate the dead. They believed that as survivors they had the obligation of making the fate of the dead known through the historical record. The act of collecting and recording in itself functioned as a symbolic gravestone or memorial for the millions of dead of the recent cataclysm who did not have graves or whose graves remained unknown to the survivors. For example, a call to the She'erit Hapletah in the U.S. zone of Germany urged the survivors to bear in mind that "every document, picture, song, legend is the only gravestone which we can place on the unknown graves of our parents, siblings, and children!"[25] Likewise, Feigenbaum encouraged his coworkers in May 1947, "let us . . . pursue our goal of erecting a great historical folk-monument [*folks-monument*] which must sanctify the memory of our murdered sisters and brothers and embody suffering, pain, and heroism of the Jews under the Nazi regime."[26] For the historical commissions of Pakhakh, writing the history of fallen partisans meant "building a monument for the unknown Jewish partisan and ghetto fighter."[27] This act was motivated by the wish of the former partisans to commemorate what they deemed "one of the most beautiful and most heroic chapters of Jewish life and fight in the bloody years of hell for our nation"[28] and by a sense of "duty among the surviving Jewish partisans to cherish with honor the last wills of thousands of their comrades who fell in the battle against the Hitlerite beasts in the plains of Eastern Europe."[29]

A further aspect of this sense of obligation toward the past lay in the wish of the commission activists to continue documentation projects that had originated during the war. The historical commission in

Achtung! Bensheimer Jdn!

Di Historisze Komisie

in undzer lager iz tejtig jedn tog in Kulturamt
jun 10 - 12 formitog.

Jdn wus wiln dercejln wegn zejer lebn in di getos,
kaceten un welder zoln zich farsztendikn mit di
chwawejrim: Titelman Josef, Minski Natan un Wohl
Herman bichdej cu farszreibn di historisze iberlebungen

Als historisz materjal wert betracht:

1. **Gwis-ejdes**
2. **Folklor (getb un kacet lider, wertlech, anekdotn fun der naci-cajt)**
3. **Bilder fun ij diszn lebn unter dem nazireżim**
4. **Dokumentn fun der naci-cajt**
5. **Muzeale chfejcim**

Dus historisze materjal betn wir iber cugeben in lokal fun der Historis zer Komisie in Kulturamt.

Regionale Historisze Komisie
Regional Komitet fun di befrajte Jidn
in Hessen   Frankfurt/M.
Sandweg 7

18⊦

Historisze Komisie
beim Jid. Komitet in Bensheim

"And thou shall tell your son!!! (Exodus 13,8) . . . It is the duty of every Jew to eternalize for history and the future generations all of your experiences during the six war years, in ghettos, camps, bunkers, among the partisans and under a false identity." The Historical Commission of the Jewish Committee in Bensheim DP camp, call for testimonies, folklore (ghetto and camp songs, sayings, anectotes), pictures of Jewish life, documents, and other artifacts from the Nazi era. (RG M1P, folder 9, frame 11, Yad Vashem Archives)

Göttingen understood its work as a continuation of the documentation project directed by the Polish Jewish historian Emmanuel Ringelblum in the underground of the Warsaw Ghetto in the years 1940–43. As Horowic explained to the officials of the municipality of Göttingen in 1947:

> The historical commissions of the Jews were born in the most difficult and tragic . . . times. Seen from a historical perspective, these commissions . . . began their work . . . as individual human beings who remained faithful despite the flames of the ghettos, of Auschwitz and other cultural institutions of the twentieth century that brought about the annihilation of the Jewish people. Under the most inhuman conditions, the Jewish historian Dr. Emmanuel Ringelblum in Warsaw collected a great amount of historical documents and buried them in boxes which were excavated only after the war. He acted in the belief that there would be a time when these documents would be brought back to light together with the remnants of the Jewish people. . . . There were many others who collected historical documents . . . of our martyrdom. These collections now constitute the basis for the research on the time of our bleeding. The present-day historical commissions have the purpose of compiling these documents and researching this material.[30]

The survivors active in the historical commissions understood their obligation toward the present as the duty to collect evidence to be used in the fight for justice in the present. Historical documentation provided a means of bringing the perpetrators to trial, making claims for material compensation, and appealing to the "conscience of the world," as Simon Wiesenthal put it.[31] Furthermore, it helped to "keep awake the . . . sense of responsibility toward the Jews," strengthen the "legal position of the Jews, and protect them against attacks by their enemies."[32]

Another key aspect of the obligation toward the present was to work against what Wiesenthal called the "coat of silence and the veil of oblivion"[33] and to demonstrate "that we have not forgotten our six million dead."[34] For Pakhakh the motivation was to ensure that Jewish fight and resistance did not fade from public consciousness.[35]

Inherent in this obligation toward the present was a heightened sense of urgency to seize the moment and get hold of the evidence as fast and as thoroughly as possible. The commission activists believed that the recollections of the recent events needed to be recorded while they were still immediate and unprocessed in order to avoid, as Feigenbaum remarked, "memory blur[ring] the important details of a difficult experience."[36] They knew that the situation of large numbers of survivors being held in provisional camps provided a convenient situation for the documentation work in the sense that, as Feigenbaum stated:

> It is clear that the Jewish settlement in Germany will sooner or later be liquidated and the people [will] come to the end of their migration. They will have to throw themselves into the struggle for their existence with all their senses. Then one will not get any testimonies out of them. . . . The current sad situation of the She'erit Hapletah in Germany, the life in the camps, the exclusion from the German economy gives an excellent opportunity for our work.[37]

Thus, he concluded, "We know that if we do not manage to seize the material now, it will practically be lost."[38] The historical work also gave a justification for the extended sojourn on the accursed soil of Europe—of Germany, the land of Amalek in particular—and it provided the Jewish DPs with an opportunity "to make use of the time spent in this . . . waiting room,"[39] as Wiesenthal expressed it. In a similar vein, the Central Historical Commission in Munich called on its coworkers not to forget that it was their "duty of honor to use the waiting time in Germany for the work of eternalizing the Jewish holiness and heroism of the latest destruction."[40] Likewise, in November 1946 Pakhakh's historical commission in Linz urged, "Brothers partisans, do not forget that you have a duty toward history and the coming generations. Do not forget that here in the desert [*midbar*, i.e., Austria] one has to make use of the time through working for history, for the future, and for those who have fallen."[41] Pakhakh's historical commission in Rome encouraged the former partisans in the DP camps of Italy to use the time spent at their last stopover on their way to Palestine to write down the history of their fallen brethren, implying that once they arrived in Palestine they would face other responsibilities.[42]

The sense of obligation toward the future among the commission activists drew from their wish to provide future generations of Jews who would not have witnessed the cataclysm themselves with an accurate and complete account of the events of Jewish suffering and heroism, of death and survival. For example, a call to the She'erit Hapletah in the U.S. zone of Germany urged, "Brother! Fulfill your duty toward the generations to come. Report to the historical commission about your survival of the concentration camps, in hiding and about partisan life, so that your children will know your path of martyrdom. Brother! Have you already fulfilled your duty? Have you visited the historical commission?"[43] For Pakhakh the obligation toward the future lay in the wish to provide future generations with a model "from which to learn how to fight and to defend the Jewish honor with a weapon."[44]

Moreover, for all commissions in the DP camps, collecting and recording of historical data was meant to constitute the basis for the work of future historians and to prevent the falsification of the historical truth by non-Jews. This motivation rose from a deep distrust against non-Jews, perpetrators as well as Allied armies, when it came to documenting crimes committed against the Jews. Non-Jews, the commission activists feared, had an interest in distorting the facts, barring access by Jewish historians to the historical evidence, and "belittling the Jewish tragedy, covering it up, and where possible, even defaming it," as Feigenbaum argued in a programmatic article in the opening volume of *Fun Letsten Hurbn* (Of the Latest Destruction), the historical journal of the Central Historical Commission in Munich. Feigenbaum further maintained that "We the remnants, the surviving Jews, have to provide the historian with the documents . . . from which he [*sic*] can draw for himself a clear picture of what happened to us and amongst us," and he concluded that the "Jews themselves must document this bloody era; therefore, historical commissions are necessary."[45] Thus, multifaceted motivations guided the commission activists in their initiatives to begin documenting the past, resulting both from their attempt to rationalize loss and survival as well as their wish to integrate their traumatic experiences into their present and future lives.

BETWEEN GRAPHOMANIA AND SILENCE: THE INTERACTION OF THE HISTORICAL COMMISSIONS WITH THE LARGER PUBLIC OF THE SHE'ERIT HAPLETAH

Contemporary observers of the She'erit Hapletah, most notably the workers of the American Jewish Joint Distribution Committee (JDC), noted at the time that the Jewish DPs in general did not remain silent about the tragedy they had witnessed but instead, out of a deep desire and almost compulsive urge, made the recent past the dominant subject of their social, cultural, and political lives in the DP camps. For example, the American Jewish historian Koppel Pinson wrote in January 1947, after having served as head of the JDC's education and culture department, in the U.S. zone of Germany:

> The DP is preoccupied almost to the point of morbidity with his past. . . . He is always ready to recount in minutest detail the events of his past or the past of his relatives. . . . With this preoccupation . . . has come a heightened historical sense that is responsible for almost passionate devotion of the DP's [sic] to the collection of historical material data on ghetto and kotzet life and death. Every DP is a private document center and every DP camp has an historical commission.[46]

Likewise, JDC field worker and YIVO affiliate Lucy Shildkret (Dawidowicz) recalled in her memoir that "the survivors had a compulsion to talk" about their wartime experiences, which they desired to "preserve . . . for history and posterity."[47]

This view corroborates the perceptions of some of the commission affiliates. They nonetheless had concerns that this obsession with the past would not benefit but instead would harm the work of the commissions. For example, Philip Friedman, the Polish Jewish historian and founder and first director of the Central Jewish Historical Commission in Łódź who had left Poland in 1946 and had followed Koppel Pinson in office, noted in 1947 that this sudden and amateurish interest of the survivors in their past bore the danger of developing into an uncontrollable "graphomania" or "plague"[48] that would very much go against the methodical and scholarly historical research pursued by the commissions.

The commissions' records also reveal that despite the apparent history mindedness of the She'erit Hapletah, the commissions faced great difficulties in motivating the survivors to engage in meticulous historical documentation and systematic research in the framework of the historical commissions. Although eventually indeed almost every DP camp in Germany, Austria, and Italy had a historical commission, this was only the result of the indefatigable efforts of the commission activists to convince the survivors of the necessity of historical documentation. Paradoxically, so it seems, the past was omnipresent in the lives of the survivors, yet when it came to documenting it systematically through compiling eyewitness testimonies, questionnaires, and documents, the majority of the survivors showed disinterest or even reluctance, and the work was left to a minority. This seems to suggest that while the survivors in general were eager to render their pasts the subject of public discourse, popular writing, artistic performance, and commemorative celebrations, they were reluctant to make it the subject of methodical and analytical inquiry and to dictate their testimonies to commission workers who would turn these personal accounts into official historical documents through stamps and signatures.

Moreover, as Philip Friedman indicated, the commission activists were aware that this sudden popular interest of the survivors in the recent past did not necessarily yield the kind of history writing that they deemed necessary for their project of documenting the recent past.

The greatest challenge for the commission activists thus lay in motivating the larger public of the She'erit Hapletah to engage in methodical historical documentation either on the level of a one-time donation of a testimony or questionnaire or on the level of long-term work as *zamlers* (collectors) of historical material. Evidence as to the concrete reasons preventing survivors from engaging in the historical work is scarce, and it remains anecdotal and is often limited to the reflections of the commission affiliates.

On the level of long-term work, for survivors, the greatest obstacle to joining the historical commissions seems to have been the psychological burden of documenting the past. "It is easy to understand how difficult the work of the employees of the Central Historical Commission is," wrote Feigenbaum in his first work report in 1946. "In a time when every surviving Jew is trying to forget the gruesome past, our employees cannot allow themselves to indulge [in forgetting]. They . . . still regularly go to the extermination camps and cemeteries, and for them it is sometimes very difficult to cope with this daily reality."[49] Feigenbaum's closest collaborator, Israel Kaplan, concurred that as a researcher for the commissions, "one constantly lives on a graveyard."[50] Feigenbaum admitted that it took a great deal of "lunacy" to work for the historical commissions. With a good portion of self-irony, he described the commission workers in the American zone as "a bunch of loafers [*batlonim*] who still today hang around graveyards, still deal with 'resettlement actions,' concentration camps and all sorts of other experiences from those dark days; some cranks who chase after someone in the street to get . . . the date of some ghetto massacre."[51] With considerable efforts, the Central Historical Commission in Munich managed to recruit a group of more than one hundred people—men and women of different age cohorts and social and educational backgrounds—for whom the desire to seize the moment to document the recent past outweighed the psychological burden of the work itself. The staff of other commissions operating among considerably smaller populations of Jewish DPs—as in the British zone of Germany as well as in Austria and Italy—only numbered a few dozen.[52]

On the level of one-time cooperation with the historical commissions, a number of factors account for the reluctance of the survivors. For one, many seem to have had what Feigenbaum called "a particularly negative attitude"[53] toward the commissions as an institution with a professional appearance that he related to a certain "inferiority complex" among the average survivors, who tended to believe that their stories were not important enough to be recorded.[54]

Many Jewish DPs seemed to have neither understood what kind of material the commissions sought nor to have grasped the significance of methodical historical work. For example, Mordechai Permutter, head of the historical commission in Leipheim, remarked after a few months of work that "the population in Leipheim does not sufficiently appreciate the importance of the historical commission, and the taking of testimonies of their experiences is very difficult."[55] Even Pakhakh's historical commissions, which addressed only the specific group of Jewish partisans, faced the problem that their target group did not "value the exceptional significance of the historical work and did not show any cooperation in collecting the historical material at a rapid pace."[56]

The commission activists observed that the willingness of the survivors to engage in the historical work waned as time went by. Some noticed a growing apathy and forgetfulness of the survivors when asked to provide information on their survival. Helen Fuchsman,[57] a correspondent for the Jewish Historical Documentation in Linz in the Ebelsberg DP camp, attributed this tendency to "a certain passivity, a negligence and a decrease in the feelings of revenge among the former Jewish inmates toward their tormentors and murderers."[58] Other activists claimed that survivors had been responsive immediately after the liberation, but their readiness to testify declined as their lives resumed a degree of normalcy. For example, Yitskhok Kvintman, secretary of Pakhakh's historical commission in Rome, remarked in October 1948 that the task of motivating the partisan DPs to testify became increasingly difficult as time went by because "the best moment for recording and writing down all the details was . . . immediately after the liberation (second half of 1945) when everything was still fresh in memory and there had been an inclination toward recording and . . . recounting among the partisans. But the driving force of the Ha'apalah [i.e., illegal immigration to Palestine] made it impossible to carry out this work." He further observed that once the survivors had settled in DP camps and their lives had consolidated, "the grounds for an organized collection work became favorable . . . yet . . . the will in many people to place their personal experiences and memories in the hands of society had weakened, and the urge to write and speak had waned."[59]

This tendency also made itself felt in the pace at which the commissions collected the testimonies. In the U.S. zone of Germany a total of 2,540 testimonies were collected between December 1945 and December 1948. More than 1,500 testimonies were collected in the course of eleven months, while slightly fewer than 1,000 were collected in the subsequent twenty-five months.[60] This seems to suggest that the survivors were more open to speak about their traumatic past when their lives were in turmoil and their memories still remained vivid, whereas the consolidation and material improvement of their living conditions made them more inclined to focus on the future and augmented their reluctance to return to the past, and the historical work conflicted with more practical imperatives of present and future such as the preparation for emigration. The contention that survivors lost interest was further complicated by the fact that as of the summer of 1946, the majority of the DPs in the U.S. zone of Germany were Polish Jews who had survived in the Soviet Union without direct contact with the Germans, and the commissions' questionnaires did not address this particular experience.[61] Another reason might have been that ever-growing numbers of survivors emigrated during 1948 and 1949.[62]

The commission activists were aware that when recruiting collaborators for their documentation work they had to compete for the attention and energies of the Jewish DPs against political parties, educational facilities, employment, recreation and entertainment, and the urge to concentrate on the future through founding families. Given the painfulness of reencountering the traumatic past through testifying, visiting the commissions was an unattractive pastime. For example, Helen Fuchsman repeatedly complained to Simon Wiesenthal that within hours the announcements she had posted for the historical commission were covered with the posters of political parties and cultural events. Therefore, she asked the camp carpenter to design a special bulletin board for the historical commission.[63] But even when she visibly posted her notices for several days, they received a weak response from potential witnesses. She visited survivors in their homes only to find that they had better things to do—be it work, entertainment, or recreation—than reencountering their past and giving a testimony.[64]

The commission activists believed that the only remedy to these problems was systematic propaganda work (*propagande arbet*) aimed at convincing the survivors that historical documentation was an imperative for moral and practical reasons. For this propaganda work the commissions chose several channels: Aware that the majority of the Jewish DPs were more concerned with the daily struggle for survival and building the future and would not contribute out of their own motivation, the Central Historical Commission in Munich instructed its workers throughout the U.S. zone "not [to] sit in their offices waiting for someone to pass by and drop a testimony or a document" but rather to "visit the residents in their apartments and establish contacts with them."[65] Consequently, commission workers toured the DP camps and used the occasions of holiday celebrations, conferences, and other cultural and social events to seek face-to-face encounters with the DP public.[66]

The Yiddish-language press and publications provided the most important vehicle through which the commission sought to reach out to the survivors. The commissions publicized their work and called upon the survivors to fulfill their moral duty and join the documentation efforts. The Central Historical Commission in Munich published its own historical journal, *Fun Letsten Hurbn,* featuring mainly eyewitness testimonies and documents, that aimed to encourage the survivors to "grab a pen and describe their wartime experiences."[67] After the publication of the first three volumes of *Fun Letsten Hurbn,* Feigenbaum struck the balance that "the journal inspires the simple Jew to sit down and describe his [*sic*] war survival. Likewise the Jewish intelligentsia appears at the historical commission to get to know its work. Thanks to the journal the collections have expanded."[68]

A further medium comprised three types of appeals distributed in the DP camps in the form of leaflets and posters, mostly handwritten but at times printed. The first type called upon the survivors from specific villages, cities, regions, ghettos, or camps as well as on people who could testify about certain war criminals to give their testimonies at the historical commission in their vicinity. An example of this most common kind of appeal read, "Attention, former inmates of concentration camp Mauthausen! All persons who know something about the behavior and deeds of Josef Giett, pictured below, born December 12, 1906, . . . guard in Mauthausen between September 1, 1944 and March 30, 1945, are requested to report to the Jewish Historical Documentation, Linz Goethestrasse 63, in writing or orally."[69]

The second type of call specified the kinds of material the commissions were collecting, since most survivors did not necessarily have a clear idea of what "historical documents" or "information" meant. Therefore, the historical commission in Bensheim near Frankfurt published a poster titled "Attention! Jews of Bensheim!" urging "Jews who want to narrate their life in the ghettos, concentration camps," to visit the historical commission in the camp. It encouraged the survivors to collect historical documents, which included "Testimonies . . . folklore (ghetto and concentration camp songs, sayings, anecdotes from the Nazi period) . . . pictures of Jewish life under the Nazi regime . . . documents of the Nazi time . . . museum objects."[70] Similarly, the historical commission in Belsen asked survivors in the British zone

Laura Jockusch

of Germany to collect "All materials and cultural treasures which give a picture of the life and [cultural] creations of the annihilated communities, pictures, photos, creations, songs, memoirs, tales and coins from the ghettos, work camps, concentration camps, and partisan [enclaves], as well as the names of the martyrs who fell and of those who passed through resettlement actions and crematoria."[71]

A third type of appeal emphasized the moral duty of the survivors to give their testimonies for the sake of documenting the recent catastrophe. For example, Pakhakh's Central Historical Commission in Rome urged former partisans in Italy and Austria:

> It is the holy duty of every surviving Jewish partisan to eternalize the memory of his fallen comrade through writing down his biography, his activity in the battle, and uncover the circumstances under which he died, in order to eternalize for the coming generations the memory of these Jewish heroes who fell—most of them not leaving behind any family member to commemorate them. This will be the best gravestone for those whose graves do not even have the names of the fallen Jewish hero inscribed. Their graves are dispersed over the woods, steppes, grounds and ways of Russia, Poland, and Lithuania. Through their paths of life, may the Jewish youth learn how to fight and die for the honor of the people, for its right to live and work as a free human being and Jew![72]

In addition to these appeals, so-called propaganda posters (*propagande plakatn*) pleaded to the survivors with visual means. In the spring of 1947, the Central Historical Commission in Munich opened a contest for the artistic design of a poster advertising historical documentation.[73] The poster that won the first prize was designed by Pinchas Shvarts and showed a dead *katsetler* (concentration camp inmate) in front of barbed wire, on his chest a scroll with calligraphically embroidered Hebrew letters quoting the beginning of the book of Esther: "And so it happened in these days . . ." (Esther 1:1). The scroll was still almost empty, and a quill in a vat of ink on top of the Yiddish slogan "Help to write the history of the latest destruction!" invited the observer to become a chronicler himself and to fill the scroll with his own history.

The poster that won the second prize was designed by P. Shuldnreyn and displayed the verse from the Hebrew Bible "Remember what Amalek did to thee!" (Deuteronomy 25:17–19) set above a clock whose face marked several episodes of the catastrophes in the Jewish past.

Each episode showed the title of the text describing the event in question: slavery in Egypt with the Passover Haggadah, the destruction of the First Temple with the Lamentations of Jeremiah (Ekhah), the expulsion from Spain in 1492 with Yehuda Ha-Cohen's (1496–1578) *Emek Ha-Bakhah* (Valley of Tears), and the pogroms in the Ukraine (1648–49) with Natan Neta Hanover's (ca. 1620–1683) *Yeven Metsulah* (The Deep Mire). The hour hand pointed at a Yiddish-language slogan, "Collect and record!" Both illustrations conveyed the image of a cyclical history of Jewish suffering, a timeless repetition of the atrocities committed by Amalek against the Jewish people. Here, the Holocaust appeared as the last link in a long chain of Jewish suffering, from slavery in Egypt to the present. The posters also conveyed the message that Jews had always responded to collective suffering by recording the events, but in the case of the latest destruction the recording was yet to be undertaken, and therefore every single survivor was called upon to become collector and chronicler and thus join the tradition of history writing as a response to catastrophe.[74] The Central Historical Commission in Munich printed the two posters in color and distributed them throughout the entire U.S. zone.[75]

The posters used in the British zone of Germany, where the historical commission was much smaller, were less symbolically loaded, displaying symbols of the destruction such as barbed wire and devastated landscapes in addition to the items that the historical commissions called upon the public to collect: Jewish cultural objects, documents, books, and photographs.[76]

Another central part of the commissions' public relations work was the visual presentation of the collected material in exhibitions. Shortly after the foundation of the Central Historical Commission in Munich, Israel Kaplan conceived the idea of establishing a "museum-archive" open to the public "in order to attract the attention of the population."[77] This idea never became a reality, most likely due to a lack of financial means and the dissolution of the DP community in Germany. However, on the occasion of the First Congress of the She'erit Hapletah on January 27, 1946, in the Munich Rathaus, which was attended by 112 representatives from all over the U.S. zone, the Central Historical Commission prepared a "fragmentary exhibition for the delegates."[78] In the context of the Third Congress of the She'erit Hapletah in the U.S. zone of Germany in Bad Reichenhall from March 30 to April 2, 1948, a second exhibition followed with the title "Jewish Life under the Nazi Regime" (*yidish lebn untern natsi-rezhim*).[79] Local historical commissions in the American and British zones of Germany followed suit.[80]

"Remember what Amalek did to Thee! Collect and Record!" Central Historical Commission, Munich, U.S. zone of Germany, 1947. (RG M1P, folder 685, Yad Vashem Archives)

"Now it happened in those days . . . [Esther 1:1] . . . Help to Write the History of the Latest Destruction." Central Historical Commission, Munich, U.S. zone of Germany, 1947. (RG M1P, folder 689, Yad Vashem Archives)

In order to record testimonies from children and youths, the Central Historical Commission in Munich urged teachers in the Jewish schools of the U.S. zone to support the historical commissions by assigning the students essays on the topic "My experiences of the Nazi occupation."[81] Likewise, the commission in Munich directed its efforts to adolescents in vocational training schools and youth groups and kibbutzim in the U.S. zone and opened essay-writing contests for children and youths.[82]

In all three countries, the commissions considered enforcing the survivors' cooperation by either promising a reward for those who would contribute or threatening to punish those who refused to cooperate. If the commissions had had the financial means to pay their *zamlers* for their contributions, the work might have been more appealing to many survivors. But there was barely enough money to pay the full-time employees. Consequently, the commissions persevered in rewarding the *zamlers* with honors, and many local commissions published the names of the collectors and the kind of items donated through their efforts.[83] The Jewish Historical Documentations in Linz and Vienna used a special badge with the slogan "I exposed a murderer" awarded together with a "diploma" that bore the name of the witness "thanks to whose testimony it was possible to bring . . . [name of the perpetrator], criminal against the Jews, in . . . [name of the place or camp] to justice."[84] In addition to these honorary rewards, the commissions repeatedly considered the possibility of applying sanctions against those who did not testify. However, these sanctions were more symbolic than anything else. For example, the commission in Vienna tried to intimidate survivors who were unwilling to cooperate by threatening to publish their names in the Jewish press.[85] It also tried to convince the JDC to discontinue its support for Jews who had not fulfilled their duty of testifying and who had thus "worked against the interest of the Jewish community." For Towia Frydman, the head of the commission, this was an irresponsible act of "sabotage," not only against the commission but also against the Jews as a whole because withholding testimony helped the perpetrators to remain free.[86] However, these sanctions seem to have been the exception to the rule. The commission activists were aware that they had nothing else at their disposal but moral inducement to encourage the survivors to contribute to their cause. Through these multifarious efforts at making a moral claim for the urgent necessity of documenting, the commissions convinced some ten thousand survivors to collect, testify, and participate in the surveys carried out by the historical commissions in the latter half of the 1940s.[87]

Collecting the Vestiges of a Shattered Past: The Research Methods of the Historical Commissions

The most fundamental premise of the commissions' methodology to document the Holocaust was the idea that sources by perpetrators and victims must complement each other. While the commission activists deemed German sources highly important for understanding the destruction of European Jews, they nevertheless found them insufficient because they presented a one-sided picture of Jewish suffering through the eyes of the perpetrators and failed to reflect Jewish responses to persecution or to give an account of the vitality of prewar Jewish life.[88] As a consequence, the commissions sought to contexualize perpetrator sources with those of the Jewish victims. Yet the activists were aware that as a result of the very annihilation process, the survivors were deprived of historical sources in the traditional sense. The only source of information they possessed was their memories, and thus the commissions deemed "the testimony of every single Jew who was saved . . . of great value"[89] for their documentation work. Therefore, collecting testimonies became a central focus of their endeavor.

Usually, as an early version of oral history albeit in written form, the witnesses did not write the testimonies themselves but instead dictated them to commission employees, and every testimony was signed by both witness and *protokolant* (protocol writer).[90] The instructions for testimony taking directed at the *protokolantn* emphasized that "the description [should] include as many facts, episodes, names of Germans, dates of actions . . . as possible. In taking testimonies on ghettos the entire Jewish life should be captured, cultural, political, social life, sanitary conditions, resistance movements, as well as the relations among the Jewish population."[91] The testimonies taken in Austria and Italy did not reflect wartime experiences in general but rather selected specific aspects: in Austria the crimes of a certain perpetrator, in Italy the experience of those who had fought "to save the honor"[92] of the Jewish people.[93]

In addition to capturing the survivors' memory through testimonies, the commissions also developed a broad concept of what served as a historical source on the Jewish experience of the destruction. In fact, as Feigenbaum explained, "every song of the Nazi period, every saying, every anecdote, every joke, every photograph and any kind of creations in the field of literature, or art, in short, everything that can illuminate the martyr path of our tragic generation,"[94] could function as a historical source and therefore needed to be collected. The commissions in Germany assembled extensive collections of thousands

Laura Jockusch

of photographs, folklore, literature, anti-Semitic writings, museum objects and Jewish cultural objects, even musical recordings of songs sung in ghettos and camps.[95]

Various kinds of questionnaires served as an additional instrument for seizing the memory of the survivors. As the largest historical commission, the Central Historical Commission in Munich proved most active in formulating and using these questionnaires among the survivors. The so-called statistical questionnaire gathered information on the fate of individual survivors, asking about experiences in ghettos and camps, loss in property, forced labor for specific firms, and corporeal punishment and medical experiments suffered as well as the injuries and disabilities that had resulted from the persecution. The so-called historical questionnaire collected information on the history of Jewish towns and settlements under Nazi occupation, their demography, major social, cultural, and educational institutions, changes in the social and economic structure under the impact of Nazi occupation, German policies of anti-Jewish legislation, mass shootings, resettlement actions, confiscations of Jewish property, and the eventual destruction of the respective town. The questionnaire also addressed the conditions in prisons, ghettos, camps, and hiding places as well as the history of resistance, revolt, and partisan fight.[96] An additional questionnaire addressed the postwar experiences of the Jewish DP population, their interaction with the Allied armies and German population, and their views of the future.[97] Another questionnaire inquired about folklore and ethnographic material, including folk songs, legends, poetry, proverbs, jokes and games, and even ways of fortune-telling, magic procedure, and superstitious believes practiced in order to avert evil.[98] Other questionnaires were directed at specific groups: one questionnaire interrogated German Landräte (district administrators) and Oberbügermeister (mayors) about the fate of the Jewish population in their districts or towns,[99] while still others interrogated members of drama groups, kibbutzim, and former partisan units. To the exasperation of the commission in Munich, however, the former partisans did not fill out the questionnaires. This might be explained by the fact that their own historical commission in Rome launched a similar survey aimed solely at documenting the experiences of partisans and ghetto fighters in 1947.[100]

From the beginning of the commissions' work, publishing parts of the collected material had been a major goal. The Central Historical Commission published a ten-volume Yiddish-language historical journal, Fun Letsten Hurbn, with a circulation of one thousand to eight thousand copies per volume and a total of more than one thousand pages, edited by Israel Kaplan. Fun Letsten Hurbn featured hundreds of eyewitness accounts, local studies of destroyed Jewish communities, folklore, documents, and photographs. While it presented a great variety of Holocaust experiences—ghettos labor, concentration and extermination camps, bunkers, hiding places, life in partisan units, and the so-called Aryan side, all of which were presented as equal—other wartime experiences were entirely blotted out, most notably exile in the Soviet Union and the history of Jews in Nazi-occupied Western and Central Europe. Equally absent were articles on individual personalities and articles judging the Jewish leadership in the ghettos, because Kaplan wanted to promote the experiences of a collective of East European Jews and create a canon of Holocaust experiences at the expense of the experiences of those who had survived outside of the Nazi orbit of power and who were not East European Jews.[101] Kaplan did not leave the testimonies in the form in which the witnesses had submitted them but instead changed the language to make them meet his literary standards. As Kaplan himself explained, "At first the mass material we publish is given to us by its authors in the form of bare facts and in a disfigured state. It is the work of whole days and nights until these materials get the form that is adequate for publication."[102] These editorial policies provoked the criticism of Philip Friedman, who called the project unscholarly and accused Kaplan of "kaplan-izing" (*kaplanizirn*) the testimonies collected by the commission, which lowered the value of the publication from a scholarly perspective.[103] However, Friedman praised the aesthetic appeal of the journal as the "most beautiful Yiddish publication in Germany" that should "serve as a model for others."[104]

In addition to the periodical the Central Historical Commission published several brochures and monographs, among them Kaplan's *In der tog-teglekher historisher arbet* on documenting the recent catastrophe and his *Dos folks-moyl in natsi klem,* an analysis of the ghetto and camp language;[105] Avrom Vaysbrod's *Ez shtarbt a shtetl;*[106] and Feigenbaum's memoir *Podolye in umkum: Notitsn fun khurbn.*[107] Other historical commissions were far less prolific. The historical commission in Göttingen, which founded its own publishing house, merely brought out two small brochures on the Jewish past in that city and Horowic's novel on prewar Jewish life in Poland.[108] The commission in Belsen published an anthology of ghetto and camp poetry and a photo album titled *Undzer khurbn in bild.*[109] In Rome, Kaganowicz published a four hundred-page study on the activities of Jewish partisans in the territory of the Soviet Union.[110] In Austria, Simon Wiesenthal published a volume with drawings and poems on Mauthausen and a work on the mufti of Jerusalem and his connections with Nazi Germany.[111] In addition, Towia Frydman prepared a history of the Jews in Austria, but it was not published until the late 1950s.[112]

The research techniques employed by the historical commissions in the DP camps—especially by the Central Historical Commission in Munich—were not entirely new. In many respects they were modeled on social science–oriented research techniques developed by the YIVO Institute for Jewish Research in interwar Poland. YIVO's influence was most notable in the commissions' use of nonprofessional *zamlers* of historical material and testimonies and in their broad understanding of what would qualify as a historical source as well as their interdisciplinary concept of research at the interface of history, sociology, and ethnography.[113] Another major frame of reference, particularly for the Central Historical Commission in Munich, were the research methods that the Central Jewish Historical Commission had developed in Łódź in 1945 under the guidance of Philip Friedman. Most of the questionnaires used in the U.S. zone were directly modeled on those of the Polish commission.[114] In the summer of 1946 Friedman left Poland and became the head of the department of education and culture of the JDC in the U.S. zone. In this capacity he became adviser and critic of the historical commissions in the DP camps, with one of his fundamental criticisms being the lack of scholars trained in the historical profession and the "popular" nature of the work. While Friedman generally acknowledged the value of the collection work carried out in the DP camps, he constantly demanded higher levels of source criticism and standards of research and better training of the collectors, which very much aggravated the commission activists in the U.S. zone.[115] Part of the conflict was rooted in the fact that Friedman was a professional historian, whereas the commission activists in the DP camps were by and large untrained in the historical profession with the exception of Israel Kaplan (who was a history teacher before the war) and instead were journalists, writers, teachers, accountants, and engineers. As long as the commissions existed, this conflict was never resolved.

Most commission activists saw themselves as preparing the grounds for the actual history writing, which would essentially occur in the future. Apart from the fact that the accumulation of data constituted an indispensable first step toward historical analysis, Feigenbaum and Kaplan were aware that they lacked the personnel, training, and material conditions that would have been necessary for historical scholarship. "Sitting on suitcases in a corridor," as Kaplan described the situation in the DP camps, "one can maybe make history, yet one cannot possibly write it."[116] Since they did not plan on staying in Europe, they understood their work as a first step toward both establishing a central memorial and a new field of historical research that would come to full fruition outside of Europe, presumably in the framework of a sovereign Jewish state in Palestine.

<h2>IN THE DESERT: THE JEWISH HISTORICAL COMMISSIONS AND THEIR SURROUNDINGS</h2>

The work of the historical commissions in and outside of the DP camps encountered challenges due to their difficult relations with the surrounding non-Jewish population, the native Jewish community, and the Jewish leadership in the DP camps. The sojourn in Germany, the land of the perpetrators, provided the greatest challenge. Non-Jewish Germans interacted with the Jewish historical commissions mainly as typesetters, printers, photographers, archivists, and municipal officials. The commission workers disdained the Germans, referring to them as Amoleykim (Amalekites), but depended on their cooperation.

When the Central Historical Commission in Munich began to consider turning to the local non-Jewish population in order to gather information, some members argued that addressing the German population was morally unacceptable and that they would "not do business with murderers"[117] even if it was for the sake of documenting the Jewish past. Others maintained that "turning to the Germans is no crime"[118] since the end goal of documenting the cataclysm justified the means. Eventually the latter view prevailed, and the Central Historical Commission combed German archives and municipalities in the U.S. zone for documents pertaining to the Jews, appealed to the German population to hand over documents, and distributed questionnaires among German majors and district administrators.[119] The officials showed alacrity in answering the questionnaires, and the survey was extended into all three Western zones. By then the administration in the larger communities had changed, and so-called *Beauftragte für politisch, religiös und rassisch Verfolgte* (Commissioners for politically, religiously, and racially persecuted) had taken office and often filed the questionnaires. The most cogent reason for the cooperation of the German officials might have been their interest in acquiring a good standing in the denazification process coupled with an awareness that acting against the questionnaire might have been politically inopportune. As becomes obvious from the answers of the officials, they were well informed about the Aryanization of Jewish property and the forced emigration, suicides, imprisonment, and deportation of the Jews in their cities or districts yet rejected any responsibility, blaming these acts on the SS, the SA, the Gestapo, and the Nazi Party, institutions that no longer existed and apparently could not be held responsible for their deeds.[120]

In the British zone of Germany where the historical commissions were much smaller, dealings with German officials proved particularly difficult as is shown in the case of Göttingen. The officials of the Göttingen municipality perceived Cwi Horowic's initiatives to uncover the Jewish past of their city as an inappropriate intrusion and surmised that Horowic sought to blackmail the city with the accusation of anti-Semitism. An internal statement of the municipality remarked, "Mr. Horowitz [sic] gives the impression that he has chosen the framework of the Jewish Historical Commission for the sake of personal gains and in order to make an existence. He counts on—and as we have seen quite rightly so—one factor supporting his unauthorized behavior: Nobody dares to be critical of him or confront him firmly because he is a Jew."[121] The officials feared that opposing the demands of a Jewish DP might harm the international reputation of the university town in times of Allied occupation. Therefore, they emphasized their goodwill toward Horowic and sought to camouflage their biases by arguing that technical and material reasons prevented them from meeting his demands.[122] Nevertheless, they obstructed his access to Nazi documents and complicated his use of the municipal archives on the grounds that he had no training in history.[123] The director of the municipal museum refused to show the exhibition on the history of the Jews of Göttingen that Horowic had compiled and refused to reopen the museum's Judaica room, which had been closed down during the Nazi period. Horowic's request to borrow Judaica artifacts from the holdings of the museum for an exhibit in Belsen was also denied.[124] The municipal authorities thwarted Horowic's efforts for a memorial at the site of the former synagogue, arguing that it was neither feasible nor necessary.[125]

In Austria, relations between the commission activists and the local non-Jewish population proved as fraught as in Germany. The activists tended to weigh Austrian society's guilt in implementing the Final Solution at least equal to that of the Germans' guilt. Wiesenthal believed that Austria, the native home of Hitler, provided a hideout for the greatest number of war criminals in Europe and that the proportion of Austrian war criminals greatly exceeded the proportion of Austrians in the Reich.[126] Towia Frydman even estimated that Austrians made up 70 percent of all war criminals involved in the Final Solution.[127] Wiesenthal asserted that in Austria virtually no family was "free of guilt toward the Jews, because [every family] had an SS, SA, or Gestapo man or Aryanizer in its ranks, [and] if the population approved of only one point of the Nazi program, that is the mass murder of the Jews."[128] The direct impetus to hunt down and help prosecute war criminals in Austria came from the fact that the Jewish DPs identified their former camp guards in the streets of Vienna and Linz.[129] Another stimulus had been the growing exasperation over the increasing leniency of the Allies and Austrian authorities toward the war criminals.[130] In addition, the commission activists encountered anti-Semitism in their daily lives, which led Wiesenthal to conclude that in Austria "anti-Semitism had in effect survived the Jews."[131] Consequently, it was necessary for postwar Austria to undergo what Wiesenthal called a "detoxication of the population" (*Entgiftung der Bevölkerung*), part of which would come from bringing the perpetrators to trial.[132] Wiesenthal and his collaborators believed that their work gave the new political system in Austria a chance to prove that a real change had occurred. "In Austria, just like in Germany, the new political course is being tested . . . and we are the needle of the barometer indicating changes in the political climate."[133] Nevertheless the Jewish DPs active in the documentation effort in Austria felt disconnected and alienated from their surroundings. For them, Austria was merely a "waiting room" that did not even provide "solid ground under the feet" and provided "no protective roof."[134]

While these conflicts between the Jewish historical commissions and the non-Jewish populations with whom they interacted were a logical consequence of the recent past, it appears that in the case of Germany the commissions had disharmonious relations with German Jewish survivors as well. For the East European Jews active in the commissions, the sojourn in the land of the perpetrators was a temporary and necessary evil—Allied occupied Germany proved safer than their countries of origin, and for many it was a step toward a new home overseas—while the German Jews who had either survived in Germany or had remigrated sought to rebuild their communities. Many work reports of the Central Historical Commission in Munich display a negative tone against German Jews, scolding them for their supposed disinterest in the documentation work.[135] However, the commission for its part undertook only very minor attempts to win the support of the German Jews: it only translated the historical and statistical questionnaires into German, and this occurred as late as 1948. These questionnaires focused on the experiences of East European Jews during 1939–45 and did not address the German Jewish experience as such. The only questionnaire that specifically related to the fate of Jews in Nazi Germany was directed not at the German Jewish population but instead at German officials. The commission's publications were exclusively in Yiddish (a language that German Jews might have understood yet certainly did not read). As a result, the reception of the Central Historical Commission's work by German Jews remained marginal and never attained a true resonance.[136]

The historical commission in Göttingen also had problematic relations with the German Jews in its direct vicinity even though it had one German Jewish member.[137] Richard Gräfenberg, the head of the Jewish community in Göttingen, in particular showed little understanding for the kind of amateur historical documentation pursued by Horowic and his commission. Born in 1870 to an old Göttingen merchant family, Gräfenberg rejected Horowic, who claimed to carry out historical research without having the expertise of a professional historian.[138] After Horowic left for Israel in November 1949, Gräfenberg defamed him as a "great swindler" and accused him of having founded the historical commission as a cover-up for his supposedly criminal activities: "He used the name Jüdische Historische Kommission für Niedersachsen to camouflage his frauds. Jüva was the name of his publishing house, like the name of the well-known American firm,"[139] by which he meant YIVO. Gräfenberg interpreted the fact that the historical commission had called upon the population to collect cultural objects and artifacts for its collection as a criminal act and accused Horowic of "embezzling Jewish property, 2,000 Marks, silverware which a German lady had given to the Jewish Historical Commission for storage. The lady had concluded from the advertisements of the Jewish Historical Commission that it was an official office to which these things had to be given."[140] While Horowic was neither a skilled researcher nor a diplomatic negotiator, the response of Gräfenberg is symptomatic of the fact that the grassroots-level documentation and collection initiatives of the DPs did not always resonate with the German Jewish public.

In addition to the difficult material conditions, the reluctance of the Jewish DPs to testify, the hostility of the non-Jewish surroundings, and the lack of cooperation on the part of the Jews who were not DPs, the commission activists often felt rejected by the Jewish leadership in the DP camps. In Germany, the Central Historical Commission constantly fought for the recognition of its work by the Jewish political leadership in the DP camps and against the impression on the part of the Central Committee and its local branches that "historical commissions are unnecessary"[141] and a "miserable nuisance."[142] The conflict arose from two fundamentally different views: those who engaged in the party politics of communal leadership in the DP camps did not see the benefit of historical documentation, and when mouths needed to be fed and political decisions needed to be made, documenting the recent past appeared of secondary importance. The commission activists on their part acted out of a deep conviction that demanded that they engage in historical work for the sake of the dead, the generations to come, and practical matters of justice and material compensation in the present.

The dilemma was, however, that the Central Historical Commission and its local branches, although funded by the JDC, depended on the local Jewish authorities in the DP camps because the distribution of JDC funds was handled by the Central Committee and its regional subcommittees.

When the Central Historical Commission convened a conference of all historical commissions in the U.S. zone in May 1947, the Central Committee did not send a representative, which only intensified the aggravation.[143] The seventy delegates even considered going on strike in order to pressure the Central Committee into more respect and better working conditions. It was Feigenbaum who rejected this suggestion, arguing:

> We cannot do the same as the teachers. They have something to threaten with, they refrain from working in the schools and the Jewish world will be in uproar because our children are without education! What do we have to threaten with? Factually, we do not even have an employer and in the leading spheres no one will not tear his hat [spadek] if the employees of the historical commissions put down their work. Most likely, people will even be content with this. It is our duty to work, and with the results of our work to force people to respect us and give us the economic possibility of continuing and expanding this work.[144]

Given these difficulties and the fact that the commissions did not plan on staying in Europe, they sought contact with Jewish research institutions in Palestine and the United States that would enable the continuation of the documentation work and the fulfillment of the goal of laying the basis for a central memorial and research institution elsewhere.

BEYOND THE DP CAMPS: THE LARGER IMPACT OF THE HISTORICAL COMMISSIONS ON HOLOCAUST DOCUMENTATION

All historical commissions in the DP camps maintained close relations with YIVO in New York, which not only had an advisory function but also embodied the cultural heritage with which most of the commission activists identified themselves.[145] Close contacts were also maintained with the World Jewish Congress, the JDC, the Jewish Labor Committee in New York, and the Jewish Agency and with the initiative around Mordechai Shenhavi (a Ha-Shomer ha-Tsair activist and member of the Mishmar Ha-Emek Kibbutz) for the establishment of a central memorial in Jerusalem, which several years later would result in the foundation of Yad Vashem.[146]

Despite the close contacts with YIVO and other American Jewish institutions, connections with Palestine proved more decisive. When it came to the question of where the documentation efforts should be continued once the DP camps had been dissolved and their populations had dispersed, the idea of leaving the "earth of the murderers of our people and soon being able to help build up our historical folk-monument as free Jews in a liberated Land of Israel"[147] appeared more compelling than transferring the collections to the United States. The foundation of the State of Israel let the idea of a folk memorial become more realistic and unleashed a rapid dispersion of the Jewish DP population, which made itself felt also among the collaborators of the historical commissions.[148]

In September 1948 Mordechai Shenhavi paid a visit to Munich and negotiated the transmission of the material to Israel, which occurred between November 1948 and the spring of 1949.[149] The Central Historical Commission in Munich was officially dissolved in January 1949, and Feigenbaum and Kaplan immigrated to Israel in the following months. In the same year the commissions in the British zone of Germany and the Central Historical Commission in Rome closed their doors and transferred their holdings to Israel. In Austria, the commission in Vienna closed in 1952, and two years later the Linz-based commission followed; both transferred their material to Yad Vashem. When Yad Vashem (Martyrs' and Heroes' Remembrance Authority) opened its doors in 1954, these collections constituted the core of its archival holdings. While Kaplan and Feigenbaum had hoped to be able to continue their research in the framework of Yad Vashem, they were disappointed to learn that Yad Vashem took the archival holdings of the commission in Munich but did not employ its former staff.[150] The Yad Vashem leadership, however, in particular its first director, the historian Benzion Dinur, sought to establish the new research institute as an academic institution affiliated with the Hebrew University of Jerusalem and consequently did not seek the collaboration of survivors who were not professional historians.[151] Although the commission activists did not receive the credit they had hoped for, by laying the basis for the Yad Vashem archives they nevertheless fulfilled their goal of helping to build a national Holocaust memorial and research institution in an independent Jewish state.

While the early documentation work undertaken by survivors in the immediate postwar years hardly left an imprint on the academic study of the Holocaust, the commissions had envisioned the writing of an "integrated history" of the Holocaust, weaving together the voices of the victims with those of the perpetrators, a form of historical narrative that has only recently become accepted in the field of Holocaust studies.[152]

CONCLUSION

The Jewish historical commissions in the DP camps of Germany, Austria, and Italy provide a poignant example of the fact that Holocaust documentation and research began immediately after the catastrophe without a period of silence that prevailed among non-Jews. The survivors active in the commissions—most of them untrained in the historical profession—took upon themselves the difficult task of reencountering their traumatic pasts through meticulously documenting the events not only because they deemed bearing witness a moral imperative but also because they believed that historical documentation would best serve their present and future political, psychological, and material needs.

Only a minority of Jewish DPs shared this imperative, however. The majority of the She'erit Hapletah in the DP camps remained reluctant to confront the recent past through documentation. In part this was due to the fact that historical work involved a psychological burden that many survivors were not able or willing to take on and because they chose to fulfill their obligations to past, present, and future in other ways, such as founding families and acquiring an education. Through multifarious public relations work that pressured the survivors into bearing witness on moral grounds, the commissions managed to collect testimonies and questionnaires from several thousand individuals, and the historical commissions became a central institution in the society and culture of the Jewish DPs in Europe.

Since the Jewish DPs formed a society in transit in an interim period that functioned as both epilogue and preface, the commission activists understood their work of documentation as a temporary and transitional phenomenon. For the commission activists sojourning in the DP camps, the documentation work endowed their survival with meaning and forged a strong sense that it had been not accidental but rather for the purpose of bearing witness and commemorating the dead. Moreover, by gathering evidence on the recent tragedy to serve the fight for justice and material compensation and to constitute the basis for future historical research, the commission activists rendered their pasts usable for their future lives outside of the camps and beyond the blood-soaked soil of Europe.

NOTES

I would like to thank Shirli Gilbert for her critical reading of this text, her insightful comments, and her helpful suggestions.

1. Jewish historical commissions were not limited to Jewish DP camps but were a European phenomenon. Historical commissions, documentation centers, and documentation projects also emerged in France, Poland, Sweden, Switzerland, Great Britain, Czechoslovakia, Romania, Greece, Bulgaria, and the Soviet Union. For a general overview on these initiatives, see Philip Friedman, "European Jewish Research on the Holocaust," in idem, *Roads to Extinction: Essays on the Holocaust,* edited by Ada June Friedman with an introduction by Salo W. Baron, 500–24 (Philadelphia: Jewish Publication Society of America, 1980), and Shmuel Krakowski, "Memorial Projects and Memorial Institutions Initiated by She'erit Hapletah," in *She'erit Hapletah 1944–1948: Rehabilitation and Struggle,* edited by Yisrael Gutman and Avital Saf, 388–98 (Jerusalem: Yad Vashem, 1990).

2. The most notable studies on the cultural, social, and political lives of Jewish DPs that mention the centrality of the historical commissions include Michael Brenner, *After the Holocaust: Rebuilding Jewish Lives in Postwar Germany* (Princeton, NJ: Princeton University Press, 1995), 28; Angelika Eder, *Flüchtige Heimat: Jüdische Displaced Persons in Landsberg am Lech 1945 bis 1950* (Munich: Kommissionsverlag UNI-Druck, 1998), 216–18; Yosef Grodzinsky, *In the Shadow of the Holocaust: The Struggle between Jews and Zionists in the Aftermath of World War II* (Monroe, ME: Common Courage, 2004), 124–28; Hagit Lavsky, *New Beginnings: Holocaust Survivors in Bergen-Belsen and the British Zone in Germany, 1945–1950* (Detroit: Wayne State University Press, 2002), 156; and Susanne Rolinek, *Jüdische Lebenswelten 1945–1955: Flüchtlinge in der amerikanischen Zone Österreichs* (Vienna and Innsbruck: Studienverlag, 2007), 101–3. For two excellent treatments of the Central Historical Commission in Munich in particular, see Zeev Mankowitz, *Life between Memory and Hope: The Survivors of the Holocaust in Occupied Germany* (Cambridge: Cambridge University Press, 2002), 192–225, and Ada Schein, "'Everyone can hold a pen': The Documentation Project in the DP Camps in Germany," in *Holocaust Historiography in Context: Emergence, Challenges, Polemics and Achievements,* edited by David Bankier and Dan Michman (Jerusalem: Yad Vashem and Berghahn Books, 2008), 103–34.

3. For an attempt to analyze the European phenomenon of early Jewish Holocaust documentation in comparative perspective considering the

cases of France, Poland, Germany, Austria, and Italy, see Laura Jockusch, "'Collect and Record! Help to Write the History of the Latest Destruction!' Jewish Historical Commissions in Europe 1943–1953" (PhD
dissertation, New York University, 2007), and idem, "Khurbn Forshung: Jewish Historical Commissions in Europe, 1943–1949," *Simon
Dubnow Institute Yearbook* 6 (2007): 441–73.

4. Report of the cultural office of the Central Committee of Liberated Jews
in the British zone, June 1946, Record group (hereafter RG) O70, folder
30, frame 19, Yiddish Yad Vashem Archives, Jerusalem (hereafter YVA).

5. Paul (Pinchas) Trepman, born in Warsaw in 1916, worked as a teacher
before the war and was active in the Revisionist Zionist Movement.
During the war he assumed the identity of a non-Jewish Pole. In 1943
he was deported and survived six concentration camps. He reached Bergen-Belsen in one of the death marches and was liberated by the British. At the end of the 1940s he immigrated to Canada, where he died
in 1987. Rafael Gerszon Olewski, born in Osienciny, Poland, in 1914,
worked as a teacher and journalist before the war. He was a committed Zionist active in the Keren Kayemet and a member of the General
Zionist Party. After the war he lived in the Belsen DP Camp, where he
cofounded and edited *Undzer Shtime,* and headed the historical commission and the Culture Department of the Central Committee of Liberated Jews in the British zone. In 1949 he immigrated to Israel. He
died in 1981. Dovid Rosental, born in Warsaw in 1919, was a journalist
before the war and a committed labor Zionist. He was a survivor of
Auschwitz and after the war stayed in the Belsen DP camp, where he
was one of the directors of the Cultural Office of the Central Committee
of Liberated Jews in the British zone. In this capacity he was also active
in the historical commission in Belsen and a member of the editorial
board of *Undzer Shtime.* At the end of the 1940s he immigrated to the
United States. See Lavsky, *New Beginnings,* 67–70. Sami Feder, born
in Zawiercie, Poland, in 1909, grew up in Germany. He studied acting
and theater in Berlin and worked as an actor and playwright. In 1934
he was forced to leave the country and return to Poland. He survived
several work and concentration camps. After the liberation from Bergen-Belsen he was active in the cultural office of the camp, led the KZ-
Teater in Belsen and wrote for *Undzer Shtime.* In 1947 he left Germany
for Paris, where he stayed until his immigration to Israel in 1960. See
Feder's autobiography *Mayn lebn* (Tel Aviv: Yisrael Bukh, 1995).

6. Rafael Olewski, "Arkhiv fun der oysrotungs tekufe finem yidntum,"
n.d., RG 294.2, reel 114, frame 0353, Displaced Persons Camps, Germany Collection, YIVO Archives, New York (hereafter YIVO DPG).

7. "Arkhiv fun der oysrotungs tekufe funem eyropeyshn yidntum baym
yidishn tsentral komitet in bergn-belzn," November 1, 1945, reel 114,
frame 0354, YIVO DPG.

8. Born in 1899 in Krakow, Cwi Horowic received a traditional Jewish
education, began to learn the furrier's trade, and then tried his hand at

tailoring, millinery, and plumbing but never practiced any of them, instead living the life of a fameless writer. In the interwar years he briefly immigrated to Palestine but was forced to return to Poland by British Mandatory powers because of his left-wing political activities. He survived World War II in the Soviet Union and returned to Poland after the war, but in 1947 he left for the British zone of Germany, where he founded a historical commission in Göttingen. In 1949 he immigrated to Israel. See S. Sh. Noam's introduction to the Hebrew edition of Horowic's novel, *Mishpahat Horovits: Ha-nefilah ha-gedolah* (Kiryat Tiv'on: Ha-Muze'on Bitan, 1973), 14.

9. Moyshe Yoysef Feigenbaum was born in 1908 in BiaŁa-PodŁaska, Lublin District, Poland. He survived several ghettos, escaped from execution and deportation to Treblinka, and survived in a bunker. In 1945 he went to Germany, and four years later he immigrated to Israel. *Leksikon fun der nayer yidisher literatur*, Vol. 7, edited by the Congress for Jewish Culture (New York: Congress for Jewish Culture, 1956–81), 342, and Dawidowicz, *From That Time and Place: A Memoir, 1938–1947* (New York: Bantam Books, 1991), 304.

10. Israel Kaplan, born in 1902 in Volozhin, Byelorussia, a graduate of Kovno University, survived Ghetto Riga and concentration camps Kaiserwald and Dachau. In 1949 he immigrated to Israel, where he died in 2003. Cf. *Lexikon fun der nayer yidisher literatur*, 8:94, and Dawidowicz, *From That Time and Place*, 304-5.

11. Protocol of the founding meeting of the historical commission in Munich, November 28, 1945, Yiddish, RG MiP, folder 2, frame 9, YVA.

12. Ibid.

13. Ibid.

14. Ibid.

15. Work report of the Central Historical Commission, May 12, 1947, reel 13, frame 0153, YIVO DPG; Work report for May 1–June 1, 1948, dated June 3, 1948, Yiddish, RG MiP, folder 7I, frame 102, YVA.

16. The teacher and writer Mejlech Bakalczuk was born in 1896 in Sernik, Polesia, and studied at the University of Kiev. During World War II he was a partisan in the Soviet Union. He returned to Poland in 1945 and left for Austria after a couple of months. In October 1947 he left for Palestine, and the following year he migrated to South Africa. Cf. *Leksikon fun der nayer yidisher literatur*, 1:230–31.

17. Michael John, "Zwischenstation Oberösterreich. Die Auffanglager und Wohnsiedlungen für jüdische DPs und Transitflüchtlinge," in *Flucht nach Erez Israel. Die Bricha und der jüdische Exodus durch Österreich nach 1945*, edited by Thomas Albrich, 67–92 (Innsbruck: Studien Verlag, 1998), especially 75; Evelyn Adunka, *Die Vierte Gemeinde: Die Wiener Juden in der Zeit von 1945 bis heute* (Berlin: Philo Verlag 2000), 58-61.

18. Statutes of Jewish Historical documentation in Linz, January 14, 1947, German, M9, folder 36, p. 1, YVA.

19. Simon Wiesenthal, "Die Rolle der Jüdischen Historischen Dokumenta-

tion bei der Verfolgung und Bestrafung der Kriegsverbrecher (Beispiel Österreich)," November 25, 1947, RG 294.4, reel 4, frames 0962–67, Displaced Persons Camps, Austria Collection, YIVO (hereafter YIVO DPA).

20. Work report of the Jewish Historical Documentation in Vienna, May 16, 1947, German, RG O-5, folder 2, YVA.

21. The journalist Moyshe Kaganowicz was born in 1909 in Ivia, Byelorussia. He survived the war as a partisan in the Soviet Union. In 1945 he reached Italy, and four years later he left for Israel. See *Leksikon fun der nayer yidisher literatur*, 8:26.

22. F. Falk, "Tsvey yor Pakhakh," *Farn Folk*, no. 20 (November 30, 1947): 4. On Pakhakh, see David Engel, *Beyn shihrur li-verihah Beyn shihrur li-verikhah: Nitsule ha-shoah be-Polin ve-ha-ma'avak 'al hanhagatam, 1944–1946* (Tel Aviv: Am Oved, 1996), 87, 198-99; Mankowitz, *Life Between Memory and Hope*, 158–60; Itzhak Zuckerman, *A Surplus of Memory: Chronicle of the Warsaw Ghetto Uprising* (Berkeley: University of California Press, 1993), 571, 585, 607–10, 637–40; and idem, *Yetsiyat Polin: Al "Ha-Brikha" ve-al shikum ha-tnu'ah ha-khalutsit* (Tel Aviv: Itshak Katzenelson House of Ghetto Fighters and Ha-Kibuts Hameukhad Publishing House, 1988), 13-15.

23. Yitskhok Kvintman, "Tsvey yor tetikeyt fun der historisher komisye bey Pakhakh," *Farn Folk*, no. 20 (November 30, 1947): 18.

24. "Informatsye Byuletin" no. 1 (November 25, 1945), RG 294.3, reel 26, folder 351, frame 0467, Displaced Persons Camps, Italy Collection, YIVO (hereafter YIVO DPI).

25. Undated call, U.S. zone, RG MiP, folder N/789,YVA.

26. Report on the first conference on Jewish historical commissions in the U.S. zone of Germany, May 11–12, 1947, Yiddish, RG MiP, folder 38, p. 11, YVA.

27. Ibid.

28. Kvintman, "Tsvey yor tetikeyt fun der historisher komisye bey Pakhakh," 18.

29. Kvintman, "A denkmol dem umbakantn yidishn partizan un geto-kemfer," *Farn Folk*, no. 27 (October 12, 1948): 10.

30. Report by Cwi Horowic on the activity of the historical commission [1947], folder 475, German Stadtarchiv Göttingen, Department of Culture (hereafter SGC).

31. Wiesenthal, "Die Rolle der Jüdischen Historischen Dokumentation," reel 4, frame 0962, YIVO DPA.

32. Ibid., frame 0963.

33. Ibid., frame 0962.

34. Ibid., frame 0967.

35. Kvintman, "Tsvey yor tetikeyt fun der historisher komisye bey Pakhakh," 18.

36. Work report of the Central Historical Commission in Munich, May 12, 1947, Yiddish, reel 13, frame 0155, YIVO DPG.

37. Ibid.

38. Ibid., frame 0154.

39. Wiesenthal, "Die Rolle der Jüdischen Historischen Dokumentation," reel 4, frames 0962–63, YIVO DPA.

40. "Vendung num. 1," May 12, 1948, RG MiP, folder 6, frame 25, YVA.

41. A. Ferkal, "Di vikhtikeyt fun der historisher komisye bay undz," *Frayer Kemfer. Tsentralorgan fun P.Kh.Kh. in Lints*, no. 1 (November 20, 1946): 7.

42. "Khaveyrim partizaner!," n.d., reel 26, folder 352, frame 0504, YIVO DPI.

43. "Yid!," n.d., RG MiP, folder 6, frames 27–28, YVA.

44. Kvintman, "Tsvey yor tetikeyt fun der historisher komisye bey Pakhakh," 18.

45. Feigenbaum, "Tsu vos historishe komisyes?" *Fun Letsten Hurbn* 1 (August 1946): 2.

46. Koppel S. Pinson, "Jewish Life in Liberated Germany," *Jewish Social Studies* 9, no. 2 (April 1947): 108–9, emphasis in original.

47. Dawidowicz, *From That Time and Place*, 303–4.

48. Philip Friedman, "Die Probleme der wissenschaftlichen Erforschung unserer letzten Katastrophe," box 13, p. 5, [October 1947], Archives of the Centre de Documentation Juive Contemporaine, Paris (hereafter CDJC). Please note: The administrative archives of the CDJC consulted here are not catalogued; the box number refers to the order in which I viewed the boxes.

49. "A yor tsentrale historishe komisye in der amerikaner zone, daytshland," January 1, 1947, and "Vu es vert gezamlt . . . a geshprekh mitn leyter fun der tsentraler historisher komisye in minkhn M.Y. Feygnboym," *Undzer Veg*, no. 57 (December 6, 1946).

50. Report on the first conference of historical commissions in the U.S. zone, Yiddish, RG MiP, folder 38, p. 6, YVA.

51. Ibid., p. 2.

52. Assessing of how many people worked for the historical commissions in the DP camps is difficult because of the high fluctuation of coworkers and the lack of accurate records. However, a rough estimate based on numerous work reports suggests that the Central Historical Commission had an average of between 70 and 120 employees in the entire U.S. zone, whereas the average of the commissions in the British zone of Germany as well as in Austria and Italy ranged between 20 and 40 employees, respectively.

53. "Barikhtn tetikeyt," in *Fun Letsten Hurbn* 10 (December 1948): 163.

54. Sixth day of the first international conference of Jewish Historical Commissions and Documentation Centers, Paris, December 8, 1947, morning session, p. 3, box 4, protocol, CDJC.

55. "Tetikeyts berikht fun der historisher komisye," in Leipheim [1947], RG MiP, folder 1, frames 8 and 10, YVA.

56. *Farn Folk*, no. 8 (February 10, 1947): 5.

57. Helen Fuchsman (née Radoszycka), born in Warsaw, received a secular high school education and worked in her mother's business until she married in 1935. During the war she was in the Vilna Ghetto and survived under a false identity together with her husband and young son. In 1945 she went to the U.S. zone of Austria, where she was active in the Jewish historical commission in Linz. In 1948 she immigrated to the United States, where she died in 1993. See the interview with Helen Foxman (Fuchsman) in Brana Gurewitsch, *Mothers, Sisters, Resisters: Oral Histories of Women Who Survived the Holocaust* (Tuscaloosa and London: University of Alabama Press, 1998), 33–46.

58. See the letters by Helen Fuchsman to Simon Wiesenthal: February 17, 1948, and March 12, 1948 (reel 5, folder 153, frames 1000 and 1016, YIVO DPA), and April 17, 1948, and May 31, 1948 (RG M9, folder 49, frames 271–72 and 334, YVA), German.

59. Kvintman, "A denkmol dem umbakantn yidishn partizan un geto-kemfer."

60. Cf. Feigenbaum's report at the first conference of Jewish documentation centers and historical commissions in Paris in December 1947, conference protocol, December 7, 1947, morning session, box 4, French, CDJC; and "Tetitkeytsbarikht fun der tsentraler historisher komisye baym ZK fun di bafrayte yidn in der amerikaner zone in daytshland tsum 20ten november 1947 fun leyter M. I. Feigenbaum," March 15, 1947, box 5, p. 1–2, CDJC. See also, "Barikhtn tetikeyt," *Fun Letsten Hurbn* 10 (December 1948): 164.

61. Mankowitz, *Life between Memory and Hope*, 19. Malcolm Proudfoot, *European Refugees, 1939–1952: A Study in Forced Population Movement* (London: Faber and Faber, 1957), 340, estimated the percentage of Polish Jews among the Jewish DPs in Germany, Austria, and Italy at 73 percent at the end of September 1947. According to Leonard Dinnerstein, *America and the Survivors of the Holocaust* (New York: Columbia University Press, 1982), 279, in Germany alone, Polish Jews made up 81 percent of the Jewish DP population in late September 1947.

62. Of the roughly 250,000 Jewish DPs who found themselves in Germany, Austria, and Italy in the summer of 1947, 190,000 had left by the end of 1949. Cf. Proudfoot, *European Refugees*, 341 and 362.

63. See the letters by Helen Fuchsman to Simon Wiesenthal: February 17, 1948, and March 12, 1948 (reel 5, folder 153, frames 1000 and 1016, YIVO DPA), and April 17, 1948, and May 31, 1948, (RG M9, folder 49, pp. 271–72 and 334, YVA), German.

64. See Helen Fuchsman to Simon Wiesenthal, February 17, 1948, reel 5, frame 1000, German, YIVO DPA; and Helen Fuchsman to Simon Wiesenthal, March 12, 1948, reel 5, frame 1016, YIVO DPA.

65. "Arbets-instruktsyes far historishe komisyes," January 27, 1947, p. 2, RG MiP, folder 6II, frame 16, YVA.

66. Cf. "Protokol 2 fun der zitsung fun der historisher komisye," December 3, 1945, RG MiP, folder 2, frame 14, YVA; and "A yor tsentrale his-

Laura Jockusch

torishe komisye in der amerikaner zone, daytshland," January 1, 1947, reel 13, frame 0189, YIVO DPG.

67. "A yor tsentrale historishe komisye in der amerikaner zone, daytshland," January 1, 1947, reel 13, frame 0192, YIVO DPG.

68. Ibid., frame 0193.

69. "Attention, former Concentration Camp Inmates of KZ Mauthausen!," reel 5, folder 148, frame 0799, n.d., German, YIVO DPA.

70. "Achtung! Bensheimer Jdn!," n.d., RG M1P, folder 9, frame 11, YVA.

71. "Arkhiv fun der oyzrotungs tekufe finem yidntum," reel 114, frame 0353, YIVO DPG.

72. "Fun der historisher komisye tsu ale partizaner!," July 20, 1947, RG AM1, folder 126, frame 0554, YVA. A similar call was published as "Tsu ale yidishe partizaner!" in *Farn Folk*, no. 14 (August 8, 1947): 11, and in Austria as "Di Centrale Historisze Komisje Bajm Farband P.Ch.Ch. in Italje. Cu ale jidisze partizaner!" in the Yiddish-language DP journal *Ojfgang* 33–34 (September 3, 1947): 7.

73. "Protokol," June 4, 1947, and "Protokol," March 30, 1947, p. 31, RG M1P, folder 2, frame 32, YVA.

74. Posters of the Central Historical Commission, RG M1P, folder 2, frames 36 and 37, YVA.

75. "Vendung num. 1," May 12, 1948, RG M1P, folder 6, frame 25, YVA.

76. See, for example, the images used in the brochure edited by the commission, *Yidishe Historishe Komisye in Getingen bey der Tsentraler historisher Komisye in Bergn-Belsn*, no. 1 (July 20, 1947).

77. "Protokol 2 funder zitsung fun der historisher komisye," December 3, 1945, RG M1P, folder 2, frame 14, YVA.

78. "Di Centrale historisze komisje," September 3, 1946, RG M1P, folder 7I, frame 8, YVA.

79. Work report for January 1–May 1, 1948 (Munich, May 5, 1948), RG M1P, folder 7I, frame 96, YVA; Work report for March 1–June 1, 1948 (Munich, June 3, 1948), RG M1P, folder 7I, frame 102, Yiddish, YVA.

80. Letter of the historical commission in Waldstadt/Pocking to the editor of *Undzer Veg*, November 29, 1946, RG M1P, folder 9, frame 10, YVA; "Protokol 3 funder driter zitsung fun di grinder fun der tsentraler historisher komisye in Minkhen," July 30, 1946, RG M1P, folder 2, frame 16, YVA; "Tetikeyts-barikht fun 24 yuni biz dem 1 oktober 1947," October 2, 1947, RG M1P, folder 7I, frame 60, YVA; "Tetikeyts-barikht far der tseyt fun 12 oygust biz dem 11ten September 1947 eynshl.," September 12, 1947, RG M1P, folder 7I, frame 58, YVA; "Tetikeyts-barikht fun 1tn yanuar bizn 1tn may 1948," May 5, 1948, RG M1P, folder 7I, frame 96, YVA; "Allgemeines Schreiben der Kulturabteilung," June 11, 1947, RG O70, file 3, YVA.

81. Central Historical Commission in Munich to the heads of vocational training schools in the U.S. zone, June 1946, Yiddish, reel 13, frame 0211, YIVO DPG; and "Kurce instrukcjes far naj ensztanene Historisze Komisjes." RG O37, folder 8, YVA.

82. "Tetikeyts-barikht farn monat yuli 1946," August 27, 1946, RG MiP, folder 7I, frame 15, YVA; "Tsu ale kibbutzim in der amerikaner zone," RG MiP, folder 10II, frame 15, YVA; "Kibbuts bne-midbar," September 17 [1947], RG MiP, folder 9, frame 3, YVA; and announcement of the contest, February 1947, Yiddish, reel 69, frame 1366, YIVO DPG. The money awarded was 100 and 50 marks for children up to the age of twelve, 150 and 100 marks for adolescents between the ages of twelve and eighteen, and 250 and 150 marks for people older than eighteen.

83. For several examples of *dankzogungn* that the local and regional historical commissions sent to individuals who had donated documents or testimonies, see June 16, 1946, p. 46; August 2, 1946, p. 47; and September 13, 1946, p. 48, all in RG MiP, folder 3, YVA.

84. "Bestätigung Jüdische Historische Dokumentation in Linz," RG M9, folder 18, frame 130, and Simon Wiesenthal to Towia Frydman in Vienna, September 25, 1947, RG M9, folder 42, frame 535, YVA.

85. For example, Jewish Historical Documentation in Vienna to Benjamin Schreiber in Vienna, January 18, 1948, RG O5, folder 2, German, YVA.

86. See Towia Frydman's letter to the JDC in Vienna, September 30, 1947, in which he claimed that a certain Mr. Wien had "acted against the Jewish community" because he had not followed the repeated request of the commission that he testify against several war criminals from Strij. As a punishment he suggested depriving this person of JDC packages for one month (RG O5, folder 2, YVA). A later letter suggests that the JDC indeed stopped its support of individuals who had not cooperated, and once they gave their testimony the supplies resumed. Cf. Towia Frydman to JDC worker Ms. Linden, Vienna, June 28, 1948, RG O5, folder 2, YVA. Commission workers were aware that the reluctance was growing as time went by, and they noticed a crisis especially in 1948; see Helen Fuchsman and Towia Frydman to the JDC in Vienna, June 28, 1948, RG O5, folder 2, YVA.

87. It is difficult to estimate how many survivors participated by completing questionnaires. By November 1947, the Central Historical Commission had received about 6,000 statistical questionnaires, whereas only 345 historical questionnaires had been received. According to Fajgenbaum's statistic, "one in twenty Jews participated," implying that roughly 120,000 Jews lived in the U.S. zone at that time (which almost corresponds with the 114,000 Jewish DPs in the U.S. zone given by Proudfoot for September 30, 1947). See Fajgenbaum's comment in the protocol of the fifth day of the conference of Jewish historical commissions in Paris, December 7, 1947, afternoon session, box 4, p. 3, French, CDJC. See also Proudfoot, *European Refugees*, 340.

88. Feigenbaum, "Tsu vos historishe komisyes?," *Fun Letsten Hurbn* 1 (August 1946): 2.

89. Ibid.

90. "Barikhtn tetikeyt," *Fun Letsten Hurbn* 5 (May 1947): 104; "Vendung num. 2," April 1947, RG MiP, folder 6, frame 20, YVA; for example, see

testimonies, RG M1E, folders 59, 193, 194, 195, 196, 197, and 198, YVA.

91. "Kurce instrukcijes far naj ensztanene Historisze Komisijes," Regional Committee Frankfurt Historical Commission, n.d., RG O37, folder 8, YVA.

92. Ferkal, "Di vikhtikeyt fun der historisher komisye bay undz," 7.

93. Along with this elitist target group, the partisan historians were convinced that the historical documents on the past of Jewish partisans "will evoke a revolution in the Jewish and non-Jewish public after their publication." Cf. letter by Moyshe Kaganowicz to Max Weinreich, YIVO in New York, Rome, October 20, 1946, reel 26, folder 352, frame 0474, YIVO DPI. Moreover, the testimonies mostly related to comrades who had fallen in battle; until August 1947 the historical commission in Rome had collected eight hundred such biographies. Cf. the guidelines for these biographies in "Tsu ale yidisher partizaner!" *Farn Folk*, no. 14 (August 8, 1947): 11.

94. Feigenbaum, "Tsu vos historishe komisyes," 2.

95. The Central Historical Commission paid particular attention to folklore, in terms of expressions, jokes, and neologisms created in ghettos and camps as well as songs that it recorded in musical notation and in a sound archive of musical recordings by survivors on gramophone records, which can be found in Yad Vashem's sound archives. For an analysis of these recordings see Shirli Gilbert, "Buried Monuments: Yiddish Songs and Holocaust Memory," *History Workshop Journal* 66 (2008): 107–28.

96. "Historisher fregboygn," reel 13, frames 0217–26, YIVO DPG. M1Q, YVA, contains 534 historical questionnaires.

97. "Tetikeyts-barikht far der tseyt fun 1 detsember 1947 bizn 1 merts 1948," March 3, 1948, RG M1P, file 71, frame 92, YVA.

98. Questionnaire on folklore material, reel 13, frames 0236 and 0227–29, YIVO DPG.

99. Questionnaire for German officials, reel 13, frame 0241, YIVO DPG.

100. "Fregboygn (tsu der oysgabe fun 'partizaner-almanakh')," [1947], reel 26, folder 352, frame 0503, YIVO DPI.

101. This editorial selectivity of Kaplan was criticized by Philip Friedman as unscholarly; see Friedman, "Dos gedrukte yidishe vort bay der Sheyres Hapleyte in daytshland," *Tsukunft*, March 1949, 151–55. For an analysis of *Fun Letsten Hurbn*, see the contribution of Boaz Cohen in this volume.

102. Israel Kaplan, *In der tog-teglekher historisher arbet: Fortrag gehaltn oyfn tsuzamenfor fun di historishe komiyes, Minkhen dem 12tn may 1947* (Munich: Tsentrale Historishe Komisye, 1947), 8–9.

103. Friedman, "Dos gedrukte yidishe vort bay der Sheyres Hapleyte in daytshland," 151.

104. Ibid.

105. Israel Kaplan, *Dos folks-moyl in natsi-klem: Reydenishn in geto un katset* (Munich: Tsentrale Historishe Komisye, 1949).

106. Avrom Vaysbrod, *Ez shtarbt a shtetl: Megiles Skalat* (Munich: Tsentrale Historishe Komisye, 1948).

107. Moyshe Yoysef Feigenbaum, *Podolye in umkum: Notitsn fun khurbn, Aroyzgegebn fun der tsentraler historisher komisye baym Ts.K. fun di bafrayte yidn in der amerikaner zone in daytshland* (Munich: Tesentrale Historishe Komisye, 1948).

108. Jüdische Historische Kommission in Göttingen, ed., *Unser Weg in die Freiheit* [Brochure] (Göttingen: No publisher, July 20, 1947), and *Jüdische Professoren und Dozenten and der Georg-August Universität zu Göttingen* [Brochure] (Göttingen: No publisher, August 20, 1947); Cwi Horowic, *Die Wacholders: Eine jüdische Familiengeschichte* (Göttingen: Jüva-Verlag, 1947).

109. Sami Feder, *Zamlung fun Katset un geto lider* (Bergen-Belsen: Tsentral Komitet fun di Bafrayte Yidn in der Britisher Zone, 1946), and Rafael Olewski, Paul Trepman, and Dovid Rosental, eds., *Undzer khurbn in bild* (Bergen-Belsen: Undzer Shtime, 1946).

110. Moyshe Kaganowicz, *Der yidisher onteyl in der partizaner-bavegung fun soviet-rusland* (Rome and New York: Tsienistisher Arbeter Komitet far Hilf un Oyfboy, 1948).

111. Simon Wiesenthal, *KZ Mauthausen* (Linz: Ibid-Verlag, 1946), and idem, *Grossmufti—Grossagent der Achse* (Salzburg: Ried-Verlag, 1947).

112. Tobias Friedman [Towia Frydman], ed., *Die Tragödie des österreichischen Judentums. Bericht und Dokumentensammlung* (Haifa: Vereinigung der Juden aus Österreich, 1958).

113. On YIVO's concept of Jewish scholarship, see Cecile Kuznitz, "The Origins of Yiddish Scholarship and the YIVO Institute for Jewish Research" (PhD dissertation, Stanford University, 2000); Lucjan Dobroszycki, "YIVO in Interwar Poland: Work in the Historical Sciences," in, *The Jews of Poland between Two World Wars*, edited by Yisrael Gutman, Ezra Mendelsohn, Jehuda Reinharz, and Chone Shmeruk, 494–518 (Hanover and London: University Press of New England, 1989).

114. Cf. Central Jewish Historical Commission, ed., *Metodologishe onveyzungen tsum oysforshn dem khurbn fun poylishn yidntum* (Łódź: CŻKH 1945). Part of the Polish questionnaire and instructions for collectors of historical material were reprinted by the Central Historical Commission in Munich as *Fregboygens far zamler fun historishe materyaln* (Munich: Tsentrale Historishe Komisye, 1947).

115. See the report on the first conference of the employees of historical commissions in the U.S. zone of Germany, May 11–12, 1947, RG M1P, folder 38, frame 1, Yiddish, YVA. Lucy Schildkret, who was closely connected with the historical commission, also reports on the disappointment of Kaplan and Feigenbaum of Friedman's lacking support and involvement; see American Jewish Historical Society, New York, Lucy Dawidowicz Papers, P-675, box 55, folder 3, November 19, 1946, English. See also Feigenbaum's fierce criticism of Friedman, RG 1258, Philip Friedman Papers, box 2, folder 63, Moyshe Yoysef Feigenbaum

to Philip Friedman, October 12, 1950, Yiddish, YIVO.

116. Report on the first conference of historical commissions in the U.S. zone, Yiddish, RG MiP, folder 38, frame 6, YVA.

117. "Protokol 2 fun der zitsung fun der historisher komisye," December 3, 1945, RG MiP, folder 2, frame 14, YVA.

118. Ibid.

119. "Barikht fun der tseyt fun 3 bizn 31 detsember 1945," RG MiP, folder 7I, frame 1, YVA.

120. MiL, YVA, contains some five hundred answered questionnaires of German officials.

121. Memorandum "Zur Frage der Jüdischen Histor. Kommission für Niedersachsen in Göttingen," n.d., folder 475, SGC.

122. Stadtdirektor Kuss to Kulturdezernent Pfauter, September 3, 1947, and note for Amtsgerichtsrat Arndt, September 3, 1947, folder 475, SGC.

123. Cwi Horowitz to Stadtdirektor Kuss, August 28, 1947; Oberstadtdirektor Schmidt to the Jewish Historical Commission, June 4, 1947; and Stadtarchiv to Oberstadtdirektor Schmidt, June 26, 1947; all in folder 475, SGC.

124. Municipality to Jewish Historical Commission, July 8, 1947; Fahlbusch to Jewish Historical Commission in Bergen-Belsen, July 17, 1947; Cwi Horowitz to Stadtdirektor Kuss, August 7, 1947; Stadtdirektor Kuss to Kulturdezernent Pfauter, September 3, 1947; letter by municipal museum to historical commission in Belsen, July 11, 27, 1947; all in folder 475, SGC.

125. Stadtbauamt to Kulturdezernent, September 25, 1947; report of the Bauausschuss, December 16, 1947; Kulturdezernent Pfauter to Cwi Horowic, January 30, 1948; all in folder 475, SGC.

126. Simon Wiesenthal, "L'importance de la Documentation Historique Juive," [November 1947], RG M9, folder 49, frame 472, YVA.

127. "Rapport de M. Tobie Frydman (Vienne). L'activité de la Commission juive de documentation historique de Vienne (Autriche)," [November 1947], RG O5, folder 10, frame 1, YVA, and Friedman, "Die grossen und kleinen österreichischen Nazis, die bei Aussiedlung und Vernichtung der Juden mitwirkten," in Die Tragödie des österreichischen Judentums, 50–53. See also Wiesenthal, "Die Rolle der Jüdischen Historischen Dokumentation," reel 4, frame 0965, YIVO DPA.

128. Undated manuscript of a speech by Simon Wiesenthal to an Austrian Jewish audience, German, RG M9, folder 41, YVA.

129. Interview with Towia Frydman in Haifa, August 11, 2005, conducted by the author.

130. Wiesenthal, "Die Rolle der Jüdischen Historischen Dokumentation," reel 4, frames 0962 and 0965, YIVO DPA.

131. Simon Wiesenthal to League for Human Rights in Vienna, October 23, 1952, RG M9, folder 31, frames 226–27, YVA.

132. Wiesenthal, "Pressekonferenz zur Lage der jüdischen DPs und der Weltlage des Judentums," [summer and fall, 1946], reel 22, folder 582,

frames 1191–95, YIVO DPA.

133. Wiesenthal, "Die Rolle der Jüdischen Historischen Dokumentation," reel 4, frame 0967, YIVO DPA.

134. Wiesenthal, "Pressekonferenz zur Lage der jüdischen DPs und der Weltlage des Judentums," reel 22, frames 1191–95, YIVO DPA.

135. "Barikhtn tetikeyt," *Fun Letsten Hurbn* 10 (December 1948): 163, 169.

136. For an analysis of the encounter of German and East European Jews in postwar Germany, see Brenner, *After the Holocaust*, 41–51, and idem, "East European Jews in Postwar Germany, 1945–50," in *Jews, Germans, Memory: Reconstructions of Jewish Life in Germany*, edited by Y. Michal Bodemann, 49–63 (Ann Arbor, University of Michigan Press, 1996).

137. In May 1947 the community had about forty members, half of whom were German-born; the leadership of the community, born between 1870 and 1895, was German Jewish from Göttingen or Lower Saxony; list of community members May 1947, collection no. 16, folder 4, SGC. Cordula Tollmien, "Nach 1945: Organisation des Überlebens und die Entstehung einer neuen jüdischen Gemeinde," *Göttingen: Geschichte einer Universitätsstadt*, Vol. 3, edited by Rudolf von Thadden and Marc-Dietrich Ohse, 733–60 (Göttingen: Vandenhoeck und Ruprecht, 1999).

138. Briefing of a letter by Stadtverwaltung to Regierungspräsident, January 5, 1948, folder 475, SGC.

139. Jewish Community Göttingen to Central Committee Belsen, January 21, 1950, collection no. 16, folder 6, frame 45, SGC.

140. Gräfenberg letter to Yanowsky Book Committee, Los Angeles, February 15, 1950, collection no. 16, folder 6, SGC.

141. Work report of the Central Historical Commission in Munich, May 12, 1947, Yiddish, reel 13, frame 0154, YIVO DPG.

142. "Vu es vert gezamlt . . . ," *Undzer Veg*, no. 57 (December 6, 1946). Work report of the Central Historical Commission in Munich, May 12, 1947, Yiddish, reel 13, frame 0153, YIVO DPG; "Tetikeyts-barikht far der tseyt fun 1 yanuar biz dem 1 yuli 1947," July 16, 1947, p. 2, RG MiP, folder 71, frame 55, YVA.

143. "Tetikeyts-barikht far der tseyt fun 26 April h.y. biz dem 12 may 1947 eynshl.," May 13, 1947, RG MiP, folder 71, frame 49, YVA.

144. Protocol of the first conference of Jewish historical commissions in the U.S. zone, May 11–12, 1947, Yiddish, RG MiP, folder 38, frame 11, YVA.

145. Protocol of the third meeting of the founders of the historical commission in Munich, July 30, 1946, Yiddish, RG MiP, folder 2, frame 17, YVA. See also "Grupe fraynt fun yidishn visnshaftlekhn institut YIVO in italye: Bashraybt ayere iberlebungen fun der tsayt fun der daytsher milkhome," *Farn Folk*, no. 6 (December 1, 1946): 12.

146. See Kvintman, "Tsvey yor tetikeyt fun der historisher komisye bey Pakhakh," 18, and idem, "A denkmol dem umbakantn yidishn partizan un geto-kemfer."

147. Report on the first conference of Jewish historical commissions in the U.S. zone, May 11–12, 1947, Yiddish, RG MiP, folder 38, frames 2–3,

YVA.

148. While the work report from June 1948 mentioned a total of forty-seven members, the work report from September 1948 referred to five members; in October and November there were only four members. Cf. RG MiP, folder 7I, frames 102 and 117–19, YVA.

149. "Khronik", *Fun Letsten Hurbn* 9 (September 1948): 107.

150. "Barikhtn tetikeyt," *Fun Letsten Hurbn* 10 (December 1948): 169–70. See the correspondence between Moyshe Yoysef Feigenbaum and Isaac Schneersohn, May 17, 1949, June 20, 1949, and September 9, 1949, box 35, CDJC.

151. On the beginnings of Yad Vashem, see Mooli Brog, "In Blessed Memory of a Dream: Mordechai Shenhavi and Initial Holocaust Commemoration Ideas in Palestine, 1942–1945," *Yad Vashem Studies* 30 (2002): 297–336; Boaz Cohen, "The Birth Pangs of Holocaust Research in Israel," *Yad Vashem Studies* 33 (2005): 203–43; idem, "Holocaust Research in Israel, 1945–1980: Trends, Characteristics, Developments" (PhD dissertation [Hebrew], Bar Ilan University, 2004); Orna Kenan, *Between History and Memory: The Evolution of Israeli Historiography of the Holocaust, 1945–1961* (New York: Peter Lang, 2003); Roni Stauber, *The Holocaust in Israeli Public Debate in the 1950s* (London and Portland, OR: Vallentine Mitchell, 2007).

152. Saul Friedländer, *Nazi Germany and the Jews*, Vol. 1, *The Years of Persecution, 1933–1939* (New York: HarperCollins, 1997), and Vol. 2, *The Years of Extermination, 1939–1945* (New York: HarperCollins, 2007), esp. 1:1–6.

Representing the Experiences
of Children in the Holocaust

Children's Survivor Testimonies Published in Fun Letsten
Hurbn, *Munich, 1946–49*

BOAZ COHEN

It's impossible to describe how we suffered

—Genia Shurz, "My Experiences during the War"

The future of surviving children was a major issue in post-Holocaust
Jewish society. Schools and educational facilities were set up in towns
and in displaced person (DP) camps, as were children's homes in
which orphaned children received care and education. Teachers were
sent from the Yishuv in Palestine to work alongside survivor teachers in these schools. Youth movements, mainly Zionist, ran their own
children's and youth groups replicating their prewar ideologies. Organizations such as the *kordinazia* (coordinated organization) in Poland
arranged for the return of Jewish children rescued by gentiles, officially where possible but clandestinely when the need arose. International
Jewish organizations such as the Jewish Agency, the American Jewish
Joint Distribution Committee, and the American Committee for the
Rehabilitation of European Jewish Children funded and contributed
to this work. All of this activity was fueled by the belief that in these
children lay the future of the Jewish people. The children were seen as
objects for care, love, and reeducation.

Less known is the fact that correspondingly, much effort was put into listening to the child survivors, recording their stories, and publishing them. By 1947 three anthologies of children's testimonies were published, bringing to the public the stories of child survivors as they told them. The appearance of such a body of books all over the Jewish world (Poland, Tel Aviv, Paris, and Buenos Aires) in Yiddish, Polish, and Hebrew shows the widespread interest in the children's Holocaust experience.[1]

This chapter tells the story of the publication and representation of children's testimonies in the first-ever Holocaust research journal, *Fun Letsten Hurbn*, published in Munich during 1946 – 48. The journal was published by the Central Historical Commission in Munich, which was established in December 1945 by the Central Committee for the Liberated Jews in Germany. The commission collected thousands of testimonies from Holocaust survivors in the DP camps, among them hundreds from child survivors of the Holocaust. The drive to collect testimonies from children was initiated by Israel Kaplan, a teacher from Kovno who together with Moshe Feigenboim led the commission. The child survivors and their stories held a strong fascination with Kaplan, whose own child survived the Holocaust in hiding and on the run.

Out of hundreds of testimonies collected from child survivors by the staff of the Central Historical Commission during its more than three years of existence, eight were selected for publication in the journal issues. What were the criteria for publication? Why were these specific testimonies chosen? Did Kaplan choose them in order to make a point, or was it instead a matter of availability? Testimonies had to be fit for print, and after years without proper education possibly not many children could recount the horrors they had experienced in a suitable way.

As for the end result, what picture of the Jewish child's Holocaust experience was the journal presenting, and what were the underlying suppositions and sensibilities behind this presentation? What can we learn from these children's testimonies about the worldview of adult DP survivors?

The *Fun Letsten Hurbn* children's testimonies offer us a glimpse into one of the earliest representations of children's Holocaust experiences and thus enrich our understanding of the dynamics of memory in the DP community and of the place of children in DP worldview.

FUN LETSTEN HURBN

Fun Letsten Hurbn (English title, *From the Last Extermination, Journal for the History of the Jewish People during the Nazi Regime*) was a

Yiddish-language journal appearing in late 1946. Edited by Kaplan, the journal featured eyewitness accounts, testimonies, documents, and photographs collected by the Central Historical Commission. The journal's aim was to "inspire every Jew from among the [Holocaust] survivors to give their testimony of their experiences under the Nazi regime." And indeed, claimed Kaplan, "Since we started with the Journal we get a wider response from survivors."[2] Somewhere between ten thousand and twelve thousand copies of the journal were published in all.

The journal was seen by Kaplan as a "people's project" (*folks arbeit*). "It is still too early for serious scientific research," he said. "Therefore, our purpose is simply a peoples [folk] journal with the participation of the masses. . . . It is the role of the people themselves to recount their experiences and fill in the great blank in our historiography." These testimonies will "furnish the historical material for the future scientific research and evaluations." The journal was to represent the "the frame of mind and experiences of the individual and the public in the destruction of a people," claimed Kaplan. "It is of course much more important to know the inner experiences, the people's frame of mind itself."[3]

In this people's project of recounting the Jewish story of the Holocaust, Kaplan gave a special place for the story of the Jewish child survivor.

ISRAEL KAPLAN AND CHILDREN'S TESTIMONIES

Israel Kaplan (1902–2003) was, as mentioned above, a teacher in prewar Kovno. Like many Jewish East European intellectuals, he studied history and wrote his thesis on the Spanish Inquisition. In the ghetto he was in charge of chronicling the ghetto's history. He went on collecting Jewish folk sayings and black humor throughout his odyssey through ghettos and camps in Lithuania, Latvia, and Germany. His urge to document and record the Jewish tragedy was so strong that even while recuperating in the hospital following liberation, he would sneak away from his bed and collect testimonies and ethnographic materials from the nearby DP camp.[4] Once the Central Historical Commission was established, he became its academic secretary and the editor of its journal, *Fun Letsten Hurbn.*

Kaplan believed that children were a distinct group whose voice had to be heard. He also believed that children had a part to play in the documentation of the past. While in the ghetto he encouraged his son to collect historical materials, such as official stamps and papers. When they were reunited in Munich, Kaplan asked his son and his

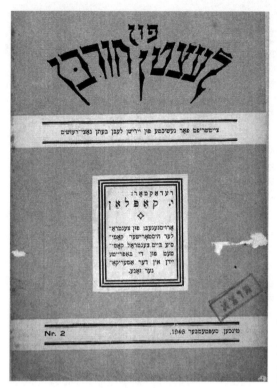

Fun Letsten Hurbn (From the Last Destruction), "A Historical Journal of Jewish Life under the Nazi Regime," edited by Israel Kaplan, Vol. 2, Munich, September 1946.

friends to reconstruct folk songs from the ghetto, which he subsequently published in the journal.

As one of the leaders of the Central Historical Commission, Kaplan initiated a project aimed at collecting testimonies from child Holocaust survivors in the DP camps. "Of great significance to our work is inspiring children to write about what they endured," he said in 1947. "We have already gotten in touch with children's camps, kibbutzim and schools for this."[5]

Kaplan explained to fellow DPs that the aim of collecting children's testimonies was not "the extraction of as many facts as possible." It was instead to record the "child's understanding, his approach and reaction to what happened to him; how the events affected him." The teachers were asked to look for the "psychological and pedagogical aspects" of the testimony to enhance their educational work. In order to enable a full understanding of the child's experience, it is imperative, he said, "not to make any corrections in these works, even in language."[6]

Although hundreds of children's testimonies were collected, Kaplan admitted that reaction to this initiative among teachers and educators wasn't so enthusiastic: "Up to now only a few have responded properly, despite the numerous reminders." He claimed that teachers were overtly shielding the children, fearing to "bring back the wounds that have already healed over." While he accepted that this was possible, he claimed that "It is nevertheless doubtful whether it is always and in every case preferable to have the young people forget their deep and meaningful experiences." He doubted "whether when they grow older the children will be grateful to their teachers for their excessive warm-heartedness." In order not to cause unnecessary pain to the children, he suggested that once teachers attempt "with the appropriate pedagogical approach" to have a child give a full version of his experiences, a copy would be deposited in a school archive, enabling teachers to consult the testimony "without causing further stress to the child himself."[7] Success in this project depended on convincing people in the camps to do the fieldwork. Even a cursory check of the children's testimonies taken by the commission shows that they come in batches from places where the teachers or United Nations Relief and Rehabilitation Administration (UNRRA) workers were won over to the project.

By the summer of 1946 the testimonies started coming in. By November 1946 the first testimony, Arieh Milch's, was published in the third issue of *Fun Letsten Hurbn*.

As mentioned above, Kaplan was not alone in his view of the importance of children's testimonies. Fervent activity in Poland and elsewhere of collecting and publishing children's testimonies also took place. This was a general evolving trend in Jewish memorial culture after the war.[8]

But besides taking part in this nascent memorial culture trend, Kaplan's interest in children's testimonies also had a personal slant. Kaplan had been transferred from the Kovno Ghetto to a work camp, leaving his wife, daughter, and son behind. Just before she was murdered by the Nazis, his wife hid their son with a Lithuanian widow. Their daughter was also hidden with a non-Jewish family that eventually handed her over to the Nazis. Although Kaplan and his son were reunited after the war, it was a difficult reunion. His son blamed Kaplan for leaving him and his mother, and Kaplan, busy with matters concerning the Central Historical Commission, found it hard to rebuild a relationship with his son.

The fate of his children haunted Kaplan, and from the first days of liberation he looked for some sign of life from them. Through his work Kaplan heard of a bright young boy participating in school plays in Orphanage No. 4, the Jewish orphanage in Kovno. He had a strong feeling that this was his lost son, Shalom, and sent emissaries to check him out. Once the boy's identity was verified Kaplan enlisted the help of Rabbi Abe Klausner, who used his contacts to get the boy to Munich. Father and son were reunited in March 1946. They were together for no more than twenty-two days before Shalom was sent to Palestine to board with his aunt and resume his schooling. Kaplan stayed in Munich to work in the Central Historical Commission and in the DP press and joined his son only two and a half years later.

Many years later Shalom told of his bitter memories from the reunion:

> He talked to me, he talked with the people I was introduced to. He never stopped talking. . . . He talked and talked, but he never asked me: "What happened to you son, what did you go through?" He didn't ask. What for? He was already working in the historical commission[;] . . . he didn't need me to tell him about the Ghetto. But as to what had happened to me, specifically to me; my experience, my pain, my fears and my distress, my worries and my apprehensions—these he never knew because he didn't ask.[9]

The ongoing correspondence between Kaplan and his son—far away in Eretz Israel—shows that Kaplan's work in the Central Historical Commission, which kept him in Europe until 1950, did not serve to build the relationship between father and son: the son constantly criticized his father for not coming to Eretz Israel, while the father repeatedly explained the importance of his historical and cultural work.

It is interesting to note that while Kaplan did not get around to listening to his son in the short time they had together and certainly did not take his testimony, he showed a growing commitment to the collection and publication of children's testimonies. As we shall see, a number of children who had their testimonies published were Kovno children and acquaintances of his son. Kaplan's private correspondence shows how much he wanted his son to write a testimony. His letters to him are replete with pleas on the matter. In May 1947, for example, after several such pleas were left unanswered, Kaplan wrote, "If you could send me your memoirs—good but as quickly as possible (two [separate] times by Air-mail) . . . write everything you went through from the beginning of the war until you reached Munich (or Eretz Yisrael). . . . If it's not too hard and if the effort will not harm

Israel Kaplan, his son Shalom (Eilati), and others.

your health—do it!"[10] But Kaplan's pleas were left unanswered. His son would not write a testimony for the journal. He was already in another world, living on a kibbutz in Eretz Israel and forging his new identity. It may also be that he didn't feel any obligation to his father's memorial project, which was keeping his father away from him in Germany.

CHILDREN'S TESTIMONIES IN *FUN LETSTEN HURBN*

Who were the children, and what did they disclose in their testimonies? What can be learned about the way in which their testimonies reached the editors of *Fun Letsten Hurbn,* and how did the editors process them?

The Children: General Characteristics

Eight children—four boys and four girls—had their testimonies published in the journal. At the time of liberation, they were nine to fourteen years old. Two were born in 1931, four in 1932, one in 1933, and one in 1936. They wrote their testimonies no more than three years after liberation. (The last published testimony, Genia Shurz's, is dated June 1948).

All but one of the children came from an area occupied by the Russians until 1941 and then by the Germans. Four of them came from Kovno; a fifth, from Warsaw, was incarcerated in the Kovno Ghetto.

Boaz Cohen

Israel Kaplan and his son Shalom (Eilati).

Two others came from Podhajce in southern Galicia. Two of the girls were cousins. As we can see, the Kovno children figured prominently in the testimonies.

Another notable feature among the testimonies was the existence of living family members. All of the children came out of the Holocaust with some family members still alive. Three survived with both their parents, the mothers of another two had survived, and two had a surviving sibling. Only two had no one from their immediate family left.

How is the predominance of the Kovno group to be explained? And is there a connection to the overrepresentation of children with surviving family members? Did the fact that they had surviving family members aid them in processing the horrors they went through? Or is it that having parents in the same circles as Kaplan helped get their testimonies noticed? Or was Kaplan, as a Kovno teacher, partial to the testimonies of his pupils and their friends, who were also the friends of his estranged son, Shalom. Or was it a combination of all these reasons?

It seems that while all of these things may have influenced Kaplan's editorial decisions, there were more mundane reasons that explain the high proportion of testimonies of the children from Kovno and of children with parents. Kaplan needed testimonies that were coherent and appropriate for print. There weren't many children who came out of the Holocaust with the ability to write an essay that could be incorporated in a journal.

The Kovno Ghetto existed well into 1944 (as did the Łódź Ghetto). In the chaos of the German retreats of 1944, there were more opportunities for survival for both children and parents. This also meant that children had a chance to receive some education, read books, and be tutored for more years then their counterparts in most Polish ghettos. From the testimonies we learn that some parents of this group were teachers. One father was a celebrated author, and the rest of the children came from middle-class and well-to-do families that usually held education in high esteem. The children tell of their parents teaching them or of studying by themselves. For example, while hiding in a gentile's house, Joseph Shuster received lessons from his father. "In quiet times we used to go out into the room, where my papa taught me to read and do arithmetic," he wrote.[11] Daniel Burstin read books supplied by the peasant he was hiding with and spoke Yiddish to the cows in the pasture. "I didn't want to forget the Yiddish language. It was deeply engrained in my heart; it was my mother-tongue. I used to converse thus with the animals: 'My dear calf, how well off you are, that you don't know and didn't know who Hitler is.' The calf or the cow used to low back at me: 'You're right.'"[12]

Children who were on the run or were hiding with non-Jewish families for more years had fewer opportunities for developing the ability to express themselves, certainly in Yiddish, which is the original language of the testimonies. The children whose testimonies were chosen for the journal had a better chance to overcome the lost years of Nazi occupation and write testimonies that were fit for publication.

Choosing the Testimonies

How were the testimonies chosen? The absence of editorial notes and protocols curtails our ability to reconstruct fully the editorial process. Yet the Central Historical Commission's archive (now in Yad Vashem), which was the clearinghouse for the testimonies collected in the DP camps, fortunately provides us with several of the testimonies in the children's handwriting and some other relevant documentation. Interweaving the printed testimonies with these materials offers answers to some of the above questions.

The first child's testimony, Arieh Milch's, was published in volume 3 of the journal (November 1946).[13] He was born in 1932 in the town of Podhajce in Galicia, a town occupied by the Russians in 1939. In July 1941 the German army occupied the town, and four days later his mother was murdered. His father, a Judenrat member ("against his will," insisted Milch), was murdered a year later. Just before the annihilation of the ghetto in 1943, Milch, his brother, and an uncle went into hiding in a gentile's house and were liberated there in March 1944. His original testimony can be found in the Central Historical Commission's archive and is titled "My Survival." It comes from Aschau bei Kraiburg, and it is a part of a group of about twenty testimonies by teenagers from the camp. Aschau was a UNRRA children's transit camp known in Yiddish as the *kinder lager*. The testimonies were written between June and August 1946. They are, as their serial numbers show, among the first testimonies obtained by the commission.[14] Most of them, like Milch's testimony, are in Yiddish, although some are in Hungarian. They were collected under the auspices of UNRRA Team 154. Milch's testimony states his present address as the "D.P. Kinder Lager Block 14." Many of the teenagers who testified with him stated that they belonged to Kibbutz Atid (Kibbutz Future) of the Zionist youth movement Hanoaar Hazioni (Zionist Youth). But Milch's testimony carries no such information.

Daniel Burstin was born in Warsaw in 1931. His eight-page testimony was published in volume 4 (March 1947).[15] Following the German occupation, his parents escaped to Soviet-occupied Kovno, where he spent the war years until the ghetto's liquidation by the Germans in 1944. Burstin, thirteen years old at the time, was sent to Germany to Landsberg and Dachau and from there with 130 children from Kovno to Auschwitz. He jumped from the train and spent the rest of the war working as a farmhand for Polish peasants. After liberation he went to Łódź and was taken into a Jewish children's home. When his mother arrived they joined the Mishmar Hanegev children's home in Ludwikowo just before it moved from Poland to the Lindenfels DP camp. The camp was home to three youth groups, each working independently of the others. Early on Burstin showed literary abilities and ended up editing and producing the group's journal together with Hadasa Rozen and Aryeh Shapira. Being older and better educated than many of the children in the group, they solicited essays, rewrote them, and copied them in fine handwriting in the journal. In 1946 he wrote the first version of his testimony, "Kovno 1944—Fragments of Liquidation."[16] Burstin makes no mention of the prewar years and the flight from his Warsaw home to Kovno; he ends his testimony with a call for revenge.

Burstin's testimony printed in the journal was longer and more complete, starting with the prewar years and ending with his reunion with his mother and their arrival in Lindenfels. His testimony was received by the Central Historical Commission on January 28, 1947. While preparing it for print Kaplan exchanged letters with Burstin, checking out several issues mentioned in the testimony. From this correspondence it turns out that the handwritten testimony was actually in Burstin's mother's handwriting. She transcribed and rewrote it for him; he apologized, "as I was deep into my studies."[17]

On the same transport from Kovno with Burstin was Jacob Lewin, whose testimony was published in volume 5 (May 1947). He did not escape and arrived in Auschwitz with the children's transport. He survived several selections and was incarcerated in Children's Block No. 29. In the winter of 1944 he was sent on a death march on foot and by train through Mauthausen and was liberated in the Austrian countryside. After the war he was reunited with his parents and brother, who had been in German camps. His detailed testimony describing his experience in the death march from Auschwitz was in an issue of the journal dedicated to the subject of death marches. His original testimony could not be traced.[18]

Rosa Pinczewski, whose testimony was published in volume 6 (August 1947), was the only child who was under German occupation since 1939. Born in Łódź in 1931, she and her family spent the first year of the war in Polaniec, where her grandmother lived. They later moved from hideout to hideout and suffered many privations. Toward the end of the war her father was killed while looking for food, and the rest of the family was attacked and killed by the people who had initially hidden them. Rosa escaped and survived by passing as a Christian. Her testimony was sent to the commission from the trade school in Greifenberg. This was her second testimony; the first was given in the children's home of the Jewish Committee of Czentochowa in July 1945.[19]

Joseph Shuster, whose testimony was published in volume 7 (May 1948), was the youngest of the group. Born in 1936, he was also a Kovno boy. He survived the war in hiding with his parents. With the help of a former non-Jewish maid they found refuge with a Christian family, and when that family would not hide them anymore the maid found them another family to hide with.[20]

Also from Kovno was Fania Olitzki (born in 1932) whose testimony appeared in volume 8 (June 1948). She was in the ghetto with her mother until its liquidation in 1944. They were taken to Stutthof, were she was saved again and again by her mother's resourcefulness. In April 1945 they were taken on a death march by foot and by boat. They miraculously survived and were liberated by the British in Neustadt.[21]

Ela Grilihes (Grillechs), Fania's cousin, also from Kovno, was born in 1933. Her two-page testimony was printed in volume 9 (September 1948). She was put in a non-Jewish children's home with a Russian alias. Her parents later died in German camps, the father in Dachau and the mother in Stutthof. After the war she was taken out of the children's home by messengers sent by her aunt, Fania Olitzki's mother, and was reunited with her brother Zvi in Munich.[22]

The testimony published in the last issue of the journal (December 1948) was written by Genia Shurz. She was born in Podhajce in

1932 and told a tale of survival by hiding in the ghetto, flight from the ghetto to a hideout in a gentile's house, and ten months spent there in deprivation with her parents and brother. Her testimony was given at Bad-Salzchlirf in June 1948.[23]

Rewriting the Children: The Question of Editing

How much editing did the printed testimonies undergo? Can the editing process be traced, and what can be learned from it?

In a general comment on his editing work, Kaplan talked of the need to rewrite the essays submitted to the journal. In one of the pleas to his son to write his testimony, Kaplan instructed him to "write in any language . . . you feel comfortable with. I'll polish it up. If you would have seen some of the 'manuscripts' I get (even from the high and mighty) and the way they come out from under my pen, they can hardly be recognized—apart from the author's name."[24] But how much polishing was put into the children's testimonies?

Each of the published testimonies was appended with a comment stating that "The work is presented with only the necessary modifications in language." But how extensive were these changes? A clue can be found in Joseph Schuster's original testimony preserved in Yad Vashem. While most of the testimony remained as Schuster wrote it, two stages, or layers, of editing can be discerned. In the first stage, style and historical details were corrected. Schuster wrote that 534 people died in the first action in the Kovno Ghetto, and the editor corrected it to 500. Later the editor reordered some paragraphs and shifted some lines. Other testimonies show no traces of such comprehensive editing. But editing was not only about language and style. Kaplan went back to the children and questioned them about their testimonies. He asked them to explain discrepancies in their stories and to provide further information on events or people mentioned in the text. Where things were unclear, he asked again. While no original letters by Kaplan were found, two letters remain in which Burstin replies to Kaplan's queries. From the answers, it is apparent that Kaplan's questions focused on Burstin's survival story. In responses to Kaplan's request, Burstin provided the address of the Pole he had hidden with and the ethnic origin of the reapers he met after jumping from the train: "they were Poles or more accurately Silesians." Kaplan wanted to understand, among other things, how a camp inmate in uniform could survive wandering around the countryside. Burstin explained that he "traveled in civilian clothes because they took away our striped uniforms in Dachau and exchanged them for civilian clothes."[25] This probably looked strange to Kaplan: Why would the Germans give the Jews a chance to blend into the countryside? Burstin explained further in cynical overtones. "It is clear that the few 'loyal' fascist Jews would not leave 131 Jewish children without any sign of their origin. Close to our being transported from Dachau they gathered us together in a big barrack and painted long wide stripes on our civilian clothes with durable red paint; on our pants, shirt and blouses. They wanted to make sure that nothing bad would happen to us on the way."[26]

The red stripes were aimed at marking out any child who might try to escape the train. In his original testimony Burstin wrote that while preparing to jump from the train the boys cut their pants and turned their shirts and jackets inside out. Kaplan wanted to ensure that the reader would immediately see the connection between this and the red stripes. He therefore added to the text the following opening sentence: "First of all we had to erase all the outer signs that we were concentration camp inmates." To Burstin's description of the cutting of the clothes he added that they were "marked in paint."[27]

Kaplan's correspondence with Burstin shows that he tried to provide the readers of *Fun Letsten Hurbn* with testimonies that were both coherent and readable. Publishing a testimony demanded getting the facts straight and clarifying any ambiguities. Kaplan regarded the published product his creation no less than the author's. "How do you like my article on Burstin?" he asked his son. "Mrs. Burstin and the son were very satisfied."[28]

CHILDREN'S EXPERIENCES

What could the readers of *Fun Letsten Hurbn* learn from the testimonies about the Jewish child's experience of the Holocaust? The testimonies recount different survival stories and different experiences, but three issues stand out: the centrality of family, the encounter with death, and relations with non-Jews.

Family

Family—its loss as well as its endurance and resilience—figures prominently in the testimonies. Daniel Burstin wrote about his feelings when transferred to Dachau without his parents: "I remained alone, without a father or mother, all alone, without a good friend."[29] Rosa Pinczewski, sent to hide with a gentile peasant, was eloquent in describing the parting from her family: "You can't imagine my parting from my parents. I will never forget it as long as I live. I can't even describe it."[30] Joseph Shuster, whose parents wanted to send him to an Aryan family, refused to part with them. He was seven years old at the time. "At first my parents wanted to send me by myself," he recounted, "but I didn't want to go because I was afraid of being left without a father and mother." Even when warned by his mother that the Germans would take him away, he refused to go by himself. He told his mother, "Mama, whatever happens to you will happen to me."[31] His insistence paid off; his mother went with him, and the father joined them later. Although they had to change hiding places, they survived the war as a family.

Genia Shurz's testimony centered on her family's efforts to keep the family together while hiding from the Nazis. At one stage, after the formal liquidation of the ghetto at Podhajce, they hid in a concealed bunker under one of the remaining buildings. They found a German who agreed to help them leave the ghetto grounds. During the escape they were found out, and a chase ensued; Shurz was knocked unconscious by one of the guards and taken for dead. Regaining consciousness, she found out that she was separated from her family. In an old ruin where she looked for shelter, she found her father. "I was overjoyed at not being alone," she said, but then she noted that her mother and brother were still missing. "I didn't want to go on," wrote Genia. "I cried over having run away from them. I was filled with a child's need for its mother." Hearing the sound of gunfire, she started shouting, "Mama, they're shooting you!" And then the unexpected happened: "Suddenly I heard a voice from far, far away: 'Geni' (that's my name). I was so happy, like a person who has lost his mother and then she rises up from the grave. I couldn't get up from weakness. So my father left me and ran to look for the voice. That is how we found each other again. I couldn't believe that I still had a mother and a brother, because you really can't grasp it. It can only be a miracle or a dream."[32]

Following this experience, the family decided to seek a hideout that would enable them to stay together. There was a gentile they knew who was willing to hide some of them. "He liked us and he told us that if we were ever in a hopeless situation we should come to him, but not everyone, just two people. But after our experience, we decided not to separate again; we would either all live or would die together."[33] He took them all in, and they stayed with him for ten hard months until liberation. But he never really forgave them for forcing the whole family on him, and this, as will be seen, made their survival very precarious.

Another major point regarding family was the parents' commitment toward their children's survival. In the testimonies the children tell of this commitment. Parents attempted, sometimes successfully, to find the children a hiding place with a gentile family or non-Jewish children's home. The children saw their parents digging bunkers for concealment, foraging for food (and sometimes dying in the attempt), and bribing guards to prevent the child from been taken away. At times the efforts had an immediate effect. Fania Olitzki and her mother were in the Stutthof camp when her mother understood that she might be sent to Auschwitz. "She gave me a wink and we both stole away between the barracks until we reached the morgue where the corpses were lying. My mother told me to lie down among the dead, and she tore off a piece of her shirt and covered my face, and threw a mound of dead people around and over me. She instructed me not to move and not to dare crawl out until she arrived. So I lay this way for over 24 hours."[34]

This was not an isolated occurrence. Olitzki's mother saved her again and again. "They took me away many times," she wrote, "but my mother would rescue me. . . . [M]ore than once she pulled me out at the last minute before they gassed me."[35] She noted that the mother was frequently punished for this.

Facing death

Death had a constant presence in the world the children lived in. They saw men, women, and children taken to their deaths in massive actions by the Germans. They saw people dying in the streets. Some lost their parents or other family members in front of their eyes. Quite a few encounters with death were more immediate or personal. The surviving children hid with other Jews in hideouts or bunkers. Often there were many people there, and silence was crucial. But what should be done with a crying baby? In one bunker in Kovno where Fania Olitzki hid, a baby started to cry. "A moment arrived when a father wanted to strangle his child," wrote Fania, but she did not disclose the outcome.[36] Genia Shurz was more forthcoming on a similar story. "In the bunker a child suffocated on my lap. It was crying, so someone stuck a rag into its mouth. After twenty-four hours the Aktion [roundup] came to an end and I saw that the child was dead. I became like a crazy person from fright. But I got used to that too."[37]

Death figured in the children's conversations and thoughts, Shurz wrote of the last night of Podhajce Ghetto's six hundred remaining Jews. "That is the most terrible moment in your life, to wait for death. People went out of their minds. My friends ran around wildly in the street. Blood flowed. People poisoned themselves, and those who didn't have poison were the unlucky ones. Very few people remained. People poisoned, killed and stabbed themselves."[38] The children did not want to die; "the desire to live . . . was so strong that we clawed at the walls."[39] She recounted the children's conversations in those harrowing nights:

One said: "It is so beautiful outside, but not for us." Another one said that he would like to be free just once more in his life and eat until he was full, and then die. Another one said: "Who knows whether there is another world and whether we will meet there." We settled between us that as soon as they started shooting us we should immediately think about meeting each other in the next world. That is how we talked all night, until morning.[40]

Rosa Pinczewski saw her mother and brother murdered by the same peasant who had hid them and was supposedly transferring them to a new hideout in the woods: "The peasant told us to get out of the cart. The peasant's brother stood by the water. Then a terrible picture began, which I will never forget. He quickly, brutally, took my mother off the cart and threw her into the water. He beat me and then my little brother cruelly."[41] This is the story as recounted in her testimony and printed in the journal. While not the end of Pinczewski's tribulations under Nazi rule, it is certainly the focal point of her narrative. At another time, Rosa told more about this harrowing moment than she was willing to divulge here. As mentioned above, Pinczewski had given a testimony two years earlier in 1945. In it she gave a more extensive and shocking account of those traumatic moments:

> Out of the bushes came Bucek's brother who lived with us in the same hut and started to shoot. I jumped first off the cart and started running toward the fields. Bucek's brother ran after me and fired. He caught up with me and held me by the hand. I pulled the gun because he was aiming at me. I asked him to spare me—but he refused. Waclaw came up to us, took the gun and as I looked on he shot my little brother. There was a full moon. I started screaming but he wanted to shoot me, I ran, fell into the water, reached the opposite bank of the stream and survived. Then I heard two more shots and my mother shouting "Help." Then there was silence.[42]

How is the difference between the two testimonies to be explained? Did the editors of *Fun Letsten Hurbn* water down the testimony on this point so as not to overly shock the readers? From an examination of her 1947 handwritten testimony in the archive, we can rule out this possibility. She certainly gave a different narration of the event. But why? It seems that the explanation lies in the time gap between the two testimonies. The first testimony was given right after liberation; events were still vivid, the pain was great, and she did not yet have any future to look forward to. In the intervening two years she became a part of a group, a community of children like herself. While the pain was still there, life was going on, and there was a future opening up. In such a setting, there was a reluctance to recount every terrible detail and reopen healing wounds.

The Rescued and the Rescuers: Jews and Gentiles

Children's testimonies open a window to the intricate relationships between gentiles and Jews during the Holocaust. The children were on the run; their fate was in the hands of strangers. Every non-Jew the child met could be his savior angel or the angel of death. The first collectors of children's testimonies commented on the way the children recounted their interactions with the world around them. As Maria Hochberg-Marianska recounted in her introduction to a 1947 anthology of children's testimonies:

> Wherever the children encountered good people, help or encouragement, they express their appreciation in words full of the warmest feelings. Every human gesture, even just the offering of a slice of bread or words of genuine sympathy, these heartfelt reactions in the terrible days of the Holocaust—none of these has been forgotten by these persecuted children. . . . In the same frank and straightforward way the children describe evil deeds and base people. . . . Bitterness and pain fill the children's recollections of those Poles who hunted them, betrayed them and handed them over to the common enemy.[43]

Children encountered gentiles who risked their lives for them. Sometimes the help was given on the basis of prewar relationships. When Joseph Shuster and his mother escaped from the ghetto, their former maid was waiting for them and took them to the hideout she prepared for them with a gentile family. After a while "the Christian took fright and demanded that we leave. We had no choice, and our former maid traveled 80 kilometers and found us a place in Visakedvar, with a Christian who knew my grandfather."[44] But, it seems, a prewar acquaintance was not always an asset. Genia Shurz was recognized by her former schoolmates when she bought food outside the ghetto. "On the way my former Ukrainian schoolmates recognized me," she wrote, "They beat me till I bled."[45]

Children and their families were also rescued by people they had no prior acquaintance with. Genia Shurz told of the gentile with whom her family hid: "The gentile had previously been a stranger to us. He had only seen us through the fence in the ghetto. He liked us and he told us that if we were ever in a hopeless situation we should come to him."[46] Hiding a Jewish family or child was a family project for their rescuers. Shuster noted that his family's survival had been facilitated by the "very clever" six-year-old daughter of their rescuer who "always guarded us well."[47]

On rare occasions help was even given by a German. While foraging for food for his family hiding in a bunker under the ghetto's ruins, Genia Shurz's brother came across a German guard. It was a moment of utter desperation: "He didn't run away from him, because he wanted to tell the German that he should take us out to shoot us. The German was amazed at how we could have survived for such a long time and he said: 'If you could survive for such a long time, I won't hand you over.' He said that we should wait in the bunker until he came to take us out of the bunker and the ghetto."[48] The German guard was true to his word and helped them escape. It was but another example of the fickleness of life in hiding. One day's rescuer could be a potential murderer the next, and vice versa. The story of the murder of Pinczewski's mother and brother by their former rescuers has already been recounted above. They were hidden for two months with this family before being murdered by them. This was not an isolated occurrence. Arie Milch recounted that the gentile he and his uncle and brother had hidden with for almost a year wanted to "hand us over to the German murderers, but the Red Army was already in our city, so he let us live."[49]

Children were also taken advantage of and let down by supposed rescuers. Pinczewski's parents sent her into hiding with a peasant woman. They paid her in advance for hiding their daughter. On the way to the woman's house they passed through a forest. The woman told Pinczewski "that she had to arrange something and had to leave for ten minutes." The girl waited for some time until she understood that the would-be rescuer would never come back. "I saw that she wouldn't return," she wrote. "I understood that she had taken the money and run away."[50] With their lives dependent on rescuers' caprices, the attitude toward rescuers could be very negative. The gentile hiding Genia Shurz's family was angry at having to hide the entire family instead of only a part of it. "He stopped giving us food," she wrote. "We began to suffer hard times, it was hot and we were hungry and thirsty." They were sure that he intended them to die. "The gentile had decided not to give us food until we died. We suffered so greatly that it can't be described. Once a day we received a small pot of food;

no bread, no water, no change of shirts. So we became filthy; the dirt ate at us. We sat that way for five months."[51] They eventually got into a heated argument, and they told him that he was "worse than Hitler." That brought some improvement in their situation. "But I was already sick, and we looked liked skeletons," she wrote. They decided that "if one of us died, we would revenge ourselves against that gentile after liberation and not let him live either."[52]

Postscript: Why Children?

The children's testimonies published in *Fun Letsten Hurbn* are survivor stories. The surviving child is naturally at the center of the story. The emphasis is on agency. The children (and their parents) take their futures into their own hands, developing survival skills: resourcefulness, sharp wits, and the ability to wiggle out of tight corners. The stories also make a strong statement regarding the parents' powerful commitment to their children. They prepare hideouts, negotiate with potential rescuers, and are highly instrumental in their children's survival.

The stories tell the reader about the gentile world where the children had to be responsible for their own survival. All types of gentiles—the good and the bad—appear in the stories. There is a tragic reason for the preponderance of stories with gentile rescuers: children who met murderous gentiles usually did not live to tell about it. It is obvious that non-Jews played a major role in the survival of Jewish children and their families. The testimonies underscore the role of moral choice made by the individual. It was a point made by Maria Hochberg-Marianska in her preface to *The Children Accuse,* an anthology of children's testimonies published by the Central Historical Commission in Poland. An individual making the right choice "prepared to make sacrifices in the interest of an innocent child, and the person's own dignity,"[53] made a world of difference for the Jewish fugitive. "From the testimonies of the Jewish children it emerges quite clearly that where will power [of the non-Jew] was directed toward a conscious goal, courage and rectitude join hands, [and] the Nazi thug is defeated in his desire to murder."[54] In a way, by juxtaposing stories of gentile rescuers with stories of gentiles who refused to help and even killed Jewish fugitives, the editors were making a point: if more gentiles had made the right choices, then many more children and adults would have been saved.

Children were the only distinct group of survivors accorded a separate place in the journal. The series about children's experiences during the war is the only one of its kind in the journal, which usually brought an assortment of testimonies and documents sometimes loosely organized around a general theme such as Kovno or death marches. Although these are children and teenagers, their testimonies are brought in their own words without an adult figure as a go-between. They are witnesses in their own right asserting a voice of their own.

How are we to explain the special place accorded to the children? Three factors stand out:

The cultural role of children in Eastern Europe. Interest in children and in children's experience was characteristic of Jewish culture in Eastern European before the war. It started in the late nineteenth century with the appearance of child heroes in the literary works of the great Yiddish masters such as Y. L. Peretz and Sholem Aleichem. Telling the story from a child's point of view brought children's experiences into the limelight of the literary and cultural scene. The child-narrator figure could be used to lay out society's failings and maladies.[55] Between the world wars this interest matured into research interest in children and their experience. This was the time of Janus Korczak who, tuning in to the experience of inner-city (poor urban) Jewish children, wrote for and about children. The YIVO Institute for Jewish Culture likewise focused on Jewish youths. YIVO ran three prize-bearing competitions in which teenagers and young people were encouraged to write essays describing their life and surrounding society.[56] By publishing these essays, YIVO accorded them a legitimate role as witnesses to current Jewish society. In this way the literary child narrator so prominent in works of Sholom Aleichem and others gave place to an authentic real-life one. The interest in children continued during the war in the work of the Ringelblum archive, where children were specifically targeted and solicited for information and essays. Once the war was over, it was obvious to the members of the Jewish intelligentsia working in the historical commissions that children had to be questioned and heard and that their experiences should be integrated into the story of the Holocaust.

The child as an authentic witness. Children were seen as having an edge on adult survivors. While adults had a reputation to uphold commitments to the dead or to fellow survivors, children were accepted as authentic witnesses unencumbered by agendas or social connections. Adult survivor testimonies, claimed Benjamin Tennenbaum, who collected hundreds of children's testimonies, are very apologetic: people feel obliged to explain the choices they made under Nazi occupation. Children, on the other hand, were innocently telling their stories, and therefore it was through them that the real story of the Holocaust could be told. While this may seem somewhat idealistic, as children also had reasons of their own to speak or to remain silent about specific experiences they went through, it was the prevalent view at the time.

Children as symbols of Jewish fate. Being young and innocent, the children epitomize the cruelty of the Nazis and their accomplices. Hounded all over towns and the countryside, they exemplified the Jewish tragedy. There was no better way of underscoring the evilness of the Nazis than by showing their most innocent victims. The children could not be blamed for exploiting non-Jews or for being politically disloyal; no apology for anti-Semitism or for Nazism could be given in their regard. In a way, they were also a major element of the Jewish indictment of the non-Jewish world for its behavior during the Holocaust and beyond.

Stories of Jewish children's Holocaust experiences were thus an important building block of post-Holocaust Jewish identity. The surviving children were a symbol of hope, a promise for the future. Their survival against all odds, as seen in their stories, spelled resilience and heroism that would be vital for the building of a viable future for the Jewish people. Israel Kaplan, by bringing forth the children's stories in *Fun Letsten Hurbn,* made an important contribution to this building process.

NOTES

This paper was researched and written as a part of the "Voices of Child Survivors: Children's Holocaust Testimonies" project of Bar-Ilan University. The project was made feasible through a grant from the Rabbi Israel Miller Fund for Shoah Research, Documentation and Education of the Conference on Jewish Material Claims against Germany.

1. Benjamin Tennebaum, ed., *Ehad me-ir u shenayim mi-mishpahah: Mivhar m'elef autobigrafiot shel yaldei Yisrael b'Polin* [One of a City and Two of a Family: A Selection from a Thousand Autobiographies of Jewish Children in Poland] (Merhavyah, Israel: Sifriat Poalim, 1947). Maria Hochberg-Marianskwa and Noe Grüss, eds., *The Children Accuse* (London: Vallentine-Mitchell, 1996), was originally published in Polish as *Dzieci Oskarzaja* (Cracow-Łódź-Warsaw: Central Jewish Historical Commission in Poland, 1947); all translations and references used here are from the 1996 edition. Noe Grüss, ed., *Kinder-martirologye: zamlung fun dokumentn* (Children's Martyrdom: A Document Collection) (Buenos Aires: Tsentral-farband fun Poylishe Yidn in Argentine, 1947), was

published as part of a series on the fate of Polish Jewry.

2. Israel Kaplan, Protocol of the first meeting of the [historical] workers of the Central Historical Commission, Munich, May 11–12, 1947, Record group (hereafter RG) 1258, file 476, YIVO Archive, New York.

3. Israel Kaplan, "Day to Day Work in the Historical Commission," 23. Lecture given at the meeting of the Historical Commissions, Munich, May 12, 1947, published by the Central Historical Commission of Liberated Jews in the American Zone.

4. Shalom Eilati [Kaplan's son], *Lahazot et Hanahar* [*Crossing the River*] (Jerusalem: Carmel, 1999), 293.

5. Kaplan, "Day to Day work in the Historical Commission," 16.

6. Ibid.

7. Ibid.

8. For an extensive description of this phenomenon, see Boaz Cohen, "The Children's Voice: Post-War Collection of Testimonies from Children Survivors of the Holocaust," *Holocaust and Genocide Studies* 21, no. 1 (2007): 73–95.

9. Eilati, *Lahazot et Hanahar*, 292–93.

10. Israel Kaplan to (son) Shalom, May 16, 1947, Shalom Eilati Private Archive (hereafter SEPA), Jerusalem.

11. Joseph Shuster, "My Experiences during the War," *Fun Letsten Hurbn* 7 (May 1948): 91–94. The original testimony is in RG MiE, file 1800, Yad Vashem Archives (hereafter YVA), Jerusalem.

12. Daniel Burstin (Burztyn), "My Experiences during the War," *Fun Letsten Hurbn* 4 (March 1947): 75–83. His original testimony is in RG MiE, file 675, YVA.

13. Arieh Milch, "My Experiences during the War," *Fun Letsten Hurbn* 3 (November 1946): 65–67. His original testimony is in RG MiE, file 159, YVA. Children's names are given as published in the English-language back cover of the respective issues. The editors of the journal did not give the names as used by the children on their handwritten testimonies but instead gave an Anglicized version. The original names are given in brackets and are the ones used in the archives.

14. Collection of Children's Testimonies from Aschau bei Kraiburg, RG MiE, files 147–63, YVA.

15. Burstin, "My Experiences during the War."

16. Burstin also illustrated the group's journal. The only existing copy was lost later (fortunately after photocopying). Interview with Daniel Inbar (Burztyn) and Hadassah Shapira (Rozen), Tel Aviv, October 4, 2006.

17. Daniel Burstin to Israel Kaplan, February 26, 1947, and March 7, 1947, RG MiE, file 675, YVA. The quotation is from the first letter.

18. Jacob Lewin, "My Experiences during the War," *Fun Letsten Hurbn* 6 (May 1947): 75–81.

19. Rosa Pinczewski (Rozia Pinczewska), "My Experiences during the War," *Fun Letsten Hurbn* 6 (August 1947): 58–61. The original testimony is in RG MiE, file 368, YVA. The testimony from 1945 is Rozia Pinczewska,

RG M49E, file 1566, YVA.

20. Shuster, "My Experiences during the War."
21. Fania Olitzki, "My Experiences during the War," *Fun Letsten Hurbn* 8 (June 1948): 85–89.
22. Ela Grilihes, "My Experiences during the War," *Fun Letsten Hurbn* 9 (September 1948): 82–83.
23. Genia Shurz, "My Experiences during the War," *Fun Letsten Hurbn* 10 (December 1948): 123–30.
24. Israel Kaplan to Shalom Kaplan, January 11, 1948, SEPA.
25. Burstin to Kaplan, February 26, 1947.
26. Burstin to Kaplan, March 7, 1947. I could not find information on the "'loyal' fascist Jews" mentioned here. In a phone interview on December 11, 2006, Burstin could not recall this matter.
27. Burstin, "My Experiences during the War," 80.
28. Israel Kaplan to Shalom Kaplan, June 8, 1947, SEPA.
29. Burstin, "My Experiences during the War," 79. After the war he was reunited with his mother.
30. Pinczewski, "My Experiences during the War," 59. She would later rejoin her parents in their forest hideout, although they were both subsequently murdered.
31. Shuster, "My Experiences during the War," 92.
32. Shurz, "My Experiences during the War," 127–28.
33. Ibid., 128.
34. Olitzki, "My Experiences during the War," 87.
35. Ibid.
36. Ibid., 85.
37. Shurz, "My Experiences during the War," 125.
38. Ibid.
39. Shurz, "My Experiences during the War," 126
40. Ibid.
41. Pinczewski, "My Experiences during the War," 60.
42. Rozia Pinczewsk, RG M49E, file 1566, in Polish, YVA. This type of testimony was usually done as an interview. The adult who interviewed the child wrote down the testimony and sent it to the Central Historical Commission.
43. Hochberg-Marianskwa and Grüss, *The Children Accuse,* xxix–xxx.
44. Shuster, "My Experiences during the War," 92–93.
45. Shurz, "My Experiences during the War," 124.
46. Ibid., 128.
47. Shuster, "My Experiences during the War," 91.
48. Shurz, "My Experiences during the War," 127.
49. Milch, "My Experiences during the War," 67.
50. Pinczewski, "My Experiences during the War," 59.
51. Shurz, "My Experiences during the War," 129.
52. Ibid.
53. Hochberg-Marianskwa and Grüss, *The Children Accuse,* xxx.

54. Ibid.

55. On this issue see, David G. Roskies, *A Bridge of Longing: The Lost Art of Yiddish Storytelling* (Cambridge: Harvard University Press, 1995).

56. See Jeffery Shandler, ed., *Awakening Lives: Autobiographies of Jewish Youth in Poland before the Holocaust* (New Haven, CT: Yale University Press, 2002).

Living in Landsberg, Dreaming of Deganiah

Jewish Displaced Youths and Zionism after the Holocaust

AVINOAM J. PATT

Some five months after the liberation in Germany, a group of young Holocaust survivors, barely removed from years of persecution and torture at the hands of the Nazi regime, moved to the estate of the virulently anti-Semitic Nazi propagandist Julius Streicher. As Streicher awaited trial in nearby Nuremberg, this group of young Zionists set about transforming his estate into an agricultural training farm, or hakhsharah, in preparation for what they hoped would be their future lives in Palestine. In the December 21, 1945, issue of the Landsberg displaced persons (DP) camp newspaper, Baruch Cheta, leader of this group, summarized the accomplishments of Kibbutz Nili:

> Not long ago, Pleikhershof was the estate and seat of one of Hitler's highest associates, the editor of the sadly famous "*Sturmer*," Julius Streicher. In the office, where for many years the great Jew-hater sat and wrote his blood-thirsty anti-Jewish articles . . . where Streicher wrote to the German people "The Jews are our misfortune" [*Di jidn zajnen unzer umglik*], can be found today the secretariat of an agricultural pioneering school, of Jewish boys and girls, coming from all corners of Europe, learning to work the land, agriculture, cattle-herding,

etc., that which is in the first line necessary in the building up of the Land of Israel. This is one of the greatest Jewish satisfactions[,] . . . to be able to see Hebrew writings and slogans, like the People of Israel live [*Am Jsroel chaj*], the strength of Israel will not lie [*Necach Jsroel loj jeszaker*, in initials, NILI], on Streicher's palace; thus we have named our new kibbutz, the first agricultural school in Bavaria.[1]

The members of the new kibbutz were thus making use of the so-called modern Jewish Haman's own personal land to prepare themselves for life in the Jewish state, beginning each day at 4:00 a.m. with the milking of cows, learning by heart the Hebrew words for cow, horse, agricultural tools, and other essential terms of farm labor.[2] The symbolic nature of the revenge exacted by the young survivors on Streicher's estate was unmistakable. However, the powerful political value of young Zionists working to build their futures in Palestine would have profound implications beyond the satisfaction experienced by the members of Kibbutz Nili.

By the middle of 1946, thousands of young kibbutz members representing all strands of the Zionist movement inhabited forty such training farms (hakhsharot) and animated political and cultural life in the DP camps of postwar Germany. Farms and kibbutzim such as Kibbutz Nili acquired widespread visibility among the DP population as a whole, to the point where military and civilian officials and workers often represented the kibbutz and hakhsharah populations as encompassing the overwhelming majority of Jewish youths.[3] Even so, most of the youths who joined such kibbutz groups had little prior experience of Zionism and next to no understanding of Zionist ideology. This chapter will address three related aspects of this phenomenon: (1) How was a situation so amenable to the Zionist project created in such a short period following the war? (2) Why did so many Jewish youths choose such a course so quickly, and why did the course they chose come to characterize the conduct of young Jewish Holocaust survivors as a whole? (3) Finally, what was the appeal of Zionism for these youths, and what did it mean to them in practice, on the everyday level, as they awaited a resolution to their stateless condition after the war?

These are not idle questions; their answers bear heavily upon the history of the establishment of the State of Israel in 1948. Following World War II the seemingly overwhelming Zionist enthusiasm of the Jewish DPs, witnessed in part by the gravitation of a significant portion of Jewish DP youths to kibbutzim and hakhsharot, was vital in informing the diplomatic decisions that led to the creation of the State of Israel as international observers representing the United States, Britain, and the United Nations weighed the desires of the large Jewish refugee population in Europe.[4] Likewise, the founders of the newly created State of Israel pointed to a clear relationship between the Holocaust and Israel, with survivors actively participating in the founding of the state. In fact, between 1948 and 1949, some twenty-two thousand DPs (seventy-eight hundred from Germany alone) were enlisted in the Haganah and sent to Palestine/Israel from the DP camps in Germany, Italy, Austria, and Cyprus to aid in the fighting there.[5] The elected bodies officially representing the Jewish DPs in Germany endorsed the conscription of young DPs enthusiastically, calling upon all able-bodied men and women between the ages of seventeen and thirty-five to fulfill their "national duty."[6] Israel's Declaration of Independence, read by David Ben-Gurion on May 14, 1948, asserted that the remnant that survived the Holocaust continued to migrate to Palestine, undaunted by difficulties and dangers, and "never ceased to assert their right to a life of dignity, freedom and honest toil in their national homeland."[7] Some framed the two seminal events in twentieth-century Jewish history as inextricably linked, as a "fateful historical reaction" that led the DPs to claim their place in a Jewish state.[8] For this reason it seems essential to understand the sources of that enthusiasm especially among young people, who bore a significant portion of the burden in the battles for Israel's independence.[9]

While there has been general historiographical consensus over the fact that the Jewish DPs presented an enthusiastic Zionist position in the years following the war, there has been considerable debate as to the source of this enthusiasm. Most scholars have accepted the dominant Zionist representation offered at the time, namely that the active steps that Jewish DP youths took to prepare themselves for migration to Palestine by joining kibbutzim and hakhsharot were a natural outgrowth of their experience under Nazi rule.[10] This thesis of an intuitive Zionism born directly from the war was affirmed in 2002 in Zeev Mankowitz's comprehensive study of Jewish DPs in postwar Germany. As Mankowitz argued, "the creation of a Jewish state in the Land of Israel was taken to be the last will and testament bequeathed by the dead to the living. . . . It signified the only real hope for the rescue and rehabilitation of the little that remained of European Jewry and, in the longer term, the promise of the Jewish future."[11] Fifty years after the end of the war, however, a group of Israeli scholars threw this chain of historical inevitability into question. In fact, some suggested that the Holocaust almost prevented the creation of the State of Israel by depriving the Yishuv (the prestate Jewish settlement in Palestine)

Avinoam J. Patt

of the European manpower reserve it so needed, making the DPs the last hope of the Yishuv to establish a state.[12] Idith Zertal and others questioned the nature of the relationship between the Yishuv and the survivors and the clandestine immigration movement at its center, concluding that the Zionists in the Yishuv had cynically manipulated the dispirited and demoralized survivors for their own political ends.[13]

A third group of scholars has similarly emphasized the importance of the postwar context but has identified features other than the activities of Zionist organizations as crucial to the development of DP Zionism. These scholars have pointed to the role of diplomatic and political developments in the mid-1940s in shaping a collective national identity among Jewish DPs. Changes in Allied policy to categorize the Jews as a distinct national group rather than as citizens of their former home countries played into Zionist hands. If Jews were indeed a nation, then they were, as Zionists had long claimed, entitled to national independence and territorial sovereignty. Thus, according to this logic, Zionism came to appear to Jewish DPs as the ideology most in tune with contemporary international political thinking.[14]

These assessments of the DP situation and the origins of DP Zionist enthusiasm have a number of shortcomings, however. They tend to describe the Jewish DPs as an undifferentiated mass with uniform wartime experiences, although it is apparent that the She'erit Hapletah (Surviving Remnant) was a population with a distinctively youthful demographic makeup that influenced its political and cultural choices.[15] From an early point following liberation it was evident that as much as half of the surviving population was under the age of twenty-five, and some 80 percent were under age forty. These young people, who were more likely to have survived years of persecution because of hardiness and selection for work, were for the most part orphaned and alone. The decisions made by young Jewish DPs have to be understood in relation to both their particular background as Jews and their universal background as young people struggling to move on with their lives in the aftermath of the Holocaust. For those youths who had survived the Holocaust in concentration and forced labor camps, in hiding, fighting with the partisans, and elsewhere, this was especially true. They were forced to confront adult decisions both during and after the war but were left without parents or family in order to make such decisions.

Most studies of the Jewish DP population have also tended to rely on sources created by either the DP camp leadership or by outside groups (such as Zionist emissaries from Palestine, the U.S. Army, and international relief agencies) to explain the choices made by youths. This is surprising considering the volume of source material created by young DPs themselves, including articles in the DP and youth movement press as well as letters, correspondence, diaries, journals, and testimonies created by kibbutz members. While sources created by outside groups who worked with the DPs may provide contemporaneous descriptions of DP youths, only through an examination of sources created by the young survivors themselves is it possible to fully understand the challenges they faced after the war and the calculations they made in determining the course of their lives after the Holocaust. Furthermore, Zionism in the DP camps has for the most part only been examined from the Yishuv perspective, asking what role DPs played in the creation of the State of Israel. Regardless of whether the state would have been created or not, Zionism filled a crucial function for the Jewish DPs and proved appealing to a number of groups in postwar Germany, who all supported the Zionist project for different reasons. This support would lead to the creation of a flourishing Zionist network in the American zone of Germany whereby survivor youths could continue the process of Zionist immersion within the framework of kibbutzim and hakhsharot, and this did in fact ultimately aid in the creation of the State of Israel.

THE JEWS IN GERMANY AFTER LIBERATION

Immediately following liberation, while most of the ten million DPs, prisoners of war (POWs), and forced laborers in Germany after the war made the decision to return home with ease, the fifty thousand or so Jewish DPs did not face such a clear decision. Unsure of what awaited them at home, often fairly certain that their families had been destroyed during the war, those who decided to stay in a DP camp also had to face the fact that this meant continuing to live with collaborators who also refused to return home. In general, Polish and Baltic Jews were the least likely to return to their home countries (although many did), while Jews from countries such as Hungary, Romania, France, and Greece were far more likely to return to their countries following liberation.[16] Jewish DPs who had made the decision to remain in Germany thus faced a choice: they could remain in the DP camp (generally German military barracks, former POW and slave labor camps, tent cities, industrial housing, and the like), or they could leave the DP camp if they chose to settle in Germany permanently, a choice that some fifteen thousand German Jewish survivors made in the summer of 1945.[17]

Some of the first Jews to encounter the surviving Jewish population, apart from the occasional Jewish Brigade soldier (a division from Palestine serving with the British Army) were Jewish chaplains

Avinoam J. Patt

serving with the American military.[18] One particularly active chaplain, Abraham Klausner, who first helped survivors catalog who had actually survived and aided in the early political organization of the She'erit Hapletah, reported to his superiors in the United States on the situation of the Jews in postwar Germany. In conducting a survey of conditions faced by Jewish DPs in Germany, Klausner visited approximately fourteen thousand Jews living in seventeen DP camps one month following liberation. He found deplorable conditions, poor accommodations, no plumbing, no clothing, rampant disease, continuing malnourishment, and a lack of any plan on the part of the American military. "Liberated but not free, that is the paradox of the Jew," Klausner concluded in a report detailing the condition of the Jewish survivors.[19] And indeed, of the approximately fifty thousand to sixty thousand Jewish survivors at the time of liberation, within the first weeks following liberation many thousands perished from complications arising from disease, starvation, and the camp experience.[20]

It had also become evident that a disproportionate segment of the surviving Jewish population was composed of young people. One month after Allied forces defeated the Third Reich, M. Winogrodzki, a Jewish Holocaust survivor freshly liberated from Dachau, composed a report on conditions for Jews such as himself in the newly created U.S. zone of occupation. Concern for the large number of young people he found among the liberated Jews in Bavaria was a prominent feature of his report. "Here in the Munich region," he wrote, "there are both large and small concentration camps with a Jewish population of ca. 50,000, of which a great number are young, for the most part without parents and therefore without existing supervision."[21] His observation was borne out by a series of reports and surveys presented by various agencies representing a broad spectrum of interests from the earliest weeks following liberation and for years thereafter in which the proportion of Jewish DPs between the ages of fifteen and thirty was consistently estimated at more than half and often above 80 percent of the total Jewish population.[22]

For those at the time who were familiar with the broadest outlines of the experience of European Jewry under Nazi rule, these statistics should not have been surprising. Every Jew within the Germans' reach had been marked for death. Avoiding the death sentence demanded quickness of foot and wit, audacity, adaptability, physical stamina, and the ability to blend inconspicuously into often hostile surroundings (in addition to no small measure of luck). Those qualities generally tend to be present in greater measure among the young than among their elders. Chances for survival were also often enhanced by absence of concern for dependent children, again a situation more common among teenagers and young adults than among those beyond the customary age of marriage. It is no wonder, then, that Jewish survivors numbered disproportionately in those age ranges. Similarly, it stands to reason that a relatively large number of Jewish DPs should have been orphans; parents whose children were teenagers during the early 1940s were already of an age where the physical and mental demands of survival were increasingly likely to prove too much to bear. Nor is it surprising that many who observed these young, largely orphaned Jews during the first weeks following liberation commented prominently on their seeming lack of direction, perhaps even their paralytic confusion, concerning how they might begin to resume normal lives. Winogrodzki summed up the situation succinctly when he wrote, "These children, who no longer have parents, do not know when and where they should go."[23]

While organizing among themselves, the DPs and chaplains such as Klausner continued to describe the poor conditions facing the DPs in letters to military authorities and world Jewish organizations (such as the World Jewish Congress and the American Jewish Joint Distribution Committee). Some former members of Zionist youth movements, such as Winogrodzki in Dachau, turned to Nathan Schwalb in the He-Halutz office in Geneva.[24] They reported poor treatment of Jewish DPs at the hands of their liberators, with Jewish DPs being denied rations, housed in camps with former collaborators, and denied freedom of movement from camps. Jewish DPs pleaded for assistance from the U.S. military government and United Nations Relief and Rehabilitation Administration (UNRRA) to rectify their miserable situation.[25]

For those Jewish DPs who chose the temporary existence of the DP camps, liberation was far from all they had hoped for. Beyond the wish for food, clothing, shelter, and security, Jewish DPs expected some validation of their survival, a sign that the outside world had not completely forsaken them. Expecting to be welcomed by the world with open arms, Jewish DPs found liberation to be a rude awakening, as they still struggled to obtain bearable living conditions and yearned for contact from the rest of the Jewish world, which had still largely been denied access to the DP camps due to the chaotic postwar situation. As Klausner had noted, the American military seemed to lack any plan for the Jewish refugees who had chosen not to return to their home countries.

The reports of continuing deprivation in the liberated camps and poor organization of recovery issued by the survivors and the Jewish chaplains serving there did eventually succeed in prompting American officials to take a greater interest in the problem of the DPs. On June

22, 1945, President Harry S. Truman dispatched Earl Harrison (dean of the University of Pennsylvania Law School) to Europe to prepare a report regarding the "needs of stateless and non-repatriable refugees among the displaced persons in Germany and to determine the extent to which those needs are being met by military, governmental and private organizations."[26] Once Harrison arrived in the camps in Germany, the Jewish DPs, along with Klausner and soldiers from the Jewish Brigade, worked to make sure that he was aware of the miserable conditions facing the Jews.[27] In his scathing report back to Truman, published in August 1945, Harrison stated that we are "treating the Jews as the Nazis treated them except that we do not exterminate them."[28] He proposed that Jews be separated in their own camps—until then they had been forced to live with other national groups and former collaborators—and to resolve their refugee status, he proposed that one hundred thousand immigration certificates to Palestine be granted immediately to the Jewish DPs. Following Harrison's report, American authorities worked to ameliorate conditions for Jewish DPs, moving Jews to separate camps and agreeing to the appointment of an adviser for Jewish affairs. Harrison's suggestions served to link the resolution of the Jewish DP situation with the situation in Palestine, thereby elevating the diplomatic implications of the Jewish DP political stance. Still, Jewish DPs had the distinct sense that their many calls for assistance continued to fall on deaf ears both in Germany and in America.

KIBBUTZ BUCHENWALD AND THE HAKHSHARAH IN POSTWAR GERMANY

Feeling abandoned by lack of contact from the rest of the Jewish world after liberation, many among the Jewish DPs resolved to help themselves. Among the liberated young Jews in Buchenwald were three former He-Halutz members who had remained active during the war in organizing groups of Zionist youths in Buchenwald and Auschwitz. Arthur Posnansky and Yechezkel Tydor, who were in the death march from Auschwitz to Buchenwald in January 1945, joined Eliyahu Gruenbaum in Buchenwald and, in the tumultuous last few months before liberation, began to plan for the postwar period.[29] The three would be central in the organization of the first kibbutz hakhsharah in postwar Germany, Kibbutz Buchenwald.

The diary of the collective group that began to come together in Buchenwald following liberation reveals the early considerations that entered the minds of the young survivors already faced with the question of where to go next. Since liberation, Posnansky had sought assistance from Nathan Schwalb at the He-Halutz office in Geneva in organizing "the hundreds of Jews, parentless, homeless, without any relatives," in Buchenwald who had remained alive and desired to go to hakhsharah but were frustrated at the lack of contact from Jewish organizations.[30] Once they had made the realization that the world seemed to have no plans for the Jews, however, Posnansky, Tydor, and the Buchenwald group proposed an option that could remove survivors who had begun to recover from the war from the squalor of the DP camp. As noted in an early diary entry,

> Perhaps for the thousandth time the Jewish committee in Buchenwald was holding a meeting on the question: Where to? A Polish Jew, a German, a Czech, a Hungarian—each faced the same burning problem: Where should the few surviving Jews of Buchenwald go? How could we ever have believed that at the end of the war the surviving Jews would have no more worries, that everything would be fine! The world, we had thought, would welcome our few survivors with open arms! We, the first victims of the Nazis. They would love us! Quickly enough, we saw that the world had other things on its mind than Jewish suffering. So where to? Comrade Posnansky put forth an idea: into our own kibbutz. To build a group of Buchenwald's youth, and find a farm where we could prepare for Palestine. A wonderful idea. There would be no lack of candidates for the kibbutz, for energy was reawakening in the survivors and seeking an outlet. From that idea sprang Kibbutz Buchenwald.[31]

The founders of Kibbutz Buchenwald pointed to the dual function of the kibbutz: on the one hand, it would assist in avoiding the temptations of black market activity and the desire to exact revenge on the German populace;[32] on the other hand, it could help train youths for the pioneering lifestyle of Eretz Israel through *shituf* (sharing), socialization, and vocational training.[33]

The early political leadership of the She'erit Hapletah, composed of many former members of Zionist youth groups who had chosen to remain in Germany rather than return to Eastern Europe, was overwhelmingly attuned to the needs of the youths in the DP camps.[34] From an early point in time, the Jewish DP leadership espoused a strong Zionist position. In many cases it was the surviving members of Zionist youth movements and political parties who undertook the self-help work and in turn became most active among those seeking to convince survivors to avoid a return to Eastern Europe. These were

Avinoam J. Patt

generally youth movement leaders who had experience leading and organizing Jewish youths both before and, in some cases, during the war. This experience made them well suited to lead the younger Jewish population that had survived life in German concentration camps. For the young Jewish survivors in the DP camps (primarily under the age of thirty-five), regardless of whether they had experience in a Zionist youth group before the war, such kibbutz groups emerged as attractive options, providing them with the camaraderie, support, and replacement family they so desperately craved.

The emerging popularity of the alternative living experiment near Buchenwald demonstrated the value of this option to DP youths and the Jewish DP leadership. Despite reservations over farming the accursed German soil and entering into relationships with German locals, the young farmers believed that the end goal—that is, the building of the Land of Israel—justified the temporary transgression of working in Germany. At the first meeting of the Conference of Liberated Jews on July 25, 1945, the representatives of Kibbutz Buchenwald argued that their kibbutz could serve as a model for the thousands of Jewish youths in Germany. With ninety-four delegates representing the approximately fifty thousand surviving Jews in Germany and Austria, the meeting was an opportunity for the Jewish DPs to state their concerns and come together as a cohesive political group.[35] While all were in agreement that *di jugnt* (the youth), as the future of the Jewish people, needed to be occupied productively to prepare for life in Palestine, others on the newly formed Zionist-oriented Central Committee were concerned that by encouraging Jewish youths to settle on farms in Germany, they could be induced to remain in Germany long term. Still, the popularity of the newly organized kibbutz groups within the camps and the belief that some productive use of time needed to be provided for the many Jewish youths in Germany demonstrated the need to expand the farming project. Thus, the Central Committee and the Zionist groups in the DP camps came to focus their efforts in the sphere of youths on vocational and agricultural training, which would largely be organized under the auspices of the kibbutz groups of the Zionist youth movements.

In response to the move of Jewish youths into the Zionist groups, at the second meeting of the Zionist organization in Bavaria on August 20 in Landsberg, the Zionist leadership decided that in addition to the official formation of a United Zionist Organization (UZO), they would authorize the creation of No'ar Chalutzi Meuchad (United Pioneering Youth), more commonly known as Nocham.[36] Such an official youth movement could systematize the loose clusters of youths who had already congregated in the various DP centers and guarantee greater membership for the UZO and Nocham, also facilitating the process of aliyah to Palestine from the DP camps.[37] In this initial period, the various Zionist youth movements agreed to participate within the Nocham framework; over the course of 1946, however, divisions would emerge and each movement (aside from Gordoniah) erected an independent apparatus in the DP camps.[38]

According to leaders of the She'erit Hapletah, Jewish youths in the DP camps had a responsibility to be productive in order to guarantee the rebirth of the Jewish people. Furthermore, as Samuel Gringauz, head of the Landsberg DP camp, suggested on Yom Kippur in September 1945, "For you, our young people, are the agents of our revenge which ought to be a proud assertion to continue life. You must readily show the world and all our enemies that despite everything we are here to stay. Your revenge must be in working and toiling for your own land. You must create and build, dance and sing, open yourselves to life, to living and labor."[39] Jewish youths thus had a duty to be the revitalizing force in the rebirth of the Jewish people after the catastrophe. As Jewish youths emerged as the most vocal and desirable element of the Jewish DP population, such a focus could also serve to empower youth, who until that time had only been the victims of persecution and dehumanization. This language of productivization would prove appealing to various groups in postwar Germany who focused on the survivor youths (and those ages fifteen to thirty in particular) as the agents of Zionist productivity for the wider DP population.

THE U.S. ARMY, UNRRA, THE JEWISH AGENCY, AND THE KIBBUTZ PROJECT

While the youth movement leaders and the DP leadership viewed life in the kibbutz and farming as therapeutic activities for survivor youths, others in the Zionist movement (and in the American zone administration) viewed the kibbutzim from a far more functional and instrumental perspective. In a visit to Kibbutz Buchenwald at the end of July 1945, Eliyahu Dobkin, head of the Jewish Agency's aliyah department and the highest-ranking Jewish Agency official to reach Germany until then, sought to convince kibbutz members eager to make aliyah that the kibbutz could have far more value as a symbolic protest through its continued functioning in Germany. As was noted in the kibbutz journal after Dobkin's visit, "Now we asked what news he had for us. His reply disturbed us greatly. For he suggested that we should remain here as a kibbutz for the time being, since our existence made us a symbol of vital political importance to the Jewish cause. . . . [E]ven if we were given the means to proceed to Palestine, there were plenty of others who would come into the kibbutz and maintain it in Germany as the next immigrant group."⁴⁰ (Ultimately the original members of Kibbutz Buchenwald were granted the aliyah certificates they desired and immigrated to Palestine in August 1945.) Both during and after the war, however, the Yishuv continued to question whether the She'erit Hapletah could really be counted on to aid in the creation of the state. Leaders doubted both the character of the surviving population and the degree of Zionist enthusiasm among the DPs.⁴¹ Nonetheless, in his October 1945 visit to the DP camps, David Ben-Gurion became convinced of the Zionist enthusiasm of the She'erit Hapletah, witnessing its early organization and initiative in the creation of training farms and kibbutzim in particular.

In October 1945 Ben-Gurion, in his capacity as head of the Jewish Agency, visited the DP camps in Germany, where the Jewish DPs welcomed him as "the personal embodiment of all their hopes for the future."⁴² Major Irving Heymont, responsible for the administration of the Landsberg DP camp, described Ben-Gurion's visit to Landsberg on October 22, 1945, and the excitement that the visit engendered among the camp population. The camp was already abuzz, for the day before the first election of the camp committee had occurred, with the Ichud Zionist slate of Samuel Gringauz emerging victorious. As Heymont related, "To add to the excitement of election day, the camp was visited by Mr. David Ben-Gurion—the head of the Zionist organization if Palestine. *To the people of the camp, he is God. It seems that he represents all of their hopes of getting to Palestine.* . . . I don't think that a visit by President Truman could cause as much excitement."⁴³

Through his meetings with General Dwight D. Eisenhower and General Walter Bedell-Smith, Ben-Gurion learned that the U.S. Army authorities did not intend to stop Jewish infiltrees from Eastern Europe from entering the American zone; sensing an opportunity, he outlined a plan that was to bring as many Jews as possible into the occupation zones that were under U.S. command.⁴⁴ In the wake of the Harrison Report, in which American authorities had been excoriated for poor treatment of Jews, American officials provided separate camps for Jews and were determined to improve conditions for Jews in the U.S. zone. Furthermore, Ben-Gurion submitted a number of suggestions to Eisenhower on how to improve the morale of the Jewish DPs, which included allowing the Jewish DPs to govern themselves, subject to the ultimate authority of the U.S. Army, and providing agricultural and vocational training on confiscated Nazi farms.⁴⁵

Other American officials were impressed by the early success of Kibbutz Buchenwald and other farms in not only improving DP morale and spiritual rehabilitation but also in providing for many of their

Major Irving Heymont converses with David Ben-Gurion during his visit to the Landsberg DP camp. Also pictured is U.S. Army chaplain Rabbi Abraham Klausner (*left*) and Abraham Glassgold, UNRRA camp director (*far right*). (United States Holocaust Memorial Museum, Photograph no. 80978A, courtesy of Sara Huberfeld)

own food needs and preparing for their future in Palestine (and not in the United States) as well as serving as a possible form of punishment for former Nazis.[46] At the time of Ben-Gurion's visit to the DP camps in late October 1945, five agricultural training settlements were already in existence, with their early success demonstrating the viability of an agricultural plan on a larger scale. Kibbutz Nili, for example, was appropriated for Jewish DPs by the U.S. Army, which ordered the evacuation of Russian and Ukrainian DPs living on the farm in October and November 1945.[47] Still, American officials had to balance their Jewish policy with the increasingly more important task of German reconstruction.

For farms to be viable, however, they needed not only the approval of American officials but also the support of a number of aid agencies, which also sought to address the issue of overcrowding and DP demoralization, while providing shelter for the increasing numbers of infiltrees being allowed to enter by American authorities. John Whiting, as UNRRA zone administrator, noting his belief that many of the DPs ultimately sought to make their way to Palestine, also con-

Avinoam J. Patt

cluded that agricultural training could be an excellent way to make use of the Jewish DPs' time in Germany and thus justified the seizure of German estates for Jewish farmers.[48] Whiting in effect became a spokesperson for the merit of these hakhsharot, arguing to military officials that "it is, in my opinion, a fact that the use of the properties by the Jewish displaced persons would increase the productivity and actually contribute more to the local German economy than present usage does."[49] Thus, he indirectly advocated a Zionist position, but not out of an overwhelming love for the idea of a Jewish state. Rather, as he saw it, Zionism came to represent a solution to his immediate problem of overcrowding, which could lead to DP demoralization, crime, black market activity, and the spread of tuberculosis.

UNRRA's support for training farms corresponded nicely with the Jewish Agency's diplomatic goals. UNRRA would be assisted in its efforts to secure land and instructors for farming projects by representatives of the Jewish Agency operating in Germany. *Shlichim* (emissaries) from the Jewish Agency attached to Haim Hoffman's delegation worked to ensure the expansion of the project. The first delegation of twenty Jewish Agency emissaries, technically working under the auspices of UNRRA, had arrived in Germany in the middle of December 1945 and worked to organize aliyah, assist the Bricha in accommodating infiltrees from Eastern Europe, facilitate agricultural and vocational training, offer political instruction, and provide Zionist education.[50] With the arrival of more *shlichim* over the course of 1946, the Jewish Agency team expanded its efforts to assist in the opening of hakhsharot. For political reasons the Jewish Agency believed that such farms, while preparing youths for life in Palestine through agricultural training, could also prove valuable by increasing the visibility of DP Zionism and isolating the pioneering avant-garde from the rest of the DP camp. For the most part, however, Jewish Agency workers adopted the largely instrumental view of the youths based on a continuing belief in survivor youths as unsuitable for agricultural labor. Haim Hoffman corroborated this view of the survivor youth as less than ideal for the type of labor required of agricultural workers, although he believed that the farms could successfully transform their residents into suitable Zionist material: "after a short time, a different type of person was created from the residents of the camps who was even closer to the Eretz Israeli type of person."[51]

Through the support of these various groups, however, the number of farms grew steadily well before the sizable influx of Jewish refugees from Poland arriving with the Bricha. By June 1946 thirty-five farms were in existence with more than thirty-six hundred inhabitants. This suggests that while the stated rationale for the creation of farms

Date of Survey	Number of Hakhsharot	Number of Inhabitants	Total population in U.S. Zone (Hakhshara Population as % of Total Population)
January 27, 1946	8	870	49,695 (1.75%)
May 31, 1946	26	2,337 (or 2,236)	67,491 (3.46%)
June 30, 1946	35	3,661	75,517 (4.84%)
September 30, 1946	36	3,515	138,551 (2.54%)
October 31, 1946	36	3,442	141,077 (2.4%)

Note. The calculations are based on the following JDC population surveys (available in the YIVO Archives): January 1946 (microfilm MK 488, Leo Schwarz Papers, reel 9, folder 57, frame 576); May 31, 1946 (microfilm MK 488, Leo Schwarz Papers, reel 2, folder 20, frames 835–41); June 30, 1946 (microfilm MK 488, Leo Schwarz Papers, reel 2, folder 21, frame 1024); September 30, 1946 (microfilm MK 483, DPG reel 3, folder 29, frame 53); October 31, 1946 (microfilm MK 483, DPG reel 3, folder 30, frame 200).

was to alleviate overcrowding, it is clear that the creation of farms preceded the large infiltration of East European Jewish refugees with the Bricha, therefore indicating that diplomatic concerns may have been as significant as demographic ones.

Just as importantly, on the diplomatic level the high visibility of the kibbutzim and hakhsharot and their manifestations of Zionist enthusiasm demonstrated to outside observers a perceived state of Palestine passion on the part of the Jewish DPs. The apparent importance of Zionism for the increasing numbers of arriving DPs confirmed the necessity of the Zionist solution for representatives of the Anglo-American Committee of Inquiry (AACI). After beginning their work in Washington and London in January 1946, in February members of the commission began visiting the DP camps in Germany and Austria as well as sites in Poland to assess the Jewish situation.[52] Notwithstanding some concerns over Zionist propaganda and manipulation, on April 20, 1946, the AACI recommended "(A) that 100,000 certificates be authorized immediately for the admission into Palestine of Jews who have been the victims of Nazi and Fascist persecution; (B) that these certificates be awarded as far as possible in 1946 and that actual immigration be pushed forward as rapidly as conditions will permit." This was the conclusion that the committee came to not only

Avinoam J. Patt

מיר װילן צוריק אין אונזער הײם ארץ ישראל

A large crowd of Jewish DPs at the Neu Freimann DP camp participate in a demonstration protesting British immigration policy to Israel. (United States Holocaust Memorial Museum, Photograph no. 96435, courtesy of Jack Sutin)

because of a lack of any other options but also because the committee genuinely believed that this was the truest expression of the Jewish DPs' desires. "Furthermore, that is where almost all of them want to go. There they are sure that they will receive a welcome denied them elsewhere. There they hope to enjoy peace and rebuild their lives." The committee based these findings in part on surveys conducted among the DPs. However, the committee also firmly believed that based on what it had observed among the Jewish DPs, they were a group ardently preparing themselves for a Zionist future. While many among the DPs were seen as reluctant to work, "On the other hand, whenever facilities are provided for practical training for life in Palestine they eagerly take advantage of them."[53]

Despite the recommendations of the AACI, however, over the course of 1946 and into 1947 diplomatic efforts stalled, and it became clear that for the majority of the youths in the kibbutzim life would continue in Germany and not on the path to Palestine. As more and more infiltrees arrived from Poland, kibbutz groups in the DP camps moved to training farms in the American zone of Germany, where they would continue life within the youth movement awaiting selection for aliyah. The massive influx of Jews from Eastern Europe, with the arrival of Jews who had survived in the far reaches of the Soviet Union and many more families, also led to a major demographic shift in the DP camps. Over the course of 1946, approximately one hundred thousand Jews from Eastern Europe were brought to the American zone of Germany by the Bricha, some one-third of them youths organized within the framework of kibbutzim of the pioneering Zionist youth movements.[54] Who were these youths in the kibbutzim, and what did they get out of this experience? What was the initial appeal of the kibbutz for those youths who chose to join the groups, and why did they choose to remain in the group rather than seek other options as time dragged on in Germany?

Jewish Youths and Zionism in the Kibbutz Groups: The Case of Kibbutz Lochamei HaGetaot al shem Tosia Altman

While Kibbutz Buchenwald and Kibbutz Nili proved appealing to young survivors eager to remove themselves from the DP camp environment in the first months after liberation, the majority of the kibbutzim by the end of 1946 were occupied by youths who had survived the war in Poland or the Soviet Union. Unlike their counterparts in Germany, many of these Polish youths had already had their first encounters with the Zionist framework of the kibbutz in Poland and were thus, to a greater extent, part of a cohesive group upon their arrival in Germany. Nonetheless, their experience of Zionism was also a work in progress that had begun to be shaped first in Poland.

Among these groups infiltrating the American zone of Germany at the end of 1945 were two Hashomer Hatzair kibbutzim organized in Sosnowiec and Bytom in Poland. Their experiences in postwar Germany would be fairly typical of those for kibbutz youths. The two groups, which united to form one kibbutz with 110 members once they reached the Landsberg DP camp, took on the name Kibbutz Lochamei HaGetaot al shem Tosia Altman in December 1945. Like many of the Hashomer Hatzair kibbutzim in the DP camps, the kibbutz was named after a fallen resistance fighter from the movement.[55] The two *madrichim* of the kibbutz, Miriam and Baruch Yechieli, who served as the guides, teachers, and spiritual leaders of the kibbutz, had returned to Poland after spending the war in the Soviet Union. The group kept a collective diary, which was commenced while the kibbutz was still in Germany, detailing the history of the kibbutz.[56] Although the youths arriving in kibbutzim such as Tosia Altman may not have known it at the time, their presence in the American zone would have significant diplomatic ramifications.

Cover page of the collective diary kept by Kibbutz Lochamei HaGetaot al shem Tosia Altman.
(Kibbutz Gazit Archive, Israel)

As was the case with the members of Kibbutz Tosia Altman, while they had been filled with hope of an early arrival in Palestine following their departure from Poland, weeks in Germany soon dragged into months, and months dragged into years. After spending fourteen months in the American zone, eight of which they spent farming the soil of Germany on a hakhsharah near Eschwege, the kibbutz left for Palestine in early 1947. They arrived there only in the spring of 1948 following a year-long internment in Cyprus. The length of the period within the DP camps raised the question of whether the kibbutz could continue as a cohesive group or would remain the most appealing option for the youths who had arrived in Germany. Still, through a focus on materials created by young Jewish DPs themselves living in the kibbutzim, it becomes evident that the time spent by the youths in the kibbutz groups was put to use in deepening Zionist enthusiasm and strengthening attachment to both the Jewish past and the Zionist future.

For many, however, the initial appeal of the kibbutz in the summer of 1945 had little to do with ideology; practical concerns were far more pressing. An early diary entry in Bytom described members who were steered to the kibbutz by the League for Labor Palestine (Ha-Liga lema'an Erets-Yisrael ha-Ovedet) and who "arrived young, without any ideological awareness and unable to understand the nature of kibbutz life. They saw the kibbutz as a practical means of aliyah to Israel."[57] The new members in both kibbutzim in Bytom and Sosnowiec, unaware of many of the meanings behind the Zionist activities in the kibbutz, had clearly not joined out of commitment to the socialist-Zionist ethic but instead saw the kibbutz as preferable to the meager options available in Poland. As one early member, Inka Weisbort, later recalled, "the negative feelings were the primary reason for joining the kibbutz: fear of loneliness, of anti-Semitism, and the threats of the outside world. . . . Positive feelings, like the better social atmosphere . . . , desire to make aliyah and . . . achieve the Zionist ideal" came only much later.[58]

The creation of kibbutzim and the choices made by Jewish youths to join them were an important part of a mutually beneficial relationship for Jewish youths and the Zionist movements in postwar Poland. While the movements viewed the kibbutzim as a method of enlisting followers and expanding the ranks of the Zionist parties, the youths who joined the kibbutzim tended to stay because of the psychological support they derived from the communal structure, which proved highly therapeutic for many of the survivors because it placed them with a similar community of youths who had undergone wartime trauma. The activity within the kibbutz, both in daily work and in education, could help to avert the depression, anxiety, and anger that were certain by-products of the post-traumatic stress disorder that many of these survivors were perhaps facing.[59] Although veteran movement activists may have been critical of the pioneering quality of the surviving youths, they were in fact dependent on these youths to reconstitute the decimated European movements.

While the Zionist ideological aspects of the kibbutz were secondary, by joining a kibbutz these youths were making a statement of membership in a Zionist organization. And membership in the kibbutz came along with the opportunity for education in Jewish and Zionist history as well as the ideology of the movement that they joined. (While many had abandoned the religion of their youth, the Jewish aspects of the kibbutz continued to hold appeal as a meaningful part of their identity.) The Zionist opportunity, however, was not merely defined by its end goal—the creation of a Jewish state in Palestine—but also came to be understood as the community provided by the kibbutz, the education it offered, the structure, and the chance to work as well as the hope for departure from Europe.

Although the members did not necessarily join for ideological reasons, this did not preclude the growth of Zionist enthusiasm. On the contrary, as members remained within the kibbutz, they learned more about their youth movement, the history of the Zionist movement, the ideas and beliefs that their movement stood for, and their new partnership in a legacy of wartime heroism. After their arrival in Germany with the Bricha, the kibbutz used the time spent in the DP camps to further their Zionist education and training. (Kibbutz Tosia Altman spent two months in Landsberg before moving to Leipheim in January 1946.) The kibbutz also provided a cultural outlet for dramatic performances, music, dancing, and writing, all of which were part of the Zionist immersion. Both in the diary and in reports to the youth movement leadership, Kibbutz Tosia Altman detailed daily Hebrew lessons, courses in Zionist and Jewish history, the history of the youth movements, and vocational and agricultural training designed to prepare the youths for their future lives in Palestine.

The daily schedule of the kibbutzim was thus run on the time of the youth movement, as was the calendar of the kibbutz. The daily activities in the kibbutz and the new interpretation of familiar events, such as Jewish holidays, had the function of reorienting members' conceptions of the past, present, and future. Kibbutz members paid special attention to the celebrations of Jewish and Zionist movement holidays in the sources they created as well as in the weekly commemoration of the Sabbath in an *oneg shabbes* (enjoying the Sabbath). As members of Kibbutz Tosia Altman noted in their diary, the *oneg shabbes,* held on Friday evenings, was a time to have discussions of literature and readings of books and newspapers and was a chance for members to present plays and performances; a successful *oneg shabbes* could keep the kibbutz discussing it for several days afterward.[60] These were common to the kibbutzim of all the youth movements regardless of the level of religious observance. In fact, Hashomer Hatzair, as a Marxist-leaning socialist group, was decidedly secular, yet the movement calendar continued to run according to the familiar Jewish holidays. The weekly *oneg shabbes* certainly did not imply observance; both Kibbutz Yosef Kaplan and Kibbutz Tosia Altman noted the Sabbath as a popular time to go to the movies in the DP camps.[61]

The celebration of holidays within the kibbutzim tended to blend Jewish and Zionist motifs; in many cases, Jewish traditions were appropriated by the movement in order to emphasize wartime heroism. On the last night of Chanukah 1945 Kibbutz Tosia Altman held a party to celebrate the holiday (with guests from UNRRA and representatives of the camp) and to bid farewell to the first aliyah group from the kibbutz. The kibbutz sang songs from the ghetto, which "described the many graves in which our families were buried. The songs told the stories of the Jewish child, on the Jewish home in Poland and Lithuania, on Janusz Korczak, who went to his death without abandoning the children he taught. The songs told the stories of the ghetto fighters whose deaths in bravery rivaled the deaths of the Maccabees."[62] Likewise, other holidays such as the 11th of Adar, Yom Tel Hai, and Purim were used as opportunities to educate the kibbutz members about the heroism of Zionist leaders. Yom Tel Hai, when the members learned about the heroism of Trumpeldor, was followed a few days later by a more light-hearted celebration of the Jewish holiday of Purim with a comical rendition of the kibbutz's play, *"Haganah."*[63] The Föhrenwald camp newspaper noted the celebration of a *"Purim-Ownt"* (Purim Evening) with the Hashomer Hatzair kibbutz in which the *"madrichim* of the kibbutz, Mirjam . . . gave a speech on the heroes of the present-day Purim, the fighters from the Warsaw, Vilna, Bialystok, and Częstochowa ghettos, as well as the partisans and the front-line fighters, who with there blood defended the honor of the Jewish people just as once before did Mordecai and Esther defend Jewish honor before King Ahashuerus."[64]

The youth movements also used holidays as opportunities to celebrate in nature with hikes, picnics, scouting games, Haganah exercises and bonfires. Approximately six weeks after the celebration of Chanukah, Kibbutz Yosef Kaplan (another Hashomer Hatzair kibbutz named after one of the founders of the Jewish Fighting Organization in the Warsaw Ghetto who was killed in September 1942) commemo-

Avinoam J. Patt

rated Tu Be-Shevat (the New Year for the trees) with a hike in the forest, capped off by a party and a celebratory bonfire. The kibbutz decided to make a contribution to the Jewish National Fund in order to plant two trees in the groves of Kibbutz Mishmar HaEmek in Palestine in their name.[65] Although they were still living in Germany, the kibbutz members were able to observe these occasions as if they were already in the Land of Israel, if not in body then at least in spirit.

The Hashomer Hatzair movement leadership also tried to maintain a sense of belonging to a larger community by publishing its own movement newspaper, which was distributed to all of the kibbutzim in the American zone. The newspaper, titled *Hashomer Hatzair*, was published in Munich in Yiddish (twenty volumes appeared between March 1946 and October 1947) and was dedicated to keeping members informed of current political debates in Eretz Israel, issues facing the movement there and in Germany, ideological concerns, the history of the movement, and the past glories of the movement during the war. In the first volume of the newspaper, Zelig Shushan, the Hashomer Hatzair emissary from the Yishuv, described his encounter with the survivors in Europe in an article titled "The Meeting with the Comrades in the Diaspora." According to Shushan, these youths carried the responsibility of those who had died to continue along the path of *halutziut* (the pioneering way). He assured the young survivors who had "seen what it is to wander on the ruins of Jewish life, on the cemeteries of your parents, sisters, and brothers," that they were "not alone in your struggle. You are comrades in a large movement, 'Hashomer Hatzair.' Your shoulder joins together with all of the shoulders of Hashomer Haztair in the entire world."[66] Such an approach pointed to the method of the movement in reframing the misery and destruction of the war as a basis for the rebirth of the Jewish people. A passage such as this, read from the newspaper to kibbutz members at an evening *asefa* (assembly), may have helped to infuse their recent trauma with an uplifting and potentially productive source of meaning.

In addition to noting the connection to Eretz Israel and making members feel a part of the community there (in time if not in space), a greater part of the newspaper continued to emphasize the heroism of Hashomer Hatzair in leading wartime resistance. As was noted in volume 2 of the newspaper (April 1946) dedicated to the three-year anniversary of the Warsaw Ghetto Uprising, "our movement was among the first to make the call for rebellion." The cover was graced by a drawing of the ruins of the Warsaw Ghetto, and the first page profiled Mordecai Anielewicz, including a selection from his last will and testament to the world: "How happy am I that I am one of the first Jewish fighters in the ghetto." The volume also included part of Abba Kovner's appeal to the Jews of the Vilna Ghetto "not to go like sheep to the slaughter"[67] as well as the hymn of the United Partisans Organization (Fareinigte Partizaner Organizatsye), "Zog Nit Keyn Mol."[68] Articles by ghetto fighters Ruzhka Korzcak, Abba Kovner, and Chaya Klinger detailed their wartime activity in the resistance. Later editions of the newspaper continued this emphasis with profiles of other resistance leaders after whom Hashomer Hatzair kibbutzim were named, including Yosef Kaplan and Tosia Altman (volumes 3 and 4) as well as leaders such as Frumka Plotnicka and Abba Kovner. The Zionism of the youth movements in the kibbutzim thus replaced the traumatic individual past of the survivors with the shared experience of wartime heroism in the ghetto revolts regardless of what members' experiences had been in the war.

Zionism in this way not only reframed the past but also provided a new way for the youths to understand their present situation. Kibbutz members came into contact with Germans on the farms and in economic exchanges; the acquisition of estates for farming and the participation of German farmhands reveals that Jewish DPs did not live in a German-free vacuum in the American zone. In April 1946 the members of Kibbutz Tosia Altman moved to a farm near Eschwege, where they engaged in agricultural training designed to prepare for their future lives in Palestine. As was the case with a number of other farms, the young farmers in Kibbutz Tosia Altman took over what had shortly before been the property of the German war machine. As they described in the diary,

> Before we came here we imagined to ourselves that on a farm can be found cows, horses, fields, etc. as is normal on every agricultural farm. How much was our disappointment to find in this place a large airport with broken plane parts scattered about, different building materials, machine parts, and the like. The building was abandoned and dirty. We were asked to clean it and bring things in order and change the place around the abandoned airfield into a blooming agricultural farm.[69]

Within a matter of weeks, however—and with the assistance of German farmers—the kibbutz members managed to acquire livestock, plant crops, and begin the operation of a fully functioning farm. Although their contact with Germans may have been more limited than those who lived in cities, they were still confronted with the reality of continued existence among their former enemies. The agricultural department of the Central Committee (established in the spring of 1946) worked to instill a "love for the soil" among the youths; the "blood-soaked" German soil would have to serve as a surrogate for the soil of agricultural labor in an abstract sense.[70] Still, farming German soil ended up having meaning for Jewish DPs on a number of levels. The DP youths in Kibbutz Nili in Pleikhershof linked farming to revenge, finding satisfaction in working the land on Julius Streicher's estate while he stood trial in nearby Nuremberg. As the leader of Kibbutz Nili wrote in the *Landsberger Lager Tsaytung*, the work was difficult, but it was done with humor, energy, and the singing of Hebrew "songs of building and struggle." With the creation of Kibbutz Nili in Pleikhershof, "the white and blue flag flies over Streicher's farm."[71] There could be no mistaking the symbolic value of this gesture by a kibbutz named "Nili," based on the acronym of the initial letters of the Hebrew verse "Netzach Yisrael Lo Yeshakker" ("the Strength of Israel will not lie"; 1 Sam. 15:29). The young farmers symbolically exacted their revenge on the "great Jew-hater," affirming the eternal presence of the Jewish people on the appropriated Nazi land. The renaming of farm buildings and livestock with Hebrew names were part of a consciously symbolic revenge for youths empowered by membership in a kibbutz and the Zionist youth movement. While Zionism could allow them to transcend their current situation through a focus on the future, when they did face Germany and Nazism they were now armed with the tools to do so. At the same time, the young farmers could take pride in their collective accomplishments, as farming provided some tangible product to their time and efforts in Germany as they waited for departure on aliyah.

After more than a year in Germany, the members of Kibbutz Tosia Altman received the news for which they had been waiting for so long: they should prepare themselves for departure. "Our joy knew no bounds. We began our preparations for aliyah, but first we thought about our departure party."[72] On December 29, 1946, the members of Kibbutz Tosia Altman held their final departure party. Yosef (Tzunik) Richter, Miriam's brother, spoke and said that "in the history of the Jews there is no example of young people like us, who only yesterday . . . left concentration camps, bunkers, and forests and now . . . have taken upon ourselves the responsibility for the future of the people."[73] The Hashomer Hatzair movement *shaliach* (emissary) Yehoshua Bruk praised the kibbutz as "the last of the first kibbutzim created after the war to leave for aliyah" and congratulated them as they received the symbol of movement graduates, the Chazak ve-Ematz (literally "strong and brave," from Deuteronomy 31:7).

On January 5, 1947, the kibbutz left the farm forever, the farm "which we established, developed, and invested great energy [in]. Here

Carrying rakes and hoes, members of Kibbutz Nili hakhsharah (Zionist collective) pass through the entrance arch on their way to the fields. (United States Holocaust Memorial Museum, Photograph no. 30025, courtesy of Ruchana Medine White)

we were educated and trained for different forms of work and therefore this period will remain engraved in our hearts. She [the farm] sealed on us the signature of productive work."[74] Their efforts on the farm were temporary, but the members sensed that the work had left a permanent impression and in ensuring their departure from Germany had been worth any physical or emotional hardship. They took a train from Eschwege via Frankfurt to the south. It was far too cold (28 degrees F) to traverse the Alps for Italy (a common border crossing route for Bricha groups), so they joined their comrades in Kibbutz Shmuel Breslaw at Hochland and awaited their departure. For many of the kibbutz members, the ten days spent at Hochland prior to leaving constituted a long-awaited vacation where the working conditions were easy and they were allowed to sleep late. Finally, on January 16, 1947, they left Hochland traveling via Leipheim. At dawn on the morning of January 17, 1947, the kibbutz reached the Austro-German border on trucks driven by members of the Bricha. As was noted in the diary, "we left forever the cursed Germany, in which we resided for 14 months, beginning in November 1945 until January 1947. Beautiful and rich experiences were our part during this period, but everyone was united in his/her thoughts on the difficult path that lay before us." The kibbutz spent two months in Italy before leaving for Palestine. On

Avinoam J. Patt

the way, they were intercepted by British forces and were deported to Cyprus, where much of the kibbutz spent one more year before departing for Palestine in March 1948.[75]

CONCLUSION: THE FUNCTIONS OF ZIONISM IN POSTWAR GERMANY

For the youths in the kibbutzim, the ideological pronouncements of Central Committee leaders such as Samuel Gringauz and Zalman Grinberg mattered little. Nonetheless, ideology provided a significant foundation for a distinctive form of DP Zionism that supported the postwar political contributions of the DPs on the diplomatic level by appealing to various groups interested in ameliorating the DP situation. On the ground, DP Zionism could succeed because it made sense both on the ideological level and the practical level; without pragmatic solutions to the most pressing needs of the young survivors, it could not have attracted and maintained the membership that it did.

It is clear that the DPs played an important role in the creation of the State of Israel so soon after the war. However, even without the retroactive knowledge that the State of Israel would ultimately be created, Zionism was highly successful in filling a positive function for DP youths in the aftermath of the Holocaust by providing a secure environment for vocational training, education, and rehabilitation and a surrogate family that could ultimately restore their belief in humanity. For the wider Jewish DP population, Zionism filled a symbolic need that had arisen for the Jewish people in the wake of tragedy even if not all would make the Zionist dream their personal reality. In the words of one survivor who intended to live in Montevideo but responded to a survey by indicating that he would make aliyah to Palestine, "I may be able to live in Uruguay, but the Jews . . . the Jews must live in Israel." Zionism in the DP camps was thus not merely a monolithic Zionism, geared solely to the requirements of the Yishuv; it filled the needs of many groups productively, therapeutically, and diplomatically.

In February 1947 the British referred the problem of Palestine to the United Nations, and following the drama of the *Exodus* Affair in the summer of 1947 and the work and report of United Nations Special Committee on Palestine, the United Nations voted for the partition of Palestine on November 29, 1947. The announcement was greeted with great enthusiasm in the DP camps, and the Central Committee declared that "on the ruins of the Diaspora will arise the Jewish state, which will represent the most beautiful ideals of our people and will give the possibility to return the Jewish masses of the historical past and the coming future. With the help of the Jewish state the Jewish camps in Germany will be liquidated and the Jewish people will return to the family of free nations after 2000 years."[76]

As hostilities broke out between the Haganah and Arab forces, the DPs were called upon to stand up in defense of the homeland they had never seen. The youths, who had proudly demonstrated their Zionist enthusiasm in the kibbutz groups, were asked to do their duty to the people on behalf of the wider DP population. At the Third Congress of the She'erit Hapletah in early April 1948, the Central Committee issued its call: "The Fatherland Calls: Do Your Duty to the People." The Zionist movement, the Yishuv, and indeed the Fatherland was calling, and in the DP camps the youth were expected to answer this call.

NOTES

1. *Landsberger Lager Czajtung*, vol. 11, December 21, 1945, Baruch Cheta, reel 1-1, p. 4, Jewish DP Periodicals Collection, YIVO Archives, New York (hereafter YIVO).

2. Ibid.

3. It is important to note that the term "kibbutz" came to represent a collective settlement that differed greatly from the kibbutzim that had been created as agricultural settlements by the Zionist movement in Palestine. After the war, the term "kibbutz" was used to refer to groups of youths, affiliated with Zionist youth movements, who presumably lived together in a collective framework. The "collective" aspects of group life in the kibbutzim of the survivors were highly variable. Agricultural hakhsharot were training farms where kibbutz groups worked to prepare for life in Palestine.

4. This conclusion has been noted by numerous scholars who have written on the Jewish DPs. See as discussed in volume introduction.

5. See Hanna Yablonka, *Foreign Brethren: Holocaust Survivors in the State of Israel, 1948–1952* (Jerusalem: Yad Izhak Ben-Zvi Press, 1994), 82. Yablonka estimates that the twenty-two thousand enlisted DPs comprised perhaps one-third of the Israel Defense Forces' sixty thousand combat soldiers during the Israeli War of Independence. The Haganah was the underground military organization for self-defense and security established by the Zionist organization in Palestine in 1920.

6. Resolutions of the Third Congress of the She'erit Hapletah, microfilm MK 483, reel 1, folder 5, frames 639–41 (Yiddish), Displaced Persons Camps, Germany Collection, YIVO (hereafter YIVO DPG). The Third Congress of the She'erit Hapletah met from March 30 to April 2, 1948, in Bad Reichenhall.

7. The Declaration of the Establishment of Israel, in N. Greenwood, ed., *Israel Yearbook and Almanac 1991/92* (Jerusalem: International Publication Service, 1992), 298–99.

8. Elimelech Rimalt (member of the Knesset for the General Zionist Party)

made such an argument in the Knesset in 1953. Quoted in Yechiam Weitz, "Shaping the Memory of the Holocaust in Israeli Society of the 1950s," in *Major Changes within the Jewish People in the Wake of the Holocaust*, edited by Israel Gutman (Jerusalem: Yad Vashem, 1996), 500. In fact, in the middle of World War II as the Nazi annihilation of the Jewish community of Europe reached its height, Benzion Dinur concluded that "the only path of escape from the fate of destruction is the return to the Jewish homeland"; see Benzion Dinur, "Galuyot ve-Hurbanan," in Dinur, *Dorot u-reshumot: Mekhkarim ve-iyunim ba-historyografyah ha-yisraelit* (Jerusalem: Mosad Bialik, 1978), 192.

9. According to Emmanuel Sivan, 21,755 soldiers arrived from Europe to join in the Israeli War of Independence in 1948. Of those soldiers who arrived in Israel in 1948, 72.5 percent were born between 1923 and 1930, while 67.4 percent of the 1940–47 arrivals and 78.5 percent of Sabras (native-born Israelis) fell into this age range. Likewise, the average age of those who died was twenty-two years old for the 1948 and 1940–47 arrivals and twenty years old for the Sabras. Emmanuel Sivan, *Dor Tashakh: Mitos, Diyukan ve-Zikaron* (Israel: Ministry of Defense, 1991), 76.

10. See Koppel S. Pinson, "Jewish Life in Liberated Germany: A Study of the Jewish DPs," *Jewish Social Science* 9, no. 2 (1947): 117. Pinson, a sociologist who had been sent to the DP camps in the American zone of Germany by the American Jewish Joint Distribution Committee to assist in the formation of an education policy for the Jewish DPs, offered one of the earliest articulations of this argument: "The events of 1939–1945 seemed to discredit completely those philosophies of Jewish life prevailing before the war which were not centered around Palestine. The Zionists were the only ones that had a program that seemed to make sense after this catastrophe. . . . Without Palestine there seemed to be no future for them. Anti-Zionism or even a neutral attitude toward Zionism came to mean for them a threat to the most fundamental stakes in their future."

11. Zeev Mankowitz, *Life between Memory and Hope: The Survivors of the Holocaust in Occupied Germany* (Cambridge: Cambridge University Press, 2002), 69. "For many, their almost intuitive Zionism stood for the warmth, unquestioning acceptance and security of home; for the more politically minded it signified the only real hope for the rescue and rehabilitation of the little that remained of European Jewry and, in the longer term, the promise of the Jewish future."

12. Evyatar Friesel "The Holocaust: Factor in the Birth of Israel?," in *Major Changes within the Jewish People in the Wake of the Holocaust*, edited by Yisrael Guttman, 519–552 (Jerusalem: Yad Vashem, 1996).

13. Idith Zertal, *From Catastrophe to Power: Holocaust Survivors and the Emergence of the State of Israel* (Berkeley: University of California Press, 1998). Yosef Grodzinsky, *Homer Enoshi Tov: Yehudim mul Tsiyonim, 1945–1951* [*In the Shadow of the Holocaust: The Struggle between Jews and*

Zionists in the Aftermath of the World War II] (Or Yehudah, Israel: Hed Artzi, 1998), 185, similarly suggested that after the war the "the Zionist activists turned to the weakest. They selected from the 'human dust' good human material for the state on the way—to take the survivors from the furnaces to the smelter." He focused on the conscription campaign in the DP camps as a particularly egregious example of Zionist manipulation of the surviving Jews. See also Zeev Tzahor, "Holocaust Survivors as a Political Factor," *Middle Eastern Studies* 24, no. 4 (1988): 432–44. Tom Segev, *The Seventh Million: The Israelis and the Holocaust* (New York: Hill and Wang, 1993), also takes this approach.

14. Dan Diner, "Elements in Becoming a Subject: Jewish DPs in Historical Context," *Jahrbuch zur Geschichte und Wirkung des Holocaust* 2 (1997): 229–48. Dan Diner, among others, has noted that at the end of the war, U.S. and British occupation officials refused to categorize Jews as a distinct people among the DPs; instead, Jews were identified as belonging to the dominant nationality of their countries of residence. The Allies only changed their approach under the impact of a series of events that occurred in 1945–46 (including most notably the publication of the Harrison Report), coming to construct Jews as a separate national group with its own particular needs and interests. See also Arieh Kochavi, *Post-Holocaust Politics: Britain, the U.S., and Jewish Refugees, 1945–1948* (Chapel Hill: University of North Carolina Press, 2001).

15. Of the studies written in English about the Jewish DPs, Mankowitz's "Politics of Education," chapter 7 in *Life between Memory and Hope*, focuses on the experience of youths in kibbutz groups. He tends to explain the Zionist choice as an intuitive response to the Holocaust. Judith Tydor Baumel, *Kibbutz Buchenwald: Survivors and Pioneers* (New Brunswick, NJ: Rutgers University Press, 1997), covers one kibbutz group whose experience was unique in that the members left Germany soon after liberation and were composed entirely of survivors from camps in Germany.

16. Zeev Mankowitz, "The Formation of She'erit Hapleita: November 1944–July 1945," *Yad Vashem Studies* 20 (1990): 27, asserts that for the most part the Jews of Hungary and Romania sought to return home following liberation, while the Polish Jews (some 90 percent of those liberated) were far more divided on the issue. Later surveys of the Jewish DP population in the American zone of Germany corroborated this information. A survey of the Jewish DP population of the 4,976 residents of Landsberg taken on October 1, 1945, indicated that 75.2 percent (3,740) of residents were Polish, while only 5.7 percent (283) were Hungarian and 3.3 percent (162) were Romanian. A survey of residents of Feldafing taken at the same time indicated that a population drop from 600 to 400 from the summer to October 1945 was attributable to the sizable repatriation of Hungarian and Romanian Jews. "Jewish DP Population Survey," microfilm MK 488, roll 8, frames 1032–37, Leo Schwarz Papers (hereafter LSP), YIVO.

17. See Ruth Schreiber, "The New Organization of the Jewish Community in Germany, 1945–1952" (PhD dissertation, Tel Aviv University, October 1995), 11. While some 36 percent of Jews from Eastern Europe did try to live in German cities in January 1946, the continuing housing shortage and reluctance of some newly formed German Jewish *keh-illot* (religious communities) to represent Jews of non-German descent made this option a difficult one. While not the rule, this was the case in Frankfurt, for example (ibid., 33). As waves of Jews began to arrive from Poland over the course of 1945 and 1946, fewer Jews made the choice to live in German cities (ibid., 55–56). German Jews also suffered from initially being denied the status of persecuted individuals and were classified as enemy nationals along with Austrian and Hungarian Jews in some cases.

18. For more on the Brigade, see Yoav Gelber, "The Meeting between the Jewish Soldiers from Palestine Serving in the British Army and *She'erit Hapletah*," in *She'erit Hapletah, 1944–1948: Rehabilitation and Political Struggle*, edited by Yisrael Gutman and Avital Saf, 60–80 (Jerusalem: Yad Vashem, 1990).

19. June 24, 1945, report of Klausner, "A Detailed Report on the Liberated Jew as He Now Suffers His Period of Liberation under the Discipline of the Armed Forces of the United States," in Alexander Grobman, *Rekindling the Flame: American Jewish Chaplains and the Survivors of European Jewry, 1944–1948* (Detroit: Wayne State University Press, 1993), 42–43. Chaplain Abraham Klausner arrived in Dachau during the third week of May. While initially reluctant to serve in Europe at all, unsure of what he could contribute in a place where the fighting had already ended, he soon made it his mission to assist the Jewish survivors in any way possible. He was eventually integral in efforts to create the Central Committee of Liberated Jews and in publishing the first lists of survivors for relatives seeking one another.

20. See Leonard Dinnerstein, *America and the Survivors of the Holocaust* (New York: Columbia University Press, 1982), 28. Slightly different statistics can be found in Irit Keynan, *Lo Nirga Ha-Ra'av: Nitzulei Ha-Shoah ve-Shlichei Eretz Yisrael: Germaniah 1945–1948* (Tel Aviv: Am Oved Publishers, 1996), 45.

21. M. Winogrodzki to Nathan Schwalb, June 18, 1945, Record group (hereafter RG) 123/Maccabi/0012, box 20, folder 4, letters to Nathan Schwalb in He-Halutz Geneva Office, pp. 88–89, Ha'apalah Project, Haganah Archives, Tel Aviv (hereafter HPHA).

22. In June 1945 two Paris-based representatives of the Jewish Agency for Palestine, Ruth Kliger and David Shaltiel, told the heads of the political and immigration departments of the Jewish Agency Executive in Jerusalem that up to 95 percent of the survivors were under thirty-five years old. Kliger and Shaltiel to Shertok and Dobkin, June 11, 1945, folder S6/3659, Central Zionist Archives, Jerusalem. A survey of Jewish DPs in Bavaria taken in February 1946 found that 83.1 percent of

their number was between the ages of fifteen and forty, with more than 40 percent between the ages of fifteen and twenty-four and 61.3 percent between the ages of nineteen and thirty-four. Jewish Population in Bavaria, February 1946, microfilm MK 488, roll 9, folder 57, frame 581, LSP, YIVO. A study by the American Jewish Joint Distribution Committee of Jews in the U.S. occupation zone in Germany more than one year after liberation found that 83.1 percent were between the ages of six and forty-four. Jewish Population, U.S. zone Germany, November 30, 1946, microfilm MK 488, folder 57, reel LSP 9, frame 682, YIVO.

23. Winogrodzki to Nathan Schwalb, June 18, 1945, RG 123/Maccabi/0012, box 20, folder 4, letters to Nathan Schwalb in He-Halutz Geneva Office, pp. 88–89, HPHA.

24. He-Halutz was created to prepare Zionist youths in Europe for life in Palestine through agricultural and vocational training and served as an umbrella organization for a number of pioneering Zionist youth movements in interwar Europe. See Israel Oppenheim, *The Struggle of Jewish Youth for Productivization: The Zionist Youth Movement in Poland* (Boulder, CO: East European Monographs, 1989). Nathan Scwhalb served as the He-Halutz representative in Geneva during and after the war. See Raya Cohen, *Bein Sham Le-Kan: Sipuram shel 'Eidim le-Hurban, 1939– 1942 [The Story of Witnesses to Destruction: Jewish Emissaries in Switzerland, 1939–1942]* (Tel Aviv: Am Oved, 1999).

25. While many Ukrainians who had collaborated with the SS continued to be well fed, the Jewish prisoners, who had always received the worst nourishment, continued to be malnourished. Insufficient food and disease were not the only concerns troubling Jewish DPs. The fact that Jewish ex-prisoners continued to be clothed in the shreds of striped prisoner garb was also troubling to the Jewish survivors who had begun to organize in order to represent their needs before the military authorities. According to testimony, "We were liberated in striped prisoners' clothes, and we are sorry to state that till now the thousands of jewish [sic] ex-prisoners have no proper clothing, underwear or shoes." See Zalman Grinberg and Puczyc to OMGUS and UNRRA, July 10, 1945, microfilm MK 483, frame 340, YIVO DPG.

26. Kochavi, *Post-Holocaust Politics,* 89; Dinnerstein, *America and the Survivors of the Holocaust,* chap. 2. Harrison's suggestions, excluding the transfer of refugees to Palestine, were implemented almost immediately by General Eisenhower, who was assisted in his work by the newly appointed adviser on Jewish Affairs, Rabbi Judah Nadich (appointed on August 24, 1945); see Kochavi, *Post-Holocaust Politics,* 93. Nadich was replaced as special adviser after three months by Judge Simon Rifkind.

27. Protocol, July 14, 1945, meeting of Executive Committee, microfilm MK 488, roll 15, frame 141, LSP, YIVO. At a meeting of the executive committee of the newly formed Jewish DP organization, Lieutenant Simon of the Jewish Brigade reported that he had recently briefed Harrison on

Avinoam J. Patt

the situation of the Jewish survivors and made sure that he was aware of the importance of free immigration for the Jews to Palestine. Harrison, he suggested, had a favorable understanding of the situation. See also Grobman, *Rekindling the Flame*, 72. Harrison was the former U.S. commissioner of immigration and the U.S. representative on the Intergovernmental Committee on Refugees.

28. Report of Earl G. Harrison to President Truman, August 24, 1945. See treatments in Kochavi, *Post-Holocaust Politics*, 89, and Dinnerstein, *America and the Survivors of the Holocaust*, chap. 2.

29. See Baumel, *Kibbutz Buchenwald*, 5.

30. Letter from Arthur Posnansky to Nathan Schwalb, May 22, 1945, folder 123/Maccabi/12, p. 83 (in German), Ha'apalah Project, Haganah Archives.

31. Kibbutz Buchenwald Diary, in Leo Schwarz, *The Root and the Bough: The Epic of an Enduring People* (New York: Rinehart, 1949), 310–11.

32. Baumel, *Kibbutz Buchenwald*, chaps. 2, 22, 27.

33. See letter from Poznansky at Huldah, September 19, 1945, in Ada Schein, "Ma'arehet ha-hinukh be-mahanot ha-'akurim ha-yehudiyim be-Germanyah ube-Austryah, 1945-1951" (PhD dissertation, Hebrew University, Jerusalem, 2001), 162.

34. See Mankowitz, *Life between Memory and Hope*, 36, and Mankowitz, "The Formation of She'erit Hapleita." A number of early leaders of the Jewish DPs in Germany, including Samuel Gringauz, Zalman Grinberg, and Leib Garfunkel (head of the organization of Holocaust Survivors in Italy) as well as the founders of the early DP Zionist youth group Nocham (United Pioneer Youth Movement), emerged from an early group of survivors from Kovno concentrated in Dachau. In the pages of *Nitzotz* (an underground publication in Dachau) both before and after liberation, the members of Irgun Brith Zion (and the editor, Shlomo Frankel) lobbied for the importance of Zionist unity, a characteristic that would be central to the early organization of the She'erit Hapletah in Germany. Gringauz, Grinberg, and Frankel were later among the most active in creating the official institutions that would represent the Jewish DPs in Germany, helping to organize the Central Committee of Liberated Jews and the UZO. Samuel Gringauz was born at the turn of the century in eastern Prussia. He was deported from Kovno to Dachau in August 1944, was active in the Zionist underground in Kaufering, and was liberated with the group near Schwabenhausen at the end of April 1945; Mankowitz, *Life between Memory and Hope*, 174. Grinberg was a doctor who had studied medicine in Switzerland. Shlomo Frankel went on to be active in the flourishing DP press, continuing to edit *Nitzotz* after liberation and then *Das Wort*. See Mankowitz, *Life between Memory and Hope*, 347.

35. Protocols, Conference of Liberated Jews, July 25, 1945, microfilm MK 483, reel 61, frames 721–27, YIVO DPG.

36. Three weeks later, on September 11–12, 1945, in a preparatory meeting in Landsberg for the upcoming Zionist conference at Frankfurt, the founding principles of Nocham and the UZO were laid out: the creation of a Jewish state; construction of the country on socialist principles; elevation of labor, agriculture, hakhsharah, and Hebrew language and culture; and aliyah by all means. The new group also took upon itself shekel collection (the membership dues of the World Zionist Organization) and called for activity on behalf of the Labor Federation (Histadrut) in Palestine; in keeping with its complete identification with the Zionist executive in Palestine, the UZO also excluded the revisionist youth movement Betar from the united camp. See Pratei Kol of First Zionist Conference in Frankfurt, October 23–24, 1945, MP-1, folder 3, Yad Vashem Archives. Yehoyakim Cochavi sees the strong influence of the Brigade in the resolutions of Nocham and suggests that the socialist language led to later divisions with nonsocialist Zionists from Poland. He proposes that Brigade soldiers also paid special attention to the question of the youths, as many of them were formerly active in Yishuv youth movements. Many of the members of the newly formed Nocham were survivors in their twenties from Lithuania and before the war had been members of Bnei Akiva.

37. Letter from Zionist center in Bavaria to Jewish Agency, August 10, 1945, folder S6/3657, Central Zionist Archives. The letter seems to suggest that Nocham was already in existence by early August. The DP Zionist group expressed concern that those who were "actively working to build Zionism in the DP camps in Germany will not have the opportunity to make aliyah . . . and all their lives, even in the worst days, they dreamt of making aliyah and building Erets Israel and therefore they have the full privilege to make aliyah."

38. This call for unity was in response to the division that existed between the kibbutz movements in Palestine and their youth movements there and in the Diaspora. The two main kibbutz movements in Palestine were Kibbutz Ha-Arzi (the National Kibbutz movement founded in 1927) and Ha-Kibbutz Ha-Me'uhad (the United Kibbutz Movement founded in 1927). Hashomer Hatzair was the youth movement of the National Kibbutz movement, while Dror and Gordoniah were affiliated with the United Kibbutz movement. Although the early leaders of the youth movements in postwar Europe strove for unity following liberation, the leaders of the movements in Palestine feared such unity, which could dilute and confuse the potential membership reservoir for the kibbutz movements organized among the youth movement groups in Europe. See Schein, "Ma'arehet ha-hinukh be-mahanot ha-'akurim ha-yehudiyim be-Germanyah ube-Austryah, 1945-1951" 163.

39. *Landsberger Lager Cajtung*, no. 1, October 8, 1945, p. 3, reel 1, Jewish DP Periodicals Collection, YIVO. For a thorough analysis of Gringauz's ideology, see Mankowitz, *Life between Memory and Hope*, chap. 8. The verse "Nikmat dam jeled hakatan od lobarah hasatan" (Satan has not

Avinoam J. Patt

yet created a fitting revenge for the blood of a small child) is taken from the Hayyim Nachman Bialik poem "'Al ha-Shehitah," written in 1903.

40. July 21, 1945, Kibbutz Buchenwald Diary, in Schwarz, *The Root and the Bough*, 322, and Baumel, *Kibbutz Buchenwald*, 49.

41. See for example, Dina Porat, "The Role of European Jewry in the Plans of the Zionist Movement during World War II and Its Aftermath," in *She'erit Hapletah, 1944–1948: Rehabilitation and Political Struggle*, edited by Yisrael Gutman and Avital Saf, 286–303.

42. Judah Nadich, *Eisenhower and the Jews* (New York: Twayne, 1953), 231. The episode is also described by Heymont.

43. Letter 19, October 22, 1945, in Irving Heymont, *Among the Survivors of the Holocaust, 1945: The Landsberg DP Camp Letters of Major Irving Heymont, United States Army* (Cincinnati: Hebrew Union College Press, 1982), 65, my emphasis.

44. Kochavi, *Post-Holocaust Politics*, 134.

45. See Meir Avizohar, "Bikur Ben-Gurion be-mahanot ha-'akurim ve-tefisato ha-leumit be-tom Milhemet ha-'Olam ha-Sheniah" [Ben-Gurion's Visit to the DP Camps and His National Outlook in the Aftermath of World War II], in *Yahadut Mizrach Eiropah Bein Shoah Le-tekuma, 1944–1948* [The Jews of Eastern Europe between Holocaust and Rebirth, 1944–1948], edited by Benjamin Pinkus, 253–70 (Sde Boker, Israel: Ben-Gurion University, 1987); Kochavi, *Post-Holocaust Politics*, 94; and Nadich, *Eisenhower and the Jews*, 238. The Jewish DPs were granted the right to self-governance by the U.S. Army in September 1946.

46. Irving Heymont, in his capacity as American head of the largest DP camp at Landsberg, also discussed the overcrowding situation with Ben-Gurion, detailing his struggles to move DPs to the new camp at Föhrenwald as so-called Jewish infiltrees began to arrive from Poland. Heymont agreed with Ben-Gurion's farming suggestion; as Heymont wrote in a letter home to his wife, "I hope he is right. Many of the people, particularly those in the kibbutzim, are anxious to get out on farms. It would also help to relieve the overcrowding and enable more people to lead a normal life. There are plenty of farmers around here who were active Nazis." Heymont, *Among the Survivors of the Holocaust*, 102. Judah Nadich, adviser for Jewish affairs, saw Kibbutz Buchenwald "as an object lesson for all those who were interested in the welfare of the displaced persons. . . . Not only was their work helping to fill their present requirements, particularly with regard to fresh vegetables, fruits, and grains, but they were successfully preparing for their future, the kind of future they greatly desired, life in a cooperative colony in Palestine" (Nadich, *Eisenhower and the Jews*, 137).

47. Jim Tobias, *Der Kibbuz auf dem Streicher-Hof: Die vergessene Geschichte der judischen Kollektivfarmen, 1945–1948* (Nurnberg: Dahlinger und Fuchs, 1997).

48. See J. Whiting, Report on Jewish DPS in the U.S. zone, folder 65, frames 7–15, roll LSP 10, YIVO. As Whiting had argued in January 1946,

A greater emphasis should be placed on the training and retraining of Jewish displaced persons both in farm schools (Hachsharoth) and in German industry. Although there has been no classification made of Jewish displaced persons by age and sex we know that there are at least several thousand youngsters who are at present occupied only in idleness and who could be placed in factories schools, or on farms. Agronomists, teachers, etc. are now available from the Jewish Agency and it would be a waste of their time as well as a waste on the displaced persons lives not to get such programs under way.

49. Memorandum from J. H. Whiting to the commanding general, U.S. Third Army, folder 65, frame 15, roll LSP 10, YIVO. On the scale of American military occupation policy, the visit of Ben-Gurion to the U.S. zone of Germany seems to have influenced the development of a unified agricultural policy for the Jewish DPs.

50. Haim Hoffman, "Ha-mishlekhet ha-eretz yisraelit le-She'erit Hapletah," *Yalkut Moreshet* 30 (1980): 19. The "political instruction" listed by Hoffman has been the subject of debate regarding the origins of DP Zionist enthusiasm before the AACI. As noted above, members of the AACI were aware of this effort by Yishuv emissaries and still concluded that the majority of DPs desired settlement in Palestine.

51. Ibid., 29.

52. "Visit of the Sub-committee to the American Zone of Austria," Vienna, February 25, 1946, RG 43, AACI, box 12, pp. 4–5, United States National Archives, Washington, D.C.

53. Report of the AACI, Lausanne, April 20, 1946, YIVO.

54. See table from Yochanan Cohen, *Ovrim kol Gvul: HaBrichah, Polin, 1945–1946* (Tel Aviv: Zemorah-Bitan, 1995), 469. Summary of "HaBricha" from Poland according to movements, July 1945–1946, Hativah Z. Netzer, box 3, folder 4, Bricha Archive, Efal, Israel. According to Cohen's calculations, 33,592 of those who departed with the Bricha were organized in kibbutzim, 6,901 were children, and 71,041 traveled in families or as individuals. This means that approximately 40,000 traveled without parents (either because they were orphaned or sent ahead) within the framework of kibbutzim and children's homes. Of those who traveled in families or as individuals (71,041), perhaps 20 percent could have fallen into the category of youths under the age of twenty-five, who were desired by the pioneering kibbutzim. Even if 50 percent (35,520) fell into this age bracket, this would suggest that roughly half of those in this age category left within the framework of kibbutzim. If we apply the more conservative (and accurate) estimate of 20 percent (approximately 14,000), then more than twice as many in this age group left within the framework of kibbutzim. On the situation in postwar Poland leading to the success of the Bricha, see David Engel, *Beyn shihrur li-verihah Beyn shihrur li-verikhah: Nitsule ha-shoah be-Polin ve-ha-ma'avak*

'al hanhagatam, 1944–1946 (Tel Aviv: Am Oved, 1996).

55. The decision to name many of the kibbutzim after the movement's resistance fighters who had died during the war was only taken at the first Hashomer Hatzair movement conference in postwar Germany at Biberach on December 10, 1945. There, several of the kibbutzim were renamed after Hashomer Hatzair resistance fighters such as Mordecai Anielewicz (the first groups from Sosnowiec and Bytom), Chaviva Reik, Yosef Kaplan (the first groups from Warsaw and Krakow), Tosia Altman, Aryeh Vilner, and Zvi Brandes.

56. Shlomo Shaltiel, ed., *HaYoman: Kibbutz Lochamei HaGetaot al Shem Tosia Altman* (Israel: Giv'at Havivah, Israel, 1997).

57. Ibid., 43. The League for Labor Palestine was the umbrella organization linking Poalei Zion (Ciyonim Sotsyalistim, or Zionist Socialists) to Dror and Hashomer Hatzair in the organization of the Bricha movement.

58. Shaltiel, *HaYoman*, 198–201.

59. For a sample of psychological studies of Holocaust survivors, see Robert Jay Lifton, "The Concept of the Survivor," in *Survivors, Victims, and Perpetrators*, edited by Joel E. Dimsdale, 113–26 (New York: Hemisphere Publishing, 1980). In the same volume, see Leo Ettinger, "The Concentration Syndrome and Its Late Sequelae," 127–62, and Dimsdale, "The Coping Behavior of Nazi Concentration Camp Survivors," 163–74. For a definition of post-traumatic stress disorder, See "Diagnosis Code 309.81," in *Diagnostic and Statistical Manual of Mental Disorders*, 4th ed. (Washington, DC: American Psychiatric Association, 1994). For a recent overview of research on the subject, see Jonathan Davidson and Edna Foa, eds., *Posttraumatic Stress Disorder: DSM-IV and Beyond* (Washington, DC: American Psychiatric Press, 1993).

60. Shaltiel, *HaYoman*, 83.

61. Kibbutz Tosia Altman in Eschwege, report to Hashomer Hatzair central leadership in Germany [n.d., probably April 1946], RG 123/HaShomer Hatzair/410, Yoman Kibbutz Lochamei HeGettaot al shem Tosia Altman, in Eschwege, pp. 319–22, HPHA; report of Kibbutz Yosef Kaplan, Kibbutz Lochamei HaGetaot al shem Yosef Kaplan, in Jordenbad, May 20, 1946, p. 188, HPHA. This raises the interesting question of the relationship of the secular youth movement to the Jewish religion. Weinberg's educational manifesto noted the importance of education in Jewish history with a focus on the historical character of religious events. In the interwar period, the approach of the movement to religion was as inclusive one; while religion was certainly not understood as the basis of group identification, members were instructed to "always identify with [their] brothers in the long black dress and never publicly insult religious ritual . . . [and] to bring the ideal of national rebirth to the synagogues and Jewish streets and plant national consciousness in the masses of our people, in these people the *shomer* should see his most holy task." From M. Zilbertal, *Ha-Hinukh Ha-Shomri: Kovetz Hinukhi shel Hashomer Hatzair, 1913–1938* (Shomer Education: An Educational

Volume of Hashomer Hatzair), cited in Zvi Lamm, *Shitat Ha-Hinukh shel Hashomer Hatzair* (The Educational Method of Hashomer Hatzair) (Jerusalem: Magnes, 1998), 70.

62. Shaltiel, *HaYoman*, 67–68.

63. Ibid., 92.

64. *BaMidbar* 4, no. 6 (March 20, 1946): 7, reel 15-11, Jewish DP Periodicals Collection, YIVO.

65. "Report of Kibbutz Yosef Kaplan to Movement Central Leadership," RG 123/HaShomer Hatzair/410, KLGYK, report of Kibbutz Yosef Kaplan, p. 176, HPHA.

66. Zelig Shushan, "The Meeting with the Comrades in the Diaspora," *Hashomer Hatzair*, March 1946, p. 8; Zelig, last name Shushan, based on Shaltiel, *HaYoman*, Yoman, 83.

67. *Hashomer Hatzair*, April 1946, p. 3, YIVO. Kovner first made his appeal to the members of the He-Halutz youth organization in the Vilna Ghetto on New Year's Eve, December 31, 1941. He declared that all the Jews who were taken from Vilna were murdered at Ponary and called upon the Jewish youths to organize for armed struggle against the Germans. Three weeks later, on January 21, 1942, the Zionist youth movements in the ghetto decided to form the Fareynigte Partisaner Organisatsye (United Partisans' Organization). Anielewicz's letter to Zuckerman was his last letter prior to dying in the uprising and seems to have been penned on April 23, 1943, to his comrade Yitzhak (Antek) Zuckerman. See [M. Kann], "Na oczach swiata" [In the Eyes of the World], Zamosc, 1932 [i.e., Warsaw, 1943], pp. 33–34, Yad Vashem Archives.

68. "Zog nit Keyn Mol" (Never Say), first verse of the song of the Partisans by Hirsh Glik.

69. Shaltiel, *HaYoman*, 96.

70. See *Landwirtschaftlecher Wegwajzer*, vol. 1, May 1946, reel 11-3, Jewish DP Periodicals Collection, YIVO.

71. Ibid.

72. Shaltiel, *HaYoman*, 123.

73. Ibid.

74. Ibid., 123–24.

75. Chronology of Kibbutz Tosia Altman from January 1947 until March 1948, in Shaltiel, *HaYoman*, 129–70:

> January 18, 1947: St. Valentina
> January 22, 1947: Milan to Rome
> January 24, 1947: UNRRA camp Cine-Citte
> February 7, 1947: Monta Maria (Rome)
> March 17, 1947: Leave Rome
> March 22, 1947–March 30, 1947: Board Ma'apilim ship *Moledet;* stopped by the British and not allowed to enter Palestine
> April 1, 1947: Arrive in Cyprus
> May 1, 1947: Arrive in camp no. 67

July 1947: Protest of the whole camp in Cypress on behalf of the *Exodus*

July 19, 1947: Wedding of Yaffa and Zvi

July 23, 1947: Hunger strike on behalf of boat *Knesset
Israel,* returned to Cyprus by the British

August 5, 1947: Avramele is born to Dvorah and Moshe
from the Belgian group

August 22, 1947: Second anniversary of kibbutz

September 2, 1947: Miriam and Baruch leave Cyprus on
September 2, 1947

September 12, 1947: Party for the babies (Mordechai
born August 22)

September 15, 1947: Rosh Hashanah

November 25, 1947: Tzippora and Azriel make aliyah
with their baby (Mordechai)

December 20, 1947: Youth aliyah, including the nine
members from kibbutz

March 1948: Last group from Kibbutz Tosia Altman
leaves Cyprus

76. *Jidisce Cajtung,* December 2, 1947, reel 1, Jewish DP Periodicals Collection, YIVO.

Face to Face

American Jews and Holocaust
Survivors, 1946–54

BETH B. COHEN

October 23, 1948. Amid a spray of water, steamboat whistles, and fog-horn blasts, SS *General Black* sailed into New York. Among its passengers were 813 displaced persons (DPs), the first admitted to the United States under the Displaced Persons Act of 1948. "Welcome to America!" proclaimed a banner atop one boat. The festive crowd included refugee agency personnel, relatives, and government officials. An army launch brought the U.S. attorney general Tom Clark, an emissary from President Harry S. Truman, to personally greet the new arrivals. The opportunity was not lost on the media: two U.S. Coast Guard cutters with photographers, journalists, radio, and public relations (PR) men accompanied the launch to capture the auspicious moment. One DP told a journalist, "We are born today. The second time in our lives."[1]

Of the 813 immigrants who arrived aboard the *General Black*, 161 were Jews, a fraction of the 140,000 Jewish DPs who emigrated from Europe to the United States during 1946–54.[2] Stories trumpeted their arrival in rosy and triumphant terms: joy at being on American soil, emotional reunions between relatives, and warm receptions by American Jewish communities. The media promulgated these images. Indeed, the heroic narrative has continued until this day. Holocaust survivors, however, often recall a very different story. The gap between these perceptions suggests a need to return to this period and explore what lies beneath the unfailingly upbeat images of DPs' first years in America. What do these stories hide? What was the day-to-day reality of the treatment and experience of Jewish refugees? It seems that the reception by American Jewry often fell far short of what the newcomers expected and needed.

This study scrutinizes a time when the term "Holocaust" had yet to occupy a central place in both American and American Jewish consciousness and identity, when the term "survivor" as an honorific was many years away from the public's awareness and lexicon. They were called "refugees," "DPs," "New Americans," "greeners," and "immigrants."[3] And their first years here were less a new beginning than a patching together of previously shattered lives. It may be comforting to accept the contemporary media accounts, fitting seamlessly as they do into our heroic image of the Holocaust survivor today, but not only does this trivialize survivors' early years here, it is also historically inaccurate.

Fortunately, a number of other sources do exist that challenge the rosy accounts provided by the contemporaneous media coverage. Among the materials I studied is a collection of refugees' case files written during the late 1940s and early 1950s by social workers at the Jewish Family and Children's Service (JFCS) in Denver, Colorado,[4] as well as those of the New York Association for New Americans (NYANA) created in 1949 to help survivors who settled in New York City.[5] These documents propelled my original study. Eventually I supplemented my research with additional agency documents as well as hundreds of transcripts and video testimonies conducted with survivors and agency personnel from 1980 through the present.[6] This allowed me to cast a wide net, to scrutinize a spectrum of experience in various locales including Boston, Massachusetts; Denver, Colorado; Cleveland, Ohio; Columbia, South Carolina; New York City; and Providence, Rhode Island. Synthesizing these various experiences and a range of sources both current and postwar yields a multilayered analysis. It reveals the kind of help, or lack thereof, that the Jewish community gave to the refugees. It throws a bright light on the American perception of their newly arrived brethren while elucidating the newcomers' expectations and sentiments about the assistance they received. Unmediated by the intervening fifty years, the case files also give shape and form to the multitudes that came to the agency for help, unvarnished by the near-sacred status as survivors that the society would later bestow upon them. All of these tools complicate the superficial and triumphant media accounts from the postwar period and contribute to a more nuanced history of this time.

In the aftermath of World War II most Jewish DPs, especially those who originally stemmed from Eastern Europe, were desperate to leave the continent, while some sought to return to their homes in Poland and Lithuania, where they were greeted by continuing anti-Semitism and violence perpetrated by their former neighbors. The rest of the world was not a welcoming place to the survivors. Few countries would admit them, including the United States, which still had restrictive immigration laws imposed in the early 1920s. Following Earl Harrison's scathing report, issued in September 1945, on conditions in the Jewish DP camps, America advocated sending the Jewish DPs to British-mandated Palestine, but Great Britain refused to lift its White Paper of 1939, which limited legal entry to Palestine to fifteen hundred visas a month.[7] In December 1945 the combined pressure from non-Zionists and the desire to set an example to the British government pushed Truman to issue a directive that eventually allowed 28,000 Jewish DPs to enter America by 1948.[8] This was followed by the passage of the first Displaced Persons Act in July 1948, which allowed entry to 205,000 DPs over a two-year period.[9] The majority of Holocaust survivors arrived in 1949 under the first Displaced Persons Act.[10]

With Truman's directive, the Jewish community readied itself for the DPs. In anticipation of an influx that would need assistance, a new agency was created specifically to resettle the newcomers around the United States. In 1946 the National Refugee Service merged with the National Council of Jewish Women's Service to Foreign Born to create the United Service for New Americans (USNA). While there intentionally was nothing in its name to suggest it, USNA was a strictly Jewish agency funded by the United Jewish Appeal.[11] USNA's goal was to work with the American Jewish Joint Distribution Committee (JDC) in Europe and, to a much greater extent, with local cooperating Jewish agencies around the country to facilitate the refugees' resettlement. When USNA realized that it could not be a national agency and also attend to the majority of DPs who remained in New York City, it established NYANA in 1949 to assist those who settled in New York.[12]

One of the first obstacles that an immigrant faced before obtaining a visa to enter America was to procure an affidavit or assurance from a sponsor, which pledged that the immigrant would not become a public charge. Previously, this fell to an immigrant's relative who, it was believed, would be best equipped to care for his or her own.[13] With his 1945 directive, Truman gave voluntary agencies the power to provide corporate affidavits for immigrants, and USNA was one of the agencies with affidavit-granting status. This was a crucial and radi-

　　　　　　　　　　　　　　　　　　　　Beth B. Cohen

A United Service for New Americans (USNA) representative greets new arrivals. (Author's personal collection)

cal step; now the Jewish community, not merely individuals, would shoulder the responsibility of assisting their immigrant brethren. In postwar America, where the memory of the Great Depression and its unemployment was still fresh, the virulent anti-Semitism of the earlier 1940s lingered, and nativist sentiment persisted, this was no mere formality. It was a commitment that the government insisted on and that the organized American Jewish community pledged to honor.

For those with relatives in the United States, of course, assurances were still expected from their American family members. Many Jewish DPs, however, had no family in the United States and thus relied on USNA to provide the needed affidavit. This was the first time in U.S. history that the government supported the concept that social service agencies could take responsibility for managing the resettlement of immigrants on a widespread basis.[14] While it was a milestone in immigrant care, it also created a multifaceted interdependency not only among the various agencies but also between the organizations and the refugees themselves, which made resettlement exceedingly complicated.

One of the first questions that arose was the issue of placement: Where would the refugees go in America? Which communities were willing to sponsor them? If a refugee arrived on an individual assurance provided by a relative, he or she went to the relative's community. Otherwise, the immigrant had little control over destination, which was determined by the JDC, USNA, and the local agencies that were expected to pull their weight in this effort.[15]

Fearful that there would be a glut of refugees in the major cities, especially New York, USNA negotiated with communities around the United States in order to persuade them to take in newcomers. The Truman administration shared USNA's plan. One of the main goals of the Displaced Persons Commission (DPC), the first federal immigrant agency established by the Displaced Persons Act of 1948, was the widespread distribution of refugees around the nation.[16] The DPC worked with affidavit-granting organizations such as USNA to resettle DPs in a way that was fair and equitable, at least to the American hosts. In order to actualize this plan, communities had to agree to accept a certain quota of DPs.

The use of affidavits to settle DPs outside of New York City may have been a vision shared by USNA, the DPC, NYANA, and the New York American Jewish community, but it was certainly not universally accepted by cities and towns around the country. The survivors did not embrace it either. True, some did not have strong feelings about destination. Some even preferred to leave the hustle and bustle of New York City behind. But many—perhaps 60 percent—did care and settled in New York City.[17]

It is no surprise that the majority of DPs felt strongly about remaining in New York City. In 1948, 40 percent of the American Jewish population, roughly two million Jews, lived in the city, which was the center of American Jewish life.[18] Jewish neighborhoods flourished, with a rich spectrum of educational, cultural, social, and religious institutions. This included a substantial Yiddish culture, both secular and religious, represented in the press, schools, theater, and radio programs that appealed to the many Yiddish-speaking newcomers. New York was also home to the majority of the country's *landsmanschaftn* (hometown social groups), which provided an important social network for survivors.[19] As more and more refugees settled there, the pull for others became even stronger.

The survivors' desire to stay in metropolitan New York dovetailed with other locales' resistance to absorbing them. It was a struggle to convince communities outside of New York City not only to accept the other 40 percent but in some instances to keep them. In 1949 Joseph Beck, executive director of USNA, "warned that USNA now faces a crucial period. We have recently reached the point where we no longer have enough assurances on a current basis to permit the continued immigration of the large numbers who are eligible to come here."[20]

Beth B. Cohen

Newcomers' Choral
Group, Worcester,
Massachusetts, n.d.
(Author's personal
collection)

The goal of maximum community participation continued to thwart
USNA's intentions.

For some communities, the idea of helping was fraught with
seemingly legitimate complications. From 1949 until the early 1950s,
Emil Salomon, the executive director of the Tulsa Jewish Federation in
Oklahoma, argued in his correspondence with USNA that Tulsa Jews
were too few and the employment opportunities too limited to absorb
the number of refugees that USNA requested of them. The language
of Salomon's letters, however, implies a different sentiment in addition
to the stated concerns over insufficient employment. When USNA
asked Tulsa to accept an additional ten refugees beyond the twenty-
four that the city expected for 1949, Mr. Salomon replied, "Following
a protracted, joint meeting of our Executive Committee and Welfare
Committee, yesterday, it was decided that we dare not increase our DP
Unit quota beyond the twenty-four Units agreed upon when you were
in Tulsa. I have already notified Mr. Edwin Rosenberg (USNA president) to this effect. The chief reason is no jobs." Salomon went on to
describe the first DP to come to Tulsa who, after three months, asked
to join his sister in New York. This man "failed utterly" in his first job
as a tailor's assistant, Mr. Salomon reported. Perhaps USNA might
send him from Tulsa to New York?[21]

Salomon's reference to the arriving Holocaust survivors as units,
while hardly an exception, seems indicative of a tendency to deper-
sonalize the new immigrants. Yes, the president of the Tulsa Jewish
Federation clearly wished to disengage from USNA and looked to find
every excuse to report the failure of the program in his city. At the
same time, virtually every agency, from USNA executive board down,
used the term "unit" to refer to the new immigrants. While it may have
been a designation initially intended for family units, it was widely

used to refer to individuals and, records show, in many instances ce-
mented an institutional attitude of distance and disengagement.

The Jewish community in Denver also sponsored refugees.
Records show that approximately three hundred newcomers settled
there.[22] While it would seem that this number constituted a respectable response for a Jewish community of sixteen thousand once again
the statistics belied the reality of the reception.[23] Denver, too, seemed
aggrieved by USNA's requests.

Despite Denver's apparent commitment to help, the JFCS had its
reservations, and Dr. Alfred Neumann, executive director, expressed
them often. An Austrian Jewish émigré, Neumann felt that Denver received more than its fair share of difficult cases. As he wrote to Arthur
Greenleigh, USNA's executive director, in January 1951, "a series of
incidents have arisen lately which we would like to bring to your attention because we feel that the continual flow of hard core cases, or
the referral of families with many children poses a grave problem in
our resettlement program." He went on to describe several cases and
maintained the conviction "that Denver has become a favorite spot
for hard core applicants."[24] Neumann also wrote to Miss Beatrice
Behrman, USNA's director of resettlement, apprising her of a difficult
situation in nearby Cheyenne. "A delegation of the Cheyenne community arrived yesterday with Mr. G [a survivor], who is trying to leave
their community since they could not handle him there any longer,"
Neumann wrote. A Cheyenne doctor diagnosed Mr. G's current illness
"as a form of a mental disturbance which caused great anxiety amongst
the Cheyenne people interested in resettlement," Neumann reported.
He also noted that "two of the three units settled in Cheyenne are in
Denver, and a third one left for Detroit." Finally, he suggested, "unless
there is absolute clarity on their part as well as on USNA's part regarding Cheyenne, Cheyenne's capacity maybe [sic] considered a waste of
time, money, and effort on the resettlement map."[25]

The belief that Denver was a dumping ground for difficult refugees provoked the Denver New Americans Committee into a debate
as to whether or not to continue "our resettlement program on the
basis of the cases sent to us."[26] Although it did continue, Neumann
threatened numerous times to cancel or impose a moratorium on the
committee's refugee program.

Neumann's attitude affected scores of survivors. The example of
Anton represents just one of many. Anton was a twenty-one-year-old
Romanian-born man who arrived in New York in 1949.[27] NYANA sent
him to the National Jewish Hospital in Denver after he became ill in
Waterbury, Connecticut, in April 1951. According to his file, he "plead-

Beth B. Cohen

ed urgently to be permitted to remain in Denver explaining how lonely he feels living by himself in Waterbury."[28] NYANA asked the JFCS if it would accept the young man on its quota in exchange for a refugee who was going back to New York.

NYANA and the National Jewish Hospital agreed that the Ex-Patients' Home (EPH) would provide proper rehabilitation for Anton. Neumann, however, concurred with JFCS casework supervisor Ralph Ross's recommendation that "placement at the EPH, because of its institutional character, would vitiate the case work goal of helping A(nton) to emancipate and become emotionally and socially autonomous."[29] Ross responded to Behrman: "After giving this plan the most careful thought and sharing our thinking fully with the National Jewish Hospital, we had come to the conclusion that it is unworkable from the casework point-of-view." Ross reasoned that "Mr. Goldstein's problem is at this point not so much one of physical rehabilitation as it is one of emotional re-education which would have to be approached by helping this deeply deprived and dependent young man towards increasing autonomy in the mastery of his environment."[30] The JFCS could not assume responsibility for Anton, Ross told Behrman. Why assume the prohibitive cost of accepting him, argued Ross, if it would provide him with the wrong type of treatment?

Behrman was not pleased that the JFCS refused to accept Anton. "I would like to point out," she responded on September 18, 1951, "that we are rather concerned that the family agency in Denver, in rejecting this case, negates the plan made by the hospital for the best rehabilitation of this young man. There are so few family casework services available throughout the country and we regret that the Denver Jewish Family and Children's Service is limited in its ability to take on a situation requiring a constructive casework job because of its present budget limitations." Behrman warned Ross that Anton's opportunities "for working through his problems in New York City, as presented by the Director of Social Service of the National Jewish Hospital of Denver, are very limited and I would say that the prognosis is not good." Nevertheless, the staff in Denver remained unmoved. "Case Closed 9/30/51," the file concluded shortly thereafter.[31]

Some of Neumann's grievances seem understandable. After all, the JFCS was a small staff of four people, and the agency had to attend to the needs of its local nonsurvivor population also. Unlike NYANA, whose sole function was to service DPs, the JFCS had other clients. At the same time, the JFCS was strengthened by a group of volunteers who helped meet the refugees, locate housing, and transport the newcomers. It is easy to sympathize initially with Neumann's agitation over the flurry of nine unexpected arrivals, for example, but his refusal to accept four of them begs a closer look. In his view, Denver could not do more. Neumann insisted to Behrman that "we are willing to go all the way out in the resettlement program." Furthermore, he said, "Our records speak for itself."[32] Yet despite such proclamations, he continued to argue with USNA over his perception of Denver as a dumping ground. He clearly felt burdened by individuals whom the agency deemed problematic, and his rejection of these newcomers reflected that.

There were communities that responded differently. Columbia, South Carolina, appears to have been one community that was willing and eager to become involved. In May 1949 the *New Neighbors* feature article "A Primer in Resettlement for Small Communities" outlined how the people of Columbia responded to USNA's appeal for help.[33] With no Jewish federation in town, representatives from the synagogues, Zionist organizations, the University of South Carolina Hillel, the Hebrew Benevolent Society, and B'nai Brith all joined together to form an executive committee that mobilized the resources of the 250-family community. The article also described the enthusiasm that had spilled over to the gentile population of 90,000. Along with planning hot meals, furnished apartments, English lessons, jobs, babysitting, and medical, dental, legal, and psychological services, the committees also enlisted help from local hairdressers who agreed to provide a free "American up-to-date hair-do" to each female newcomer.[34]

The Columbia community's rally to meet the challenge of resettlement stands in sharp contrast to Tulsa. Since this initial impression of Columbia was gleaned from a PR piece in *New Neighbors*, it begged for a closer look. The field reports of USNA representatives' visits to Columbia in the USNA's archives, however, do reinforce the PR story.[35] Why was Columbia so ready to help when others did so reluctantly if at all? Perhaps it was because the number of affidavits that the community agreed to provide was, in fact, less than ten. Undoubtedly, it was easier to manage such a small number trickling in over two years. The role of local advocacy seems more important: an ambitious young Columbia couple, Mr. and Mrs. Bank, spearheaded the effort. They saw it as their mission to bring refugees to South Carolina and to take a personal interest in them. This is a distinct departure from the New York City and Denver agencies' strict policy against the professionals fraternizing with the clients. In a letter to USNA in 1950, Dena Bank wrote: "One of our DPs had his first birthday in America last week. He's single—25 years old—and without any relatives anywhere. We had a real party at our house for him—with candles, cake, ice cream etc. He was so very grateful—we really enjoyed the party."[36] The secre-

Beth B. Cohen

tary of the Columbia refugee committee, Mrs. Hannah Rubin, took a similarly warm and personal approach. In an interview half a century later, she recalled her contact with a refugee family. Rubin assumed responsibility for the first DPs, the M. family, she said. "They became independent very soon. Within two years they were functioning on their own," she noted, echoing the way in which so many in the American community judged the refugees' success.[37]

Rubin remembered how the housing market affected their program. Faced with the imminent arrival of their sister, one of the refugee families living in a one-room apartment sought a larger accommodation. The search went unrewarded until two Jewish businessmen suggested a solution and offered the family access to an unused shack attached to their fast-food establishment. Rubin and the refugees cleaned and painted their new home. The newcomers settled into the town, worked hard, and became respected members of the community. Rubin's involvement with the M. family was personal. In fact, the relationship continues to this day. She "was really glad to help them," she explained; she "felt very close to the family." She summed up the experience by saying, "It was a real pleasure to be able to do it."[38] From Rubin's perspective, the Columbia program was effective on many levels. She was proud of her direct help to the immigrant family and of their rapid adjustment to life in the United States.

Looking at the Columbia example from the perspective of the refugee family reveals a more ambiguous story. The young sister (now Mrs. G.) who joined the M. family in 1949 recalls, "People were very nice. There was nothing more they could have done," which suggests that despite the community's efforts, the reality fell short of the DPs' needs.[39] Thinking about the help she received, she remembers how people "brought them old clothes. We had to smile and say thank you," while others "didn't care to know about us." The hierarchical nature of the relationship predominated. "You're not human, not equal, you're a 'greener.'" She believes this changed in the 1960s, "when we didn't need anything from them."[40] The recipient of the community's help viewed the so-called successful reception quite differently. From her perspective, her hosts treated her as a second-class citizen. From the local population's vantage point, however, the program was a triumph. The arrival of the small group of refugees, and the Banks' charismatic leadership seemed to infuse the entire town with a sense of collective purpose.

What happened when the refugees' American relatives, rather than communities, were the sponsors? The response was very mixed. Sponsorship brought together families who were blood relatives but had never met and who often had vastly different expectations of each other and their new relationship. Sponsors in New York City furnished 77 percent of all individual affidavits, but again statistics did not necessarily reflect the qualitative kind of support that the refugee needed or wanted.

Many individuals felt obliged to provide the affidavits, which were the DP's ticket out of Europe, but clearly never intended to make a commitment beyond this.[41] Indeed, once the refugees arrived, despite written promises of help, such help was not ongoing. The NYANA files are rife with entries such as "[the sponsor is] a distant relative who was in no position to help as she was a worker herself"[42] and "relatives could not meet the obligation they had agreed to."[43] In one situation, the caseworker recorded that the sponsor "had kept Mr. H. for three weeks and has paid for her family physician but she cannot go further. Mr. H. is her relation not her husband's. She personally has no funds at her disposal and her husband feels that he had done more than he was under obligation to do."[44]

At times the refugees felt that their American relatives had legitimate reason for withdrawing their financial commitments. One client stated that his cousin "has been unemployed for some weeks and is receiving unemployment insurance."[45] Another sponsor who accompanied the newcomer to his meeting at NYANA was upset when he told the caseworker that "he was proud to have his relatives here . . . but he really could not do anything and as proof of this he showed us various receipts from a loan he had been granted."[46]

The most common pattern in the NYANA files appears to be the relative who offered limited help to start but then did not continue. Sometimes this was due to stretched financial resources, and at other times the affiant grew tired of the burden of being needed by the newcomer. In other cases, as occurred with Mr. H., the arrival of the new refugee generated familial tensions. Sometimes the survivors themselves expressed the need to stand on their own feet and had no expectations of their relatives once the survivors arrived here. It is also possible that once word got out in the community that agency relief money was available, the DPs, either independently or with pressure from their sponsors, approached NYANA for aid. Certainly, few relatives kept their financial commitment. The fact that nearly 90 percent of survivors on relatives' affidavits turned to NYANA attests to that.

Mrs. K. was among the 90 percent who requested help from the New York agency. She and her husband chose to immigrate to the United States over Palestine because the pull of family in America was so strong. Her husband's uncle sponsored them, and they fully expected their uncle to take Mr. K. into his thriving business. When this did not happen, the couple turned to NYANA. "Yes," the agency

Seven DP families arrive in Oakland, California. (Author's personal collection)

would help, Mrs. K. recalled in 1998, fifty years after her arrival in 1998, "if she would agree to be resettled outside of New York." Both dire need and disappointment drove her decision. She agreed without hesitation.[47]

Financial aid was one thing, emotional support another. The new-comers needed to feel that finally they were not alone in the world, that someone, especially *mishpocha* (family), cared. Therefore, when moral support went undelivered (as with Mrs. K.), the rift could be irrepa-rable. One NYANA caseworker observed that her client didn't want to have anything to do with his relative and noted "how much he and his wife resented him for not even inviting him for a seder, something which they had been longing to attend for years, which they didn't have after they lost their parents."[48]

The night that Mrs. S. arrived in New York in 1946 is still a painful memory more than fifty years later. Her cousin greeted her at the dock and brought her home. Their arrival there coincided with the airing on television of *The Milton Berle Show.* It was "very, very very popular, everybody was watching," Mrs. S. recalls. "It was such an excitement like who knows what was going on. And I came the first night—and instead of talking to us, she left us and went to watch Milton Berle."[49]

Cecile is still bitter when she recalls her first day in America from a distance of more than half a century. Their sponsor, her husband's uncle, was supposed to meet his new family at the boat. No uncle appeared, nor did any of his five married children. With thirteen dollars to their name, the family took a cab to his address in Brooklyn. Upon reaching the home, they found it dark. A neighbor told them that a day earlier "the Kanters left for Florida, they're not home." Sonia greeted this news with bewilderment. "They know we are arriving the next day, they get a cable, none of the children are waiting for us. The uncle picks himself up with his wife and leaves for Florida. . . . That [her husband] is his nephew, his brother's son."[50] "I was devastated," she said. She could not fathom this attitude. After all, she pressed on, "they were not ignorant, they know what happened—they know the family was killed. They are not anxious to see, they are not interested to—see somebody an—and—-cheer up those people, to know we are here for you, I'm glad you survived?"[51]

This longing for family was often one-sided. Those far from the horror of Europe had limited imagination about what this need meant, while those who had passed through it were desperate for family connections. For many American relatives, however, the pledge of sponsorship only went so far. The very gesture might seem to imply interest, but when the refugees came face-to-face with their kin, the reception could be chilly. Perhaps some American families simply could not face the staggering loss of the Holocaust when confronted by the refugees. Others may not have wanted the emotional or economic burden of the newcomers. This could lead to irreconcilable grief on the part of newcomers. After all, family was often the primary reason cited by many survivors who chose America over other destinations.

For some, their American family did not disappoint. Fritzie recalls her aunt and uncle with much devotion. "If she was my mother," Fritzie comments, "I couldn't love her more and she couldn't have been better to me. . . . I came to a loving family . . . a family that opened their arms to me and did the best they knew how." And, she adds, "I really was one of the lucky ones."[52]

Rochelle echoes similar sentiments. When other DPs heard of those who had family in the United States, she remembers that they remarked, "Oh, they are lucky, they are going to relatives and they will be so good and. . . . I didn't say anything because I didn't know my relatives. . . . I'd—couldn't say if they will be good to me or not good to me . . . I couldn't say. How would I know? I never knew them and they . . . didn't know me either." As it turns out, she too believes that she was one of the fortunate ones. "My relatives," she states emphatically, "were very, very, very good to me." But she was in contact with others who immigrated at the same time whose experiences differed sharply from her own. Her friends confided in her quite simply that "the relatives weren't good."[53]

When sponsors reneged on their commitments, when refugees

arrived on community assurances, or when the newcomers were desperate, they sought help from agencies such as NYANA or the Jewish social service agencies. How did the agencies respond? In many ways, the Jewish institutional response to the New Americans was far-reaching and radical. Never before had cooperating communities been called upon to participate in this manner, to accept refugees into their midst, offer financial aid, locate housing, find jobs, provide social casework services, extend medical care, or advise on immigration laws. It is not surprising that USNA prided itself in the mid-twentieth century for leading the way in progressive, humanitarian immigrant care. In 1950 USNA president Edwin Rosenberg lauded American Jewish communities for making possible "an era of magnificent accomplishment."[54]

Survivors, however, experienced the process very differently. The intent of the agencies' approach may have been innovative and well meaning, even recognizing that survivors "had suffered the unspeakable brutalities of Hitler's death camps."[55] What was delivered, however, often fell short of newcomers' expectations and left them wanting. When the hosts were confronted with these New Americans, the essential fact that they were unlike any preceding immigrants often eluded those who were committed to helping them.

The Jewish agencies insisted that they were addressing many facets of the DPs' adjustment. In actuality, the primary focus of the agencies was on finding work and getting the refugees off of relief. The belief that employment was the first necessary step in the road to becoming productive Americans was widely accepted and was deemed both practical and effective. As Arnold Askin, NYANA president, announced at NYANA's second annual meeting in 1951, "I think it is significant, as a measure of the speed with which the immigrant can become part of the mainstream of our economic and cultural life to point out that of the 38,000 people who have received NYANA's help during the past two years, 31,000 have become fully independent, self-sustaining members of the community."[56]

Askin and his constituents basked in the glow of both NYANA's and the refugees' apparent success in becoming acculturated. Askin's remarks are telling, however, both because of what he chose to emphasize and what was left unsaid. His statement certainly describes NYANA's perceived accomplishments. But Askin did not mention that speedy acculturation also furthered other agency goals. It minimized the DPs' financial and emotional dependence on NYANA and guaranteed that no refugee would become a public charge. Also unsaid was NYANA's policy that limited financial help to one year. Once a newcomer was self-maintaining—and the sooner the better—the file ended with the words "Case Closed," thus ending the agency's relationship with the client.

Because of the agencies' focus on the immediate future, the trauma that the DPs survived was often obscured, minimized, or ignored. References in the archives to wartime experiences appear so infrequently that I often asked myself, as I read through the archives, if these were the case histories of Holocaust survivors. Why is so little mentioned about violent separation from and murder of dear ones; total rupture from prewar life; years in ghettos, in concentration camps, or in hiding; the aftermath of wandering in search of family; and living in DP camps? There was deafening silence on these matters. And, at the same time, their immigrant clients were clearly suffering. In more than 50 percent of the files, illness, much of which developed once the survivors were in America, prevailed.[57]

Many of the refugees' illnesses appear to have been psychosomatic: headaches, dizziness, backaches, and chest pains for which physicians could not find any organic basis. Skin rashes were also fairly common. More than one survivor described himself as having a "nervous heart." Depression is a common theme in an extraordinary number of the early files.

It is no surprise that survivors suffered from symptoms that today are associated with post-traumatic stress disorder (PTSD).[58] What is surprising is that the social workers and physicians, including psychiatrists, made little connection between the numerous somatic complaints and their clients' recent histories. Although professional conferences of the day addressed the issue of trauma, the workers seemed quite averse to delving too deeply into the source of their clients' pain. Even when survivors suggested a link between their emotional struggles and Holocaust memories, the professionals generally paid little heed.[59]

In one instance a fifty-year-old woman arrived in Denver alone. Her husband and daughter had been killed in Europe, and she was determined to reclaim some semblance of her former life as a successful cosmetologist by studying for a Colorado license in this field. Her dreams of opening up a small shop of her own remained distant as she struggled with preparing for the exam in English as well as with the JFCS attitude that her time would be better spent by taking a job. During this period Mrs. F. lived alone in a rundown hotel in the city, anxious for companionship but unsure as to how to expand her social circle. She began to manifest a number of ailments for which there seemed to be no organic basis. Finally, the agency recommended psychiatric treatment. The psychiatrist's assessment after their initial

Beth B. Cohen

meeting was that Mrs. F. suffered from depression due to menopause. He treated her accordingly.[60]

Mr. H. was a widower who arrived in New York City in August 1949. His sponsor was the woman mentioned earlier whose husband felt that they had more than met their obligation to their brother-in-law. Mr. H.'s wife (his sponsor's sister) was murdered in 1942, and he continued to struggle with this loss. The examining physician wrote:

> Mr. H, 43 years old, was examined by me on June 1, 1950. The patient told me that he had never been seriously ill before, and that he had developed no complaints during 4 years in concentration camps but that his complaints started after his liberation. He has been here for 9 months, and complains now that he perspires excessively, that sometimes he has a weakness in his hands and gets severe headaches.
>
> He attributes his complaints to the severe emotional upsets he has suffered during the last 10 years. He says that he would gladly do any kind of work, but that he is unable to find any position in this country. He told me in particular that it is not his complaints which keep him from working, but the impossibility to get a job.
>
> He seemed slightly depressed, but did not show any signs of a deep depression. On physical examination there was no evidence of an organic disease of the nervous system but he showed increased perspiration and some trembling of the hands, disappearing when distracted.
>
> This patient suffers from a psychoneurosis with depressive and hysterical symptoms. I told him that the best way to get over his complaints would be to start a new life here by getting a regular occupation, and that his chances for recovery would not be good if he would have to spend the whole day without useful work. To this he reacted rather violently, saying that this meant an accusation that he was not willing to work. Nothing of this kind has been expressed by the examiner. It is my opinion that this patient should be put to work as soon as feasible and should continue in any case the training course which he is taking now.[61]

In both the cases of Mr. H. and Mrs. F., work was seen as a remedy for the client's ills. In fact, this was the primary goal for which the agency strove and the gold standard by which the agencies judged their success, as Askin eagerly announced at the NYANA annual meeting. What Askin failed to mention, however, was that NYANA policy limited financial help to a maximum of twelve months. After that, needy clients were referred to the Department of Welfare, and their file ended with "Case Closed." Thus, while many, though by no means all, refugees did express the desire to find work as quickly as possible, there was also tremendous pressure to achieve this.

Becoming self-sustaining, however, did not address the emotional needs of the refugees. In a letter to his social worker at the JFCS, a young man, Yakov, expressed his feelings about his new life in Denver. After describing his satisfaction with his office job and his progress in English, he continued:

> This is one side of the medal. The other side is not hot. Am very disgusted and from day to day am getting worse. Very nervous. I feel some kind of nostalgy [sic]. Not for my country. The word "my country" doesn't exist to me. I miss my lost family, my friends and the system of living. I can't get adjusted here regardless of my attempts. I really drive myself very hard in order to get Americanized but this is useless. My trying has no success as yet and I don't think that will ever have. There is a wall of customs, characters and attitudes. I do not have anything in common with my surrounders [sic]. They will never understand me even if I speak a better English than they do. It's a terrible problem to me. Furthermore, I don't seem to see a sense in life and little by little I lose the courage to live and that worries me. We all can take only so much and I am only a human.[62]

The example of Yakov illustrates how one immigrant seemed to be adjusting according to the agency's standards: employment, housing, learning English, and getting on his feet. Nevertheless, he clearly felt a sense of despair rather than one of achievement. And Yakov was not an isolated example.

Why would social workers and trained professionals ignore what seemed like the obvious source of their clients' suffering? Why was the Holocaust so glaringly absent from the social workers' reports and from their approach to treating their clients? How did they miss the obvious? Was it simply that their training in the late 1940s and early 1950s precluded a more nuanced, insightful approach?[63] Is this only obvious through a twenty-first-century lens? I think not.

What argues most tellingly and persuasively for the possibility that the professionals could have behaved differently was the simple fact that in a few cases they indeed did. One exception shines brightly as an example of an institutional or quasi-institutional program that served a number of young people well. The JFCS in Boston decided in 1946 to experiment with placement strategies for refugee children who were beginning to arrive in the United States. The agency created a special New American unit at an already existing Jewish summer camp, Camp Kingswood, in Bridgton, Maine. Beatrice Carter, JFCS case consultant and camp supervisor, delivered a paper to a national social work conference in which she stressed the therapeutic nature of this initiative. Slightly separated from the regular girls' camp, this unit was intended to offer a supportive setting in which the youths "are able to utilize many of the skills acquired in European experiences to master the rugged environment, which the new camp site offers."[64] This special program began with seven children in 1946 and by 1949 had grown to include nineteen orphans.

Leonard Serkess was a young social worker whose involvement with the New Americans began in 1947 at the summer camp. Speaking in 2002, he noted the staff's response to the refugees' attitude toward food. "One of the biggest problems we had was the kids would steal food and bring it back to the tents. And we tried to explain to them, there was a mild language problem, mild, because we had enough people that could convey the different languages, that there would be plenty of food," he remembers. Still, "they found it hard to believe. There was a perpetual hunger. . . . [T]hey just never felt secure that there would be enough food for them."[65] The staff recognized the special significance of food for the young DPs and allowed for it. The manner in which the camp staff responded to this and other issues reflects its attempts to understand the psychological aspects of these children's behavior.

The camp gave the young people a great deal of latitude in their actions. "So, if they got angry and urinated on a tree . . . we were out in the woods," explains Mr. Serkess, "you could allow more freedom." That tolerance and understanding pervaded the camp. The youngsters spent some of their time learning English, and there were also art therapists and opportunities for creative expression.[66] At the end of each summer, the New American unit published a collection of their stories, essays, and poetry.

Robert B., a sixteen-year-old orphan, was sent to Camp Kingswood in the summer of 1947. Because like so many others he wanted to remain in New York City, he was initially reluctant. Before long, however, he found a place for himself in Maine partially because it was a summer camp and partially because he was among others like himself. "You're on the lake, you can go swimming," he reminisces. "It was very milk and honey . . . and we had each other. I'm pretty sure there was an element of isolation, of loneliness." Still, Robert reflects, "I just don't recall wallowing in it. I mean, there were so many things to do and so many positive things."[67] Robert's remarks emphasize the camp's ideology. Although the summer experience was therapeutic in nature, the staff discouraged their campers from dwelling too long on their traumatic past.

The camp's philosophy, as described by a visiting journalist from the *Boston Herald,* was "to help these young folk face and forget their pogrom experiences."[68] Today this principle would be considered naive. In the context of the time and the message to forget the past that most adult DPs received, however, it was exceptional. What was extraordinary was the camp's approach: in order to move ahead, the unit's young people were encouraged through various art therapies to face their past. In addition to story writing and poetry, the adolescents were also allowed to create and perform a play based on their lives during the Holocaust. In a collection of campers' short stories printed at summer's end, one boy wrote a piece titled "Why We Put the Play On," which describes the unusual production:

> Other people rehearse for weeks and then put on a medio-cre show. Not so with us. To this day we don't even have a name for our show. We needn't—because it just simply is the showing of part of our life experience. One day Szmul came out with the idea of a play about concentration camp events, and, in talking, he had already acted out parts of the future play. At first we were stunned and resented to be overcome again by the flood of evil memories. Then we resolved to face once more the reality that had been. We only needed to pass out roles, never learned any parts and never twice said quite the same words during the life-like rehearsals. Within a week we were ready to perform in front of the entire camp. During that week we had little time for classes. We lived only partly in the present. Some of us sang the songs of the concentration camps; some, who were to act as Nazis, sang the songs which before we so often had heard and hated. Then the Friday night came. We were deeply steeped into the past and we played from our hearts. People were impressed. We were asked to perform in other camps. That, we could not do. We did some-thing to ourselves by acting as we did. Something we cannot now "re-enact." In some way we are freer now to live for the future.[69]

Although many of the youths did seem to live for the future, not all of

Beth B. Cohen

them did. Robert described Danny, a young boy at Camp Kingswood who had witnessed the murder of both of his parents and had survived afterward in the forests of Poland. He did fairly well at the summer camp, where he could spend much of his time outdoors. Back in Boston, however, he had difficulty functioning. After a suicide attempt, Danny was sent to a school for troubled boys in Pennsylvania. Even the most progressive and supportive environment of the JFCS was no match for the traumas of the recent past that tormented him.[70]

Were it not for an unexpected turn of events, the New Americans at Camp Kingswood who subsequently arrived in Boston might all have been placed in foster care. However, in January 1948 the JFCS created Bradshaw House, a group home for the young refugees in Dorchester, then a primarily Jewish neighborhood of Boston. Bradshaw House became the first of two group homes that the JFCS established for New Americans in the Boston area. This afforded the teens a way to continue living with other DP orphans while still under adult supervision. "They clung and were very supportive of one another," emphasizes Mr. Serkess.[71] Indeed, Robert B. spoke about how he, even as a college student, continued to spend weekends with friends who were still in the group home.

Mrs. Beatrice Carter's approach highlights the difference that individuals could make in a communal organization. Her exceptional devotion to these young people stands out. A number of examples support the impression that under Carter's leadership, the staff of the JFCS in Boston responded to this refugee group differently from their counterparts elsewhere. In addition to the availability of social workers and psychiatrists and the willingness to use them, the innovative program at Camp Kingswood allowed the youngsters to be together in a particularly tolerant environment. The residential home also offered a transitional place where the orphans could step into the world of America yet still retreat to each other's company. It was a circle of friendship and mutual understanding that they share to this day.

Aside from these structures, the social workers' attitudes appeared to have transcended the traditional professional-client relationship. Beatrice Carter is one example. Leonard Serkess is another. When he married, he invited all of the children. "We had twenty-two of the kids at our wedding," he remembers. Moreover, the newlyweds brought trinkets from their honeymoon for each of the teens. "We wanted them to feel that my getting married was not separating from them but we were bringing someone in . . . an acquisition for them," Serkess explains.[72]

The Boston agency, unlike others, believed that their New American orphans needed treatment that differed from conventional approaches and created special programs accordingly. Other policies already in place for their local clients benefited the New Americans as well. One was a strict rule about clothes. The staff believed that only new clothes should be given to foster children, and this was extended to the newcomers. Nothing secondhand would do. A seemingly small gesture, this was profoundly important to the teenagers, Serkess states.[73] In other ways too, the agency showed a unique respect for its charges. Art therapy was an integral part of the agency's treatment for all children, both native and refugee. Mrs. Dora Margolis, the director, insisted that only the agency's clients' artwork should be used to decorate their offices. Thus, the teenagers' work was among those framed and displayed on the JFCS walls. In many ways, this approach stood in marked contrast to that of the Denver agency.

Sometimes, even this agency had its limits. After working feverishly to overcome the gaps in his high school education, Robert applied to four colleges. Three accepted him, including Harvard. He turned to the JFCS to help him pay his tuition bill. He recalled his dismay when Mrs. Carter told him, "You can't go to college, you have to go to work."[74] The young man persisted in pursuing his goals, working first at a law firm and later as a laborer in construction and as a dishwasher at Camp Kingswood to pay for a part of his college tuition. In the end, JFCS helped as well. It turned out to be a wise investment. Robert finished college and medical school and became chief of cardiac surgery at Boston University Medical Center. He pointed out that his case was not exceptional, noting that many of the orphans achieved professional and financial success. While noting the help he received, he acknowledges that the Holocaust shadowed all of these children's lives, making them "very vulnerable to certain things that we had a very difficult time coping with." Of their group of approximately twenty-five orphans who were together in camp and the home, two committed suicide, and another two were institutionalized. Most have a sad story behind the good one, he suggested.[75]

The example of the orphans and the JFCS in Boston illustrates that alternatives in both attitude and approach toward the newcomers were indeed possible. Perhaps the attitude was more sympathetic because these were youngsters rather than adults, although other accounts of child survivors indicate that the treatment they received was not necessarily more compassionate than that toward adults.[76] As was the case of Columbia, South Carolina, it seems that this more generous approach was due to the organization's leadership and staff. In this case, the professionals were acutely aware that these newcomers were unique and used cutting-edge techniques to help them.

Beth B. Cohen

The case of the young adults in Boston also illustrates another important—and misunderstood—aspect of survivors' first years in America. That the young people needed to and did express their feelings about their wartime experiences challenges the commonly accepted perception that survivors could not speak about those experiences in the immediate aftermath of the Holocaust.[77] My research shows that there is close to universal agreement among survivors that no one—neither their relatives, the social workers, nor the outside world—wanted to hear about the Holocaust. The DPs' reactions to this are vivid. "We were very bitter," recalls one camp survivor. Because "in the beginning—in the beginning the people in America didn't want . . .," he says, his voice failing. "We started to tell stories, nobody wanted to listen. And if somebody listened, they thought that we are . . . we told them stories that it is not true. From the first minute I spoke," he continued, "when I came to America, when I told the people, they thought I'm crazy . . . they didn't want to listen."[78]

One new arrival, a writer for the Yiddish daily the *Forverts,* was invited to speak at a fund-raising event for a women's organization in Baltimore in 1949. She looked out at her audience and told them that their faces reminded her of her mother, whom the Nazis had murdered. The organization's president quickly interrupted her and reminded the guest that the bad memories were in the past. As the hostess urged the band to resume playing, the survivor fled, resolving never to speak publicly about her experiences again.[79]

Another was ready to talk, but when her American cousin asked her if she had orange juice for breakfast in Auschwitz, she knew that she could not and would not share her story with her American family. "People had no—no understanding," said Hanne, explaining her cousin's crushing insensitivity and ignorance. Perhaps more telling, she added, they "didn't really want to know."[80]

A.'s experience confirms that as well. None of her relatives believed the extent of the atrocities she had witnessed. She agreed, too, that Americans weren't ready to hear. She posed a possible reason. "They felt guilty for a number of years," she suggests, "Jews and non-Jews." But she also remembers that American "Jews were also complaining that they suffered . . . they didn't have enough meat and sugar." The attempt to equate their wartime experiences with survivors or to suggest that they empathized with their European relatives' suffering because of their own did not sit well with the newcomers. To the newcomers, this signaled a deep, even unbridgeable chasm between the two groups and reinforced the belief that their American hosts did not care to hear about what survivors had endured. This prevented one woman from talking to her relatives. "I saw the lack of understanding in the first years, so I decided not to waste my time," she states. It was too "emotional to open my wounds," she explains.[81]

The conspiracy of silence started not with the survivors but with their relatives, the agencies, and the greater society. Some tried to broach the subject with their American kin. For others, the topic never came up. One woman, whose father was the only child out of his large family who survived Auschwitz, wondered, "How could the relatives not ask about their murdered aunts and uncles?" But they didn't. And the silence hung like a curtain separating the newcomers from their hosts. "No one asked," said Amalie Sandelowski with finality.[82]

Certainly there were survivors who chose not to speak. Some simply could not. Bernie Sayonne of Denver believes that many of his friends were quiet because they could not shake the internalized fear of persecution that shadowed their lives in America; better to keep a low profile, some survivors reasoned, than to become a possible target of anti-Semitism.[83]

What these sources make excruciatingly clear is how little the outside world encouraged survivors to talk or seemed interested in learning about their Holocaust experiences. Even simple sympathy about the past was rare and, for that reason, is important to note. When it happened, it was deeply appreciated and remembered. One survivor recalled her despair after arriving in America. She mourned her murdered family so intensely that she could not stop weeping. At night she screamed from her nightmares and woke her young cousins, who would ask, "Why are you crying?" The young woman told her relatives. Their response was simple and direct. "Cry, if this will help you," they encouraged her. Moreover, her aunt told her, "I know it's not easy for you, but we love you and we want you to be happy." Their understanding meant a great deal. "I appreciate those words what [sic] she said to me," recalled the woman in an interview nearly forty years later. "Til now I remember them," she emphasized.[84] Such instances are glaringly absent from survivor testimonies. But it exemplifies that survivors could and would speak, especially when encouraged with sensitivity and kindness.

For the vast majority, this did not happen. "We, the survivors, even me, I'm talking personally, I wanted to, I wanted to talk about it," emphasizes Mrs. G., who settled in Washington, D.C., in 1949. Why did she want to talk about? Because, she said, "in the most horrible times during the Holocaust, we used to sit and talk to each other, the women, hungry, cold, all the women used to say, please don't forget us. If you survive," she was instructed to "tell the world of what happened." Mrs. G., as do others, takes this obligation seriously. "Those women

Beth B. Cohen

Holocaust survivors at a wedding celebration, Providence, Rhode Island, 1950. (Author's personal collection)

asked me to talk about it," she affirms.[85] And talk she did. But at first it was with other refugees, not her American family, that she spoke. She recalls "five, six couples, survivors coming to our house on the Sabbath, having a little lunch, what did we talk about? . . . [C]omparing each other's suffering, telling how it was, talking about how by miracle we survived this selection and that selection and in a way, I think this was really beneficial to us . . . we didn't keep it inside."[86]

Many, many instances both in the case files and in oral histories reveal that the newcomers not only wanted but also needed to speak about their experiences and did so within their own circles. It would take many years before their stories found an audience beyond their own. Then they would be heard, recorded, filmed, and embraced as testimony to the human spirit. In the postwar period, however, the outside world was deaf to what survivors had to say.

CONCLUSION

One hundred forty thousand of the surviving remnant of European Jewry immigrated to America. This work explores the experience of those men, women, and children in their first years in America and Americans' first face-to-face confrontation with the Holocaust through those who survived. It illuminates a time before survivors were survivors in their own eyes and those of the greater society and before the term "Holocaust" had become ubiquitous.

If the only impressions we had of their reception was gleaned from contemporary media reports and Jewish organizations' accounts or from the place of honor that survivors hold in our society today, we would be led to believe that America had welcomed survivors warmly and that the refugees had acclimated without delay. It is a comforting thought from many perspectives. But, unfortunately, it is false.

As this chapter shows, the postwar reality was exceedingly complicated. For many survivors, this era was imbued with vast and irrevocable loss. By focusing on an external and uniformly happy ending, the complex and arduous period immediately after the Holocaust has been trivialized, minimized, and obscured. It has been reinvented into a story that is heartening but untrue.

This myth hides another painful truth. It masks the way that survivors were treated when they arrived in America. How can we understand an orphan banished from a foster family's home, the downward spiraling of a family when its case was closed because the year was up, or a new arrival waiting at the dock for a sponsor who never shows? These are not stories of triumph or of welcome.

Undoubtedly, these postwar immigrants, battered as they were in body and spirit, presented an enormous challenge to their hosts. The Jewish communities' response to the Holocaust survivors in America, however, was shaped by other concerns and other receptions in immigration history. But these New Americans were unlike any immigrants before them.

Conventional wisdom holds that the survivors themselves wanted to move on, forget their past and live normal lives after the chaos they had recently experienced, and that their memories were too raw, too painful, to confront. Thus, they repressed them and forged ahead, becoming successful survivors. But this was not always the case. Yes, many survivors did go forward, but it was hardly a seamless progression. There were those whose energy was depleted. There were those whose grief prevailed. Even when survivors seemed to be acculturating according to plan, a host of ailments cropped up unbidden. Births, eagerly anticipated, evoked loss that could not be staved off. Other pitfalls materialized. The road was bumpy and fraught with dangers. Over and over, survivors emphasize the difficulty rather than the ease that characterized this period.

Despite what refugees felt, despite the enormous bureaucratic ef-

Beth B. Cohen

forts, the world around them was largely unsympathetic to the pain they harbored. Other concerns occupied people's attention. America was caught up in the postwar mood and firmly desired to leave World War II behind. After all, the refugees were not the only ones who had been in Europe. American troops returned to civilian life eager to rejoin society. And it was expected that the newcomers, grateful to be in the United States, would do the same.

The postwar Jewish community was growing and increasingly becoming part of the American mainstream yet was mindful of the virulent anti-Semitism of the earlier part of the decade. The refugees, as immigrants, threatened the host community not just because they flocked to the main urban centers and competed for jobs but also because they embodied the Old World sensibilities that the American-born Jewish community eschewed. Some claimed that they could not confront survivors because of guilt. They distanced themselves from this tangible reminder that they had been safe in America, had been spared Hitler's wrath, while European Jewry burned. Others simply did not believe the depths of the Holocaust's atrocities. Some simply did not want the burden of relatives they did not know or care to know.

Reassuring as it would be to have the contemporaneous media images of warmth and welcome confirmed, the records reveal otherwise. They highlight the range of reception and the caesura between the refugees' and the American Jewish community's perception of this story. Yes there were those who opened their doors and those who turned their backs and an entire spectrum of response in between. This shows that survivors' battles, despite or sometimes because of the help they received, were not over once they reached America. This is hardly a simple story. On the contrary, the particular historical experience of Jewish DPs in postwar America was complex.

NOTES

The author wishes to thank Rutgers University Press and the United States Holocaust Memorial Museum for permission to quote from her book Case Closed: Holocaust Survivors in Postwar America (2007).

1. "813 European DPs Arrive in New York," *Washington Post,* October 31, 1948, M4.
2. Leonard Dinnerstein, *America and the Survivors of the Holocaust* (New York: Columbia University Press, 1982), 288. These figures are based on records from the Jewish communal agencies such as USNA. They include European refugees and also those from Shanghai, China, as well those who went first to Palestine/Israel and then came to the United States.

3. I use some of these contemporary terms. I also use "survivor." Even though this designation entered our vocabulary later, its usage here is a reminder that the refugees were different from previous immigrants.

4. These are housed at the American Jewish Historical Society (Center for Jewish History, New York City).

5. This included 150 case files from the JFCS (Denver, Colorado) housed at the American Jewish Historical Society (New York City) and 250 files from NYANA (New York City).

6. The majority of these are at the United States Holocaust Memorial Museum (USHMM), Washington, D.C. A smaller number are from the USC Shoah Foundation Institute for Visual History and Education, and some fifty are interviews conducted by the author.

7. On the White Paper, see Aaron Berman, *Nazism, the Jews, and American Zionism* (Detroit: Wayne State University Press, 1990), 66–70; Arieh Kochavi, *Post-Holocaust Politics: Britain, the U.S., and Jewish Refugees, 1945–1948* (Chapel Hill: University of North Carolina Press, 2001), 60–64; and Michael Marrus, *The Unwanted: European Refugees in the Twentieth Century* (Oxford: Oxford University Press, 1985), 152–53, 274–76. For more on the Anglo-American Committee of Inquiry, see chapters 4 and 7 in this volume.

8. For a contemporary demographic analysis of Jewish DPs and DP camps, see Kurt Grossman, *The Jewish DP Problem: Its Origin, Scope, and Liquidation* (New York: Institute of Jewish Affairs, 1951). For background on the DP question that includes, but is not limited to, Jewish DPs, see Mark Wyman, *DPs: Europe's Displaced Persons, 1945–1951* (Ithaca, NY: Cornell University Press, 1998), pt. II; and Haim Genizi, *America's Fair Share: The Admission and Resettlement of Displaced Persons, 1945–1952* (Detroit: Wayne State University Press, 1993).

9. This included all DPs, not only Jews, although the perception by the general public was that most DPs were Jewish.

10. According to USNA and NYANA records, approximately 110,000 Jewish refugees arrived during 1948–52, as noted in Dinnerstein, *America and the Survivors of the Holocaust*, 288.

11. For a history of USNA, see L. C. White's *300,000 New Americans* (New York: Harper's, 1957) in which he also discusses the National Refugee Service, created during the 1930s to aid refugees fleeing Hitler.

12. For a history of NYANA, see Josh Friedland, *The Lamp beside the Golden Door: The Story of NYANA* (New York: NYANA, 1999).

13. During the war the U.S. Committee for the Care of Children was permitted to sponsor refugees.

14. Dinnerstein, *America and Survivors of the Holocaust*, 113–14.

15. Records show that immigrants sometimes moved from their destined community to another locale, but they relinquished their right to financial support from their new community when they did so.

16. According to USNA records, DPs eventually went to forty-six states.

17. White, *300,000 New Americans*, 316–18.

Beth B. Cohen

18. Ben B. Seligman and Harvey Swados, "Jewish Population Studies in the United States," in *American Jewish Year Book, 1948–1949*, Vol. 50, edited by Harry Schneiderman and Morris Fine (Philadelphia: Jewish Publication Society of America, 1949), 667, 683, 717 (based on the 1940 census).

19. Studies of *landsmanschaftn* include Daniel Soyer's *Jewish Immigrant Associations and American Identity in New York, 1880–1939* (Cambridge: Harvard University Press, 1997), which provides an excellent analysis that examines the societies and their influence on the immigrants' identity and acculturation through 1939; a work produced as a Works Progress Administration (WPA) Yiddish writers' project, *Di yidishe landsmanschaftn fun nyu york* (New York: Yiddish Writers' Union, 1938), edited by I. Rontsch, which is the most comprehensive contemporary description of *landsmanschaftn* in the 1930s; Hannah Kliger's *Jewish Hometown Associations and Family Circles in New York: The WPA Yiddish Writers' Group Study* (Bloomington: Indiana University Press, 1992), which offers an edited English translation of Rontsch's study with foreword and afterword; and "The Present State of the Landsmanschaften," *Jewish Social Service Quarterly* 15 (1939): 360–78, which gives an English synopsis of Rontsch's group's work.

20. "Report from the Executive Director," *New Neighbors* 2, no. 2 (1949): n.p.

21. Letter from Emil Saloman, Director, Tulsa Jewish Federation, to Al Meyers, USNA Field Representative, July 6, 1949, 1945–64, file 405, American Jewish Joint Distribution Committee Collection, American Jewish Joint Distribution Committee Archives, New York, New York.

22. According to the case files of the Jewish Family and Children's Services (JFCS), Denver, and the American Jewish Historical Society, Newton Centre, Massachusetts, and New York, New York (hereafter JFCS/AJHS).

23. Letter to Arthur Greenleigh, Executive Director, USNA, from A. Neumann, Executive Director, JFCS, Denver, January 10, 1951, Record group (hereafter RG) 246, microfilm MKM 24.30, YIVO Institute for Jewish Research Archives (hereafter YIVO).

24. Letter to Beatrice Behrman, Director of Resettlement, USNA, from Alfred Neumann, Executive Director, JFCS, Denver, June 20, 1951, RG 246, microfilm MKM 24.30, YIVO.

25. Ibid.

26. Ibid.

27. RG I-065, box 21, file 1852, JFCS/AJHS.

28. Ibid.

29. Report by R. Ross, Casework Supervisor, RG I-065, box 21, file 1852, JFCS/AJHS.

30. Letter from R. Ross, Casework Supervisor, JFCS, to B. Behrman, USNA, August 31, 1951, RG I-065, box 21, file 1852, JFCS/AJHS.

31. Letter from B. Behrman to R. Ross, September 18, 1951, RG I-065, box

21, file 1852, JFCS/AJHS.

32. Letter to Beatrice Behrman, Director of Resettlement, USNA, from Alfred Neumann, Executive Director, JFCS, Denver, December 6, 1951, RG 246, microfilm MKM 24.30, file 707, YIVO.

33. "A Primer in Resettlement for Small Communities," *New Neighbors* 2, no. 2 (1949): n.p.

34. Ibid.

35. Columbia Field Reports to USNA, 1950, RG 246, microfilm MKM 24.53, file 1333, YIVO.

36. Letter from Dena Banks to Milton Krochmal, Community Relations Department, USNA, March 30, 1950, RG 246, microfilm MKM 24.53, file 1333, YIVO.

37. Hannah Rubin, telephone conversation with the author, January 28, 2002.

38. Ibid.

39. B. G., telephone conversation with the author, January 30, 2002.

40. Ibid.

41. Approximately 77 percent of those going to New York arrived on individual affidavits.

42. Case file H.B.-51, NYANA Archives, New York, New York (hereafter NYANA).

43. Case file A.D.-52, NYANA.

44. Case file H.B.-51, NYANA.

45. Case file 324-49, NYANA.

46. Case file 390-51, NYANA.

47. C. K., RG 50.549.02*0012, February 24, 1998, Postwar Testimonies, United States Holocaust Memorial Museum Archives (hereafter USHMM).

48. Case file 398–51, NYANA.

49. B. S., RG 50.549.02*0011, February 22, 1998, Postwar Testimonies, USHMM.

50. C. K., RG 50.549.02*0012, February 24, 1998, Postwar Testimonies, USHMM.

51. Ibid.

52. F. Fritzshall, RG 50.549.02*0020, September 22, 1998, Postwar Testimonies, USHMM.

53. C. K., RG 50.549.02*0012, February 24, 1998, Postwar Testimonies, USHMM.

54. "A Summing Up," *New Neighbors* 3 (1950): 4.

55. Ibid.

56. Address by NYANA president A. Askin, NYANA Second Annual Meeting, April 5, 1951, Executive Board Meetings, NYANA.

57. This included any type of illness mentioned that either kept the newcomer from working or required medical attention. Sometimes both spouses in the same file were ill, which would make the figure even higher.

58. There is a wealth of sources on PTSD. For PTSD related to Holocaust survivors, see Yael Danieli, ed., *International Handbook of Multigenerational Legacies of Trauma* (Norwell, MA: Kluwer Academic, 1998); Leo Eitinger and Robert Krell, *The Psychological and Medical Effects of Concentration Camps and Related Persecutions on Survivors of the Holocaust* (Vancouver: University of British Columbia Press, 1985); Charles R. Figley, *Trauma and Its Wake: The Study and Treatment of Post-Traumatic Stress Disorder*, Vol. 1 (Milton Park, UK: Taylor and Francis, 1985); Mardi Jon Horowitz, ed., *Essential Papers on Post Traumatic Stress Disorder* (New York: New York University Press, 1999); and Andreas Maercker, ed., *Post Traumatic Stress Disorder: A Lifespan Developmental Perspective* (Seattle, WA: Hogrefe and Huber, 1999).

59. For a discussion of mental health worker's treatment of refugees, see chapter 7 in Beth B. Cohen, *Case Closed: Holocaust Survivors in Postwar America* (New Brunswick, NJ: Rutgers University Press, 2007).

60. Case file report, box 16, Mrs. F. (no file number), RG I-065, JFCS/AJHS.

61. Letter from Dr. S. to NYANA Social Worker, June 2, 1950, case file 324–49, NYANA.

62. Report by S. J., April 11, 1949, box 6, file 2433, JFCS/AJHS.

63. For a history of social work, see John Ehrenreich, *The Altruistic Imagination: A History of Social Work and Social Policy in the United States* (Ithaca, NY: Cornell University Press, 1985), chaps. 1–2; Carel Germain, "Casework and Science: A Historical Encounter," in *Theories of Social Casework*, edited by R. W. Roberts and R. H. Nee, 5–32 (Chicago: University of Chicago Press, 1970); James Leiby, *A History of Social Welfare and Social Work in the United States* (New York: Columbia University Press, 1978), chaps. 1–13; and Roy Lubove, *The Professional Altruist: The Emergence of Social Work as a Career, 1870–1930* (Cambridge: Harvard University Press, 1965).

64. Beatrice Carter, "Social Case Work with the Adolescent in a Program of Social Case Work with Displaced Persons," paper read at the National Conference of Social Work, Atlantic City, 1950, cited in Beatrice Glanz, "Factors in the Adjustment of New American Children in Their First Year in the United States" (Unpublished master's thesis, Simmons College, 1950), 27.

65. Leonard Serkess, interview by the author, tape recording, Newton, Massachusetts, February 27, 2002.

66. Ibid.

67. Robert Berger, interview by the author, tape recording, Brookline, Massachusetts, February 5, 2002.

68. Robert Graham, "Dachau Victims Transformed into Husky Americans in Maine," *Boston Sunday Herald*, August 1, 1948, 6.

69. Harry Plow, "Why We Put the Play On," in *Twice Born*, edited by Joshua Rosenberg, writings from the New Americans Unit, Camp Kingswood, Bridgton, Maine, Summer 1948, p. 21.

70. Berger interview.

71. Serkess interview.

72. Ibid.

73. Ibid.

74. Berger interview.

75. Ibid.

76. See chapter 5, "Unaccompanied Minors," in Cohen, *Case Closed*.

77. See Milton Bergman and Milton Jucovy, *Generations of the Holocaust* (New York: Columbia University Press, 1982); and T. L. Brink, ed., *Holocaust Survivors' Mental Health* (New York: Haworth, 1994).

78. N. Salsitz, RG 50.549.02*0052, July 5, 1999, Postwar Testimonies, USHMM.

79. H. Taube, interview with the author, tape recording, Rockville, Maryland, December 2, 2004.

80. H. Liebman, RG 50.407*0086, August 10, 1996, Postwar Testimonies, USHMM.

81. A. Salsitz, RG 50.549.02*0054, July 8, 1999, Postwar Testimonies, USHMM.

82. A. Sandelowski, interview by the author, tape recording, Providence, Rhode Island, March 3, 2000.

83. B. Sayonne, interview with the author, tape recording, Denver, Colorado, December 19, 2002.

84. E. Beder, RG 50.091*0004, August 27, 1984, National Council of Jewish Women Oral History Project, Cleveland, Ohio, USHMM.

85. N. Godin, RG 50.549.01*0009.60, December 14, 1995, Postwar Testimonies, USHMM.

86. Ibid.

Perceptions of Jewish Displaced Persons as Criminals in Early Postwar Germany

Lingering Stereotypes and Self-fulfilling Prophecies

MICHAEL BERKOWITZ
AND SUZANNE BROWN-FLEMING

In August 1961 the young American Jewish theologian Richard L. Rubenstein interviewed Dr. Heinrich Grüber, the Protestant dean of East Berlin, known for his opposition to Nazism and his postwar efforts to foster reconciliation between Christians and Jews. Grüber lamented that "many of the brothels and risqué night clubs . . . [were] now in Jewish hands." It was Grüber's feeling that "after what had happened [during the Third Reich], they [Jews] ought not to do these things, as it made the work of ending anti-Semitism so much harder." Rubenstein concluded that in Grüber's mind, "there was an objective relationship between Jewish behavior and Antisemitism."[1] In his now-famous tract *After Auschwitz: Radical Theology and Contemporary Judaism,* Rubenstein reflected that "here was a Christian who had almost died because of his efforts on behalf of Jews—the Nazis kicked out his teeth and at one point he was left for dead in Dachau—yet he was incapable of seeing Jews simply as normal human beings with the same range of failings and virtues as any other group."[2]

In the wake of the resounding Nazi defeat, many if not most Germans understood that it was no longer appropriate, at least outside their confidants, to refer to the Jewish remnant in their midst by the racial terms that were ubiquitous in the Third Reich. Informal and later compulsory restraint on public speech and publications did not mean, however, that well-entrenched stereotypes were expeditiously quashed, as Rubenstein would learn during his 1961 visit to Germany. One of the ways that Germans in the postwar period dealt with Jews— and especially Jewish displaced persons (DPs)—was to perceive and treat them as criminals or as persons with an inordinate propensity toward criminality.[3]

According to surveys taken the Office of Military Government, United States (OMGUS), in the American zone in 1946, 39 percent of the total population was either intensely (18 percent) or moderately (21 percent) anti-Semitic.[4] Alongside older forms of anti-Semitism, new strains appeared. The post-Holocaust issues of guilt, restitution, and reparations as well as the creation of the State of Israel (1948) under-girded what Werner Bergmann and Rainer Erb recognize as "second-ary" anti-Semitism. In postwar surveys, Bergmann and Erb conclude, Germans made it clear that above all, they wished for an end to the "annoying" debate about the past, the guilt associated with it, and demands for reparations.[5] Rabbi Philip Bernstein, adviser on Jewish Affairs to General Joseph McNarney, commander in chief of United States Forces, European Theater (USFET),[6] detected this attitude even among German clergy, whom he expected would be less prone to anti-Semitism.[7]

In the days leading up to and especially after the Nazi surrender, such a predisposition had a symbiotic relationship with the desperate circumstances in which Jewish survivors found themselves as well with as the occupying forces' preconceptions. In this way Germans could assure themselves that Jews had rightly been and should remain objects of contempt, that Jews had been the root cause of their defeat, and that Jewish DPs were the source of postwar distress. While it was no longer good form to talk about Jews as defiling the Aryan race, it was acceptable to label Jewish DPs as crooked, as responsible for and profiting from the sea of crime in which Germans felt themselves to be immersed, and as exacerbating Germans' misery. In July 1947 Phillip Bernstein reported that:

> The reasons assigned for the emergence of the new anti-Sem-
> itism in Germany fall into several distinct categories. . . . Ger-
> mans and indigenous Jews consider the Jewish DPs as a pro-
> vocative element in the German scene. . . . Stemming as they
> do from East European Jewry, they are the type with whom the
> German is either not familiar or whom he has traditionally re-
> sented. The Jewish DPs are believed to be the hub of the black
> market. Some German workers . . . have swelled the ranks of

anti-Semites because they were dispossessed to make room for the Jewish DPs. The Germans are [made] uneasy by the presence . . . of people to whom they owe a colossal debt, and relieve themselves of their guilt by proving to the world that the Jews deserved their fate under the Nazi regime.[8]

Stereotypes of Jewish DPs as morally lax, natural criminals and black marketers, leftist agitators, and communists were commonplace. Anton Rupert Sittl of Munich alleged, for example, that "KZ [*Konzentratzionslager*] Jews possessed coupons that allowed them to buy new Mercedes Benz and Opel cars straight off the factory lot, for a mere 4,000 to 6,000 deutschmarks. [They] turned around and sold the cars for 100,000 deutschmarks."[9] In the British zone the following rumor circulated:

> The most successful of all black marketers in Germany [was a Jew who had survived the death camps and] who got hold of a million sewing machine needles after they had vanished from the Singer factory in Darmstadt while under the American Military Government control. The DP was able to smuggle the needles to Italy and sell them to the Necchi Company in return for the American sales rights in the Necchi sewing machine. He then emigrated to America, set up a commission order office in New York, and within two years had made much more than a million dollars.[10]

Such perceptions of excessively privileged or powerful Jewish DPs flourished in a heavily war-damaged Germany coping with an influx of expellees, refugees, and DPs, only a small minority of whom were Jewish.[11]

In 1946 the DP population in Germany, Austria, and Italy, Jewish and otherwise, increased significantly. East European states, with the consent of the Allied Control Council under the terms of the 1945 Potsdam Agreement, forcibly expelled roughly 12 million ethnic German citizens (Volksdeutsche) to Germany. Around 8 million ethnic Germans came to the Western area of Germany, most to the American zone. The Jewish DP population increased from 50,000 to 145,000 in 1946 alone. The numbers of Jewish DPs under United Nations Relief and Rehabilitation Administration (UNRRA)[12] or U.S. Army care in camps or urban centers peaked at approximately 250,000 in early 1947 and declined thereafter. But even at its peak, the Jewish DP population never exceeded more than 10–20 percent of all uprooted Europeans categorized as DPs. In the American zone, for example, 80–90 percent of DPs were Christian (predominantly Roman Catholic), and 10–20 percent were Jewish.

By the summer of 1947, about 182,000 Jewish DPs lived in Germany, 80 percent of them from Poland. The majority of the remaining 20 percent came from Hungary, Czechoslovakia, the Soviet Union, and Romania. This group of Jewish refugees, East European nationals who sought refuge from the Nazis in the Soviet Union in 1939, escaped death in the Holocaust, but many returned to their homes only to encounter rampant anti-Semitism. Thus, they sought refuge once again in the western zones of occupied Germany.[13] Most DPs were sent to (or situated themselves in) the British and American zones of Germany. In the British zone, 9,000 (of 12,000 total) Jewish DPs lived in the Hohne-Belsen camp.[14] The American zone contained several camps of approximately 5,000 inhabitants each to accommodate the total Jewish DP population of some 150,000 (this number fluctuated). These included Jewish DP camps in Landsberg,[15] Feldafing,[16] and Föhrenwald (Bavaria) as well as mixed camps in Pocking and Leipheim (Bavaria), Frankfurt-Zeilsheim, Wetzlar, and Eschwege (Hesse). About one-fourth of Jewish DPs lived not in camps but in cities. Munich, for example, had up to 7,000 Jewish DPs. A little more than 1,000 Jewish DPs lived in the French zone, and Jewish DP camps also existed in Austria and Italy.[17]

By October 1948 fewer than 85,000 Jewish DPs remained in Europe, many having immigrated to the new State of Israel, formed on May 15, 1948. Between 1945 and 1952, approximately 136,000 Jewish DPs would immigrate to Palestine, later Israel.[18] From 1946 to 1953, between 80,000 and 100,000 entered the United States under the 1946 Truman Directive and Displaced Persons Acts of 1948 and 1952. Other Jewish émigrés went to Australia, the United Kingdom, France, and elsewhere. As of 1952, only 12,000 Jewish DPs remained in Germany, a tiny percentage of which were of German nationality prior to the war. In 1959 the Jewish community in the Federal Republic (mostly of East European origins) numbered a mere 23,000.[19]

Most scholarly studies of anti-Semitism reveal that anti-Semitic prejudice consisted overwhelmingly of projection on the part of non-Jews, having little or nothing to do with Jews' own thoughts or activities.[20] There is an important but nevertheless problematic caveat for this period. While Jewish DPs did not disproportionately participate in the black market when compared to other DPs or native populations, they were indeed involved in the black market and thus were technically violating the law. These facts notwithstanding, this chapter argues that allegations of so-called Jewish criminality not only had to do with the deeds of Jews in black and gray markets but also with the pro-

Michael Berkowitz and Suzanne Brown-Fleming

tean nature of anti-Semitism. While previous varieties of anti-Jewish prejudice were transformed into something more genteel, they still preserved the irrational fear and disdain of the Jew as the archetypal outsider, easily melding into "the Jew as a criminal menace."[21]

An example of lingering prejudices toward Jewish DPs was the uproar surrounding the camp in Zeilsheim, an industrial suburb of Frankfurt-am-Main that housed thousands of IG Farben workers during the Third Reich. After the war, the Hoechst Factory (a pharmaceutical company) replaced IG Farben facilities in Zeilsheim. In 1945 the U.S. Army ordered approximately 1,300 working-class Germans out of their homes (without their furniture) in order to make room for the Jewish DP camp.[22] For army officers, the requisitioning of some 300 German homes for Jewish DPs was a "hot problem" that "no one wanted to touch."[23] Occupation officials knew that a "Jewish DP smuggling ring" operated out of Frankfurt-Zeilsheim. They discovered its existence after arresting Polish Jewish DPs Martin Amsterdam and Markus Goldberg, who were illegally crossing the American zone border with the help of German national Otto Krecht. Their Opel vehicle contained 2.216 million reichsmarks. Distressed army officials alleged that several members of the Zeilsheim ring had communist sympathies.[24]

The presence of Jewish DPs in Zeilsheim greatly disturbed Roman Catholic priest Father Rupp, who wrote to Bishop Dirichs of Limburg to describe alleged goings-on in the "Jewish quarter" (Judenviertel): "Nearly 5,000 Jews have been put into their own camp. They have their own so-called 'police.' The German police referred an official report regarding the production of false German money to the Americans, who ignored it for the last four months. Then, after renewed urging from the German police, the Americans conducted a raid. But they did not find anything."[25]

"The black market activity in Zeilsheim—in the Jewish quarter—is notorious," Father Rupp relayed to Bishop Dirichs[26] and subsequently to American bishop Aloisius Muench, papal emissary and Catholic liaison to OMGUS.[27] In a separate letter, Father Rupp told Bishop Muench that prejudice against the Jewish DPs stemmed not only from their "Jewishness" but also from their "Russian" way of thinking.[28]

Six days later, Bishop Muench received a petition from a Catholic priest named Father Brim that was also signed by sixteen Zeilsheim Catholics. In great detail—indeed, on a street-by-street basis—it described the requisitioning of Zeilsheim homes for "Polish Jews." It also described in detail the living conditions of now-displaced Germans. It should be noted that according to one contemporary American Jewish chaplain and several residents, overcrowding in the Jewish camp was also atrocious.[29] The Brim petition included political arguments. Imploring Bishop Muench for help, these sixteen Zeilsheim Catholics told Muench of rumors that more homes would soon be requisitioned for Jews. They warned of the negative political effects that any new confiscation would have:

> The Communist Party places itself in the middle of these critical days by holding a meeting in Zeilsheim . . . to give the impression that only they endeavor to ease the situation in Zeilsheim. [The Communists] successfully strengthen this impression. After repeated evacuations, fear and resignation have set in among those Germans affected. They have become mistrusting and inclined toward radicalism. This showed itself in recent elections, when voices in favor of Christian Democracy declined, and opposition to the Christian Democratic Party grew. Stoppage to these requisitionings must be achieved. This is the only way to stem the tide of radicalism and avoid the moral pitfalls of so many persons living in unnaturally close proximity. We Zeilsheim Catholics beg you for help.[30]

Bishop Muench had already attempted to intervene even before receiving this petition by writing to General Joseph T. McNarney to describe the "problematic" situation.[31] When roughly one-third of Zeilsheim's homes still remained occupied by Jewish DPs in April 1948, Father Rupp wrote to Muench again, this time to report the dire consequences that befell Germans forced to live among Jewish DPs. Zeilsheim was now world-famous for its black market, said Father Rupp. "Some of our good farming community [*Bauernschaft*] have mixed themselves up in such activities," lamented Rupp, implying the common anti-Semitic stereotype that Jews corrupted Germans. "Our working-class Germans turn to Jews, who have lots of cash, to earn a little on the side. Even children participate, and thereby lose the correct understanding of money's true value," Rupp stated. In the autumn of 1948, the U.S. Army dismantled the Zeilsheim camp.[32] Father Rupp reported that even the departure of the Jewish DPs was disastrous. In a long letter, he described the manner in which "Ukrainian-Jewish, Lithuanian-Jewish, and Polish-Jewish DPs," as they evacuated the Zeilsheim camp, packed furniture, bedding, and china belonging to "simple German workers who had to count every penny."[33] Ironically, Muench's secretary, Robert Deubel, informed him that "some German

Michael Berkowitz and Suzanne Brown-Fleming

Jewish DPs gather in a central square of the Eschwege DP camp following a raid by American military police searching for contraband, ca. June–August 1947. (United States Holocaust Memorial Museum, Photograph no. 44865, courtesy of Esther Kacs Livingston)

families did not want to go back to their homes, because in some instances they received better accommodations in the meantime."[34]

Added to the accusations of Jewish DPs as corrupt, careless with German property, and excessively involved in communist and black market activity was a great amount of sexual tension and anxiety in general and sexuality-related fears centered around Jewish DPs in particular. Germans told Captain Malcolm Vendig, the U.S. military governor of the Landkreis Dachau in May 1945, that they were afraid that women from the DP camps would initiate a massive outbreak of venereal disease.[35] There was palpable alarm over the presence of black U.S. soldiers and resentment over the fact that German women fraternized with American GIs.[36] A poignant example referencing Jews specifically again came from Father Rupp of Zeisheim. In April 1948 Father Rupp wrote a letter to Bishop Muench that implicated Jewish males as sexual predators who took advantage of innocent German girls, a staple anti-Semitic argument. "Many good families have fallen to the ways of Mammon," he wrote. "Over one hundred young German girls live among Jews, in primitive conditions. Pregnancies outside of marriage result from this. To date, four or five civil marriages have taken place between German girls and Jews," wrote Rupp.[37] From the Jewish perspective, the decimation and persecution experienced during the war prompted an understandable tendency to flaunt convention in this new day of freedom. German Jewish survivor of Auschwitz Erwin Tichauer recalled a "mass wedding" held in a barn and attended by the military governor of Bayreuth, "a Jew from Brooklyn." It was "a glorious wedding" attended by other officials. Tichauer offered no apology for the fact that "all the brides were in advanced stages of pregnancy."[38]

In some cases, Germans also viewed Jewish children as active or potential criminals with disdainful and even dangerous habits. A study at the Kloster-Indersdorf displaced children's center in the outskirts of Munich, under the auspices of UNRRA, cited "lying and stealing" as "not unusual" among any group of children numbering 200–300, but it was nonetheless "especially difficult to treat [the] problem" of children who had been compelled "to lie and steal for survival."[39] In June 1947 the Catholic sisters of Cloister Bad Wörishofen asked Bishop Muench for help in ridding their two cloisters-turned-infirmaries, Josefsheim and Kneippianum, of displaced children. The sisters implied that most of the displaced children there were Jewish. Sister Reifsmeier told Bishop Muench, "I can assure you all the sisters carried out their duty of Christian love for their neighbor [*christlicher Nächstenliebe*], despite suspicion and mistrust. It is heroic for the sisters to dutifully remain at their posts. . . . The sisters must remove the crucifixes from each room because the current patients do not like

Michael Berkowitz and Suzanne Brown-Fleming

them. . . . It is easy to see that the routines of our Order are greatly disrupted."[40] Bishop Muench responded by writing to General Clarence R. Huebner, who replied that it was "not considered advisable that the property in question be released at the present time because of the unavailability of a suitable alternative location." Furthermore, added Huebner, an army investigation revealed that 242 tubercular children of all faiths received treatment at Josefsheim and Kneippianum.[41] Huebner suspected the sisters of shading the truth, telling Deubel that "untrue allegations [were] made by some Bad Wörisfhofen people about the real situation there."[42]

Sister Fernanda Weip laid bare her hostile feelings toward the Jewish children in her care in a letter to Bishop Muench. Sister Weip, who had contacted Dr. Philipp Auerbach,[43] Bavarian state commissioner for restitution, to demand the removal of DPs from Josefsheim and Kneippianum, told Bishop Muench, "[Auerbach] personally pleaded to the military government in Munich for our rights as order nurses, and will have *his* Jews moved from our houses."[44] When in August Jewish DPs still remained at Kneippianum, she complained bitterly to Bishop Muench: "German personnel who have worked with our order nurses for years are being replaced by DPs," presumably some of whom were Jewish. "These boys, aged between fourteen and eighteen, have no upbringing whatsoever. The sisters must defend themselves against physical abuse and stealing, and often without success," she stated.[45]

The tendency on the part of some Germans and OMGUS officials to lump Jews together with communism and to characterize them as inherently dangerous and threatening meant, naturally, that they regarded the steady influx of Jewish DPs as undesirable. In his weekly intelligence report from the headquarters of the U.S. Third Army, titled *The Modern Wandering Jew,* Vincent la Vista described the mass movement of Polish Jews into territory under the control of the Third Army as "financed and fostered by Zionist groups." Although there appears to be nothing illegal about giving refugees money, in this rendering it is given sinister overtones in that La Vista mixed this statement with the charge that Jews who evaded "transient camps" made their way because of "false papers" supplied to them from "Kibutzes."[46] "Jewish infiltrees" in the "thousands" who had "been indoctrinated in Poland" were sent to the U.S. zone "without authority" and "without the knowledge of the UNRRA," La Vista's report stated.[47] He referenced such activity as a form of "espionage."[48] Interestingly, La Vista defined a "Kibutz" as "a Jewish group organized in Poland to train its members in the fields of endeavor which they intend to pursue, once they have arrived in Palestine."[49] La Vista also suspected "an organized crossing of the border (150–200 a day) for the purpose of joining the

Polish Army in Munich."[50] As incredible as it sounds, La Vista's report also recited information, given to La Vista by the "camp police at Feldafing," that plans existed to establish a "Jewish state" in Bavaria "if Palestine is inaccessible." Each "infiltree," wrote La Vista, "is well-groomed in the stories told [to] American authorities," supposedly a result of the "specific instructions they had received in Poland."[51] The American La Vista had no appreciation for the irony in his own characterization of the movement of Jews whose "main desire [was] to get to Palestine, whether it be through legal or illegal means," as an "underground railroad,"[52] a term used for the routes that American slaves took in order to gain freedom in the North.

La Vista's report characterized the "method of operation of the Jewish displaced persons camps" as purposefully exploitative of the black market, as "black market sales of rations drawn from the UNRRA [were], in the opinion of this writer, the largest source of income for both the Jewish underground and the legitimate Jewish relief organizations [now] operating in Italy," he wrote. While the report did not blame UNRAA or the American Jewish Joint Distribution Committee, La Vista did believe that these two organizations were "used" by "unscrupulous individuals and agencies" that "maliciously used the names of both organizations to their personal or collective advantage."[53] La Vista's report recognized the Vatican as the "largest single organization involved in the illegal movement of immigrants," but he condoned Vatican illegal activity as "propagation of the [Roman Catholic] faith," made respectable by its accompanying anticommunist stance.[54] Despite the fact that Jews' urge to reach Palestine was palpable, there was little cognizance of what prompted their desperation. "Illegal" Jewish population movements were seen as more pernicious than the attempt by former Nazis to escape to South America.[55] La Vista dismissed threats facing Jews in Poland as "hearsay"[56] and did not see their material situation as dire.[57] He described Jews in Munich as "well dressed, well fed, rosy checked [sic] and with plenty of money."[58] Interestingly, La Vista was mimicking, if not plagiarizing, the controversial assessment of Britain's general Sir Frederick Morgan, the first head of UNRRA.[59] As has been discussed by Leonard Dinnerstein and Joseph Bendersky, the renowned and bigoted General George S. Patton help set the tone of derision and insensitivity in dealing with Jewish DPs,[60] which would have to be undone by a succession of special advisers to the American occupation forces and the implementation of the Harrison Report.[61] To Patton and other authorities, fighting communism and "anarchism" and "restoring normal communications and law and order" was paramount, even if it meant "having some Nazis work for us."[62] Nevertheless, some individual Jews whom

Michael Berkowitz and Suzanne Brown-Fleming

he believed rose above the general character of the DPs impressed Patton.[63] Rather than seeing temporary residence in Germany as the only alternative available to the majority of Jews who were there, La Vista, similar to other observers, portrayed Munich in particular as not only a safe haven but also as a spot that afforded Jews the opportunity to take advantage of the unwitting Germans, who were depicted as victims of the DPs.[64]

Bishop Muench also blamed the dissatisfaction of Germans on Jewish DPs, even placing blame for growing anti-Semitism on Jews themselves. In 1950 Monsignor Paul Tanner sent Muench an un-flattering National Catholic Welfare Conference report on Jewish af-fairs in Germany. Muench's response to Tanner was this: "There is some growth of anti-Semitism, but as elsewhere it is a reaction to Semitism—the requisitioning of hundreds of homes for Jewish Displaced persons, the damage done to the property during the oc-cupancy, the exorbitant claims that are now being made under the res-titution law, black marketeering, the defense of smutty publications by Jewish printers and publishers etc."[65] When OMGUS officials req-uisitioned the Catholic seminary in Dieburg to provide housing for Jewish DPs, Bishop Muench worked in tandem with Bishop Albert Stohr of Mainz to restore the Dieburg seminary to German seminar-ians. Bishop Stohr told Religious Affairs officer Captain Kenny that so-called Ostjuden (Eastern Jews) "severely damaged" the Dieburg building, adding that German civilians in Dieburg were "very bitter" at having their homes requisitioned "for the Jews." He asked that Kenny make repair materials available to restore the seminary, including new bedding, desks, and chairs. Otherwise, said Bishop Stohr, the "libera-tion of the Jews would become a psychological burden for civilians." The bishop told Kenny that he also heard complaints from Germans in the town of Lampertheim: "The civilian population is on the edge of despair. The Jews sit in beautiful and spacious homes (sources as-sure me that a single Jew lives in a three-room home), while seven or eight expelled Germans live in one room, married couples and chil-dren together. One can imagine the negative effect on morality. One could easily see that under these circumstances, a new anti-Semitism grows, anti-Semitism perhaps even stronger than that of National Socialism." Bishop Stohr suggested that Ostjuden be evacuated from private homes in Lampertheim and placed instead in larger buildings, such as schools or soldiers' barracks. "This has the advantage," he ar-gued, "that Germans thrown out of their homes would no longer have to watch [them] rob and sell off their entire household, which Jews are doing in a shameless manner."[66]

Malcolm Vendig observed that Germans tended to evade their

own responsibilities for the situation of DPs as well as their role in producing an atmosphere of brutality. Certainly, thought Vendig, a number of forces about which Germans felt anxious were at play, such as the specter of communism, the large number of foreign forced laborers and prisoners of war in the their midst, and the presence of occupation forces that included an unsettling number of "American colored troops."[67]

On May 6, 1945, Vendig wrote in his diary, "the public safety and displaced persons problems are the most critical now faced by this detachment, and they complicate each other. The majority of complaints and disturbances which occur result from looting, pillaging, and general hell-raising by displaced persons. . . . The displaced persons are inadequately fed, clothed, and housed. . . . Hungry, ragged people know only the laws of their own needs and of their long-fed resentment."[68] He listed several specific examples of lawlessness especially precipitated by hunger. Vendig reported "Russian" DPs (possibly including Jews) in the town of Egeln to be "unmanageable" and responsible for "looting," the killing of pigs, and possession of "unknown quantities of firearms with which they terrorized [Egeln's] population."[69] In April 1945 in the town of Dalldorf, the *Bürgermeister* (mayor) complained to Vendig that "DPs were taking eggs" from Germans. But when Vendig asked about the quantity of eggs being distributed to hungry DPs, the mayor answered Vendig with "a puzzled stare,"[70] seemingly unaware of the obvious relationship between food hoarding on the part of Dalldorf authorities and citizenry and so-called lawless behavior on the part of DPs.

Similarly, in late April 1945 in Tarthun, the first postwar *Bürgermeister*, Ehrling Sinka, told Vendig that he "spent over a week recovering from black eyes given him by DPs." Upon further questioning, it came out that Sinka had been charging DPs for food that Vendig's detachment "had ordered [Sinka] to furnish them." Vendig commented wryly, "the new *Bürgermeister* was given our ideas on that subject."[71] Sinka did not acknowledge the relationship between appropriate food distribution and "criminal" behavior on the part of DPs. Likewise, in Escherhausen in April 1945, Vendig found that "no provisions had been made for the reception of DPs and those [DPs] directed there were uncared for." Upon questioning the *Bürgermeister* and receiving answers that were "unsatisfactory," Vendig jailed the *Bürgermeister* and charged him with "disobeying mil[itary] gov[ernment] orders." Incidentally, upon conducting a search of the *Bürgermeister*'s home, Vendig found that "a large quantity of food was on hand in the house."[72]

For both Germans and Jews during the immediate postwar

months, the reversed power dynamic in their relationship made the world seem strangely disordered. At the Deggendorf DP camp, a survivor from the Netherlands recalled "a small group of captive German soldiers who had been stripped of their insignias [and] ordered to work for the Jewish displaced persons." One morning, she remembered, she "heard a knock at [her] door . . . [and] there stood a man in a German uniform holding a stack of chopped wood. His resemblance to my father was immense: middle aged, slim, with the lean oppressed face—just as I remembered him in the hospital. Without saying a word I gave him a slice of bread. He took it silently. I looked around if somebody had seen me, not being sure of my deed. Every time he brought me wood, I repaid him with a slice of bread."[73] Hungry Germans now found themselves in the position of asking for food from the very same persons their regime and sometimes they themselves had sought to exterminate. Other inversions of the previous order were striking, such as the fact that a number tattooed on an arm sometimes entitled survivors—formerly subject to varying degrees of brutal treatment that usually culminated in death—to "tender care" and "plenty of food."[74] Typically expelled from positions of authority over Germans under the Nazi regime, a number of Jews now assumed positions as policemen, and some of them were keen to exploit the benefits. Survivor Michael Bernath of Hungary, after the war living temporarily in the Poppendorf DP camp, wrote that "to be a police officer those days had many good side effects. First[,] I never had to stay in line for food or whenever a person had to stay in line. Police had the edge above all the rest[;] and besides[,] my words were the final words and I got paid for it. . . . I am telling you I had it made," he remembered.[75]

In many respects, the Nazis had succeeded in turning Jews into their enemies. That fact that Jewish survivors should have by all rights hated the Germans passionately is rarely admitted. "Nearly all" children at Kloster-Indersdorf "had one attitude in common—that of intense hatred of the Germans and all that was German. It was extremely difficult to help the children with these feelings, when everything in their daily life was surrounded by the German atmosphere, and when they had to continue living in Germany after the liberation. The staff of the Center often wondered what damage was being caused and how the rehabilitation process was being slowed by these factors," reported Indersdorf employee Greta Fischer.[76]

For similar reasons, some Jewish DPs refused to work. Renowned historian Arno Lustiger, himself a DP, recalled that the American army tried to compel the Jewish DPs to work in areas that benefited the community at large. The army "thought the DPs shouldn't loaf around

Two men stand outside a kosher butcher shop on the Ismaningerstrasse in Munich that was vandalized in an anti-Semitic attack, 1947. (United States Holocaust Memorial Museum, Photograph no. 58612, courtesy of Alex Hochhauser)

without work, but should participate in the construction of the German economy," remembered Lustiger. He and others rejected army overtures in this regard. "That was an abstruse idea that we should help the Germans built their economy, when they themselves destroyed it with their own guilt and their own crimes," asserted Lustiger, a Polish Jewish survivor of Auschwitz, Gross-Rosen, and Buchenwald.[77]

Aggressiveness and defiance of authority on the part of survivors still in Germany as DPs is evident in numerous accounts. Survivor Jonas Landau, a former partisan who was originally from Stolpce, Poland, explained such behavior poignantly. He acknowledged that "some of our behavior was perhaps difficult to understand. However, after living in the woods for a couple of years—the ghetto and then the woods—our manners and general behavior were not the best." After an incident in which he became drunk and loud, prompting a visit by the hotel manager, "it seems I threatened to throw him down the staircase and showed him a small pocket knife," Landau recalled.[78]

Certainly the fact that former Nazis were often recruited as police[79] and that SS men were among the supposedly reconstituted, de-Nazified local governments[80] dissuaded survivors from believing that the occupation power represented a new order in which they would

Michael Berkowitz and Suzanne Brown-Fleming

German police on horseback conduct a raid to suppress Jewish black market activity on the Moehlstrasse in Munich, May 1949. (United States Holocaust Memorial Museum, Photograph no. 58636, courtesy of Alex Hochhauser)

be fairly treated. One observer of the DP camps wrote that "the most shattering thing" she observed was to see Jewish DPs in the midst of "former SS men, Gestapo, Nazi party members, Polish voluntary labor—not slave laborers but Poles who offered their services voluntarily to the Reich for a wage—Russian voluntary labor, [and] Yugoslavian fascist soldiers[,] all of whom disguised themselves as displaced persons and [entered DP] camps to escape detection."[81] Certainly it was predictable that victimized Jews suspected Germans of "working for" such persons.[82] In this atmosphere of unrest and depravation, crime was rampant and came in many guises, and conflict between German police and DPs sometimes resulted in violence.[83] Indeed, a great deal of tension existed between Jewish DPs and Allied-approved German police, who conducted overzealous raids, sometimes accompanied by German shepherd dogs, on Jewish DP camps. In Stuttgart, for example, a German policeman shot a member of the Jewish camp police, causing a riot in March 1946. Only a month later, riots broke out in Landsberg.[84]

Jewish survivors openly acknowledged Jewish involvement in black market activity. For example, while Dr. Auerbach denied the collective charge that "all" Jewish DPs were black marketers in a April 26, 1949, speech to the International Council for Christians and Jews (ICCJ)[85] in Munich,[86] he still acknowledged illegal activity taking place in Jewish DP camps. In 1947 he wrote a report to political adviser Robert Murphy criticizing the Displaced Persons Central Committee (DPCC), the survivors' organization and principle representative body for Jewish DPs,[87] telling Murphy, "I accuse the Central Committee of being guilty of the black market bargains made by Jewish citizens . . . because it did not allow the proper distribution of goods among the 25,000 Jewish DPs placed in towns and communities."[88]

Survivors often discussed the moral complexity of engaging in black market activity in memoirs. William Eisen, a survivor from Warsaw, wrote of his time at the Landsberg DP camp:

> Naturally, the black market flourished there. When the demand for goods is high and the supply is low, as it was in postwar Europe, the black marketeers surface. There was nothing that a person wanted that couldn't be bought—for a price. I felt that, for the sake of my family, I needed to earn a lot of money quickly if we were to ever be anything more than DPs, so I actually attempted to take advantage of the situation. I went out one morning with some yard goods [cloth] that I was going to sell at an exorbitant price. With the money I was "going" to earn, I intended to buy more goods and pyramid my meager possessions into a fortune. After two days of standing around waiting to be approached because I didn't have the courage to make the initial advance, and feeling like I was the worst of criminals, I gave up "my life of crime." I realized I just wasn't cut out for that type of life and went back to the profession that had always kept me alive during the worst of times: tailoring.[89]

On the part of Jewish participants, black marketeering could be rationalized as a transitional means of earning a living, as an essential step along the way of establishing oneself in a legitimate business. The director of the DP camp at Gnadenwald, reported German Jewish survivor Erwin Tichauer, was a "large scale black marketer—and eventually wound up on Wall Street."[90]

A prerequisite for activity on the black market was simply having something to sell or trade. At times, Jewish DPs found themselves in possession of items and even food for which they had no or little use, and this prompted their activity in the black market. A report from Dachau on May 27, 1945, asserted that there was "a belated avalanche" of food, "far surpassing the needs of the diminished camp population."[91] Bernard Novick, chief of police in the DPs camp Lichtenau-bei-Kessel (Hesse), recalled that he "went out and bought beef and butchered it and sold it in the DP camp. It was illegal all the way, but people had to eat. We used to get the UNRRA rations, which [consisted of] oatmeal and canned foods; and you get tired of that stuff. The first two weeks the camp food was a great thing. Then we couldn't eat. So we bought meat. Then, of course, we had access to Americans, more sources; so we found cigarettes; we found coffee. The Germans loved it; so we traded with them."[92]

A number of Jewish survivors found themselves with precious commodities upon their first encounter with American soldiers. Initially, it seemed that the GIs were willing to give away "whatever they had: cigarettes, chocolates, all kinds of canned food—sardines, corn beef, cheeses."[93] Oscar Lichtenstern, a survivor from the Netherlands, found that the conditions in Bamberg were appalling, but "in contrast, food allowances are good and plentiful and everyone even received cigars or cigarettes."[94] It also was possible for survivors to be both given food and paid for work;[95] sometimes this was the incentive for staying on.[96] Exploiting one's trade or expertise with the demands of the black market was common, as in Heidenheim-an-der-Brenz, north of Ulm, where "shoemakers, tailors, [and] butchers worked overtime" while "the black market was booming."[97]

Simon Sterling, a survivor from Szurowicz, Poland, traded in dresses and fur hats in Lemberg; the "black market" there was simply a "bazaar."[98] Immediately after the war, the Russian army had set him up brewing beer in Lopatin.[99] He ventured to the American zone upon hearing from other survivors that they had been treated "wonderfully," given food, drink, and good care. "The Americans," he was told, "gave us [food] to eat and the Americans gave us cigarettes and there's nothing better than the Americans. So we figured[,] let's go to the Americans."[100] He was not disappointed; he was resuscitated both psychologically and physically. Whereas he had gotten used to identifying himself as "a Greek," he was now told by a Yiddish-speaking American soldier that there was neither fear nor shame in calling himself a Jew. He recalled that after enjoying as much food, drink, and coffee as could be consumed, "we were so happy, you know, happy; we were like doped up in ourselves."[101]

When Sterling reached the Föhrenwald DP camp, he was given a position as "a kind of judge," one of three survivors placed in this role. Primarily, robbery cases were brought before him. The other two men had legal backgrounds as opposed to Sterling, who saw himself as "the easiest of them all. I always told them, try to look at it through his eyes.

Try to see what he did with his thoughts and reasons. I always wanted to let them go."[102] Other Jews showed similar understanding of their coreligionists who bent or broke the rules. At the Pocking DP camp, Fannie Stern Selig was in charge of "free food coupons" and was supposed to dispense them to the camp's one hundred yeshiva students. Other Jews, who were not studying, made themselves look like yeshiva *bochers* (boys, or boy students) and were not rebuffed. Selig "knew that they were getting more than they were entitled but she closed her eyes[,] for she felt that the young men needed more food."[103]

In the eyes of Jewish survivors, in addition to feeling compelled to act as they did, any sense of guilt for wrongdoing was balanced by their awareness that black marketeering was not an exclusively Jewish concern. Similarly, the American forces knew that non-Jews, whether East European or German, were active in the black market, although accusations of German wrongdoing were greeted more skeptically than charges against Jews and Poles.[104] Even American soldiers contributed to the atmosphere of lawlessness; Germans complained of theft and lewd behavior, and officials themselves thought that the troops' possession of bicycles and motorcycles were indicative of wanton pilfering.[105] "Polish tradesmen," one survivor wrote, "used to enter abandoned homes, loot or 'shnorrer' whatever they could lay their hands on, anything which would sell, such as clothes, blankets, dishes, furniture and, of course, food if they could find any. After looting these homes, they returned to Poland and transacted business."[106] It is not surprising that this view of marauding Poles bears great similarity to countless accusations against Jews except that most Jews lacked a home to return to. Some Jews also recognized that consistent with behavior in the ghettos and camps, Jews continued to "steal food from each other,"[107] that they were victimized by crime, not simply benefiting from it.

Many Jews had no choice but to participate in the black market because they found that Germans would sell them neither food nor clothing.[108] Certainly this was exacerbated because many Germans refused to comply with requests for foodstuffs. American forces were frustrated by German shopkeepers who turned away DPs with ration cards.[109] Moreover, the policies set by the occupying forces were sometimes quite slippery, such as this statement "regarding the ethics of handling confiscated goods": "Goods may properly be used by the individual who confiscates them, or given in return for something which can be used directly, but any officer or enlisted man guilty of selling confiscated goods for personal gain is liable to a general court martial."[110] This policy must have contributed to the kind of barter system that characterized the black market in Feldafing and other DP camps.[111]

There is little if any evidence that survivors saw the black market as a permanent solution to their problems or that any of them wished for their own children to follow this kind of livelihood. Indeed, the vast majority wanted desperately to immigrate to Palestine and the United States. From the perspective of the American and British occupying armies, the very attempt by Jews to flee to Palestine and even to immigrate to the United States and other Western countries was also perceived as a type of criminal behavior. By its very nature, then, the American Jewish Joint Distribution Committee was "illegal" in that it fabricated the backgrounds of refugees so as to facilitate their emigration.[112]

It is a savage irony than that Nazis were held accountable for only a fraction of their crimes, while a more genteel version of anti-Semitism in the postwar order nurtured the "crooked" taint of Jewry.[113] It was, indeed, a topsy-turvy world in which a Jew might be a policeman on the street among gentiles, and a previously fatal yellow star could grant one access to chocolate and cigarettes. Many Germans clung to the fiction that the decimated Jews somehow remained threatening. The Jewish DP was often imagined to be abusive of Christians; capable of disguising his Jewishness in order to control key positions in the postwar German order; responsible for radical communism; capable of dishonesty, intrigue, and even murder; careless with German property; responsible for psychologically burdening Germans; overfed and overhoused; sexually predatory in nature; without shame or modesty; politically unreliable; physically abusive; a smuggler; Russianized in his way of thinking; rich; and greedy. On a number of levels the fact of German and Jewish coexistence and cooperation is of greater importance than the prejudice and occasional flashpoints of violence. The stereotype of Jewish criminality, however, continued to inform and sometimes inflame the tumultuous immediate postwar period.

Notes

I wish to thank the following institutions that supported my research and writing for this project in invaluable ways between 1995 and 2005: the United States Holocaust Memorial Museum's Center for Advanced Holocaust Studies, especially its Fellowship and Summer Research Workshop Programs, Robert Ehrenreich, Director of the University Programs Division, and Paul Shapiro, Director of the Center; the University of Maryland–College Park, most especially its Department of History, the Joseph and Rebecca Meyerhoff Center for Jewish Studies, and professors James Harris and Marsha Rozenblit; the staff of the Department of Archives, Manuscripts & Museum Collections, at the Catholic University of America; the German Historical Institute and German-American Center for Visiting Scholars in Washington, D.C.; the Holocaust Educational Foundation; the Friedrich-Ebert-Stiftung; the Center for German and European Studies at the University of California–Berkeley; and the German Academic Exchange Service. I also thank my coauthor, Michael Berkowitz. The opinions expressed in this chapter are exclusively those of the author and are not to be construed as official statements of the United States Holocaust Memorial Museum.

1. Richard L. Rubenstein, *After Auschwitz: Radical Theology and Contemporary Judaism* (Indianapolis: Bobbs-Merrill, 1966), 48–52.
2. Ibid., 57.
3. For studies employing this perspective, see Atina Grossmann, *Jews, Germans, and Allies: Close Encounters in Occupied Germany* (Princeton, NJ: Princeton University Press, 2007); Eva Kolinsky, *After the Holocaust: Jewish Survivors in Germany after 1945* (London: Pimlico, 2004); Suzanne Brown-Fleming, *The Holocaust and Catholic Conscience: Cardinal Aloisius Muench and the Guilt Question in Germany* (Notre Dame, IN: University of Notre Dame Press, 2006); and Michael Berkowitz, *The Crime of My Very Existence: Nazism and the Myth of Jewish Criminality* (Berkeley: University of California Press, 2007).
4. Jeffrey Herf, *Divided Memory: The Nazi Past in the Two Germanies* (Cambridge: Harvard University Press, 1997), 204–5. See also Richard L. Merrit, *Democracy Imposed: U.S. Occupation Policy and the German Public, 1945–1949* (New Haven, CT: Yale University Press, 1995), 132–40.
5. See Werner Bergmann and Rainer Erb, *Anti-Semitism in Germany: The Post-Nazi Epoch since 1945*, translated from the German by Belinda Cooper and Allison Brown (New Brunswick, NJ: Transaction, 1997).
6. This position was created in the wake of the September 1945 Harrison Report, the report of an investigative committee set up by President Harry Truman and led by Earl G. Harrison, dean of the faculty of law at the University of Pennsylvania. The Harrison Report criticized treatment of Jewish DPs under U.S. control, "in concentration camps in large numbers under [U.S.] military guard instead of SS troops." As a result, Jewish DPs were recognized as a separate national category. Exclusively Jewish DP camps were created in the American zone, largely in Bavaria, Württemberg, and Northern Hesse. See Michael Brenner, "Displaced Persons," in *The Holocaust Encyclopedia*, edited by Walter Laqueur, 152–53 (New Haven, CT: Yale University Press, 2001).
7. Berkowitz, *The Crime of My Very Existence*, 195.
8. Memorandum titled "A Program to Deal with Anti-Semitism in Germany" from Rabbi Phillip S. Bernstein to General Joseph McNarney, commander in chief, USFET, July 16, 1947, folder 1, box 117, document 13, Records of the Office of the Adjutant General, General Correspondence & Other Records 1945–1949 (hereafter OAG-GC), Records of

the Executive Office (hereafter REO), National Archives and Records Administration, College Park, Maryland (hereafter NARA).

9. Letter from Anton Rupert Sittl, Munich, to Muench, Kronberg, January 21, 1948, Collection 37, box 128, folder 4, Cardinal Aloisius Muench Papers (hereafter Muench Papers), American Catholic University Archives, Washington, D.C. (hereafter ACUA).

10. Douglas Botting, *In the Ruins of the Reich* (London: Allen & Unwin, 2005), 300.

11. UNRRA statistics for September 1945 showed that of approximately 1.5 million uprooted European citizens remaining in Germany, Austria, or Italy, roughly 50,000 (3.6 percent) were Jewish. These 50,000 Jews who had survived the Holocaust came from all parts of Europe. See Michael Brenner, *After the Holocaust: Rebuilding Jewish Lives in Postwar Germany*, translated by Barbara Harshav (Princeton, NJ: Princeton University Press, 1997), 139.

12. UNRRA was one of three major international organizations engaged in welfare operations for DPs. The others were the International Refugee Organization and the American Jewish Joint Distribution Committee.

13. Yehuda Bauer, *Out of the Ashes: The Impact of American Jews on Post-Holocaust European Jewry* (New York: Pergamon, 1989), 45.

14. The standard work is Hagit Lavsky, *New Beginnings: Holocaust Survivors in Bergen-Belsen and the British Zone in Germany, 1945–1950* (Detroit: Wayne State University Press, 2002).

15. Located in military District V in Munich (activated by OMGUS on September 28, 1946), Landsberg, site of former barracks for the German Wehrmacht, became an exclusively Jewish DP camp in October 1945. Between mid-September 1945 and late July 1949, the number of Jewish camp residents fluctuated between 5,079 and 2,150. See Angelika Königseder and Juliane Wetzel, *Waiting for Hope: Jewish Displaced Persons in Post–World War II Germany*, translated from the German by John A. Broadwin (Evanston, IL: Northwestern University Press, 2001), 233.

16. Located in the military District V in Munich on the shores of the Starnbergersee, 35 kilometers southwest of Munich, Feldafing was the former site of Nationalpolitische Erziehungsanstalten (National Political Training Institutes, or Napola), a National Socialist training school for Nazi elite. Set up on May 1, 1945, to accommodate three thousand Hungarian Jewish women liberated at Tutzing on April 29, the camp also housed non-Jewish Russian, Polish, Hungarian, and Yugoslav former concentration camp inmates until August 1945. Between September 1945 and May 1951, Feldafing was an exclusively Jewish camp. From December 1951 until March 1953, the Feldafing camp was under German administration. See Königseder and Wetzel, *Waiting for Hope*, 225–26. See also Angelika Heider, "Das Lager für jüdische 'Displaced Persons' Feldafing in der amerikanischen Besatzungszone, 1945–1951" (Master's thesis, Technical University of Berlin, 1994).

17. Brenner, *After the Holocaust*, 135–37.

18. After May 15, Jewish DPs immigrated to Israel from Germany and Austria at the rate of four thousand per month. See "Interim Report of Advisor on Jewish Affairs," William Haber to Kenneth Royall, Army Secretary, October 28, 1948, folder 17 (H), box 8 (1948 A–Z), Classified General Correspondence of the Political Advisor (hereafter CGCPA), Office of the Political Advisor to Germany, Berlin (hereafter OPAG-B), Record group (hereafter RG) 84-State Department, NARA.

19. Brenner, *After the Holocaust*, 41.

20. See Albert Lindemann, *Esau's Tears: Modern Anti-Semitism and the Rise of the Jews* (Cambridge: Cambridge University Press, 1997); see also Alan Steinweis's review of *Esau's Tears* at www.h-net.org/reviews/show-rev.cgi?path=16305880493317.

21. Berkowitz, *Crime of My Very Existence*, 1–23.

22. Brenner, *After the Holocaust*, 94; letter from Father Rupp, Frankfurt-Zeilsheim, to Muench, Kronberg, April 19, 1948, Collection 37, box 128, folder 5, Muench Papers, ACUA.

23. Muench Diary entry, January 6, 1947, Vol. 5, p. 43, Series 1, box 1, folder 5, ACUA.

24. Memorandum from Major General W. A. Burress to Chief of Staff, Frankfurt, January 9, 1947, folder 6, box 117, document 10, OAG-GC, REO, RG 260, OMGUS, NARA.

25. Letter from Father Rupp to Bishop Dirichs, January 15, 1947, Collection 37, box 69, folder 6, Muench Papers, ACUA. Rupp sent the letter to Muench in Kronberg.

26. Ibid.

27. Bishop of the diocese of Fargo, North Dakota, at the time that Pope Pius XII (1939–58) appointed him papal visitor to Germany, Aloisius Muench would come to hold a number of high-level positions in Germany between 1946 and 1959. He remained Pope Pius XII's apostolic visitor to Germany until 1947, after which he was appointed Vatican relief officer seated in the suburb of Kronberg, near Frankfurt-am-Main (1947–49), Vatican regent in Kronberg (1949–51), and finally Vatican nuncio (papal diplomat and dean of the Diplomatic Corps) to Germany (1951–59), stationed at the nunciature in Bad Godesberg, a suburb of the Federal Republic's capital, Bonn. Cardinal Muench was also the U.S. National Catholic Welfare Conference's liaison representative to the U.S. Army in occupied Germany from the summer of 1946 until the end of occupation in 1949. See Brown-Fleming, *The Holocaust and Catholic Conscience*.

28. Letter from Father Rupp to Muench, November 24, 1948, Collection 37, box 128, folder 8, Muench Papers, ACUA.

29. Brenner, *After the Holocaust*, 13.

30. Letter from Father Brim, cosigned by sixteen Zeilsheim Catholics, to Muench, Kronberg, January 21, 1947, Collection 37, box 127, folder 9, Muench Papers, ACUA. This petition reflects German Catholic concern about the appeal of communism to the German working class if

living conditions did not improve.

31. Letter from Muench, Kronberg, to General Joseph T. McNarney, Berlin, January 15, 1947, Collectin 37, box 124, folder 3, Muench Papers, ACUA. According to Joseph Bendersky, McNarney was unsympathetic to Jewish DPs, urging President Truman to order all the DP camps closed with the exception of those for a small group of "persecuted" Jews, meaning the small percentage of Holocaust survivors identified as such during the summer of 1945. McNarney did not include the large numbers of Polish Jewish DPs fleeing westward after 1946. See Joseph W. Bendersky, *The Jewish Threat: Anti-Semitic Politics of the U.S. Army* (New York: Basic Books, 2001), 363.

32. Brenner, *After the Holocaust*, 94.

33. Letter from Rupp to Muench, November 24, 1948.

34. Memorandum titled "Zeilsheim" from Robert Deubel to Muench, Kronberg, July 4, 1949, Collection 37, box 128, folder 12, Muench Papers, ACUA.

35. War Diary, May 17, 1945, RG 09 Liberation .014*02, Malcolm A. Vendig papers relating to postliberation Dachau (hereafter Vendig Papers), United States Holocaust Memorial Museum Archives, Washington, D.C. (hereafter USHMM).

36. Daily records, France, June 18, 1944–July 16, 1944, Aug. '44 Record of Events, 4 Hrs., Record of Events, August 5, 1944, [time] 1530, Vendig Papers, USHMM.

37. Letter from Rupp to Muench, April 19, 1948, Collection 37, box 128, folder 5, Muench Papers, ACUA. The word "Mammon" is a common term in rabbinic literature denoting "money, goods, or wealth." In parts of the New Testament, "Mammon" is also personified as an "object of false devotion."

38. Letter from Rupp to Muench, April 19, 1948.

39. Greta Fischer papers (hereafter Fischer Papers) related to Kloster-Indersdorf displaced children's center and to UNRRA's postwar work in Europe, RG 19.034*01, p. 26, USHMM.

40. Letter from Sister Ant. Reifsmeier, Josefsheim, Bad Woerishofen, to Muench, Kronberg, June 20, 1947, Collection 37, box 37, folder 1, Muench Papers, ACUA.

41. Letter from Lieutenant General C. R. Huebner, Chief of Staff-USFET, to Muench, Kronberg, July 11, 1947, Collection 37, box 37, folder 1, Muench Papers, ACUA.

42. Letter from Robert Deubel to Muench, July 14, 1947, Collection 37, box 37, folder 1, Muench Papers, ACUA.

43. Philipp Auerbach, an Orthodox German Jew and a survivor of Auschwitz, Gross-Rosen, and Buchenwald, was Bavarian state commissioner for restitution and chair of the Association of Jewish Communities in Bavaria. He was among the most prominent leaders of German Jewry in the early postwar years. In January 1951 he became a member of the newly founded Central Council of Jews in Germany. Due to a

series of accusations including forgery and embezzlement (which Auerbach denied), German authorities arrested him a few months later. In August 1952 five German judges (three of whom had connections with the Nazi Party) sentenced Auerbach to two and a half years in prison and ordered him to pay a fine of twenty-seven hundred deutsche marks. That August, Auerbach committed suicide. See Brenner, *After the Holocaust*, 135–37.

44. Letter from Sister Fernanda Weip, Kneippianum, Bad Wörishofen, to Muench, Kronberg, July 20, 1947, Collection 37, box 37, folder 1, Muench Papers, ACUA. My emphasis.

45. Letter from Weip to Muench, August 3, 1947, Collection 37, box 37, folder 1, Muench Papers, ACUA.

46. "The Modern Wandering Jew," typescript copy of excerpt from Weekly Intelligence Report No. 35, pp. 1, 2, 3, USHMM. This appears to be taken from the Vincent La Vista report "Illegal Immigration Movements in and through Italy" to Herbert Cummings, May 15, 1947, RG 19.003*01, USHMM.

47. "The Modern Wandering Jew," 2.

48. Ibid., 4.

49. Ibid., 1.

50. Ibid., 1.

51. Ibid., 3.

52. Ibid.

53. "Vincent La Vista Report on illegal immigration in and through Italy," RG 19.003*01, May 15, 1947, pp. 9–10, USHMM.

54. Ibid., 2

55. Ibid., Appendix, 3.

56. "The Modern Wandering Jew," 2.

57. Ibid., 4.

58. Ibid., 2.

59. "UNRRA Aide Scents Jews' Exodus Plot; Morgan Charges Maneuver to Quit Europe, Doubts Pogroms; Statements; Protests," *New York Times*, January 3, 1946, 1, 2. Apparently the same reports that Morgan used were also the background for "The Modern Wandering Jew."

60. Abraham J. Klausner, *A Letter to My Children: From the Edge of the Holocaust* (San Francisco: Holocaust Center of Northern California, 2002), 23–24.

61. "Jews in U.S. Camps Held Ill-Treated: Military Government Men in Germany Are 'Incompetent,' Chaplain Declares," *New York Times*, November 22, 1945, clipping in item 2, box 1, Rabbi Philip S. Bernstein Collection, Advisor on Jewish Affairs, Rush Rhees Library, Rare Books, Special Collections & Preservation, University of Rochester, New York.

62. "Remove Patton from Germany," *New Republic* 113, no. 14 (October 1, 1945): 420.

63. Berkowitz, *The Crime of My Very Existence*, 197–219.

64. Ibid., 1–2.

65. Letter from Muench, Bad Godesberg, to Monsignor Paul Tanner, Washington, March 17, 1950, Collection 37, box 114, folder 6, Muench Papers, ACUA.

66. Letter from Bishop Albert Stohr, Mainz, to Captain Kenny, OMGUS-Wiesbaden, August 6, 1947, Collection 37, box 141, folder 3, Muench Papers, ACUA.

67. Daily Report, Group V, April 23, 1945, OMGUS Report, RG 09 Liberation .014*08, Vendig Papers, USHMM.

68. War Diary, May 6, 1945, RG 09 Liberation .014*02, Vendig Papers, USHMM.

69. Report of April 25, 1945, OMGUS Report, RG 09 Liberation .014*02, Vendig Papers, USHMM.

70. Report of April 24, 1945, OMGUS Report, RG 09 Liberation .014*08, Vendig Papers, USHMM.

71. Report of April 23, 1945, OMGUS Report, RG 09 Liberation .014*08, Vendig Papers, USHMM.

72. Daily Report, April 8, 1945, RG 09.014*08, Vendig Papers, USHMM.

73. "The Postwar Years; A Sequel to As I Remember," RG 02*143, p. 8, USHMM.

74. "Holocaust Survivor: A Mother Writes to Her Children," RG O2, file 030, p. 62, USHMM.

75. Michael Bernath, "Christians Revenge on the Jews," RG 02.096, p. 122, USHMM.

76. Fischer Papers, RG 19.034*01, p. 26, USHMM.

77. See Brenner, *After the Holocaust*, 90–95.

78. "Jonas Landau: Memoirs," RG 02.214, p. 41, USHMM.

79. Report of March 5, 1945, by Lt. Morse, RG 09.-14*06, Rough notes and rough transcript of April 1945 war diary, Vendig Papers, USHMM.

80. Daily Report, 0001–2400, April 2, 1945, RG 09.14*08, Vendig Papers, USHMM.

81. Helen Waren letter concerning displaced persons, RG 19.002*01, pp. 1–2, USHMM.

82. Ibid., 27.

83. UNRRA records relating to a riot in a displaced persons center in West Stuttgart, RG 19.030*01, report of incident at UNRRA DP center 502, March 29, 1946, by David Clearfield, USHMM; Joseph Levine, "My Work in Germany with Jewish Survivors of World War II," RG 19.020*01, p. 45, USHMM.

84. See Brenner, *After the Holocaust*, 53. See also Frank Stern, *The Whitewashing of the Yellow Badge: Antisemitism and Philosemitism in Postwar Germany*, translated from the Hebrew by William Templer (New York: Vidal Sassoon International Center for the Study of Antisemitism at the Hebrew University of Jerusalem, 1992).

85. Chief Justice Charles Evans Hughes founded the National Conference of Christians and Jews in 1928. With central offices in New York City, its purpose was to promote "justice, amity, understanding and cooperation among Protestants, Catholics and Jews." In 1947 Hughes founded the

International Council of Christians and Jews (ICCJ) with headquarters in Geneva, Switzerland. The president of the new ICCJ, Dr. Everett R. Clinchy, received Clay's blessing to go to Europe and set up local chapters of the ICCJ in the American zone. Letter from Everett R. Clinchy, New York, to General Lucius D. Clay, Berlin, August 16, 1947, box 117, folder 1, document 15 (AG 000.3 Religion), OAG-GC, REO, RG 260, OMGUS, NARA.

86. Memorandum titled "For Your Information" containing an excerpt from *Muenchner Merkur*, April 27, 1949, "Dr. Auerbach Attacks Scharnagl," Religious Affairs Branch (Miscellaneous), box 163, NARA.

87. The DPCC was officially recognized by the Americans as the authorized representative of Jewish DPs in the American zone and had offices in Munich's Deutsche Museum (German Museum).

88. He then called the DPCC a "state within a state" that supported Zionist party interests and created dissension among Jewish DPs. See report titled "The Position of the Jewish DPs" by State Commissioner Philipp Auerbach, June 23, 1947, box 6 (June–September 1947), folder 4 (no title), CCGPA, OPAG-B, RG 84-State Department, NARA.

89. William Eisen testimony, RG 02*136, p. 121, USHMM.

90. Jonas Landau: memoirs, RG 02.214, p. 45, USHMM.

91. War Diary, May 27, 1945, RG 09 Liberation .014*02, Vendig Papers, USHMM.

92. Memoir of Bernard Novick, in "Strangers in the Heartland," Survivor testimonies compiled by Donald M. Douglas, RG 02*142, p. 56, USHMM.

93. Sonja Haid Greene, "Between Life and Death (My Memoirs)," RG 02.112, p. 96, USHMM.

94. Oscar Lichtenstern, "My Struggle for Survival 1940/45," RG 02*118, p. 25, USHMM.

95. Diary: Fannie Stern Selig, RG 19.012*01, p. 30, USHMM.

96. "The Story of Two Sisters," RG 02*168, p. 43, USHMM.

97. "Jonas Landau: memoirs," RG 02.214, p. 46, USHMM.

98. "A Survivor's Story: Simon Sterling," RG 02*156, pp. 107–8, USHMM.

99. Ibid., 98.

100. Ibid., 112.

101. Ibid., 114.

102. Ibid., 128.

103. "The Story of Two Sisters," RG 02*168, p. 44, USHMM.

104. War Diary, May 23, 1945, Detachment Diary, June 14, 1945, Detachment Diary, June 20, 1945, RG 09 Liberation .014*02, Vendig Papers, USHMM; Report of January 15, 1945, by Lt. Morse, RG 09.-14*06, Rough notes and rough transcript of April 1945 war diary, Vendig Papers, USHMM.

105. War Diary, May 31, 1945, RG 09 Liberation .014*02, Vendig Papers, USHMM.

106. "The Story of Two Sisters," RG 02*168, p. 36, USHMM.

107. "Diary: Fannie Stern Selig," RG 19.012*01, p. 27, USHMM.

108. Helen Waren letter concerning displaced persons, RG 19.002*01, p. 9, USHMM; Daily Report, from 0001–2400, March 8, 1945, Oberkassel, Germany, RG 09.014*08, Vendig Papers, USHMM.

109. War Diary, May 18, 1945, RG 09 Liberation .014*02, Vendig Papers, USHMM.

110. War Diary, May 7, 1945, RG 09 Liberation .014*02, Vendig Papers, USHMM.

111. Erwin Tichauer, *Totenkopf und Zebrakleid: Ein Berliner Jude in Auschwitz* (Berlin: Metropol, 2000); Records relating to Joseph Levine and his work at the Regensberg displaced persons camp, RG 19.020*01, "Life in Regensburg," p. 1, USHMM.

112. Vincent La Vista report on illegal immigration in and through Italy, RG 19.003*01, May 15, 1947, pp. 5–6, USHMM.

113. War Diary, June 2, 1945, RG 09 Liberation .014*02, Vendig Papers, USHMM.

The Reshaping of Jewish Communities and Identities in Frankfurt and Zeilsheim in 1945

LAURA J. HILTON

INTRODUCTION

Amid chaotic conditions in immediate postwar Germany, Jews in the city of Frankfurt-am-Main and the camp for displaced persons (DPs) at Zeilsheim rebuilt community life and struggled to define their place in the postwar world. But their actions were circumscribed by the boundaries established by the military occupation, the international debate over Palestine, and the reality of the ravages of the Holocaust on their physical and mental well-being. Despite these obstacles, Jews in postwar Germany worked immediately to rebuild community organizations, re-create their identities, and influence policy development, clearly demonstrating that besides victims they were also survivors.

Temporally, many DP studies move through 1945 quickly, eager perhaps to deal with the years when the number of Jewish DPs in Germany swelled to more than 250,000. Yet this year was very important in several respects. First, Jews in Germany wielded political agency very quickly in the postwar period. They influenced three key policy decisions that directly affected the development of their community and its identity: classification as Jews, inclusion in local decision making, and the establishment of separate Jewish camps. The military's initial refusals to recognize Jews as a nationality and to provide camps solely for them acted as a catalyst for a growing sense of community and support for Zionism, particularly among DPs. Occupation authorities built on the lessons learned from the aftermath of the Harrison Report in ongoing policy discussions and decisions. An early example of this was the outcry in December 1945 when the United States suggested measures to stem the flow of Jews from Eastern Europe into its zone of occupation and to house them in separate camps. Within several days this was shelved, and the refusal to admit additional movement of Jews into the U.S. zone was not implemented until April 1947.

Second, during 1945 the dominant perception of Jews as helpless victims shifted. Jews were also survivors, perhaps best indicated by their identification as the She'erit Hapletah (Surviving Remnant).[1] As survivors, they were a problem with no easy solution for the military and their partner, United Nations Relief and Rehabilitation Administration (UNRRA). Many of the tactical troops who had liberated the camps were demobilized or redeployed. The later waves of American soldiers who entered Germany had an increasingly negative perception of Jews and an increasingly positive viewpoint of Germans, setting the stage for future tension. UNRRA, with its mandate to assist repatriation, had limited sympathy and few resources for a population determined to remain in camps, rejecting return to their prewar homelands.

Third, Jews in 1945 Germany implemented the Yiddish phrase *mir zaynen doh* (we are here).[2] This phrase had multiple meanings. It was a call to resist the Nazi attempt to annihilate the Jewish people. It was also a password in the Zionist struggle for a Jewish homeland. Most importantly in the postwar period, it served as a symbol of strong conviction that those who died in the Holocaust did not die in vain, that the world would learn from this experience. During the immediate postwar period, Jews in Germany created political, religious, cultural, and educational institutions to foster a sense of community, a visible and public reminder of their presence. For DPs, this community building served to strengthen support for Zionism, which sustained them until mass resettlement began in 1948. Rebuilding was different for German Jews as they focused on the painful process of reestablishing their lives and communities within Germany.

Despite the recent growth in scholarship about DPs, geographic and temporal weaknesses remain. Geographically, this chapter focuses on the Jewish communities of Frankfurt and Zeilsheim, both of which lay in Hesse in the U.S. zone. Focused studies of the Jewish community of Frankfurt-am-Main and the DP camp at Zeilsheim provide starting points for examining the re-creation of Jewish life on German soil. Despite their unique position in the postwar period, these two communities and Hesse have been understudied within DP literature. Hesse was the only one of the three states in the U.S. zone of occupation that shared borders with all three other zones of occupation (British, Soviet, and French). It was a massive transit area, as Jewish DPs traveled searching for relatives and also traveled from the other zones as they became much less desirable places to live. In addition, Frankfurt offers not only a specialized local study for the reintegration of Jews into urban German life but also an interesting microcosm of the relations among the U.S. occupation forces, Jewish DPs, and the local German population, given Frankfurt's status as military headquarters. Zeilsheim is likewise important to examine since it was one of the largest Jewish DP camps outside of Bavaria and was one of the few camps where occupation forces requisitioned hundreds of small private homes and farms from the local population.[3]

Liberation and Material Conditions

Within the U.S. zone, the military initially found only about thirty thousand Jewish survivors, many of them weak from years of malnutrition and slave labor, exacerbated by the death marches during the final months of the war. The troops who liberated concentration camps in the spring of 1945 described the inhabitants as walking skeletons, with sunken chests and feverish eyes and clinging to life by a slim thread. These survivors were extremely malnourished, were often plagued with contagious diseases such as typhus, and were struggling mentally and emotionally to cope with the enormity of their losses both individually and collectively. Unlike other DPs, many of whom were repatriated during the summer of 1945, they almost overwhelmingly had nothing to which they could return. Family, homes, businesses, and personal possessions had all been brutally taken from them.[4]

The situation in which they found themselves was incredibly unstable. The internal economy was on the verge of collapse. Shortages of food, coal, and adequate housing were acute. More than one hundred major urban areas lay in ruins, the communication systems were devastated, and only about 10 percent of the railway network remained intact. In addition, damage to utilities was widespread, and the materials to rebuild them were in short supply. Food shortages, due to lack of adequate seeds and fertilizer and the loss of the agriculturally rich eastern states, were extreme.[5] Within its western zones, four hundred million cubic meters of rubble needed to be cleared away, 10 percent of which lay within Hesse.[6] In Frankfurt, streetcars did not operate until June, and electrical and gas lines took months to repair.[7] Given the intense bombing campaigns, many residents of Frankfurt lived in cellars or partially destroyed apartments and made daily trips to the few still-working hand pumps to bring water back to their homes.[8] As one American soldier described, "Frankfurt itself is another of those complete wrecks. It's a pile of bathtubs, mud, bricks, radiators, timber and roofless buildings. It's wrecked in the downtown area, the residential area, the slums, industrial area—everything."[9]

Yet within weeks of liberation, despite all the material and psychological hardships, Jews who continued to survive took action to protect what remained. They battled with occupation authorities to recognize "Jewish" as a legitimate nationality and to establish separate camps for Jews. The military initially rejected both of these demands, since such recognition had an implicit connection to the contentious issue of a Jewish homeland in Palestine.

POLICY DEVELOPMENT: REPATRIATION, STATELESSNESS, AND THE ISSUE OF JEWISH NATIONALITY

Given the sheer numbers of DPs and the serious shortages of material provisions, the main goal of occupation authorities in the spring and early summer of 1945 was to quickly repatriate them. By July 31, 1945, 4.1 million of the 6.4 million DPs located in the western zones were back in their homelands. As this process continued, the existence of 70,000 DPs who had not been classified by nationality became more visible. At least 20,000 of the 70,000 were Jews who claimed statelessness as their status.[10] Many took this drastic action expecting that this curious existence of having no officially recognized nationality would not persist.[11]

The concept of statelessness proved to be complicated on multiple levels. Despite earlier memos urging consideration of this very problem, as of September 1945 no clear UNRRA or military occupation policy existed for the long-term care of stateless DPs.[12] Both institutions defined stateless loosely as "the status of persons as to whom no government acknowledges the existence of that bundle of reciprocal rights and duties called citizenship."[13] Since statelessness was a relatively new concept, neither institution knew how to approach it. On a practical level, it meant both the lack of internationally accepted travel documents and a government to protect rights for those who claimed this status.[14]

As repatriation continued, leaving behind those who refused it, the Jewish presence became more visible. By November 1945 the American Joint Jewish Distribution Committee (JDC) estimated that ninety thousand Jews existed in Germany, only ten thousand of whom were native Germans. Of the eighty thousand nonnative Jews, an estimated seventy-two thousand rejected repatriation.[15] Yet occupational officials continued to steadfastly oppose acknowledging "Jewish" as a national classification. The military had an approved list of nationalities and geographic entities by which DP camps were organized in order to facilitate repatriation; "Jewish" was not on it.[16] Therefore, Jews who came from Poland were considered Polish and were placed in camps with other Polish DPs, a potentially dangerous situation. As Arno Lustiger explains, "In the camp, we were supposed to sleep under the same roof with these murderers—sometimes they were even worse than the Germans."[17]

This refusal to recognize Jews as a separate nationality was directly linked to the issue of whether a Jewish liaison officer should be attached to the Office of Military Government, United States (OMGUS), in Germany. Early military planning had built liaison officers into the control, care, and repatriation of DPs.[18] In June 1945 American Jewish voluntary agencies made the first call for Jewish liaison officers. A letter from the American Jewish Conference (AJC) to the secretary of war explained: "No doubt the military authorities are doing everything possible to assist the Jews in Germany. However, their needs are of such a nature that those who care for them must have an intimate knowledge of Jewish life in Europe and of its religious, traditional and cultural background."[19] UNRRA also refused to appoint Jewish liaison officers.[20]

Despite being rebuffed, influential American Jews such as Rabbi Stephen Wise continued to press General Dwight D. Eisenhower for separate camps because the needs of Jewish DPs were being neglected and their classification by their prewar nationalities was placing them in harm's way.[21] Eisenhower's reply was blunt: "This Headquarters does not agree that the assignment here of a Liaison Officer for Jewish displaced persons would materially assist such persons and regrets that it cannot accept the proposal. Liaison Officers attached to this Headquarters are selected on nationality basis and it is considerably undesirable on many grounds to have one specially designated for Jews."[22] "Jewish" was not an acceptable nationality; therefore, liaison officers were not deemed necessary.

These two related issues galvanized Jews within Germany into action. They organized a gathering in July 1945 with the assistance of the Jewish Brigade,[23] and this gathering became the basis of Jewish political organization in the U.S. zone. Delegates at this first meeting of the Central Conference of Liberated Jews (CCLJ) voiced fierce opposition to repatriation and a strong desire for resettlement.[24] Leib

Laura J. Hilton

Pinkusewitz, the representative for Frankfurt, stated that DPs had enacted positive changes in terms of food and housing. But they desired more than material needs; they wanted a homeland. "We have no intentions whatever to remain in Germany. All other nations are removing their sons from Germany, giving them a home in their own fatherland. Whither are we to go? The countries we came from do not spell home to us. There our dearest ones were butchered. Our only way leads to Eretz Israel. Not until we come to Eretz Israel will our life have any meaning."[25] The conference culminated with the representatives issuing a series of fourteen resolutions including demanding the immediate establishment of a Jewish homeland, recognition as a member of the United Nations (UN), and unity among survivors.[26]

The quick establishment of the CCLJ demonstrated that Jews were actively engaged in shaping their future and in building a sense of unity as a people. The foundation of this unity was their shared experience of the Holocaust regardless of their national, ethnic, or religious background. They had all been targeted as Jews, and as Jews they sought to rebuild their communities, to explain to the world what had transpired, and to ensure that the world never forgot.[27] Although Zionism was an important component of this unity,[28] it was not the core of identity for all Jewish DPs. For instance, Orthodox Jews had a considerable presence in DP camps, as did other forms of Judaism.[29] Yet many DPs supported Zionism in a general sense as a necessary step to preserve Jewish life and community in this postwar world.[30] Although many Jewish DPs in Germany wanted to present a strong, coherent, unified identity to the rest of the world, political, religious, social, and cultural tensions lay under the surface.[31]

Just two months after liberation, Jewish DPs had the political means to protect their community and the will and unity to create a sense of Jewish identity and community.[32] They also demonstrated their ability to work with American voluntary agencies to influence policy development, most notably by the pressure they placed on President Harry S. Truman to respond to their difficult situation and the aftermath of the Harrison Report.

THE HARRISON REPORT AND ITS IMPACT: PALESTINE, SEPARATE CAMPS, AND THE ADVISER ON JEWISH AFFAIRS

The months of August and September 1945 were the turning point in the development of Jewish policy. A flood of letters and reports from prominent American Jews, Jewish voluntary agencies, and Jews in Germany asked President Truman to improve living conditions and to appoint liaison officers to help Jews resettle and to provide legal assistance. In response, Truman sent Earl Harrison to Germany. Harrison's report, received by Truman in late August, harshly critiqued the conditions within Jewish DP camps. The report stated that Jews lived behind barbed wire, still wore concentration camp uniforms, and remained isolated from the world. Harrison focused on the lack of rehabilitation and resettlement programs and stated that the solution to the problem was the opening of immigration to Palestine.[33] As a result, Truman ordered Eisenhower to enforce U.S. Army policies protecting and providing for Jewish DPs on all levels.[34]

The powerful impact of the Harrison Report focused attention on resettlement and Palestine. After Truman read Harrison's full report, he sent a letter to Clement Attlee, the British prime minister, requesting that Britain issue to Jewish DPs in Germany and Austria one hundred thousand visas for travel to Palestine. Truman believed that this measure was a short-term solution and that the division of land (part of the long-term solution) could be dealt with by the UN. In response, Attlee asserted that the situation of Jewish DPs was not necessarily connected to the issue of Palestine and refused to increase the number of visas issued.[35] At this stalemate, Truman proposed an Anglo-American Committee of Inquiry to survey the Jewish DPs and make policy suggestions.[36]

The U.S. military responded immediately to the report by issuing a directive concerning Jewish treatment. It reaffirmed that no person of Jewish faith would be repatriated against his or her wishes, provided for the establishment of exclusively Jewish camps, and mandated that "wherever necessary, suitable accommodation will be requisitioned from the German population."[37] The directive emphasized that tactical troops and OMGUS must give Jewish DPs and persecutees priority in terms of material needs. Although the army still would not recognize "Jewish" as a nationality, they did establish exclusively Jewish camps, such as Zeilsheim. Several of the resolutions passed by the CCLJ in July had already come to fruition.

The Harrison Report also resulted in the establishment of a new position, the special adviser on Jewish affairs, attached directly to headquarters, as a compromise on the issue of liaison officers. To avoid elevating "Jewish" to the status of a recognized nationality, the military appointed Judge Simon Rifkind as the first special adviser on Jewish affairs in early October 1945.[38] During his tenure, Rifkind served as an advocate for Jews in Germany and became the focal point for lobbying by Jewish voluntary agencies and the CCLJ within Germany, particularly during the negotiations concerning infiltrees.

Laura J. Hilton

The United States made one final major policy decision in 1945, namely whether to stop the westward flow of Jews into their occupation zone from Eastern Europe. Infiltrees were mainly Jews who had either returned to Eastern Europe following liberation or survivors who were in territory held by the Soviet Union at war's end. Given the hostility and violence toward Jews across Eastern Europe, ironically Germany seemed a safer temporary haven; therefore, beginning in December 1945, infiltrees began to move en masse into the U.S. zones of Germany and Austria. These new arrivals caused considerable concern amid the military, UNRRA, and voluntary agencies by stretching already thin resources in the middle of winter. Initially, the military called for an investigation and recommended that the infiltration be stopped immediately.[39] However, military authorities were at a loss as to how the infiltrees already within the zones should be handled. As a stopgap measure, they issued this directive:

> Jews recently infiltrating into US Zone will be temporarily cared for in segregated installations separate from United Nations Displaced Persons Camps or Jewish Centers for Persecutees who are military responsibility. They will be given reasonable care pending establishment of firm policy. United Nations Displaced Persons who were willingly repatriated in the past and who have again infiltrated into US Zone will not be accorded United Nations Displaced Persons' status or treatment.[40]

This directive caused outrage among Jewish DPs and Jewish voluntary agencies.[41] Their lobbying pushed the United States to reverse this directive less than three weeks later. On December 28 military authorities declared that "a displaced person has a right to UNRRA assistance, and this right is not lost by reason of an unsuccessful attempt at repatriation." In addition, Jewish postwar refugees were entitled to UNRRA assistance because "if their internal displacement (i.e. displacement from their homes) occurred during the war it is immaterial that their external displacement (i.e. displacement across national frontiers) only occurred post-war."[42] Despite fierce British criticism of this policy, the United States did not want to risk the negative publicity that would have accompanied banning Jewish refugees from entering its zone.[43]

Underneath the policy layer, complex relationships were developing among DPs and outside observers, such as military personnel and workers for UNRRA and voluntary agencies. Despite the ingenuity demonstrated by DPs in shaping policy and in rebuilding community life, most outside observers still saw DPs primarily as victims who needed assistance to make their lives normal and needed to escape the behaviors that had been necessary for survival. As Oscar Mintzer, JDC worker, stated, "They have lived and been treated as animals, and much of the animal is in them now. Many of them are dirty, even filthy. Their moral standards are shot to hell. They connive, and finagle, and contrive—all the time. They lie and cheat and steal. They had to do this under the Nazis to remain alive, and our crazy red tape and regulations, particularly Army and UNRRA, are making them continue this in order to survive."[44] UNRRA workers expressed similar perception of the DPs and their behavior: "The camp atmosphere constantly calls forth reactions similar to those they made in their former period of subjugation. . . . When there is overcrowding, lack of clothing and food in camps, these people are reminded of the previous deprivations of their physical necessities."[45] A UNRRA worker and psychiatrist who worked with Jewish youths in the DP camp at Föhrenwald observed that feelings of isolation, depression, and loneliness were very common, as was strong hostility toward attempts to control their behavior.[46] Each of these observations demonstrates that many of the perceptions of the Jewish DPs were negative, rooted more in their victimization at the hands of the Nazis and their collaborators than in their survival.[47]

While many of these workers comprehended, at least on a superficial level, what Jews had endured during the Holocaust, they were impatient for the survivors to heal and lacked understanding of psychological effects of displacement and their typical coping mechanisms. One psychologist believed that people who had been displaced shared certain characteristics: separation from family and community, fear of the destruction and bombing of society, and uncertainty about what the future held. In his opinion, these characteristics led to, in general, regression from adult to less mature behavior.[48] Yet the establishment of political institutions, cultural and religious organizations, and educational facilities within months after liberation indicates another explanation. While some DPs were seriously mentally and emotionally scarred by their wartime experiences and in some cases retreated from the world, other DPs worked quickly to rebuild their communities and desired the respect of their fellow human beings, not their pity.[49]

Even so, often these early efforts at rebuilding themselves and their communities were not known or recognized by outsiders. Ralph Segalman stated in his psychological analysis of DPs that a year after liberation, all Jewish DPs remained in crowded barracks with no recreational, vocational, or educational opportunities. He also charged that items that instilled personal pride, such as eating and writing utensils, books, and musical instruments, were nonexistent in the camps. Segalman criticized the lack of leadership among the camp population, claiming that the only individuals who rose to the occasion were ex-partisans or members of the Jewish Brigade.[50] Essentially, Segalman drew incorrect conclusions based on faulty and overgeneralized evidence. These false assumptions led to a reinforcement of a negative view of Jewish DPs solely as victims, almost beyond the pale of human assistance.

Another dimension to the perception of DPs is the comparisons that Allied troops made between the DPs and the native German population, which typically placed the Germans in a much more favorable light. A compelling explanation for this ongoing disconnect was provided by Captain C. E. Jack of DP Detachment Eight. His report delineated several key factors that explain why GIs viewed Germans more favorably. First, Germans looked and acted closer to "civilized" beings. Jack believed that the overall appearance of the Germans tended to be better than that of the DPs. In addition, the image of DPs living in crowded, often unsanitary camps contrasted sharply with Germans living in private homes. For U.S. soldiers, often young and away from home for the first time, Germans represented that which they missed. A study commissioned by the U.S. War Department traced the shifting attitudes of American soldiers toward the Germans. For example, in April 1945, 20 percent of American soldiers stated that they had strong hatred of German civilians; by August 1945, this number had dropped to 10 percent.[51] This evidence of their shifting, more positive attitude toward the Germans reinforces Jack's analysis. The second major factor raised by Jack was that few DPs could speak English or German well. When the military conducted interviews with DPs who did not speak English, very often either the interpreters were Germans or the DPs were unable to make themselves clearly understood. The lack of communication ability placed DPs at a disadvantage and reinforced the military's negative perception of them. Jack believed that American military personnel had quickly forgotten the Germans' inhumane treatment of the DPs.[52]

This last point requires additional clarification, as it set the tone for Jewish DP life in Germany for several years to come. The original combat troops who had liberated the DPs from inhumane conditions and who had seen the walking skeletons tended to be more considerate and understanding of their situation. The few American occupation officials who understood the persecution endured by Jewish DPs were unable to change attitudes within the military on their own.[53] One DP noted the change in how he and other DPs were treated by new troops in comparison to his liberators at Dachau, who had treated them with generosity and sympathy. He believed that the newer troops had little comprehension of the overwhelming destruction wrought by the Third Reich, particularly on Jews and slave laborers, and that only those of first-generation American status who encountered DPs of their own ethnic or religious background were likely to demonstrate understanding of their needs.[54]

EARLY RECONSTRUCTION OF JEWISH LIFE IN FRANKFURT

When U.S. troops entered Frankfurt in late March 1945, they initially found a tiny Jewish community of 106 persons among the rubble. By the time Sergeant Joseph W. Eaton arrived in April 1945, 162 people in Frankfurt had identified themselves as Jews, 56 of whom survived the war in hiding. Eaton identified an immediate problem: their uncertain legal status. Most of them were German in national origin, and the tactical troops were treating them as ex-enemies and not as persecutees despite clear directives to the contrary. He forwarded his observations to Rabbi Judah Nadich, who then included them in a larger report to the World Jewish Congress (WJC).[55] The information provided by Eaton and Nadich then prompted Arieh Tartakower to raise this issue directly with the War Department. He strongly recommended that the army must classify all Jews, regardless of national origin, as persecutees in accordance with its stated policy.[56] This designation would assure all Jews in Germany of material aid from and legal protection by UNRRA (regardless if they lived within or outside of the assembly centers) and would entitle them to a higher daily food ration than that of the German civilian population (2,500 calories per day versus 1,300). This information chain demonstrates not only the importance of actions by members of the U.S. military but also how experiences on the ground helped to shape larger policy decisions.

Individual initiative during this crucial period proved to have a positive impact on this tiny Jewish community. Eaton continued to interact with the growing Jewish community of Frankfurt, which by June 1945 totaled 300 persons. This stood in stark contrast to its size

Laura J. Hilton

prior to the beginning of the Third Reich; in 1933, Frankfurt was the second-largest Jewish community in Germany.[57] In order to ascertain their nationalities and their needs, he conducted interviews with several members of the community. He discovered that 100 were of Polish origin, 150 were German Jews of mixed marriages who had previously lived in Frankfurt, and 50 were stateless Jews who had been transported from the Theresienstadt Ghetto to Frankfurt.[58] This was a pattern replicated in many other former centers of Jewish life in Germany whereby native Jews, some of whom had not identified themselves previously as Jews, were often outnumbered by foreign Jews, particularly from Eastern Europe.[59] He also interviewed Dr. August Adelsberger, who had been appointed as a member of the civilian advisory council to represent Jewish interests by the ranking OMGUS officer in Frankfurt, Lt. Colonel Howard Criswell. Criswell believed that this was necessary to ensure that the requests of the Jews for food, shelter, and assistance were heard by the *Bürgermeister*, Wilhelm Hollbach, and the short-lived city council, but he acted of his own accord. No military directive mandated that local government structures include a representative of the Jewish community.[60] According to Eaton and Adelsberger, this representation was successful in that the DPs received additional food rations.[61] In this instance, a directive—based on common sense rather than precedent and issued by one individual within the OMGUS structure—offered supplemental material assistance to the Jewish community of Frankfurt.

Although this illustrates the cooperation that could exist between OMGUS and the survivors of the Holocaust, relations between OMGUS and the Jews of Frankfurt remained strained concerning both housing and negative perceptions of Jews. Initially Jews in Frankfurt were housed in several hotels and dwellings seized by the military from supporters of National Socialism.[62] But as additional OMGUS personnel arrived on May 1, they requisitioned this housing for their own use. They did assure the Jews that they would be allowed to return to the area on June 1. However, by that date OMGUS personnel had changed, and the new personnel told the returning Jews that they could not collect their belongings. In addition, since building materials were so scarce, their requests for replacement housing were denied. This illustrates the difficulty that Jews had with shifting OMGUS personnel and unwillingness to enforce directives that placed housing DPs at a higher priority than the needs of the local German population.

Although Criswell, the initial OMGUS commander in Frankfurt, made accommodations for meeting the needs of Jews, his successors were less concerned. In fact, the civilian advisory council of Frankfurt seemed at times more willing than OMGUS to accommodate the needs of their Jewish residents. In one instance, they offered trucks and gasoline to retrieve five hundred deportees from Thereseinstadt, but OMGUS refused to issue the necessary travel documents. In addition, when former active Nazis returned to Frankfurt, the city advisory council was willing to evict them from their property but could not secure the obligatory OMGUS permission to requisition the structures. Frustrated, Eaton noted that "many realize that most of these happenings are understandable, as the complex conditions of war in Germany do not allow an immediate satisfactory solution of all individual problems. But there seems to be a general reproach that the Americans make too little effort to distinguish clearly between Germans, and especially Nazis, and those who have been their enemies and victims."[63] This inability or unwillingness to address issues on community or individual levels complicated Jewish–U.S. Army relations for the entire occupation period.[64]

At the heart of these problems lay acute shortages, particularly that of available safe, clean housing. Most tactical units and OMGUS officials were reluctant to requisition housing from the Germans despite overcrowded and unsanitary living conditions for Jews. Although OMGUS had issued clear directives that mandated such requisitioning, in August 1945 the local German population had much better living conditions than those of Jews.[65] The issue of assigning German housing to DPs was very prickly. Officials were cautioned to "use discretion in assigning German billets to DPs."[66] An uneasy stability existed between U.S. troops and the Germans, and army officials usually were not willing to risk antagonizing them to obtain better housing conditions for Jews.

Despite the obstacles placed in their path, the Jews living in Frankfurt began to reestablish their community as their ranks gradually increased. By September 1945 more than one thousand Jews lived in Frankfurt.[67] A committee of Jewish citizens, including Adelsberger, acted as a liaison between DPs and both OMGUS and the city council, encouraged attendance at religious services, published a newspaper, and organized classes in Hebrew. According to one DP, another main task was to assist survivors in the search for family members and to establish a distribution system for supplies from the JDC. Already by May 5, 1945, religious services began to be held on a regular basis at the synagogue in Baumweg 5–7 where the committee's offices were located.[68] In addition, the Westend synagogue, which was one of the few to partially escape the fury and destruction of Kristallnacht (The Night of Broken Glass), was opened after repairs.[69] For the native Jews in Frankfurt, these were efforts to rebuild their *Gemeinde* (commu-

Laura J. Hilton

nity) and to ensure that the Jewish presence in Germany persisted, contrary to the goals of the Third Reich.[70] But pressure was building from another contingent, those who believed that it was necessary to establish a Jewish homeland in Palestine. In order to provide agricultural training for them, the Jewish committee, with the assistance of OMGUS, obtained a number of small cottages and land in the Taunus suburb of Frankfurt. Despite the importance of these institutions in reinforcing a sense of unity, it was seen as a temporary living situation by many, particularly nonnative Jews, and serious dissatisfaction with their inability to emigrate was widespread.[71]

Since allocation of food was based on one's nationality or classification as a DP, the issue of uncertain persecutee status continued to be of serious concern for German Jews in Frankfurt.[72] Adelsberger persisted in lobbying OMGUS to clarify the status of German Jews.[73] However, the military, in many instances, did not understand or make the effort to understand their circumstances. This is evidenced by Dr. Adelsberger's observation to the WJC: "True, they had been freed, to live without fear of persecution, but they were no better off than the other Germans. In fact, they were in principle even worse off." He explained these Jews were persecuted for twelve years in the most inhumane way by their fellow Germans, and thus it was even more important that they receive additional rations. It was as if they were deprived doubly, once at the hands of the Third Reich and then at the hands of the occupation forces. Adelsberger made contact in Frankfurt with representatives of both UNRRA and the JDC, but the established pattern of treating German Jews as ex-enemies initially prevented them from rendering assistance.[74] The Jewish Council also contacted the city council of Frankfurt in an attempt to settle the issue. The request asked that all Jews, regardless of whether they were religious or whether they belonged to a Jewish *Gemeinde,* be considered as persecutees.[75] However, until the aftermath of the Harrison Report, the army's implementation of policy still remained unchanged.

Once again, information gathered firsthand proved crucial in highlighting policy inconsistencies. Adelsberger's report prompted Leon Kubowitzki, secretary general of the WJC, to write to John J. McCloy, the undersecretary of war. Kubowitzki noted that according to Supreme Headquarters Allied Expeditionary Force (SHAEF) regulations, all Jews should be treated as persecutees regardless of current or previous nationality.[76] The Combined Displaced Persons Executive (CDPX) sent out a general message to all theater chaplains regarding the status of German Jews. "This . . . does not mean that German Jews are not to be regarded as Germans. It does mean that certain classes of Germans will be given the same assistance granted to United Nations displaced persons."[77] But this enforcement targeted only army chaplains until the firestorm unleashed by the Harrison Report.

Occupation personnel who conducted evaluations of the Jewish community in Frankfurt were pessimistic regarding its future. Rabbi Robert Marcus, a U.S. Army chaplain, wrote that although elections were recently conducted and officers for a Jewish Council were chosen, discord among members of the committee existed. In fact, they had asked Marcus to mediate several of their disagreements, which stemmed from conflicts between German Jews and East European Jews. Marcus was of the opinion that the caliber of leadership among the DPs was only average.[78] Eaton noted that almost all of the surviving German Jews were not "full Jews"—that is, they were married to Christian Germans or were children of mixed marriages—implying that their efforts to rebuild were problematic. He claimed that upon liberation Polish, Hungarian, Russian, and Lithuanian Jews were refused assistance by the Frankfurt committee, and consequently they ended up in nationality-based camps and were often mistreated. "Luckily, I met a couple of these Jews and through them met about 150 of them or a little more, went to work and got them jobs with the American Army and thus solved the problem of the Jewish D.P.'s in Frankfurt."[79] His judgment is interesting, as it indicates how little comprehension most military personnel had of the short- and long-term problems facing Jews in postwar Germany.

Samuel Schmidt, a representative of Vaad Hatzala, provided another view of the Frankfurt community. Upon arriving in August 1945, he was pleasantly surprised to find that newspapers contained notices of where German Jews returning home should register and that religious services were being held regularly. Accustomed to reading of the horrors suffered by European Jews, he expected to find a broken and hopeless people. Instead, he found a strong community that was in the process of rebuilding. However, he attributed the vitality of Jewish life in Frankfurt not to the survivors themselves but rather to U.S. Army private Philip Tulipan. According to Schmidt, Tulipan had secured housing, jobs, and food for the community.[80] Schmidt's stereotypes were not confirmed, and yet he held on to them, namely by attributing the vitality of the Jewish community in Frankfurt to an army private rather than to the Jewish Council or the Jews themselves. Certainly the work of Tulipan was instrumental in assisting the community's acquisition of goods, housing, and services, but the Jews then did the rest on their own.

As their numbers swelled, the Jewish community in Frankfurt found it increasingly difficult to provide sufficient material assistance and housing. In addition, as the native population was overwhelmingly outnumbered by nonnative Jews, tensions between the two groups increased, particularly over planning for the future. Some Zionists criticized native Jews who wished to rebuild in Germany. By August 1945, the number of Jews within Frankfurt and the surrounding environs rose to at least seven thousand, forcing authorities to devise at least a temporary solution to the housing problem. According to Schmidt, Tulipan secured houses consisting of workers' barracks from the IG Farben plant, located eleven miles west of Frankfurt in Zeilsheim. However, the elected committee refused at first to move to the requisitioned housing. Schmidt stated that "With the help of the Creator, I managed to liquidate the strife peacefully and the elected Committee took over the administration and all survivors went to the new home in Zeilsheim. By that time, UNRRA had come in with a Jewish team to help out."[81]

Schmidt's explanation fails to mention that while many of the non-German Jews chose to move into Zeilsheim, most of the German Jews remained in Frankfurt. Material conditions in the city had improved slightly. According to Oscar Mintzer, a member of the JDC, by late October 1945 rubble still lay everywhere, but trolleys were beginning to run, and some electricity had been restored.[82] The Jewish community in Frankfurt dropped back down to 320 people by December 1945. Their living conditions were adequate but crowded, and the Frankfurt Jewish Committee continued to care for their needs.[83] As the vast majority of Jews in the area sought care in Zeilsheim or in one of the large Jewish camps in Bavaria, the Jewish community within Frankfurt continued to be fairly small in comparison and was almost exclusively Jews of German origin.[84]

ZEILSHEIM

A combination of population pressure and the Harrison Report pushed the occupation authorities to found the DP camp at Zeilsheim. When it officially came into existence on August 22, it already had 600 inhabitants. By October 6, the population had swelled to 1,093. The majority of people who moved into Zeilsheim did so with the idea that it was a temporary stop on their way to Palestine.[85] Some within the military also operated on this assumption and clearly did not understand the international political questions that this involved. As one report stated, "We express again our hope that early arrangements can be made to move at least 700 of these persons to Palestine before the advent of cold weather."[86] Given the tight visa restrictions placed by the British on Palestine, this desire was quite unrealistic. Due to the constant influx of DPs in and out of the camp as they searched for

The initial group of Jewish DPs to arrive in Zeilsheim, August 1945. (United States Holocaust Memorial Museum, Photograph no.89516, courtesy of Alice Lev)

lost relatives and friends, a firm head count was difficult to obtain, but Sadie Sender, the JDC representative assigned to Zeilsheim, estimated that the camp had 3,000 inhabitants by the end of December 1945.[87]

The issue of providing sufficient housing highlights tense relations among the Jews of Zeilsheim, their German neighbors, and the military. Zeilsheim was originally formed by requisitioning one-story brick workers' barracks from the IG Farben complex.[88] Then, in order to alleviate overcrowded conditions, in October the military authorized the construction of new houses. However, as UNRRA housing inspector J. Trevor Guy reported:

> Evidence of deliberate "slow-down" and poor construction on the part of the Germans set to the task of completing some of the buildings is apparent. First, the contractor has insisted that it will require three months to construct one of the buildings due to the time required for drying out. Such a building can be easily erected in three weeks at least and can be dried out in a few days. . . . Secondly, the mortar (the word is used very loosely) consists of sand, water and very little lime if any.

Laura J. Hilton

It is believed that no cement at all has been used in the mortar of the buildings now under construction. It is evident that better methods of construction were used in buildings put up prior to the Allied occupation.[89]

Therefore, since housing could not be constructed quickly enough to accommodate the DPs, the military requisitioned 217 houses close to the barracks in accordance with the directive issued after the Harrison Report.[90] This allowed some of the larger barracks to be converted into use as schools and recreational halls and for other cultural and vocational purposes.[91] It also made Zeilsheim dissimilar to many of the major Jewish DP camps that consisted almost exclusively of barrack-style housing.[92] Following their eviction, "most of the Germans came in at night . . . and removed all their furniture and bedding. Before this practice could be stopped, a considerable amount of such equipment had been taken. These are almost impossible items to obtain under the present circumstances and the movement of persons into homes was considerably complicated and impeded by this activity on the part of the Germans."[93] Since Zeilsheim lay within the environs of United States Forces, European Theater (USFET) headquarters, M. Leib, its UNRRA director, lodged an official complaint with OMGUS in Frankfurt over the Germans' actions:

> Despite explicit instructions, which I helped prepare, the Germans moved out their furniture and fixtures, removing even electric fixtures, ovens, etc. . . . The movement of the furniture was carried on under the noses of the German civil police. In fact, they literally turned their backs when they saw the furniture being moved. The action of the police was nothing less than a conspiracy to defeat the order of evacuation given by Military Government.[94]

This entire exchange illustrates the problematic relations among UNRRA, the U.S. Army, the Germans, and the DPs. The U.S. Army was the highest authority, and the German civil police came under its jurisdiction. UNRRA's only recourse for ensuring compliance with their orders to the German people was to depend on U.S. Army enforcement. Yet as stated earlier, the Army was reluctant to increase tensions between it and the German population; therefore, the military did not prioritize the needs of Jewish DPs despite multiple directives clearly establishing and reiterating this policy.[95]

As in Frankfurt, the Jewish population in Zeilsheim quickly established key community institutions: hospitals, cooking facilities, arrangements for clothing distribution, educational and vocational training, and cultural and religious activities. A hospital consisting of a large waiting room, an examining room, and ten beds was founded early in October 1945 and was staffed primarily by the DP doctors and nurses. Both the examining room and the dispensary were stocked with equipment and medicine from UNRRA and army stocks.[96] A UNRRA nutritionist who inspected the cooking facilities in late October estimated that inhabitants were receiving mandated rations in terms of calories per day; breakfast and dinner consisted of cold rations, while lunch was normally a hot meal. Although the DPs had expressed a desire to cook for themselves in their own homes, a food distribution system that would allow such normalcy was not in place.[97]

Similar to other camps, the DPs of Zeilsheim established a political structure soon after it opened.[98] They elected a camp committee to oversee tasks such as the distribution of supplies, to act as a liaison between the DPs and UNRRA, and to operate as a forum for community concerns.[99] One of its subcommittees, which dealt with culture and welfare, tried to combat feelings of despair by organizing events and programs that helped to bring the community together and focus on the future, particularly preparation for immigration. The subcommittee also organized small Hebrew and English classes, secured rehearsing facilities for a dramatic circle,[100] and set up an educational program, including a nursery, a compulsory grade school, and adult vocational and educational training. Camp inhabitants began to print a weekly newspaper and rehearsed both a jazz orchestra and a regular orchestra. To alleviate idleness among the DPs, the committee offered vocational training at a tailor shop, a beauty parlor, and a barbershop.[101]

Despite the lack of religious items, schoolbooks, and other equipment, the community was slowly building a unified yet multifaceted sense of Jewish identity. Many of the materials taught in class and the themes of theater performances emphasized the longing for Palestine and the attempt to cope with the Holocaust. This was fueled as well by continued contact with members of the Jewish Brigade, Jews arriving in the camp with the assistance of Bricha, and David Ben-Gurion's visit to the camp in October 1945.[102] According to Judah Nadich, 90 percent of DPs in Zeilsheim stated their intention to immigrate to Palestine.[103] One DP inhabitant noted that a self-sufficient life was developing, almost a Jewish island in Germany, with its own school system, political parties, sport and youth organizations, and religious institutions.[104] The DPs organized Sabbath celebrations, a wedding, and even a competitive soccer match. Oscar Mintzer of the JDC attended the "first full-fledged wedding with all the trimmings" at Zeilsheim in

One of many wedding portraits taken at the DP camp at Zeilsheim. (United States Holocaust Memorial Museum, Photograph no. 89664, courtesy of Alice Lev)

November 1945. The DPs fashioned a *chuppah* (wedding canopy) out of an army blanket with blue ribbons sewn in the shape of the Star of David. According to Mintzer, this ceremony evoked strong emotions from all participants. "The symbolism and significance of the occasion was terrific, and we all felt it."[105]

Despite these signs of returning normalcy, Alfred Fleischman, a representative from the AJC, warned that idleness in the camps was widespread and that "the complete absence of a planned program of any kind represents a grave and great danger." He noted that the UNRRA team running the camp was operating at 50 percent and that the JDC had only one representative in the camp who was also responsible for additional Jewish communities in the area.[106] To Fleischman, the DPs of Zeilsheim were people who needed to be helped, and shortage of that outside help placed their future in jeopardy.

This view was shared by Samuel Schmidt of Vaad Haatzala who was very concerned with ensuring that the religious needs of the survivors were being met. "I am beginning to make some progress in organizing our religious Jews. . . . As soon as I secure a *Shochet* [ritual slaughterer] for them the camp kitchen is going to be koshered and the entire camp will have kosher food. At present they have one kosher kettle where food is prepared for those who want kosher and are willing to forego meat."[107] He extended his efforts to rebuild religious life by asking the WJC for assistance in securing *seforim, tefillin, taleisim,* and *mezuzahs*.[108] Most of these religious objects had been destroyed during the reign of the Third Reich and were unavailable throughout much of Europe.

The impact of Zionism within Zeilsheim was central to the creation of an identity within the DP camp. Whereas the political control of the Jewish community in Frankfurt was held primarily by German Jews, leadership in Zeilsheim during this period was dominated by East European Zionists. They established two kibbutzim, both of which operated on a communal basis and stressed training for life in the homeland. The smaller kibbutz, composed of 75 members, focused on agricultural training, while the larger, with 250 members, focused on vocational training.[109] Sadie Sender believed that the Zionists were the only population with a strong organization.[110] She interpreted support for them among the non-Zionists as a fervent belief that a homeland was necessary even if they had alternative immigration plans, evidenced in part by large numbers of students in English-language classes. She also noted that the prewar political divisions among Zionists had been put aside to focus on the goal of securing Palestine as a homeland.[111]

Many of the Jews who lived in Zeilsheim had shed their old nationalities, a process that was not recognized in a world organized by nations. Some had espoused a new identity, that of Zionism or statelessness. But others were not certain that immigration to Palestine was the best choice; therefore, they did not identify themselves as Zionists. What is certain is that most inhabitants felt a larger connection to their community at Zeilsheim and to the larger European Jewish community. The JDC conducted a survey trying to understand the feelings and dynamics of this DP community. The thirteenth question asked, "What is the cohesive power that keeps these people together?" The answers indicated that "It is not citizenship. Hitler succeeded to a considerable measure in dividing Jews from their non-Jewish neighbors. They do not feel [that they are] Poles or Slovaks; the only idea or loyalty that united them is the Jewish group consciousness."[112] Although Zionists believed that since the times were so nationalistic the only way for Jews to survive was to create their own nationalism and with it their own nation,[113] an alternative identity coexisted in the camp. The larger Jewish group consciousness was the shared experience of the Holocaust; this was the core of the Jewish identity at Zeilsheim.[114]

Members of the Zionist youth group stand in front of the Shoah memorial in Zeilsheim, 1945. (United States Holocaust Memorial Museum, Photograph no. 89599, courtesy of Alice Lev)

CONCLUSION

As 1945 came to a close, the situation on the ground in Germany began to stabilize. OMGUS officials and UNRRA teams were in place. Additional voluntary agencies and their representatives were assisting with relief and rehabilitation. Amid conflicting images of the DPs, Jews within Zeilsheim and Frankfurt were rebuilding their lives, their identities, and their communities. Their resilience stands as evidence of the strength of their message, *mir zaynen doh*, the message of the She'erit Hapletah. In the process of rebuilding communities and identities and shaping policy decisions, Jews in immediate postwar Germany reminded the world not only of the inhumanity they had faced but also of their determination to survive and actively ensure the revitalization of Jewish life in Germany, in emigration, and, most importantly, in Palestine.

NOTES

1. The term "She'erit Hapletah" references a biblical passage describing the Jews who survived the Assyrian conquest. It had previously been used in a variety of contexts including the partisan song "Zog Nit Keyn Mol," written by Hirsh Glik, in documents produced by the Jewish Historical Commission of Vilna in the interwar period and during the Russian Civil War. In the postwar context, the term was first used in July 1945 in a printed volume of survivors' names produced by DPs in Dachau.

2. See Abraham Peck, "Unsere Augen haben die Ewigkeit gesehen," in *Überlebt und unterwegs: Jüdische Displaced Persons im Nachkriegsdeutschland* (Frankfurt: Campus Verlag, 1997), 31–32.

3. Zeilsheim had an average population of at least three thousand throughout its existence from 1945 to 1948.

4. For a thorough overview of liberation from the point of view of the U.S. military, see Robert Abzug, *Inside the Vicious Heart* (Oxford: Oxford University Press, 1987).

5. Occupation forces established strict rationing and conservation systems that allocated roughly 1,000–1,300 calories per day to the German civilian population, 2,300 to DPs, and 2,500 to those designated as persecutees. Wolf-Arno Kropat, *Hessen in der Stunde Null* (Wiesbaden: Historischen Kommission für Nassau, 1979), 201–205; Dexter Freeman, *Hesse: A New German State* (Frankfurt: OMGH, 1948), 41–42.

6. OMGUS, "Report of the Military Governor," No. 1, August 20, 1945, pp. 4, 9–10, Military History Institute (hereafter MHI); "Aus Trümmern zum Wiederaufbau," in *Hessen: Kultur und Wirtschaft*, edited by Georg August Zinn (Wiesbaden: Erasmusdruck Max Krause, 1952), 167.

7. *Magistratsakten*, folder 1060/1, Stadtarchiv Frankfurt-am-Main (hereaf-

Laura J. Hilton

ter SFM).

8. Percy Knauth, *Germany in Defeat* (New York: Knopf, 1946), 9–10.
9. Letter to his mother, May 13, 1945, folder Personal Correspondence, May–June, 1945, Howard J. Silbar Papers, MHI. For an overview of 1945 in Frankfurt, see Madelen Lorei and Richard Kirn, *Frankfurt und die Drei Widen Jahren* (Frankfurt: Verlag Frankfurter Bücher, 1962), chap. 1; and Günter Mick, *Den Frieden Gewinnen* (Frankfurt: Waldemar Kramer, 1985), 33.
10. OMGUS, "Report of the Military Governor," No. 1, July 1945, MHI.
11. Joel Sack, *Dawn after Dachau* (New York: Shengold Publishers, 1990), Introduction.
12. See, for example, Letter regarding nonrepatriable DPs, June 1945, Record group (hereafter RG) 331, box 54, entry 47, National Archives and Records Administration, College Park, Maryland (hereafter NARA); and OMGUS, *DPs, Stateless Persons and Refugees,* U.S. zone, September 20, 1945, pp. 2–3, MHI.
13. Memo to A. H. Robinson from Louis C. Stephens, November 1, 1945, Possible Statelessness of Baltic Displaced Persons, folder 013.1/D Displaced Persons: Balts, PAG-4/3.0.11.0.0, box 6, United Nations Archive (hereafter UNA).
14. Louise Holborn, *The International Refugee Organization* (London: Oxford University Press, 1956), 174. Hans Frankenthal relates in his memoir *The Unwelcome One* (Evanston, IL: Northwestern University Press, 2004), his response to the local authorities of Schmallenberg who demanded that he and his brother claim a nationality in order to receive ration cards: "The answer is 'stateless.' I don't want to have anything more to do with this country" (85).
15. Department of State Memo 1503, December 20, 1945, RG 84 (POLAD), file 840.1, box 138, NARA.
16. Acknowledgment of Jews as a separate and officially recognized nationality within the U.S. zone of occupation was not politically acceptable in the summer of 1945. The British government, extremely concerned about its control in the Middle East, did not wish to anger the Arabs in the region.
17. Michael Brenner, *Nach dem Holocaust: Juden in Deutschland, 1945–1950* (München: C. H. Beck, 1995), 92. See also Angelika Königseder and Juliane Wetzel, *Waiting for Hope: Jewish Displaced Persons in Post–World War II Germany,* translated from the German by John A. Broadwin (Evanston, IL: Northwestern University Press, 2001), 17–18.
18. The SHAEF Outline Plan of June 1944 gave liaison officers the task of identifying nationals, supervising their activities within camps, and registering them in anticipation of speedy repatriation. Memo, SHAEF, CAD, February 1944, Subject: Refugees and Displaced Persons, box 11, SHAEF 1943–1945, McSherry Papers, MHI.
19. Letter from American Jewish Conference to Henry Stimson, Secretary of War, June 26, 1945, folder D59/5, Relief—Camps—Appointment

of Jewish Liaison Officers to Germany—Correspondence and Misc., 1945–1946, Manuscript Collection (hereafter MSC) 361, WJC, American Jewish Archives (hereafter AJA).

20. "Position of Jews in Germany," Minutes of meeting between WJC representatives, Governor Lehman (executive director of UNRRA), and U.S. congressmen, held June 28, 1945, folder 4, box D6, WJC, AJA.

21. Cable from Stephen Wise to Dwight Eisenhower, August 3, 1945, folder 5, box D59, WJC, AJA.

22. Cable S-16667, from USFET Main from CDPX, signed DDE, to UK base, U.S. embassy, August 10, 1945, folder 5, box D59, WJC, AJA.

23. Jewish Brigade soldiers first had contact with Jews in May 1945, providing material support and a boost for morale. They helped organize a meeting of Zionist representatives in June in Bavaria; this grew into the larger conference in July. Zeev Mankowitz, *Life between Memory and Hope: The Survivors of the Holocaust in Occupied Germany* (Cambridge: Cambridge University Press, 2002), 42–44, 49–51. See also Königseder and Wetzel, *Waiting for Hope*, 20–21, 83–84.

24. This initial meeting involved ninety-four DPs as delegates speaking on behalf of forty thousand Jewish DPs in camps in Germany and Austria. Yehuda Bauer, "The Organization of Holocaust Survivors," *Yad Vashem Studies* 8 (1970): 153.

25. Minutes of the Business Session of the Conference of Liberated Jews in Germany (American and British occupation zones), St. Ottilien bei Landsberg am Lech, July 25, 1945, WJC MS 361, Box D61, folder 1, AJA.

26. All fourteen resolutions can be found in Robert Hilliard, *Surviving the Americans: The Continued Struggle of the Jews after Liberation* (New York: Seven Stories Press, 1997), 118–21. In dramatic fashion, on July 26 they presented these resolutions in the ruins of the famous Munich Bürgerbräu beer cellar, the floor of which was strewn with torn Torah scrolls. Their ideas were echoed by observers from voluntary agencies, such as Dr. Israel Goldstein who, after touring living situations in the U.S. zone during the first week of August 1945, made the following suggestions: house Jews in camps solely for Jews, provide assistance in searching for relatives and friends, think ahead in terms of their educational needs, and issue policies quickly at the highest level of OMGUS. Letter from Dr. Israel Goldstein to Herbert Lehman, August 11, 1945, folder D59/4, Relief-Camps—Authorities—Correspondence and misc., July–December 1945, Small Collection 291-AJJDC, AJA.

27. The issue of the She'erit Hapletah was readdressed by historian Abraham Peck in "An Introduction to the Social History of the Jewish Displaced Persons' Camps," *Proceedings of the Eighth World Congress of Jewish Studies* (1981): 189–94. In 1947 the issue was raised by Koppel Pinson in "Jewish Life in Liberated Germany," *Jewish Social Studies* 9 (1947): 102–3. See also Margarete Myers, "Jewish Displaced Persons Reconstructing Individual and Community in the US Zone of Occupied Germany," *Year Book*, Leo Baeck Institute, vol. 42 (1997): 311–12;

and D. Rosenthal, "She'erit Hapleytah, the Remnant That Was Saved," *Midstream* 36, no. 6 (1990): 25.

28. In his analysis of the formation of the She'erit Hapletah, Zeev Mankowitz refers to the Zionist call for a homeland as a "moral claim on a civilized world" and strongly links the establishment of a homeland to the rebuilding of Jewish identity. Zeev Mankowitz, "The Formation of She'erit Hapleita: November 1944–July 1945," *Yad Vashem Studies* 20 (1990): 351–61.

29. Eva Kolinsky, "Experiences of Survival," *Year Book*, Leo Baeck Institute, vol. 44 (1999): 269–70.

30. For example, Arno Lustiger remembers, "My mother and sister were very sick and my leaving them was out of the question. So my bad conscience made me actively support the Brichah—the illegal immigration to Palestine." Brenner, *Nach dem Holocaust*, 138–39. Lustiger remained in Frankfurt and served on the Jewish community council.

31. This issue of multifaceted identities of DPs is also addressed in Cilly Kugelmann, "The Identity and Ideology of Jewish Displaced Persons," in *Jews, Germans and Memory*, edited by Y. Michal Bodemann, 65–76 (Ann Arbor: University of Michigan Press, 1996); see also Pinson, "Jewish Life in Liberated Germany," 114.

32. Leo Walder Schwarz, *The Redeemers* (New York: Farrar, Straus, & Young, 1953), 34–35.

33. Earl Harrison, "The Harrison Report," *Department of State Bulletin* 13 (September 30, 1945): 456–63. Harrison had served as the American representative to the Intergovernmental Committee on Refugees and as dean of the Law school at University of Pennsylvania. In 1946 he became the head of the Citizens Committee for Displaced Persons, which was concerned with immigration opportunities for DPs to the United States.

34. Truman to Eisenhower, August 31, 1945, ibid., 455 (letter precedes the report). This report provoked serious controversy when it was published, and the debate over its truthfulness, generalizations, and political message has continued through historians' interpretations. See Leonard Dinnerstein, *America and the Survivors of the Holocaust* (New York: Columbia University Press, 1982), 39–49; Abraham Hyman, *The Undefeated* (Jerusalem: Gefen, 1993), 45–55; Mark Wyman, *DPs: Europe's Displaced Persons, 1945–1951*, 2nd ed. (Ithaca, NY: Cornell University Press, 1998), 135–37; and Malcolm Proudfoot, *European Refugees, 1939–52: A Study in Forced Population Movement* (Evanston, IL: Northwestern University Press, 1956), 325–30.

35. Attlee had only been in power for six weeks when he received this letter from Truman.

36. Harry S. Truman, *Memoirs*, Vol. 2, *Years of Trial and Hope* (Garden City, NY: Doubleday, 1956), 139–45. Arieh Kochavi, "The Displaced Persons' Problem and the Formulation of British Policy in Palestine," *Studies in Zionism* 10, no. 1 (1989): 31–35. See also Dinnerstein, *America and the*

Survivors of the Holocaust, 73–80; Yehuda Bauer, *Out of the Ashes: The Impact of American Jews on Post-Holocaust European Jewry* (New York: Pergamon, 1989), 47–48, 50–51.

37. AG 354.1 GEC-AGO, Subject: Special Camps for Stateless and Non-repatriables, USFET Headquarters, August 22, 1945, box 2, PAG-4/3.0.11.0.1.6, UNA.

38. As a temporary measure, U.S. Army chaplain Rabbi Judah Nadich had served in this capacity until Rifkind was named. For Nadich's early reports on Jewish DPs, see RG 19.036 (Nadich Papers), United States Holocaust Memorial Museum Archives, Washington, D.C. (hereafter USHMM). Rifkind served in this position until May 1946 and was succeeded by Rabbi Philip Bernstein, who served until August 1947. Following Bernstein's tenure, which was the longest, he was succeeded by Louis Levinthal (August 1947–January 1948), William Haber (January 1948–January 1949), Harry Greenstein (January–October 1949), and Major Abraham Hyman (October–December 1949). For additional information, see Königseder and Wetzel, *Waiting for Hope,* 34–36.

39. Cable SC 6173 from USFET Main, December 6, 1945, Subject: Zeilsheim Jewish Center near Frankfurt, box 9, folder Infiltrees, 5.11.1945–27.2.1946, PAG-4/3.0.11.3.0, UNA. UNRRA was bound to follow this directive, as it was under the authority of USFET.

40. Cable S-34347 from USFET, December 10, 1945, Subject: Interim Measure relative to the question of offering haven in US zone to persecuted persons from outside Germany, folder Jewish Problems, 7–12.1945, PAG-4/3.0.11.3.0, box 13, UNA.

41. An interesting and detailed personal account of this process is provided by Herbert A. Fierst in the transcription of his memoirs, *A View of the Jewish Problem from the Pentagon and State Department,* Herbert A. Fierst Papers, 1996.A.294, USHMM. As Fierst notes, the improvements in living conditions that had been achieved due to the Harrison Report were now placed in jeopardy, as camps' resources were stretched beyond their limits.

42. U.S. State Department, "Development of Policy on DPs," December 28, 1945, folder D.P. 9: 10, PAG-4.2, box 78, UNA. See also the extensive memo on this subject dealing particularly with overcrowding at Feldafing and Landsberg, December 27, 1945, RG 338, entry ETO-G-5, folder 383.7-3 (Jews), box 42, NARA.

43. Kochavi, "The Displaced Persons' Problem and the Formulation of British Policy in Palestine," 34–35.

44. Oscar Mintzer, *In Defense of the Survivors* (Berkeley, CA: Judah L. Magnes Museum, 1999), 47.

45. Report on Displaced Persons at Zeilsheim to JDC Representatives by Miss Sadie Sender [hereafter Sender Report], December 25, 1945, folder AJJDC, Correspondence, Memoranda and Miscellaneous Materials describing conditions and repatriation of Displaced Persons in Europe, Small Collection 291-AJJDC, AJA.

46. Becky Althoff, "Observations on the Psychology of Children in a D.P. Camp," *Journal of Social Casework* 29, no. 1 (1948): 19.

47. Atina Grossmann, "Trauma, Memory and Motherhood: Germans and Jewish Displaced Persons in Post-Nazi Germany, 1945–1949," *Archiv für Sozialgeschichte* 38 (1998): 229, makes this point in her comparative study of narratives of victimization of Germans and Jews in the postwar period.

48. Edward Shils, "Social and Psychological Aspects of Displacement and Repatriation," *Journal of Social Issues* 3, no. 2 (1946): 3–9.

49. Paul Friedman, a psychoanalyst who worked with Jewish DPs in Europe, Cyprus, and Palestine, was one of the few who recognized and emphasized the resilience he saw in DPs as survivors. See Friedman, "The Road Back for the DPs," *Commentary* 6, no. 6 (1948): 502–10.

50. These assumptions may have been rooted in the struggle to understand why so few Jews had taken up arms directly against the Third Reich. Ralph Segalman, "The Psychology of Jewish Displaced Persons," *Jewish Social Service Quarterly* 23, no. 4 (1947): 361–69.

51. Samuel A. Stouffer, Edward A. Suchman, Leland C. DeVinney, Shirley A. Star, and Robin M. Williams Jr., *The American Soldier: Combat and Its Aftermath*, Vol. 2 (Princeton, NJ: Princeton University Press, 1949), 564–66.

52. Report by Captain C. E. Jack, DPS, 2nd ECA Regiment, "DPs vs. German Authorities," July 8, 1945, Ret. Army Bulletin Collection, James Robertson Papers, MHI.

53. "Statement of the Executive Staff of UNRRA U.S. Zone Headquarters," n.d., PAG-4/3.0.11.3.0, box 9, folder Confidential Report on DPs: 4, UNA.

54. Simon Schochet, *Feldafing* (Vancouver: November House, 1983), 82–83.

55. Sgt. Eaton to Nadich, April 24, 1945, MSC 361, WJC, box D63, folder 7, AJA.

56. Tartarkower to Major General Hilldring, Director, CAD, War Department, June 25, 1945, MSC 361, WJC, box D61, folder 1, AJA.

57. Cilly Kugelmann, "*Befrieung—und dann?,*" in *Nach der Kristallnacht*, edited by Monica Kingreen (Frankfurt: Campus Verlag, 1999), 436. The 1933 Jewish community of Frankfurt was between thirty-one thousand and thirty-seven thousand persons.

58. Theresienstadt was located on the border between Greater Germany and the Protectorate of Bohemia and Moravia. The Third Reich sent prominent and elderly Jews from Germany, Austria, and Western Europe to this ghetto, established in November 1941.

59. Tension between native and foreign Jews in Frankfurt continued to exist during the postwar period. For example, in October and November 1946 German Jews instituted strict requirements for membership on their board and voting rights ranging from a year's residence in Frankfurt and three year's membership in a German Jewish community to

pre-1933 residency. Jay Geller, *Jews in Post-Holocaust Germany, 1945–1953* (Cambridge: Cambridge University Press, 2005), 50–51.

60. Hollbach had been the editor for the *Neueste Zeitung* and the *Illustriertes Blatt*. He remained as temporary mayor until OMGUS appointed Kurt Blaum as *Oberbürgermeister* (mayor) in early July 1945.

61. Eaton, DP & PW Detachment, 12th Army Group, report dated June 10, 1945, titled "The Jewish Community of Frankfurt," MSC 361, WJC, box D63, folder 7, AJA; Letter from Acting Bürgermeister Hollbach to Fürsorgeamt, May 15, 1945, folder 7047/6, Vol. 1, SFM.

62. Alon Tauber, "Die Entstehung der Jüdischen Nachkriegsgemeinde, 1945–1949," in *Wer ein Haus baut, will bleiben*, edited by G. Heugerber (Frankfurt: Societäts Verlag, 1998), 98.

63. "The Jewish Community of Frankfurt," AJA. The city advisory council of Frankfurt was formed by OMGUS officials in April 1945 and was initially composed of the head of the Catholic Church in Frankfurt, two Protestant ministers, the director of IG Farben, the general manager and another representative of the local Chamber of Commerce and Industry, an interpreter, a representative of the Communist Party, and August Adelsberger. See Rebecca Boehling, *A Question of Priorities* (Providence, RI: Berghahn, 1996), 81–85. See also Leonard Krieger, "The Inter-Regnum in Germany, March–August, 1945," *Political Science Quarterly* 64 (1949): 507–32.

64. Boehling states in her examination of occupation policy that Colonel Robert Phelps, Criswell's immediate successor, complained that he and his men were not in agreement with much of the "prevailing policy" emanating from headquarters. See Boehling, *A Question of Priorities*, 126.

65. USFET, *Displaced Persons: Occupation Forces in Europe Series, 1945–1946* (EUCOM: Frankfurt, 1947), 26.

66. Directive issued October 24, 1945, folder Directives Issued by Public Safety Division, OMGHE, 8.1945–5.1946, RG 260, OMGUS, file 8/53–2/2, NARA.

67. Boehling, *A Question of Priorities*, 80.

68. Brenner *Nach dem Holocaust*, 139; Rachel Heuberger and Helga Krohn, eds., *Hinaus aus dem Ghetto: Juden in Frankfurt-am-Main, 1800–1988* (Frankfurt: S. Fischer, 1988), 201–2; Lynn Rapaport, "The Cultural and Material Reconstruction of Jewish Communities in the Federal Republic of Germany," *Jewish Social Studies* 49, no. 2 (1987): 138.

69. Brenner, *Nach dem Holocaust*, 140. The Westend synagogue, on Freiherr-von-Stein Street, was the site of High Holiday services in the autumn of 1945. "Wiederweihe des ersten jüdischen Gotteshauses in Frankfurt am Main," *Frankfurter Rundschau* 1, no. 13 (1945): 1.

70. For a similar reaction from Hans Frey in the British zone, see Brenner, *Nach dem Holocaust*, 70–71.

71. Pfc. Akiva Skidell to members of office committee, August 20, 1945, MSC 361, WJC, box D62, folder 2, AJA. Skidell was a well-known so-

cialist and Zionist. See Deborah Dash Moore, *GI Jews* (Cambridge, MA: Belknap, 2004).

72. SHAEF, Administrative Memorandum No. 39, "Displaced Persons and Refugees in Germany," revised April 16, 1945, in Proudfoot, *European Refugees,* Appendix B, para. 32.

73. "The Jewish Community of Frankfurt," AJA. For descriptions of the rebuilding of Jewish communities in other major cities in Germany in the immediate postwar period, see Brenner, *Nach dem Holocaust,* 63–68.

74. Adelsberger to WJC, July 6, 1945, MSC 361, WJC, box D61, folder 1, AJA.

75. Letter to City Council, November 21, 1945, folder Displaced Foreigners, folder 7407/1, SFM.

76. Kubowitzki to McCloy, July 26, 1945, MSC 361, WJC, box D61, folder 1, AJA.

77. Cable: GE CDPX 383.7, CDPX to Communications Zone, to the attention of theater chaplains, July 20, 1945, MSC 361, WJC, box D63, folder 7, AJA.

78. Chaplain Marcus to Office Committee, August 21, 1945, MSC 361, WJC, box D62, folder 2, AJA. For additional explanation of these types of conflicts, see Brenner, *Nach dem Holocaust,* 69–77.

79. Eaton to Sarah Friedman, June 1945, MSC 584, Samuel L. Haber, box B5, folder 2, AJA.

80. Schmidt to his wife, August 15, 1945, box 853, folder 2 of 2, AJA. Vaad Haatzala was a Jewish voluntary agency founded by the Union of Orthodox Rabbis in the United States and Canada that was primarily concerned with rebuilding Orthodox Jewish life among the DPs.

81. Report of Schmidt, July 5–September 19, 1945, box 853, folder 2 of 2, AJA. A UNRRA team was in the camp on August 22 when it officially opened. The work of Private Tulipan is also cited in Earl Harrison, "The Last Hundred Thousand," *Survey Graphic* 34 (1949): 469–73. According to Harrison, Tulipan organized housing in hotels for DPs within Frankfurt, and when these hotels were requisitioned for use by the occupation authorities, he secured apartment buildings in Hoechst, which would become the heart of the DP camp at Zeilsheim.

82. Mintzer *In Defense of the Survivors,* 38. In November 1945 Mintzer also stumbled upon the Jewish cemetery in Frankfurt, which was being slowly repaired by non-Jewish Germans by orders from the mayor.

83. Report, OMGH, LK & SK Marburg, RG 260, file 8/5-1/4, folder OMGH LSO Marburg District, NARA.

84. Tauber "Die Entstehung der Jüdischen Nachkriegsgemeinde, 1945–1949," 100, estimates that this Jewish community averaged 600–700 inhabitants in 1946, 600–680 in 1947, 680–750 in 1948, and 800–850 in 1959.

85. Det. E-2 Reports for August 25 and October 6, 1945, RG 260, OMGUS, file 8/190-3/6, NARA.

86. Det. E-2 Report for September 15, 1945, RG 260, OMGUS, file 8/190-

3/6, NARA.

87. Sender Report, AJA.

88. The workers' barracks at Zeilsheim consisted of fourteen wooden structures and ten brick structures. Until the Jewish DPs' arrival, German POWs were housed in the wooden barracks. Johannes Winter, "Die Hauptstadt des Schwartzmarkts," *Frankfurter Rundschau—Zeit und Bild,* August 30, 1988, 1, 11.

89. Folder Guy's Reports, September 45–January 1946, dated October 24, 1945, PAG-4/3.0.11.3.0, box 46, UNA.

90. Florian Ritter, "Das 'Displaced persons'—Lager in Frankfurt am Main/Zeilsheim," in *Wer ein Haus baut, will bleiben,* 111. This was also in line with an official directive of October 28, 1945, that called for a minimum of thirty-six square feet of living space per person. Zisman Papers, RG 19.047.03*03, USHMM.

91. "Report from Major Alfred Fleischman," November 30, 1945, MSC 361, WJC, box D61, folder 2. AJA. Fleischman was an AJC representative sent to tour DP camps in Germany. He arrived in Germany on October 28 and visited Zeilsheim on November 2.

92. Lustiger discusses the unique nature of Zeilsheim in Brenner, *Nach dem Holocaust,* 92–93.

93. "Report from Major Alfred Fleischman," AJA.

94. Leib to Sheehan, October 24, 1945, Subject: Evacuation of German homes, PAG-4/3.0.11.3.4, box 19, folder 17.00 General, UNA.

95. Sender Report, AJA. The tension over the requisitioned homes continued until the camp was closed in 1948. For many complaints from Germans, see Abteilung 509/Akte 2029: Eingabe wegen Freigabe des als Lehrhof Zeilsheim, in Hessisches Staatsarchiv. For a wider analysis of relations between Germans and Jewish DPs, see Leonard Dinnerstein, "German Attitudes toward Displaced Persons (1945–1950)," in *Germany and America: Essays on Problems of International Relations and Immigration,* edited by Hans Trefousse (New York: Columbia University Press, 1980).

96. Headquarters Regional OMGUS, Land Hessen-Nassau. Det. E-2, Marburg, Weekly OMGUS Report No. 12 for week ending October 6, 1945, RG 260, NARA.

97. Report by Jane Grant, Nutritionist, UNRRA, October 24, 1945, file 8/56-1/5, folder DP Camps, UNRRA RB Kassel, RG 260, OMGUS, NARA. Irving Heymont also observed this tug of war between cleanliness and ensuring "normality" in the DPs lives; Heymont, *Among the Survivors of the Holocaust, 1945: The Landsberg DP Camp Letters of Major Irving Heymont, United States Army* (Cincinnati: Hebrew Union College Press, 1982), 16.

98. For additional information about the political organization of DP camps, see Jacqueline Giere, "We're on Our Way, but We're Not in the Wilderness," in *The Holocaust and History,* edited by Michael Berenbaum and Abraham J. Peck (Bloomington: Indiana University Press,

1998), 702.

99. For example, requisitions for clothing from the German economy and U.S. Army stores for the DPs at Zeilsheim were made early in October. Most DPs were wearing lightweight makeshift clothing not suitable for winter. It is important to note that this request contained no clothing for children, which underlines the devastating demographic impact of the Holocaust. It was not until November 1945 that children were found in larger numbers within the camp at Zeilsheim with the arrival of infil-trees from the East, some of whom had survived with all or part of their families intact. Memo from MG Frankfurt-am-Main to MG Headquarters, October 4, 1945, folder Food and Supply Office, file 17/16-3/12, RG 260, OMGUS, NARA.

100. Nadich Report, November 29, 1945, MSC 361, WJC, box D62, folder 4, AJA. According to Koppel Pinson, who was the Education Director for the JDC in Germany and Austria from October 1945 to September 1946, all Jewish DPs were encouraged to speak Yiddish and to learn Hebrew as part of the unifying process; Pinson, "Jewish Life in Liberated Germany," 112.

101. Sender Report, AJA.

102. Mankowitz, *Life between Memory and Hope*, 65–68. Zeilsheim also received international attention due to a September 1945 visit by Eleanor Roosevelt during her campaign to forge an International Declaration of Human Rights. Grossmann, "Trauma, Memory and Motherhood," 299.

103. Judah Nadich, Chart of camps, folder 2, RG 19.036, Judah Nadich Papers, USHMM.

104. Brenner, *Nach dem Holocaust*, 136; Mintzer, *In Defense of the Survivors*, 40–41. For an explanation by an inhabitant of the camp at Feldafing of the explosion of culture and committees in the camps, see Kolinsky, "Experiences of Survival," 256, and Myers, "Jewish Displaced Persons Reconstructing Individual and Community in the US Zone of Occupied Germany," 312–15. For a view from the American Jewish Conference representatives, see Memo to Simon Rifkind, December 13, 1945, folder Infiltrees, 11.1945–2.1946, PAG-4/3.0.11.3.0, box 6, UNA.

105. Mintzer *In Defense of the Survivors*, 46.

106. "Report from Major Alfred Fleischman," AJA.

107. Samuel Schmidt to his wife, September 10, 1945, box 853, folder 2 of 2, AJA.

108. Press Release No. 59E, September 4, 1945, MSC 361, WJC, folder D3/10, Vaad Haatzala, reports and releases, 1944–1945, AJA. For an in-depth analysis of the rebuilding of Jewish religious life, see Judith Baumel, "The Politics of Spiritual Rehabilitation in the DP Camps," *Simon Wiesenthal Center Annual* 6 (1989): 57–79.

109. Zionism also encouraged other types of vocational training in addition to agriculture so that workers would be able to contribute to their new nation. Myers, "Jewish Displaced Persons Reconstructing Individual

and Community in the US Zone of Occupied Germany," 320. "Report from Major Alfred Fleischman," AJA. For information on other kibbutzim, see Judith Baumel, *Kibbutz Buchenwald* (New Brunswick, NJ: Rutgers University Press, 1997).

110. Multiple examples of quickly constructed strong Zionist organizations exist, most notably the establishment of a Zionist Committee in Dachau immediately after liberation that demanded that the blue and white flag be hoisted alongside national flags. See Mankowitz, *Life between Memory and Hope*, 38.

111. It is important to note that while the majority wanted to immigrate to Palestine, others wished to resettle in Canada, Great Britain, or the United States, most commonly to be reunited with family members however distant. Sender Report, AJA; see also Pinson, "Jewish Life in Liberated Germany," 117.

112. Fourth Version, October 30, 1945, MSC 361, WJC, box C105, folder 6: JCBA: V Jewish Displaced Persons, 1945, AJA.

113. Report Delivered at World Jewish Congress Administrative Committee, July 1945, speeches by Nahum Goldmann (file 13–14) and Jacob Robinson (p. 51), MSC 361, WJC, box C109, folder 12: PWPP: Report Delivered at WJC Administrative Committee, AJA.

114. Another illustration of this shared unity is noted by Ruth Gay, *Safe among the Germans: Liberated Jews after World War II* (New Haven, CT: Yale University Press, 2002), 62–63, in a list of camp newspapers: "Our World, Our Goal, Our Word, Our Hope, Our Front, Our Courage, Our Voice, Our Struggle, and of course, Our Way. As the names indicate, these newspapers were not addressing a general public. They were written by Jews for one another, Jews who were bound by their wartime sufferings, for whom these papers were a forum."

The Experience of the Displaced Persons in Bergen-Belsen

Unique or Typical Case?

Hagit Lavsky

Bergen-Belsen was founded by the Nazis in 1943 as a prisoner of war and concentration camp. It was located in Lower Saxony, not far from Hanover, between the towns of Bergen and Belsen and eventually transformed to become one of the most horrific death camps. From the winter of 1944 on, ten thousand prisoners died there from starvation and disease. When the British forces liberated the camp on April 15, 1945, they were shocked to encounter the horrors, and the camp became the symbol of Nazi atrocities. Parallel to their efforts to bury the ten thousand corpses and the fourteen thousand survivors who died after liberation, they embarked on caring for the thirty thousand barely alive inmates and transformed the nearby German military camp into a hospital and camp for displaced persons (DPs), housing Jews and Poles. Many of the DPs returned to their homelands (particularly France, Belgium, Holland, and Czechoslovakia), and in 1946 the remaining Poles were transferred to other camps. Thus, Bergen-Belsen (or in the shortened version "Belsen" used by the survivors) became an exclusively Jewish camp, with about twelve thousand DPs, and was the biggest camp in Germany and the center for the survivors in the British zone of occupation in northwestern Germany, while most of the Jewish DPs concentrated in the American zone in southern Germany.

This chapter illuminates the experiences of the Jewish DPs in Bergen-Belsen, placing it within the comparative perspective of the Jewish DPs in the American zone. To what extent can the in-depth study of a certain case, and in many ways a unique one, be used to represent the common experiences of the DPs in post-Holocaust Germany?

THE BRITISH ZONE

Following the end of the war in Europe on May 8, 1945, the Allies established in June 1945 the Allied Control Commission, which assumed control over Germany and divided it into four zones of occupation (Berlin was also divided among the four Allies). Northwest Germany was placed under British control and included the future federal states of Schleswig-Holstein, Hamburg, Lower Saxony, and North Rhine-Westphalia and the Ruhr region. Covering 97,000 square kilometers and with a population of 22.3 million, the British zone was the densest in population compared with the American zone in the South and the Russian in the East, each covering 107,000 square kilometers and with populations of only 14.3 million and 17.3 million, respectively. (The French received a small area including the Saar region on the southwestern border.)

In the face of the devastated German economy the burden that fell upon the Allies was enormous, particularly in the British zone. The region was poor in agricultural resources, and its industrial infrastructure had been largely destroyed in the war. These factors together with the deindustrialization and demilitarization policies of the Allies created a shortage of industrial merchandise that could be exchanged for food supplies. Even the most basic needs of the dense population could not be met. The British economy, which had itself suffered a severe setback during the war, was now being asked to shoulder responsibility for the survivors, too.

The DPs—people uprooted by the war, including Jewish and other survivors of concentration camps—presented a special problem. Despite the agreement signed in the autumn of 1945 transferring responsibility for the DPs into the hands of United Nations Relief and Rehabilitation Administration (UNRRA), the problem continued to bother the occupation authorities. The British, even more so than the Americans, looked for ways to lessen the burden posed by the DPs and the local German population. The DPs were urged to return to their countries of origin. Those of Western countries did so as soon as possible, but many DPs from Eastern Europe hesitated, and severe restrictions were imposed in the hope of getting them to comply. Their numbers indeed dropped by millions after the mass repatriation movement, but more than a quarter million DPs were still present in the British zone alone in February 1947.[1]

THE BRITISH POLICY REGARDING THE JEWS

The Jews in the British zone constituted approximately .08 percent of the total population. Because the Jewish remnant was so small and the economic burden so heavy, the authorities were not as attentive as they might have been to the specifically Jewish aspects of the problem.

The Jewish survivors' starting point upon liberation was much lower than of the non-Jewish DPs. Most of the Jews had been in the death camps or had taken part in death marches from which they emerged barely alive, while the majority of the non-Jews had been in forced labor camps and were comparatively better off physically and mentally. Thus, the preferential treatment that was supposedly enjoyed by all DPs, which was not enough in any case, was even less adequate for the Jewish DPs.

For German Jews, the problem was compounded. Those who had been liberated from concentration camps were recognized as victims of the Nazis, but the liberated Jews, who were usually older and in worse health than their German counterparts, had no families to whom to return, no sources of income, and no social connections to assist them. In addition, there were some German Jews who had survived in their hometowns without being deported. As such, they were not included in the "victims" category and were treated as ordinary Germans.[2]

The whole situation could have been changed after the initial chaos had died down and an official occupation policy was instituted or as various issues were brought to the attention of the military government. Yet this was not the case because of the overall British approach to specifically Jewish problems. From the very beginning, the British ignored the Jewishness of the victims of the Nazis. However horrific their testimonies in connection with Bergen-Belsen and regardless of the compassion they felt for the victims of the Nazis as human beings, they did not even bother to mention that most of the victims were Jews.[3] As a result, the British adopted a policy whereby the Jews were treated just like all the others in terms of their nationalities, and this was true even in respect to German Jews. According to British policy, there were only two legitimate categories: (1) enemy Germans and Nazi collaborators and (2) victims of the Nazis and Allied collaborators.

Since Jews were not recognized as a separate category, they did not enjoy any special status and were not entitled to better treatment by the authorities. For Jewish DPs this meant being pressured on the subject of repatriation. Polish Jews, who constituted the majority of the survivors, were placed in Bergen-Belsen together with Polish forced labor survivors, and German Jews went back to being under the jurisdiction of German municipalities, as was the case for all other German citizens.[4] This attitude meant that the authorities turned a blind eye to the specific needs of the Jews as Jews in regard to their individual physical needs as well as their spiritual needs to be part of a community after losing their families and being left alone in the world. This situation also made it difficult for any Jewish relief mission to operate and to tend to the special needs of Jewish survivors.[5]

At first, there was not much difference in this respect between the British and the American policies. However, the Americans, following the recommendations of Earl G. Harrison, the special envoy appointed by President Harry S. Truman, introduced in the summer of 1945 strict segregation between Jews and non-Jews. The new policy placed Jewish DPs in the American zone in camps of their own, appointed special Jewish advisers, worked to improve the living conditions of Jews, and equated the status of German Jews with that of the Jewish DPs. The British, in contrast, stubbornly held to the principle of nonsegregation, only starting slowly to implement reforms at the end of 1945, a process that took several months. The appointment of special Jewish liaison officers and a Jewish adviser was delayed until the spring of 1946, and the transfer of the non-Jewish inmates from Bergen-Belsen took place as late as June 1946.[6]

THE JEWISH POPULATION IN THE BRITISH ZONE

When the war ended, about half (40,000) of the Jewish survivors in western Germany were to be found in the British zone, most of them in Bergen-Belsen, the largest of the concentration camps liberated in Germany and subsequently the largest DP camp. These numbers were reduced by the time two months had passed through death and repatriation and then stabilized at 12,000 Jews out of 18,000 DPs in Bergen-Belsen. By the end of 1946 there were about 16,000 Jews in the British zone, of whom some 9,000–10,000 resided in Bergen-Belsen besides some 5,000–6,000 in the cities.[7] The rest, some 1,000–2,000 DPs, were scattered among forty-five small camps or assembly centers. Twenty-one of the camps were very tiny, with fewer than 10 DPs each; fourteen camps held up to 50 persons; four camps held up to 200 persons; and three camps held 350–800 each.[8] The British were generally strict about movement to and from their zone and tried to prevent illegal entry into territory under their aegis. Thus,

Hagit Lavsky

the size of the Jewish population did not grow in the wake of the Bricha, the escape movement from Eastern Europe.

The population in the American zone developed along quite different lines. Due to the supportive American occupation policy and the implementation of the Harrison Report, the Jewish remnant was joined by the growing influx of Jewish refugees fleeing from Eastern Europe. This mass migration was destined to Palestine or the Western democracies, preferably the United States. However, the road out of Europe was virtually blocked. The only option was to join the DP population, which exerted pressure on the Western governments and especially the British Mandatory authorities in Palestine. DP camps in the American zone became the last resorts for those seeking a way out of Europe, and the population of these camps grew very rapidly.[9] By the end of 1946, in the wake of the frantic exodus from Poland after the Kielce pogrom of July 1946, the total number of DPs in Germany rose to 180,000, of whom around 160,000 were to be found in the American zone alone. The DP population in Germany reached a peak in the spring of 1947 after the arrival of refugees from Czechoslovakia, Hungary, and Romania. At that time, there were about 190,000 DPs in western Germany (out of a total of 250,000 in Germany, Austria, and Italy), of whom some 175,000 were in the American zone alone.[10]

As already mentioned, most of the DPs—survivors as well as those who joined them during the Bricha—were East Europeans predominantly from Poland, and the new arrivals changed the demographic composition entirely, particularly in the American zone. The original group of survivors at the time of liberation consisted exclusively of Jews who had experienced the concentration camps firsthand, with almost no children or elderly among them. By the end of 1946, nearly two-thirds of the DPs in the American zone were refugees, many of them repatriates from the Soviet Union, which brought in married couples, children, and old people with diverse wartime experiences.

The dispersion of these great numbers in the American zone was quite different from that in the British zone. Here there were a few large-scale DP camps—Pocking, Landsberg, Feldafing, and Föhrenwald—as well as many smaller camps and also clusters of camps, such as those around Ulm or Stuttgart. There was no single big concentration of the DPs as there was in Belsen, and the population within these camps hardly exceeded five thousand or six thousand (Pocking, with 7,000–7,500 DPs, was an exception), half the size of Bergen-Belsen's Jewish population.[11]

Belsen's Jewish population was marked by its relatively numerical stability due to the British refusal to admit refugees from the East. This stability also affected the camp's sociodemographic character, which was unique from the outset. Owing to the fact that the Belsen concentration camp served as a waiting camp for exchange Jews, there were relatively many children there, some accompanied by a parent, others alone. Transports from death and forced labor camps who arrived up until the very last moment before liberation also contributed to the population makeup, which was not typical of the She'erit Hapletah (Surviving Remnant). There was an exceptionally high ratio of women and a large proportion of children (nearly five hundred) who were either survivors of Belsen or transferred just before liberation from Buchenwald and Theresienstadt.[12]

In Bergen-Belsen, as in the American zone, Polish Jews were the dominant element. There was also a large group of Hungarian Jews — about three thousand — who had survived Auschwitz and constituted at least one-quarter of the camp's Jewish population. Most of the Hungarian Jews were Orthodox and together with the Polish Hasidim formed a strong Orthodox core. In the American zone the footsteps of Lithuanian survivors were much more noticeable, and the presence of an extreme Orthodox segment was much less pronounced than in the British zone.[13]

Another feature that distinguished the British zone from the American zone was the proportion of the DPs from Eastern Europe relative to German Jews in the overall Jewish population. In the American zone, the new established communities were made up by and large of East European Jews, while the big new communities in the British zone were made up mainly of German Jews.[14] This situation, combined with the problems caused by the British rule, created a unique give-and-take relation between German Jews and DPs in the British zone.

THE ROLE OF JEWISH WELFARE ORGANIZATIONS

British policy as well as the size, the demographic profile, and the kind of dispersion that characterized the British zone had in their turn a special impact on the policies and patterns of activities of the Jewish welfare organizations, which played generally a major role in the rehabilitation process experienced by the DPs. The American zone, being the largest concentration of Jewish survivors in Germany, also became the focus for the welfare activities. Most organizations placed their headquarters in the American zone, and their agencies in the British zone were considered affiliated branches. Thus, every development occurred in the British zone later and in smaller dimensions than in the American zone. The British policy described above put additional odds on the road of welfare activities earmarked toward Jews, thereby contributing to their limited scope. On the other hand, the very same British policy lent a special emphasis to the needs of the Jews in the British zone, thus triggering on the part of British Jewry a great effort on behalf of Jewish DPs and German Jews alike.

The Jewish welfare emissaries were late in arriving due to the reluctance of the military authorities to admit civilians into Germany. The first Jews from the outside world who came to the DP camps were soldiers and officers as well as chaplains of the liberating armies and of the Jewish Brigade. The absence of any formal Jewish delegation for weeks and months after liberation added to the survivors' deep sense of bitterness. They felt abandoned by their own people. Once the emissaries did arrive, however, they fulfilled an important function in helping the survivors to help themselves.

The American Jewish Joint Distribution Committee (JDC) was the largest and most important organization in this welfare system. The first JDC relief team entered Buchenwald in June 1945. The entry of the JDC mission to Bergen-Belsen was even later, in early July.[15] Shipments of goods started to arrive only later and were often delayed, causing severe shortages that were felt most of all in the British zone, where the special needs of the Jews were not recognized and where UNRRA supplies were particularly inadequate because German Jews were not listed as entitled to UNRRA support.[16]

During 1945–48 the JDC spent more than $7.32 million on relief efforts in Germany and Austria and shipped all kinds of needed goods to Germany. In addition, the JDC mobilized hundreds of American Jewish field workers for its operations in Germany, most of them in the American zone.[17] JDC operations in the British zone were mainly financial and less personal, and most of the JDC's emissaries there were Jews from Canada, England, or other countries. Nevertheless, the unsympathetic attitude of the military authorities lent an American Jewish presence in the British zone special significance.[18]

The help from Palestine came even later than that from the American Jews. The first team of 20 persons of the welfare groups sent by the Jewish Agency for Palestine (JAP) reached the camps in the American zone on December 11, seven months after liberation.[19] The British zone had to wait even longer. The first JAP emissary, Kurt Lewin, arrived in Belsen in March 1946 almost a year after liberation.[20] By May 1946 there were 10 emissaries in the British zone, 4 of them in Bergen-Belsen, and the number changed very little over the coming months despite the growing number of emissaries to Germany, reaching 152 by the second half of 1947, most of them in the American zone.[21]

The Palestine emissaries were delegates of various political parties and kibbutz movements. They saw themselves as representatives of both the Jewish Yishuv and of their respective movements, and their ultimate goal was to prepare the survivors for life in Palestine. Physical conditions in the camps had already been improved by the time they arrived, and the work of the Jewish welfare agencies was already in full swing. The Palestinian emissaries thus concentrated not on welfare but rather on Zionist education, pioneer training, political activism, and aliyah. These activities were pursued along party lines, with the emissaries trying to recruit people to their respective parties.[22] The emissaries in the British zone were an exception, however, in that they did not allow their political views to affect their work. Zionism was their common goal, especially confronting the British antinational and restrictive policy, so political party interests were laid aside even if this meant drawing fire from their own political parties.[23]

The relatively minor role played by the Palestine emissaries in the British zone was shaped by several factors. For one, when they arrived (almost a year after liberation), Bergen-Belsen and the British zone as a whole were already organized along clear Zionist lines and in full unity. Moreover, as already mentioned, the bulk of the survivors lived in the American zone, so the British zone was lower on the Palestine emissaries' scale of priorities.[24] Thus, they were not trailblazers but instead pursued their work within the general framework of cooperation and unity.

The chief feature distinguishing the relief work in the British zone in comparison with the American zone was the presence of Anglo-Jewish people there. The most important agency working in the British zone was the British Jewish Relief Unit (JRU), organized by the Jewish Committee for Relief Abroad (JCRA), founded in 1943. The first JRU team entered Bergen-Belsen in August 1945.[25] By April 1946 there were sixty-eight JRU workers in Germany, and by the summer the figure grew to ninety-two, the great majority of them in the British zone, and many of them were members of Zionist youth and pioneer movements.[26]

The financial basis of the JRU was very limited, and its activities were based on the material support of the JDC, which encountered endless problems in organizing and shipping essential provisions from America. Restrictions imposed by the British also impeded the ability of the JRU to improve living conditions in any substantial manner. Thus, most of its energies were devoted to mental and spiritual rehabilitation, medical care, and community work, playing a dominant role in reviving Jewish religious, cultural, and social life in Germany.[27] The JRU was also significant in mediation between the survivors and the German authorities, due to the fact that many JRU volunteers were of German origin and spoke German fluently.[28] Some of the volunteers, such as Henryk Van Dam, who served as the legal adviser for German Jews,[29] and E. G. Lowenthal, JRU field director for Germany, eventually settled in Germany and went on to become important figures in the German Jewish community.

Another unique feature that helped the survivors in the British zone in dealing with the extra hardships experienced there was the political assistance of British Jewry. The two most important bodies in this sphere were the British section of the World Jewish Congress (WJC) and the Board of Deputies of British Jews. They exercised political pressure on the British authorities in London on behalf of the Jewish survivors in the British zone, and slowly their pressure bore fruit, such as in matters of nominating the Jewish adviser and facilitating relief work in the Jewish communities.[30]

Jewish adviser Colonel Robert Solomon did not settle in Germany but instead traveled back and forth. Consequently, he remained in the job for the whole period in contrast to the high turnover among the American Jewish advisers.[31] In this way, Solomon helped to smooth relations with the British military authorities.[32] It was due to his initiatives that the British embarked on the Grand National operation of legal aliyah from the British zone in 1947 that enabled six thousand DPs to make their way to Palestine.[33] He also contributed greatly to the cooperation between the British military authorities and the JRU within their effort to relieve the hardship of the German Jews and allow them to organize.

The efforts of the British Jews on behalf of the survivors were characterized throughout by a deep sense of affinity. Proximity to Germany enabled frequent visits and telephone calls, which led to the development of personal relationships.[34] JRU workers stayed in Germany for longer periods than the workers of the JDC because it was easier for them to go home for a vacation and then come back refreshed.[35] On the whole, although the JDC was indispensable, there is no question that the JRU and British Jewry constituted a far more dominant presence in terms of personnel numbers, activities, and connections with the authorities and the survivors thanks to the political advantages and geographical proximity.

The external Jewish welfare and political work in post-Holocaust Germany was marked by cooperation between Zionists and non-Zionists, a dramatic shift in the Jewish world as it confronted the horrors of the Holocaust and the vastness of the DP problem. This cooperation was especially pronounced in the British zone at a time when the British adopted a hard-line policy with respect to the Jews in Germany and Palestine alike. On the one hand, the aim was to achieve segregation and introduce a separate apparatus for Jewish relief work through diplomatic channels, meanwhile carrying on as best as possible under the constraints of British policy. On the other hand, a concerted effort was made to implement what seemed at the time (not only to the Jews, as the Harrison Report manifested) as the one feasible solution to the Jewish problem: opening the gates of Palestine.

SELF-ORGANIZATION

The survivors in Bergen-Belsen were quick to organize and to establish a framework for Jewish self-government. By sheer luck, nearly half of the survivors arrived in the Bergen-Belsen death camp just a few days before liberation. Therefore, despite the horrible conditions prevailing in the camp, most of them were still in reasonable physical shape, and many were young people who belonged in their past to Zionist youth movements and were preparing for a life of pioneering in Palestine. They spoke Hebrew and knew Hebrew songs and had a significant impact on the mood in the camp because they had a real goal and were full of hope.

On April 25 a provisional committee was formed with Yossel Rosensaft as the chairman.[36] The provisional committee functioned until the First Congress of the She'erit Hapletah met in Bergen-Belsen in September 1945 and elected the Central Committee. Committee members came and went, but the main persons stayed active in the Central Committee throughout the existence of the camp.[37] They constituted an extremely diverse group. Many of them were intellectuals, representing a wide range of political beliefs and degrees of religious observance. Most had been active in communal affairs before the war, and quite a few had been Zionists. However, none had actually been a leader in the past, and few knew each other before the war.[38] The organization of Jewish DPs in Bergen-Belsen was thus a spontaneous phenomenon that gave birth to a new set of leaders with no legacy of former leadership but with a common goal. In the face of harsh conditions and hostility toward Jewish cohesiveness, embracing Zionism provided a strong focal point around which the survivors could rally. The early elected Jewish leadership thus became a cornerstone for national unification that encompassed all the Jews in the British zone.

Soon after its election, the provisional committee sat to work to construct a framework for the whole of Germany. On July 8, 1945, a conference was held in Bergen-Belsen that was attended by fifty-four representatives of the camps in the British and American zones as well as representatives of the JDC and the JRU.[39] A committee was elected at this forum to represent the Jewish DPs in contacts with the military authorities, the Allies, and the United Nations and to pose three demands: unrestricted emigration for those who refused to be repatriated; the provision of necessary infrastructure for cultural, educational, and vocational centers in the camps that would operate until emigration became possible; and recognition of the committee as the authorized representative of all Jews in the American and British zones.

Eight days later, on July 16, 1945, a second convention took place, this time of British zone representatives only but including representatives of the Jewish communities outside the camps. By this time the provisional committee established in Bergen-Belsen seems to have extended its authority over the whole of the British zone. At this forum, a subcommittee was elected to prepare for a general Jewish congress in Germany.[40]

These conventions were not really about Zionism. The goal was to organize a united front against the strict rules laid down by the British, to improve living conditions in the camp, and to speed up the liberation process. However, in the time between these gatherings and the next convention in September, the Zionist spirit seems to have strengthened and become much more intense for a variety of reasons, both positive and negative.

One of the leading positive factors was the cultural and educational activity of the provisional committee, which was clearly Zionist in orientation and did wonders for the overall mood. A school and a kindergarten were already operating in Bergen-Belsen and in nearby Celle by June, and the teaching staff came from among the survivors. The entire curriculum was in Hebrew, and Land of Israel studies were a major component.[41]

The first issue of *Unzer Sztyme* (Our Voice), one of the first Yiddish newsletters to be published in post-Holocaust Germany, appeared on July 12.[42] Behind it stood three provisional committee members: Rafael Olewski, David Rosenthal, and Paul Trepman. *Unzer Sztyme* carried a vibrant Zionist message that spread throughout the British zone.

Around this time, the first soldiers of the Jewish Brigade from Palestine appeared in the British zone. Their immediate involvement in Jewish cultural activity, schools, and pioneer training programs strengthened the Zionist fervor that had already taken root. These soldiers constituted practically the only contact with the Jewish world outside Germany, which made them particularly influential and increased the survivors' desire for a connection with Zionism and the Land of Israel.[43]

British Jews sent in by the JRU also bolstered the Zionist spirit. The JRU was not a Zionist entity but, as already mentioned, most of its workers held Zionist beliefs and belonged to Zionist organizations. The same held true for the military chaplains who came to Belsen. The post-Holocaust pro-Zionist consensus of the Jewish world, which embarked on a mission to rehabilitate the She'erit Hapletah, was particularly strong among British Jews. In 1943 presidential campaigns for the Board of Deputies of British Jews were fought on Zionist versus non-Zionist lines. The winner was a prominent Zionist, Professor Selig Brodetsky, a member of the World Zionist Executive. The strictly Orthodox Agudat Israel movement also began to reevaluate its anti-Zionist thinking and at the convention of its British branch in May 1945 declared the rehabilitation of Holocaust survivors and resettlement in Palestine mutually dependent. One of the heads of the Central British Fund, which organized and financed the JCRA, was the well-known Zionist Norman Bentwich. The chief rabbi of Great Britain, Joseph Hertz, who set up the Chief Rabbi's Religious Emergency Council for European Jews, was a long-standing Zionist, too.[44]

Aside from these positive reasons for embracing Zionism, there was also an element of defiance. The intransigence of the British liberators on many issues and the harsh living conditions to which the Jews were subjected in the British zone—and this included survivors as well as rescue teams from abroad—created a wall of resistance that helped to reinforce the Jewish national struggle.[45]

The British also disrupted Jewish attempts to organize. All requests for a general Jewish congress were turned down. No separate Jewish representational bodies were recognized, and no delegations were allowed to visit Bergen-Belsen from other parts of Germany or abroad. The attitude of the British is perhaps best exemplified by their refusal to use the name "Bergen-Belsen" although the DP camp was only a short distance from the liquidated death camp. In all British documents, it is referred to as the "Hohne camp," Hohne being another small town nearby.

Through their actions, the British liberators thus defeated their own purpose. Their anti-Jewish policies created a broad Jewish front inside and outside Germany aimed at the achievement of immediate Jewish national goals. From here, the move to long-range national goals was only a matter of time.

On July 25, 1945, a general assembly was held in Munich that was supposed to address issues of concern to both the American and the British zones. In practice, it was run by the leaders of the American zone alone and failed to establish a united organization for the whole of Germany. However, now that a separate framework had been cre-

Hagit Lavsky

ated for the American zone, the leaders of Bergen-Belsen realized that they would have to be more forceful in convening a congress for the British zone.[46] Without applying to the authorities, the congress was scheduled for September 1945 in a deliberate attempt to circumvent the British prohibition on delegates from abroad. The idea was to take advantage of the many Jewish leaders and journalists allowed into Germany as participants or observers at the Lüneburg trials (of Nazi criminals from Bergen-Belsen), about to open on September 17.

The congress took place as planned on September 25–27 without obtaining British permission. A total of 210 delegates representing a population of 40,000 Jews from forty-two camps and communities convened at Bergen-Belsen. Theoretically various zones of occupation were participating, but this time the American zone was absent, and the congress was run by the leaders of the British zone. Representatives of many Jewish organizations were present too, mostly from Great Britain.

The Bergen-Belsen congress convened under the Zionist flag, which had already been adopted as the Jewish flag throughout the post-Holocaust Jewish world. The congress was also united in its call to "Open the Gates of Palestine."

The Bergen-Belsen congress, which started out as a general assembly of the She'erit Hapletah, focused in the end on the British zone alone, laying the foundations for a more solid organizational structure: a seventeen-person Central Committee was elected, representing the entire region, with its headquarters in Bergen-Belsen. Yossel Rosensaft was elected chairman, with Norbert Wollheim as his deputy and the representative of the communities. Berl Dov Laufer was appointed organizational secretary; Hadassa Bimko was appointed head of the Health Department; Rafael Olewski, Paul Trepman, and David Rosenthal were appointed as heads of the Culture Department and editors of *Unzer Sztyme;* and Sami Feder, founder of the KZ Yiddish theater that gave its premiere at the congress, was appointed theater director. Rabbi Israel Moshe Olewski represented the Orthodox sector, and Rabbi Zvi Helfgott was the authority on rabbinic issues. Shmuel Weintraub of Hapo'el Hamizrahi (the religious Zionists) and Karl Katz of the Bremen community took charge of the Economic Department, which handled the allocation of food, clothing, and housing.[47]

In September 1945 the congress thus gave birth to an active national organization that appeared as a united front demanding free immigration to Palestine. This demand was not surprising considering the background described above and especially following Earl G. Harrison's recommendation to solve the Jewish DP problem through immigration to Palestine.[48] The DPs' demand became increasingly militant as time went on, with the DPs resorting to demonstrations, strikes, and even violence. When David Ben-Gurion, the head of the Jewish Agency, arrived at the end of October 1945, he already found a cohesive and determined Jewish entity ready to join the Zionist struggle for immigration to Palestine.[49]

The Central Committee was made up almost entirely by inmates from Bergen-Belsen and at first served both the British zone as a whole and the Belsen camp. In March 1947, however, a few months before the Second Congress of the She'erit Hapletah, a special committee was set up just to deal with Belsen.[50]

Although representatives of Belsen were in the majority and Belsen was by far the largest center of Jewish population in the British zone, the purpose—albeit unspoken—of the Central Committee was to represent all the Jews in the zone regardless of political, social, or cultural divisions.[51] Representatives of every party were thus included. Other camps and communities also enjoyed representation.

The Central Committee was basically a very centralized organization. Against the backdrop of harsh conditions, British hostility, frequent anti-Semitic outbursts by the Germans and the non-Jewish DPs, scarce welfare resources, and the prospect of a long struggle for freedom—an authoritarian, all-embracing framework—was regarded as the only solution. The Central Committee set out to be the sole governing body of the Jews in the British zone, responsible for internal affairs and serving as liaison with world Jewish organizations and the British authorities.[52] To achieve this goal it embarked on a broad range of semigovernmental activities, partnership with world Jewish organizations, political activism, and diplomatic efforts on behalf of the survivors.

In its bid to become the exclusive instrument of Jewish national self-government, the Central Committee worked on several fronts. It battled against the divide-and-rule policy of the British and against the German authorities' efforts to hinder its involvement but also against excessive intervention on the part of world Jewish organizations. The Central Committee claimed that it understood more so than those on the outside the needs and wishes of the survivors and that control over supplies and sharing in the management of welfare and rehabilitation projects were crucial. Internally, the Central Committee deemed a centralized apparatus essential for preserving unity and equality and ensuring that protégées of certain organizations were not singled out for preferential treatment.

In seeking to become the main governing and representative body, the Central Committee went through various phases of development and suffered a number of setbacks, especially during the first years of existence. By the eve of the second congress in July 1947, however, it was well on its way to reaching its goal of controlling almost every aspect of life—health, education and cultural activities, allocation of supplies, chief rabbinate, Jewish police, etc.—and enjoyed wide acceptance among the survivors. The authority of the Central Committee extended throughout the British zone with special emphasis on cooperation between the Belsen camp and the Jewish communities and catering to the needs of both the DPs and the German Jews.[53] Once the Central Committee was accepted as the national leader by all Jewish world organizations, the British were the only ones who refused adamantly to recognize the committee as the sole and exclusive representative of the DPs and the German Jews. The maximum that the British were ready to accept was the recognition of a committee representing Bergen-Belsen alone. Not long after the second congress of July 1947, when the United Nations voted on November 29, 1947, in favor of the partition of Palestine, the British no longer stood in the way of the Central Committee, which stopped insisting on unified leadership. In fact, the DPs and German Jewish communities chose separate paths, the DP leadership promoting emigration and liquidating the camps, and the Jewish community leadership supporting continued life in Germany.[54]

The organization in the American zone, though not less Zionist oriented, did not have to face American hostility and could not govern all of the dispersed camps in the larger American zone, each of which had its own independent committee. Therefore, the Central Committee of the American zone was less cohesive and in a worse condition to exercise authority in its bid for centralization and exclusiveness toward the DPs, the external Jewish organizations, and non-Jewish authorities. (The American military authorities recognized the Central Committee in the American zone as the official representative of the Jewish DP population there in September 1946.) Hence, the organization in the American zone was less unified and less militant than that of the British zone.[55]

EVERYDAY LIFE AND NEW BEGINNINGS

Our study is a case study, and indeed Bergen-Belsen was one of a kind due to its size, its sociodemographic composition, and its centrality within the British zone, which differed radically from the American zone, where most of the DPs were concentrated. Still, the processes generated in this camp exemplify the unique situation of the Jewish survivors, DPs, and immigrants after the Holocaust. While living without an inviting absorbing society, their personal rehabilitation processes were inseparably combined with the formation of a new society struggling both for its collective identity and for its members' rehabilitation. The various activities, institutions, and organizations and the formation of economic, political, social, educational, religious, and cultural systems and of a culture of memory were all inseparably interwoven with many conflicts and struggles that accompanied the development of new internal and external as well as Jewish and non-Jewish channels of communication.

We should note that it was precisely the difficult conditions of life in the camps that produced various initiatives and improvisations. In contrast to the widely accepted stereotypic images of the devastating consequences of the Holocaust and of the welfare-dependent life with its forced or willful idleness and black market, there were also other aspects to life in the camp.

The basic condition of living in barracks endured for many years. People slept, ate, and dressed in a single room; cooked in a common kitchen; and washed in common bathrooms. However, over the course of time, people managed to make their rooms resemble a normal flat by adding furniture, dishes, and electrical equipment for light, heating, and cooking. They added paintings and hanged curtains, either self-made or bought, and exchanged for other commodities.[56]

Vocational training was only one of many ways in which camp inmates earned their living. Many people offered their skills or were employed by UNRRA and the Jewish welfare services: teachers, nurses, policemen, clerks, locksmiths, technicians, shoemakers, bakers, etc. They were paid by extra JDC rations, which they could use in exchange for other commodities.[57] Others who had prior experience in various trades were able to offer their services locally or to open workshops and shops of various types in the camp. These shops were called canteens, and on walking through the streets in Belsen (or for that matter reading the advertisements in *Unzer Sztyme*) one could find services being offered for hairdressing (for men and women), dry-cleaning, shoe repair, printing, and chauffeuring. These small businesses were the natural response to a growing demand that increased in quantity and diversification among the camp dwellers along with the process of establishing families and settling down. Thus many people, though not becoming rich, managed to improve their living conditions and to accumulate property for their current use or for their entrepreneurial endeavors as well as for their future.[58]

The most important incentive to emerge out of the despair and deep depression and loss was establishing new families, compensation for the loss of relatives and families in the Holocaust. The drive to regain a sense of normal life quickly overcame obstacles of poor

Hagit Lavsky

health, uncertainty concerning the fate of relatives, and loneliness. The natural way to fight despair, to make the grim present appear somewhat brighter, and to face an unclear future was to find love and friendship. Living together in the barracks meant that there was constant contact between people and an ongoing opportunity to approach each other on a personal level. Young widowers and widows met and shared their grief, grievances, and fears. During the first year after liberation there were numerous weddings, sometimes up to 6 in a single day, even 50 in a week. During 1946 there were 1,070 weddings in the British zone alone.[59] With the weddings, new families were formed and babies were born. By 1948 the 1,000th Jewish baby was born in Belsen. For early 1948 the statistics numbered 1,278 children up to the age of three and in Belsen alone there were 934 children in this age range.[60]

Family life became a vital basis for physical and mental rehabilitation. Struggling with Holocaust traumas was postponed. Raising children reflected the combination of individual and collective aspects of life in the camp. These children were not only a source of personal joy for their parents but also became the center of the camp's social and public life. Around them and their families the whole social and cultural system was built.

Already shortly after liberation a handful of survivors began to organize schools for the children who were among the survivors, which was an exception for Belsen. During the following months, soldiers of the Jewish Brigade and JRU, ORT, JDC, and JAP emissaries joined in and helped to develop the educational system initiated by the survivors. By March 1946 there was a network of educational institutions in Belsen, including kindergarten and primary school; a Hebrew high school; two Talmud Torah schools, a Beth Jacob girls' school, and a teachers' seminar; a yeshiva; a vocational school; a people's university; and an orphanage. In addition to the formal institutions there was a great variety of informal education that operated through the various youth movements and kibbutzim.[61]

Everyday life in its public expressions and the intensive literary and theatrical activities revealed the will to commemorate and preserve the Holocaust memory along with the desire to revive the formerly vital Jewish culture and tradition. The DPs coupled this activity with the aspiration to establish a new Jewish national sovereignty in Palestine. Among the many DPs there were quite a number of outstanding thinkers, Orthodox and liberal, who were occupied with the attempt to explain the disaster that had befallen the Jewish people and to draw consequences as to the meaning and mission of Jewish life thereafter. These people took an active part in the leadership, and

Schoolchildren marching in the Bergen-Belsen camp. (Yad Vashem Photo Archives)

moreover, they wrote intensively, created, and expressed their thinking in many forms: in newspapers, in the realm of education, and in their cultural performance and political activity. Their lessons found a fertile ground among their fellow survivors, who longed for some form of self-respect, meaning, and a sense of belonging within the emptiness and often demoralizing existence as DPs.

As already mentioned, in July 1945 shortly after the liberation, the first Yiddish publication in the British zone, *Unzer Sztyme*, appeared and developed to become the official organ of the Central Committee. It was meant to serve as the main tool for expressing the concerns and the wishes of the survivors, to become the central voice of the Belsen leadership inwardly and outwardly, to encourage the Jewish discourse with worldwide participation, and to become the channel for bringing the best of Jewish culture and national aspirations to the attention of the survivors. In the course of the years it grew in size and diversity and was read by most of the survivors in the British zone and by many outsiders. It was followed by many other periodicals and other publications. Besides publication activities involving periodicals there were many other cultural initiatives in the spheres of theater, public libraries, book publishing, concerts and entertainment evenings, lectures, chess clubs, sport games, etc. Such a vibrant cultural activity was even more pronounced in the American zone, which was richer in human resources.[62]

Much emphasis in cultural and social life was put on the Zionist-nationalist aspects, but this was not as an antithesis to traditional Jewish culture. It was carried out in a unique version that tried to integrate them together. Hence, in contrast to prevailing impressions that most Holocaust survivors abandoned religion because they lost their faith as the consequence of their Holocaust lesson, religious life in the camp had a prestigious status. Rabbis actively participated in the leadership of the camp and of the British zone at large, and spontaneous yearning for Jewish religious traditions was felt throughout the camp, which could be conceived as a link in a long Jewish chain. Thus, in spite of disagreements, many accommodations were found and played out in the course of time, as most residents wished for a public life that would have a Jewish character. On the other hand, previously anti-Zionist ultra-Orthodox inhabitants wished in the context of the new special circumstances to become an integral part of the national body. This was manifested in their active participation in both the organizing committee and in cultural and educational life. This does not mean that everything was smooth and agreed-upon; there were many antagonisms and difficulties. However, the common wishes to construct some form of Jewish respectful existence in the present and for the future overcame to a certain degree these difficulties.

Intensive debates and political orientations and affiliations served as social cohesive glue, forming various groups that segregated and contested and even struggled with each other. The political activities in the camp served as a most important vehicle for creating an intimate and defining framework separated from and contrasted with other such frameworks. These political settings were a crucial sociocultural space for nourishing an active involvement in public life, for building genuine motivation in the survivors to hold to an important cause, and thus for acquiring a renewed sense of belonging, of feeling they were once again, despite everything, masters of their own destiny and heading forward toward the future.

Hence this civil society grew from the bottom up. It started with individuals who were developing their families, but these individuals were searching to become involved in something that would go beyond a basic personal identification. In this sense they yearned to belong to a wider worldview, which the political parties could supply. The enthusiastic political activities, with their separatist inclinations, were in this context a positive factor in the process of developing a new shared public life. It was precisely the clear and salient identity given by the political activities and debates that gave some color and meaning to the individuals, each in their own group, and that deeply fermented public life in the camp. This intensive schismatic activity created a form of national consensus in the camps and pushed to the margins the nonbelonging groups (such as the Jewish socialist and non-Zionist labor union Bund), excluding them from the She'erit Hapletah as an exclusive group. Alternatively, this same process pulled toward the inside whoever stood in the past at a certain distance, such as the extreme Orthodox party Agudath Israel, which was formerly an anti-Zionist party. Inside this evolving national consensus—Jewish and Zionist alike—the excluding, separatist system served as a life elixir.

THE CASE OF BERGEN-BELSEN
REPRESENTING THE SHE'ERIT HAPLETAH

The concept of She'erit Hapletah refers to Holocaust survivors in general but focuses specifically on those survivors who, having been forced by postwar conditions to stay in DP camps, have become an exterritorial immigrant population. This not only involves what they had experienced in the Holocaust but also relates to the postwar conditions that they were living in. They lacked any control over their fate and destiny, lived in difficult conditions in a deadlocked trap. They were a small enclave cut off to a large extent from the external world in detested Germany and exposed to anti-Semitic taunts by German and other nationalities, and thus they were deeply vulnerable and easily demoralized.

The study of the She'erit Hapletah has attracted the attention of historians due to its unique location at the crossroads between the Holocaust and the establishment of the State of Israel and because of the role that the Holocaust survivors' issue played in the political struggle of the Zionist movement and in the international arena.

Studying individuals and public life in the Bergen-Belsen DP camp exposes the Zionist spirit that dominated life there and reveals that the national leanings of the She'erit Hapletah was neither a manipulative effort by external forces nor a constructed ideology, formed as the only possible consequence of the Shoah, but instead was a spontaneous creation born in the context of the issues, experiences, and struggles within and in relation to the camp and its surroundings. This national leaning might be called a functional Zionism that the survivors used, discovered, interpreted, and implemented as a renewed kind of Zionism in the context of their own experiences and struggles.

Life in the camps in general became a greenhouse for a new Jewish national identity and the formation of a shared public life while providing a unique setting for a new discourse. Lacking any prior assumed organizational styles or agreed-upon norms, codes, or behavioral habits, they had to create and negotiate these among themselves. The survivors' sole common ground was their past and present difficult experiences and their deep desire to achieve, once again, a free, normal life. Here then developed a unique paradigm of public Jewish life that had to dictate to itself new, or renewed, norms and values and struggled to crystallize and achieve a common goal.

The detailed analysis of the survivors' experiences and activities in one DP camp unveils the various mechanisms involved in the formation of such a community in transition. Through their own mutual experiences they started a process of shaping and experimenting with a new complex post-Holocaust Jewish national identity. What was unique for the British zone was that the rehabilitation mechanisms were combined with a tough British policy and therefore formed the centralized organization of the DP community. The paradoxical outcome of the British policy was that Jews had no choice but to get organized in a national and militant fashion, assisted and backed by world Jewish organizations. The Jews related their struggle to improve their living conditions (and their demand to be released from their new trap) with a more general Jewish struggle for national recognition. This linkage was ipso facto tied up with the struggle with the British on the other front, the British Mandate in Palestine. The organizational constellation in the camp, which made Zionism the center of political activity, was based on the obvious functional advantages of Zionism at that time. Zionism was the only political agent that could supply an operational ready-made organizational and ideological paradigm, some hope for the future, and a cause worth fighting for. It is no wonder, then, that the leadership emerging right in the beginning and persisting throughout the camp period consisted mainly of young Holocaust survivors who were former political activists, mostly in Zionist organizations.

Zionism as such did not characterize the Central Committee in the British zone alone, but its composition and patterns of activities were quite different from the American zone. Its centralized functioning, its pluralistic makeup, its being the representative of the DPs and the communities alike, and its militant Zionist activity were all in contrast with the type of organization in the American zone.

The educational system activity in Bergen-Belsen illustrates the dynamics of shaping national consensus. The atmosphere in most of the educational institutions was nationalistic. The most dominant and determining factor in its operation was the survivors themselves, led by the Central Committee and enjoying the cooperation of external organizations in fostering a Zionist atmosphere. The group of emissaries from Palestine arrived in Belsen only after most institutions were already at the peak of their activities. Representatives of the JDC provided basic equipment, and agents of the JRU provided professional

The Second Congress of the Liberated Jews in the British zone, Bad Harzburg, July 1947. (Yad Vashem Photo Archives)

and organizational skills alongside much active support in the Zionist mode of the educational system.

This Zionist bent of the external organizations was the outcome not only of the fact that even the emissaries of non-Zionist organizations happened to personally be Zionists but also because these organizations recognized the functional importance of the national spirit as an important mechanism for elevating the morale of the DPs and preparing them for the future. It thus seems that the She'erit Hapletah held an active role in the creation of a pro-Zionist cooperation among the entire Jewish public in the free world in these years.

One of the more interesting phenomena in the organizational processes of the camp community in the British zone was the reciprocation and collaboration that took place between the DPs and the local Jewish communities organizations. We have already pointed at some of the special circumstances of this area that stimulated this cooperation and helped establish it on a national and even a militant basis, among which was the British policy, the funneling power of the Central Committee in Bergen-Belsen, its stable population, and its living together in comparison to the scattering mobility and multiplicity that characterized the American zone.

These circumstances were relevant not only for the camp community but also for the renewing local Jewish communities in spite of the fact that in many respects there were many differences between them and the DPs. The relatively large Jewish communities established in the British zone—Hamburg, Cologne, Düsseldorf, and Hanover—were all established by Jews of German origin who had been hidden or had returned from the concentration camps. They were composed of an aging and ill population who could hardly think of the possibility of immigrating and building a Jewish life elsewhere. Notwithstanding, and perhaps as a consequence, in building these communities they were wishing for some sort of a new Jewish identity that would relate to their vanished Jewish past and would give some taste of continuity with that past. Their leaders understood that their ability to provide an answer to the complex needs involved in building a new Jewish life in Germany was dependent to a large extent on their integration with the overall national Jewish organizations in the local as well as the international context. Thus, at the beginning of 1946 the Jews of the British zone started to organize on the basis of regional states, which soon after turned into the parent organization of the entire British zone in cooperation with the Central Committee. At the same time they acted under the banner of a Zionist-nationalistic struggle alongside their struggle for international recognition of the local Jewish community in Germany. The issue of the future of Jews in Germany thus turned into an integral part of the Central Committee agenda. It is no coincidence that the Jewish communities of the British zone were the ones that created the foundations for the establishment of the Central Council of the Jews in Germany, founded in 1950.

Despite all that was unique for the British zone, the experiences of the survivors there and their responses represent the She'erit Hapletah in general. It is possible to define as nationalistic the various active responses of these Holocaust survivors to the situation in which they found themselves, a situation they referred to as liberated but not free. It developed into a major axis point as they confronted and struggled with myriad obstacles on their road to freedom. The struggle for freedom was identified and closely combined with the Zionist struggle for Jewish sovereignty in Palestine. It grew from the inside and received much encouragement from and collaboration with many Jewish organizations.

This was true to a large extent regarding all Jewish DP communities in Central Europe. However, it is reasonable to assume that in the British zone in Germany it was particularly noticeable due to the special circumstances and because Britain stood as an obstacle to the Jewish cause on all fronts at once. It is thus possible that in the British zone, more than in the American zone, there was much collaboration among the various Zionist parties, between Zionist and non-Zionists, and between the DPs and the communities of German Jews.

The She'erit Hapletah in general, and the survivors of Bergen-Belsen in particular, embodied both the horrors of the Holocaust and the challenges toward which the discourse concerning the future of the Jewish people was directed. In this sense the DP camps served as an active meeting place of national solidarity despite many differences, a phenomenon that is unique in Jewish history.

NOTES

1. *Volks- und Berufszählung vom 29. Oktober 1946 in den vier Besatzungszonen und Groß-Berlin* (Berlin: Duncker and Humboldt); Werner Abelshauser, "Die Rekonstruktion der westdeutschen Wirtschaft und die Rolle der Besatzunspolitik," in *Politische und ökonomische Stabilisierung Westdeutschlands, 1945–1949,* edited by Claus Scharf, Hans Schröder, and Hans Jürgen, 1–17 (Wiesbaden: F. Steiner, 1977); John E. Farquharson, *The Western Allies and the Politics of Food: Agrarian Management in Postwar Germany* (Warwickshire and Dover, NH: Berg, 1985); Arieh L. Kochavi, *Post-Holocaust Politics: Britain, the United States & Jewish Refugees, 1945–1948* (Chapel Hill: University of North Carolina Press, 2001).

2. Ursula Büttner, "Not nach der Befreiung—die Situation der deutschen Juden in der britischen Besatzungszone, 1945–1948," in *Das Unrechtsregime—Internationale Forschung über den Nationalsozialismus, Band 2: Verfolgung—Exil—Belasteter Neubeginn,* edited by Ursula Büttner, Angelika Voss, and Werner Johe, 373–406 (Hamburg: Christians, 1986).

3. Hagit Lavsky, *New Beginnings: Holocaust Survivors in Bergen-Belsen and the British Zone in Germany, 1945–1950* (Detroit: Wayne State University Press, 2002), 51–52.

4. Büttner, "Not nach der Befreiung."

5. Report by S. Rurka, September 1945, Henriques Collection, Belsen Reports, Wiener Library Institute of Contemporary History, London (hereafter WL). See also Norman Bentwich, *They Found Refuge* (London: Cresset, 1956), 176–77.

6. Directions by the Headquarters, Prisoners of War & Displaced Persons Division, Control Commission Germany (British Element), November 19, 1945, Foreign Office Papers (hereafter FO), file 1049/81, British Public Record Office, Kew (hereafter PRO); Chilento (UNRRA) to Brotman and Viteles, March 8, 1946, FO, file 1013/1948, PRO; announcement by the police, August 29, 1946, YIVO microfilm JM reel 10.374, frame 1576, Yad Vashem Archives (hereafter YVA). As for the American

policy, see Leonard Dinnerstein, *America and the Survivors of the Holocaust* (New York: Columbia University Press, 1982).

7. Adler-Rudel, Memorandum of June 28, 1945, collection A140, file 272, Central Zionist Archives, Jerusalem (hereafter CZA); Memorandum on resettlement of Jews, by Colonel Solomon, May 1946, FO, file 945/384, PRO; Report submitted by the Central Jewish Committee, British zone, to the director-general of UNRRA, August 23, 1946, Record group (hereafter RG) O70, file 6, YVA. Calculation based on the official census of 1946; see *Volks- und Berufszählung.*

8. According to UNRRA statistics for June 1946. See Wolfgang Jacobmeyer, "Jüdische Überlebende als Displaced Persons," *Geschichte und Gesellschaft* 99, no. 3 (1983): 421–52.

9. Dinnerstein, *America and the Survivors of the Holocaust,* 278–84.

10. Ibid.; Yehuda Bauer, *Flight and Rescue: Brichah; The Organized Escape of Jewish Survivors of Eastern Europe, 1944–1948* (New York: Random House 1970); idem, *Out of the Ashes: The Impact of American Jews on Post-Holocaust European Jewry* (New York: Pergamon, 1989), 104-32.

11. Bauer, *Out of the Ashes,* 104-32. A detailed listing of all the camps and assembly centers, with exact locations and numbers, appears in Angelika Koenigseder and Juliane Wetzel, *Waiting for Hope: Jewish Displaced Persons in Post–World War II Germany,* translated from the German by John A. Broadwin (Evanston, IL: Northwestern University Press, 2001), 215-55.

12. Lesley H. Hardman, *The Survivors: The Story of the Belsen Remnant* (London: Valentine, Mitchell, 1958); Isaac Levy, *Witness to Evil: Bergen-Belsen, 1945* (London: P. Halban, 1995); Derrick Sington, *Belsen Uncovered* (London: Duckworth, 1946); letters of Rabbi Isaac Levy, *Jewish Chronicle,* May 4, 1945, 1, and June 8, 1945, 1; Hadassa Bimko-Rosensaft, "The Children of Belsen," in *Belsen,* published by Irgun sheerit Hapleita me'haezor Habriti Israel (Tel Aviv: Irgun, 1957), 98–108; Paul Trepman, "Monthly Report," *Unzer Sztyme* 5 (November 29, 1945): 6–8 (esp. 7); Eryl Hall Williams, *A Page of History in Relief* (York, UK: Sessions Book Trust, 1993), 28–29, quotes estimates ranging from 237 to 700 for the number of orphaned children; Thomas Rahe, "Jüdische Waisenkinder im Konzentrationslager Bergen-Belsen," *Dachauer Hefte* 14 (1998): 31–49.

13. Letter by Rabbi Klein, *Jewish Chronicle,* June 22, 1945, 14; letter by Rabbi Levy, *Jewish Chronicle,* May 4, 1945; Sington, *Belsen Uncovered,* 202.

14. Michael Brenner, *After the Holocaust: Rebuilding Jewish Lives in Postwar Germany,* translated by Barbara Harshav (Princeton, NJ: Princeton University Press, 1997), 45; Lavsky, *New Beginnings,* chap. 5.

15. Bauer, *Out of the Ashes,* 30, 41–42; Rosensaft to E. Warburg, November 11, RG O70, file 17, YVA.

16. Bauer, *Out of the Ashes,* 30, 41–42; Brotman-Viteles report, March 29, 1946, RG O70, file 6, YVA.

17. Bauer, *Out of the Ashes,* xviii.

18. Bimko-Rosensaft, "The Children of Belsen," 37; Vida Kaufman, "An American in Belsen," in *Belsen*, 152–55.

19. Haim Yahil, "The Activities of the Palestine Mission for She'erit Hapletah, 1945–1949," Parts 1 and 2, *Yalkut Moreshet* 30 (November 1980): 7–40, and 31 (April 1981): 133–76.

20. Ibid.; The Histadrut Zionit Ahida in Bergen-Belsen to the JAP, Paris, April 2, 1946, RG L10, file 232I, CZA.

21. Report on emissaries, May 26, 1946, RG S86, file 343, CZA; JAP mission Diary no. 3, February 9, 1947, RG S25, file 5231, CZA; Irit Keynan, *Lo nirga ha-ra'av: Nitzolei ha-sho'ah u-shelihei Eretz-Yisrael, Germaniyah 1945-1948* [Holocaust Survivors and the Emissaries from Eretz Israel: Germany, 1945–1948] (Tel Aviv: Am Oved, 1996), 197–205.

22. Keynan, *Lo nirga ha-ra'av*, 117–31.

23. Bichler to comrades, [December 1946], RG S6, file 1911, CZA; Lewin to Behar, July 2, 1947, RG S6, file 3658, CZA; Z. Zamarion (Halpern), "A Shaliach in Belsen," in *Belsen*, 177–81.

24. Many letters of complaints testify to the absence of regular contact with either the JAP headquarters in Jerusalem or with the mission's center in the American zone. See, for example, Chomsky to Behar, August 20, 1947, RG S6, file 1627, and many others in RG S86, file 284, CZA. JAP correspondence with the British zone occupies only a very small section of the Emissaries Archive (RG S86) in CZA. See also, Yahil, "The Activities of the Palestine Mission for She'erit Hapletah, 1945–1949," part 1, 147–51.

25. Levy, *Witness to Evil*, 103.

26. List of field workers of the JCRA, May 10, 1946, Schonfeld Papers, file 130/1, Special Collection Division, Hartley Library at the University of Southampton; Central British Fund, *Annual Report 1946*, 3, Central British Fund (CBF) Collection, WL.

27. Central British Fund, *Annual Report 1945, Annual Report 1946,* and *Annual Report 1947,* CBF Collection, WL; Reports by Rabbi Goldfinger, January and March 1946, and by Reverend Carlebach, October 20, 1946, and December 7, 20, and 31, 1946, Henriques Collection, Brunswick Reports, Hamburg Reports, Lübeck Reports, WL.

28. D. S. Norman, Military Government Berlin, to Headquarters, Control Commission Germany (British Element), December 11, 1945, FO, file 1050/1491, PRO; a meeting of British Military authorities, May 20, 1946, FO, file 1049/418, PRO; report by Lily Holt, July 8, 1946, Henriques Collection, Kaunitz Reports, WL; Lowenthal, Field Director, Germany to Germany Dept., JCRA, June 14, 1947, Henriques Collection, Reorganization of Communal Life, WL.

29. B. Weingreen, Report on Jews in the North-Rhine Region, October 15, 1945, Henriques Collection, LV North Rhine-Westfalia, WL; memorandum on the German Jews in Germany, December 4, 1945, FO, file 945/384, PRO; memorandum from Henriques to Solomon, August 10, 1946, FO, file 1049/368, PRO; Central British Fund, *Annual Report*

1946, 5, WL.

30. Control Commission Germany (British Element) to all Military District Headquarters, November 19, 1945, on segregation of Jews, FO, file 1049/81, PRO; Zone policy instruction no. 20, December 4, 1945, RG O70, file 6, YVA; report on a visit of the Parliamentary Committee headed by Secretary Hynd to Bergen-Belsen, January 21, 1946, RG O70, file 5, YVA; N. Barou of the World Jewish Congress to A. Skeffington (Control Office for Germany and Austria, London), March 8, 1946, RG O70, file 16, YVA; Robertson, Control Commission Germany, Berlin to Street, War Office, May 7, 1946, FO, file 945/384, PRO.

31. Nadich stayed from August to November 1945, Rifkind from October 1945 to March 1946, Bernstein from May 1946 to August 1947, Levinthal from June to December 1947, etc.; finding a replacement was always difficult. See Haim Genizi, *Yo'etz u-mekim: ha-yo'etz la-tzava ha-amerikani ule'she'erit hapletah* [The Adviser on Jewish Affairs to the American Army and the Displaced Persons, 1945–1949] (Tel Aviv: Moreshet, 1987); Central British Fund, *Annual Report 1945*, *Annual Report 1946*, and *Annual Report 1947*, WL.

32. See, for example, Major Murphy to Displaced Persons Headquarters, April 15, 1946, FO, file 1030/307, PRO; Robertson to Solomon, May 2, 1946, and notes on a proposal for the resettlement of Jews by the adviser Colonel Solomon, May 8, 1946, FO, file 945/384, PRO.

33. Central British Fund, *Annual Report 1947*, 2–9, WL; see also Lavsky, *New Beginnings*, chap. 12.

34. Rosensaft and Wollheim to Kubowitzky, [July 1947], World Jewish Congress Papers, file 9A, CZA; Shlomo Shafir, "Der Jüdische Weltkongress und sein Verhältnis zu Nachkriegsdeutschland, 1945–1967," *Menora: Jahrbuch für deutsch-jüdische Geschichte* 3 (1993): 210–37; Josef Rosensaft, "Our Belsen," in *Belsen*, 24-51; Norbert Wollheim, "Belsen's Place in the Process of 'Death and Rebirth' of the Jewish People," in *Belsen*, 52–66; Noah Barou, "Remembering Belsen," in *Belsen*, 81–86; and Alex L. Easterman, "They Were Liberated but Not Free," in *Belsen*, 87–93.

35. On the high JDC American employee turnover, see Bauer, *Out of the Ashes*, xx–xxi.

36. Rabbi Levy's letter to the *Jewish Chronicle*, May 4, 1945, 1, shows that the committee was active well before the transfer to the military camp, which took place from April 24 to May 19. The first entry in the committee's protocol book is June 24, 1945, RG O70, file 1, YVA.

37. Rafael Olewski, "A Blat yiddische Geschichte in haintiken Deutschland," *Unzer Sztyme* 2 (August 15, 1945): 30–31; List of the members of the Central Committee of Bergen-Belsen and the British zone, in *Belsen*, 195–97; *Yiddisher Heftlings-congress in Bergen-Belsen, 25–27 September 1945* (Bergen-Belsen: Zentral Yiddisher Komitet, 1945).

38. Rafael Olewski, "Roich," *Unzer Sztyme* 11 (July 12, 1946): 7–8.

39. Report on the conference, RG O70, file 25, YVA.

40. Ibid.

41. For further details about the educational system, see Lavsky, *New Beginnings*, chap. 10.

42. It was preceded by *Tehiat Hametim* [The Resurrection of the Dead], first published in Buchenwald on May 14, 1945. See Zeev Mankowitz, "The Formation of She'erit Hapleita: November 1944–July 1945," *Yad Vashem Studies* 20 (1990): 337–70.

43. On the Jewish Brigade soldiers, see information in *Unzer Sztyme* 1 (July 12, 1945): 10-11. On the desire for connections with Zionism and the Land of Israel, see Jacob Landa, "Mit wos kenn man undz traisten?," *Unzer Sztyme* 2 (August 15, 1945): 38–39.

44. Resolutions of Agudath Israel convention in London, May 21, 1945, FO, file 1050/1491, PRO; protocol of the conference of British Jewish organizations held in London on the Jewish DP problem, May 23, 1945, RG C11, file 13/17/2, and draft decision by the Board of Deputies of British Jews, July 15, 1945, RG C11, file 13/16/3, Board of Deputies of British Jews Archive, London.

45. Report by Sadi Rurka, September 1945, Henriques Collection, Belsen Reports, WL.

46. Jewish Telegraphic Agency report on the Munich congress, July 31, 1945, RG O37, file 19/1, YVA; Yehuda Bauer, "The Initial Organization of the Holocaust Survivors in Bavaria," *Yad Vashem Studies* 8 (1971): 127–57; Mankowitz, "The Formation of She'erit Hapleita."

47. *Yiddisher Heftlings-congress in Bergen-Belsen, 25–27 September 1945*, and the appendix in *Belsen*, 195–97, differ with regard to many of these appointments. See also the protocol of the first meeting of the committee, October 3, 1945, RG O70, file 1, YVA.

48. The Zionist leadership under Ben-Gurion and Weizmann still hoped for a change in the Mandatory immigration policy (the 1939 White Paper policy). In her book on Bergen-Belsen, Joanne Reilly, while presenting her arguments against Zionist historiography, is mislead by the false assumption as if Zionism in 1945 meant exclusively the struggle for a Jewish state. See Joanne Reilly, *Belsen: The Liberation of a Concentration Camp* (London and New York: Routledge, 1998), 145–91.

49. David Ben-Gurion's report on his visit to the camps at a meeting in London, November 6, 1945, RG S25, file 5231, CZA.

50. In his memorandum of May 1946 (FO, file 1049/367, PRO) Colonel Solomon, the Jewish adviser, writes about an official subcommittee for the Bergen-Belsen camp, although in practice the Central Committee and the Bergen-Belsen Committee were one and the same. On the Bergen-Belsen Committee, see the appendix in *Belsen*, 195–97. The establishment of a subcommittee seems to have been connected with the struggle for the British recognition.

51. On the need for unity, see B. Laufer, "Milchome der Zersplitterung," *Unzer Sztyme* 5 (November 29, 1945): 29.

52. Rosensaft in a meeting with British Parliament Commission in Bergen-

Belsen on January 20, 1946 (report dated January 21), RG O70, file 5, YVA; Viteles and Nurock on the Central Committee, in a Jewish survey meeting, April 1, 1946, FO, file 1050/1491, PRO; protocol of a meeting of all the committees and the communities, May 9, 1946, RG B1, file 6, Community of Hanover Archives, Zentralarchiv zur Erforschung der Geschichte der Juden, Deutschland, Heidelberg (hereafter ZAH); Rosensaft to La Guardia, director general of UNRRA, August 23, 1946, RG O70, file 6, YVA.

53. Circular on Central Committee handling of affairs in various communities, December 16, 1945, RG O70, file 64, YVA; report by Wollheim, January 21, 1946, RG O70 file 5, YVA; reports by Wollheim, March 14 and April 8, 1946, RG O70, file 63, YVA; Central Committee circular, July 31, 1946, RG O70, file 13, YVA; protocol of a meeting of Jewish committees and communities in Bremen, May 9, 1946, RG B1, file 6, ZAH; Hanover Jewish Committee to Central Committee, July 15, 1946, and November 17, 1946, Henriques Collection, Hanover Papers, WL; Announcement on a German newspaper put out by the cultural department for the communities, *Unzer Sztyme* 14 (October 2, 1946): 28.

54. On negotiations up until recognition, see Sir Brian Robertson to Gilmore Jenkins, January 9, 1947, FO, file 945/399, PRO; Jenkins to Robertson, February 14, 1947, FO, file 1049/890, PRO; Wollheim to Barou, May 30, 1947, and Barou to Rosensaft, August 1, 1947, World Jewish Congress Papers, file 9A, CZA; Dallob to Katzki, January 21, 1948, on the British authorities finally recognizing the Central Committee as representative of the camps, RG 7A, file C-48.009, Givat Joint Archives, Jerusalem; Report on the second congress of the She'erit Hapletah, including a synopsis by Josef Rosensaft, on two and a half years under British control, *Unzer Sztyme* 22 (August 20, 1947): 15–16; protocol of the Central Committee executive, planning for liquidation, November 28, 1948, RG O70, file 4, YVA.

55. For the American zone, see Zeev Mankowitz, *Life between Memory and Hope: The Survivors of the Holocaust in Occupied Germany* (Cambridge: Cambridge University Press, 2002), 101–30.

56. Announcement by the Bergen-Belsen Committee regarding the use of electricity, YIVO microfilm JM reel 10.374, frame 1573, YVA.

57. Report of the JDC, *Central Committee of Liberated Jews in the British Zone of Germany, 1945–1947: Activities Report Submitted to the Second Congress of Sh'erit Hapletah* [Bad Harzburg, July 1947].

58. Interviews with Ze'ev and Rachel Fischler (1994), Avraham Greenbaum (1992), Arieh and Sonia Havkin (1993), Michael Klodowsky (1997), and Yitzhak Kerbel (1993), Oral History Division, Institute of Contemporary Jewry, Hebrew University of Jerusalem.

59. Brotman-Viteles report, March 29, 1946, RG O70, file 6, YVA; Report of the Chief Rabbinate, *Unzer Sztyme* 16 (December 15, 1946): 32.

60. Report of the JDC, *Central Committee of Liberated Jews in the British Zone of Germany, 1945–1947*, 31–35; JDC report, September 29, 1947,

RG O70, file 35, YVA; JDC statistics for the British zone, January 1, 1948, RG O70, file 17, YVA.

61. Lavsky, *New Beginnings*, chap. 10.

62. Mankowitz, *Life between Memory and Hope*, chap. 7; Jacqueline D. Giere, "We Are on Our Way, but Not in the Wilderness," in *The Holocaust and History: The Known, the Unknown, the Disputed and the Reexamined*, edited by Michael Berenbaum and Abraham J. Peck, 699–715 (Bloomington: Indiana University Press, 1998).

Jewish Observance in Amalek's Shadow

Mourning, Marriage, and Birth Rituals among Displaced Persons in Germany

MARGARETE MYERS FEINSTEIN

Much has been written about the theological implications of the Holocaust and the responses of religious leaders to the problem of how to explain God's apparent absence. Focusing on the displaced persons (DPs), Gershon Greenberg has written about the efforts of DP rabbis to make sense of their recent experience, and Judith Tydor Baumel has examined the politics of Jewish religious aid groups in the DP camps,[1] but little has been done to study the role of religion among the wider Jewish DP community. Jewish DPs tended to gravitate to the religious practices of their prewar homes. Although they differed in beliefs and levels of observance, Jewish survivors shared a need to mourn and commemorate their dead and to sanctify their marriages and births.

An examination of life-cycle observances among Jewish DPs in postwar Germany illuminates the role that religious rituals played in creating social bonds among survivors, shaping identity, and reclaiming their agency. By providing opportunities for the retelling of their Holocaust experiences, Jews who had survived the war years in different ways (for example, in hiding, as partisans, in concentration camps, or through flight into the Soviet Union) were able to form collective memories of their families' fates. Rituals reaffirmed Jewish identity, and their performance in the land of their persecutors proclaimed the endurance and continuity of the Jewish people.

Mourning the dead and providing for burial were often the first communal religious acts after liberation. Ernst Landau's transport was liberated near Feldafing by U.S. soldiers who immediately brought their Jewish chaplain to meet with the survivors. In an open field, the few rabbis who were in the transport together with the chaplain led an estimated fifteen hundred survivors in their first religious service in freedom. With no *kippot* (religious head coverings) to cover their heads for worship, these survivors improvised: "We put the jacket of the concentration camp uniform on or just put our hand on our head."[2] Since everyone had lost most of their families, they first recited a memorial prayer for the dead. Those who knew that their parents had been murdered or no longer had hopes that they had survived said the mourners' Kaddish.[3] Landau recalls that "it was the most moving religious service I have ever experienced."[4]

The Kaddish touched an emotional chord in the survivors; virtually all were in mourning for their parents. Traditionally recited in a public congregation consisting of at least ten Jewish adult males, known as a minyan,[5] the prayer often had a consoling effect, demonstrating to the mourner that he was not alone and was building a sense of community.[6] Despite his then anger at God, Elie Wiesel helped to organize a minyan to say Kaddish after the liberation of Buchenwald: "That Kaddish at once a glorification of God's name and a protest against His creation, still echoes in my ears." Praise and protest mingled in the hearts of the worshipers. The communal nature of the minyan finds expression in Wiesel's language. He writes not of his personal feelings about this Kaddish but rather of the collective experience: "It was a thanksgiving for having spared *us,* but it was also an outcry. 'Why did You not spare so many others?' There were no joyous embraces, no shouts or songs to mark *our* happiness, for that word was meaningless to *us. We* were not happy."[7] With liberation the struggle for mere survival had ended, and mourning could begin. Even while some raged against God they offered the prayer of Kaddish, honoring the memory of their dead and forming a Jewish community of mourners.

Bergen-Belsen survivor Pearl Benisch recalls an impromptu address at a Belsen DP camp assembly by Rivkah Horowitz, the leader of the Beth Jacob school, an ultra-Orthodox girls' movement affiliated with Agudath Israel. While endorsing the Zionist program of the Jewish camp committee, Horowitz exhorted the survivors to live for more than immigration to Palestine:

God has chosen us to live. Why us? We don't know, but we

know that we were chosen, chosen to continue the chain of Jewish heritage by living a pure and moral life, by following in our parents' footsteps and embodying their creed. . . . Dear sisters and brothers, we were left in this world to say a collective *Kaddish* for all those who are gone, to sanctify Hashem's Name and theirs by continuing to live as they did. In spite of all our enemies, we are here, alive! *Am Yisrael chai*! Our nation is destined to live.[8]

Horowitz appealed to the memories of the dead parents to inspire the survivors to lead devout lives; this type of rhetoric would be used repeatedly by the religious parties to try to win support for their programs. She also connected the recitation of Kaddish to the survivors' duty to remember their parents and to maintain Jewish traditions and life.

The shared experience of loss and a need to commemorate the dead led the survivors to join together to recite the mourners' prayer. Benisch describes the reaction of the assembled DPs to Horowitz's words, "Echoing her note of determined hope, the whole assembly rose, and a spontaneous *Kaddish* reverberated from the walls. There was not a dry eye in the audience, but neither was there a despairing heart."[9] The mourners' prayer united Jewish survivors, whether Orthodox or secular, in their sorrow and often consoled them. The persistence of religious ritual expressed their determination to create a vibrant Jewish community.

The centrality of Kaddish in survivors' worship was only part of the survivors' obligation to the dead. Proper burial was also an immediate concern. Liberating troops quickly buried the dead they found in mass graves, frequently forcing former concentration camp guards to do the physical labor. While the humbling of the once proud guards had an appeal to survivors, their uncaring handling of the corpses was still an affront to their victims. According to Jewish tradition, corpses were to be given the utmost respect until burial in order to preserve the dignity of the dead. Likewise, it was traditionally considered a great privilege to assist in the preparation and burial of the body.[10] Certainly the vanquished guards did not ensure the dignity of the dead; moreover, as non-Jews their very handling of the body was a violation of Jewish law.[11]

After liberation, tens of thousands of Jews continued to die of epidemics as well as gastrointestinal illness caused by eating foods that their starved bodies were unprepared to digest. No longer at the mercy of their tormentors, the survivors did their best to bury the dead with dignity. At Bergen-Belsen, a group of Beth Jacob teachers and students, themselves still recovering from typhus, dug a shallow grave for one of their comrades. Benisch observed their efforts: "The girls filled the grave and recited *Kaddish* for their friend. A *minyan* or so of girls, barely alive themselves, glorified God's Name, proclaiming their gratitude for having the merit at last, for the first time in the Valley of Death, to bring their friend to a *kever Yisrael* [Jewish grave], to provide a Jew with a dignified Jewish burial."[12] In the women's camp, there were no men to create the requisite minyan, so these devout women took on the duty for themselves.

Many of the men who emerged as the DP leadership began their community service by tending to the needs of the dead. Survivors were determined to provide Jewish burials for unburied concentration camp inmates and for death march victims. For example, eight days after liberation, the man who would become the president of the Jewish community of Neunburg vorm Wald oversaw the burial of 220 victims of Nazism at the town's cemetery.[13] The continuing deaths after liberation led to the formation of traditional burial societies as one of the first Jewish institutions in postwar Germany.[14] The DP rabbinic council in the U.S. zone of occupation reported in October 1945, "We have also done our brotherly duty for our martyrs beginning with fencing in the cemeteries and erecting memorial stones for our tortured brothers and sisters."[15] A German Jewish survivor who went to Lübeck after his liberation became active in the Jewish community there. "Our first task was to bury the dead in the old Jewish cemetery. We buried them in a special section of the cemetery; I think there were sixty to a hundred who had died soon after the Liberation."[16] In assuming this responsibility, these leaders were performing one of the greatest duties in Judaism, caring for the abandoned dead. That these acts occurred on German soil heightened their significance. In the land of their persecutors, survivors performed Jewish rituals, affirming Jewish values and the continuity of tradition.

By reburying their dead, DPs reclaimed control of their lives. DPs had to win the cooperation of Allied military governments or local German officials to acquire the manpower, equipment, and/or land necessary for exhumation and burial. The ability to accomplish these tasks in the face of Allied and German recalcitrance only highlighted the survivors' determination to exercise their agency. Allied commanders, overwhelmed with the problems of maintaining order, feeding and clothing civilians, and reconstructing the German infrastructure, often had little patience for DP requests. In June 1945 Wolf Weil entered Germany illegally after searching for surviving family in Krakow and was immediately asked to take a leadership role in the Jewish community of Hof. His first task was to secure the burial of

Margarete Myers Feinstein

more than one hundred death march victims whose bodies still lay in the surrounding forests. The local American commander refused to permit the burial of the dead, yet Weil would not be intimidated. With obvious satisfaction, he states, "I finally carried out everything, and [the American commander] himself was even present. Today, the memorial stone, with the inscription that 142 concentration camp inmates are buried here, is still standing."[17]

Even when Allied officers were sympathetic, they were often hampered by questions of jurisdiction and military protocol. In August 1945 Dr. Richard Bahr approached American Public Safety Officer Captain George J. Ganer for help reburying death march victims. Ganer wrote to his superior, "Inasmuch as [Bahr] requests that local Gemeinde officials be ordered to assist him in the disinterment and transportation of corpses to a regular cemetery this becomes a matter out of our jurisdiction. While we realize that it is not our place to make suggestions to higher Headquarters we feel in many ways that this is a desirable project and are sending him to see you in the hope that you may be able to assist."[18] Ganer was moved enough that he boldly and impertinently recommended a course of action to his superiors. Unfortunately, the record does not show whether Bahr was ultimately successful in his efforts.

Some survivors did succeed in gaining the cooperation of local Germans in honoring the dead. In either the autumn of 1945 or early spring of 1946, the mayor of Neunburg vorm Wald granted DPs permission to rebury some Jewish remains in a corner of the town cemetery. Exhuming the bodies themselves, the Jews transported the corpses on blankets to the new burial site.[19] The first thing that the well-known German Jewish journalist Karl Marx did upon his return to Düsseldorf was to demand that the city council put up a memorial plaque to the murdered Jews. In 1946 the city complied. Marx's widow recalls, "It was the first act that gave us a little satisfaction, a tiny consolation."[20] The reassertion of the dignity of the dead was a source of pride for the living. The ability to perform the essential tasks of Jewish burial symbolized the continued expression of Jewish values and community.

The efforts of DP representatives in one Bavarian community to secure the close cooperation of military government and German officials resulted in a noteworthy event. The reinterment of thirty-nine victims of a death march from Buchenwald was a ceremonial occasion that spoke to the rehabilitation of the survivors and their will to determine their future.[21] The victims had been murdered on April 13, 1945, and were subsequently buried in six mass graves. Two of the graves were plowed up even though the German landowner had known that

DP police carry a wreath to a memorial for Jewish victims at the Dachau concentration camp. (United States Holocaust Memorial Museum, courtesy of George Gerzon [Gerzon Trzcina])

Jews were buried there. The Jewish Committee of Tirschenreuth had long sought the reburial of these victims, but it was only when the local U.S. military government officer, Captain Lyle Mariels, became involved that the reburial took place. An orphan raised in a foster home in the predominantly Jewish neighborhood of Portland, Oregon, Mariels was a champion of the disadvantaged and was sympathetic to Jewish concerns.[22]

Mariels ordered former Nazis to exhume the bodies on August 19, 1946. The coffins had a round-the-clock honor guard of American Constabulary troopers and Jewish DP policemen, in keeping with Jewish tradition that the deceased be attended until burial as well as a safeguard against anti-Semitic vandals.[23] On the morning of August 20, a funeral procession including representatives of the regional military government, local United Nations Relief and Rehabilitation (UNRRA) workers, the *Landrat* (a German regional official), the mayors of the surrounding towns, and members of the neighboring Jewish committees drove through a number of towns along a sixty kilometer stretch to the Jewish cemetery in Floß. Leading the procession were three Jewish DP policemen displaying the Zionist flag, a blue Star of David bordered by horizontal blue stripes on a white background. The coffins, carried on a UNRRA truck, were decorated with flowers and

Margarete Myers Feinstein

wreaths. Mariels had ordered that shops along the route be closed and that German residents line the streets with their heads bared. In the cities of Tirschenreuth and Floß the procession was accompanied by a band.

This event was a departure from prewar Jewish traditions. Reinterment is generally discouraged in Jewish law and practice; however, the circumstances of the mass graves created legally permissible reasons for reinterment. Rabbi Ephraim Oshry of Kovno ruled that whoever moved the body of a Holocaust victim to a Jewish cemetery did so for the deceased's honor and therefore performed a great service.[24] Both the floral decorations and the musical accompaniment of the funeral procession were contrary to Jewish funeral practices. Traditionally, funerals are to be simple, "without excessive show."[25] Memorial gifts of charity or of religious objects to the synagogue are considered more appropriate and enduring than flowers.[26] The report of the Tirschenreuth Jewish Committee, however, expressed great satisfaction with the effects of the flowers and music, commenting that "The procession made an exceptionally deep impression on the entire German population."[27] Indeed, the scene appears to have been designed with the Germans in mind.

The procession had the air of a state funeral. With uniformed Jewish police officers and a fully manned armored car leading the way, the president and vice president of the Jewish Committee rode next in the military governor's car, physically representing the alliance between the Jewish DPs and the military government. Behind them followed military and UNRRA vehicles and then trucks bearing the coffins. The rear was brought up by local German officials and Jewish survivors. The participation of the denazified German officials, their attendance undoubtedly encouraged by Mariels, signaled their understanding that postwar Germany was expected to repent for Nazi crimes and to honor Jewish dead, yet they were in a subservient role as humbled students of democracy.

The intended message to the German population was that these were the bodies of dignified and innocent people, worthy of honor. The Jewish policemen demonstrated Jewish respectability.[28] As the vice president of the Jewish Committee stated at the graveside later that day,

> Our procession . . . today has once again brought sharply before the eyes of the German population of this district how the Hitler regime dealt with innocent people. It is a belated honor, a belated rehabilitation for the Jews who did no wrong and were forced to give up their lives simply for their faith, for

holding fast to the traditions of their fathers. But it is the survivors' tribute for that silent martyrdom, that silent heroism; it is an admonition to Germany to acknowledge finally the infamy of the past and finally to find the path to true tolerance.[29]

Sadly, the German population quickly repressed the memory of this event, obscuring the origins of the mass grave in the Floß cemetery. However, what is significant for our purposes is that the Jewish Committee of Tirschenreuth sought to honor the dead in a way that would be comprehensible to the German population. The DPs chose to venerate the dead in a ritual code that was understandable not only to Jewish survivors but also to the nation of their persecutors.

At the cemetery, the ceremony was more clearly designed for the nearly eight hundred survivors who had accompanied the coffins. The coffins were placed in the ground, and a minute of silence was observed for the six million Jewish dead. A cantor from Hof sang the memorial prayer for the dead, "El Male Rahamim." Various officials offered words of empathy and solace. An elderly Jew, a rarity among the survivors, led the assembled mourners and dignitaries in Kaddish. The prayer was followed by the singing of the Zionist anthem, "Hatikvah," and this concluded the service. The juxtaposition of the mourner's prayer with the Zionist song was echoed in the speech that had been offered by the vice president of the Tirschenreuth Jewish Committee:

> For us the death of these Jews shall be a warning and reminder, a guidepost and a guiding principle for the future of a new Judaism, for the future of our children. We want to identify our errors through the sorrows of the past and to learn from our mistakes. We know that only those nations are respected who have their own land; that only those nations are respected who are strong enough to defend their security and freedom with their own land, and to earn the respect that every nation is due. . . . Let us now take our leave from our brothers with the vow, never to remain in Europe, the part of the earth where our fathers experienced so many and unheard of persecutions, the part of the world that is soaked through and through with Jewish blood, dampened millions of times by Jewish tears. Let us be a true union of brothers forged together by the fire of destruction, strong in faith in our own strength, and let us put all of our dreams and efforts, all of our talents to use in building our own land, our own home, so that we can erect on our

Margarete Myers Feinstein

own soil, our own ground, a secure future for our children and children's children.[30]

The connection between the dead of Europe and the need for an independent homeland in Palestine was made explicit in this speech and was demonstrated symbolically in the juxtaposition of Kaddish and "Hatikvah," the future anthem of the State of Israel. As Zeev Mankowitz notes, "the creation of a Jewish state in the Land of Israel was taken to be the last will and testament bequeathed by the dead to the living. . . . It signified the only real hope for the rescue and rehabilitation of the little that remained of European Jewry and, in the longer term, the promise of the Jewish future."[31] Religious observance created a space for the performance of this ethnic identity and its political expression, Zionism.

Postwar Zionist politicians frequently pointed to the murdered Jews of Europe as evidence for the need for a Jewish state, but religious leaders also made similar connections. In an announcement for the memorial service (Yizkor) on the last day of Passover 1948, the Bergen-Belsen DP rabbinate encouraged survivors to attend in order to commemorate not only "our dear parents, children, sisters, brothers who were murdered in the sanctification of God's Name by Nazi butchers" but also "the heroic fighters, the holy ones who daily fall in the Holy Land at the hands of various enemies, who want, God forbid, to deliver a death blow to the Yishuv [Palestinian Jewry] and simultaneously the entire Jewish people." In that crucial time between the United Nations vote for the partition of Palestine in November 1947 and the declaration of the State of Israel in May 1948, Jewish soldiers were engaged in frequent battles. The DPs understood that their hopes for emigration depended on the soldiers' victory. For many DPs, the fate of the Yishuv was the fate of the entire Jewish people. The announcement concluded, "Let us gather in order to pray to God in the image of the spilled blood of our sacrifices, so that we may be worthy of the merit of the holy deceased for final victory and complete redemption, may it be speedily in our day, Amen."[32] The identification of the European DPs with Jews in Palestine was expressed in this call to prayer, as was the connection between the past of the Holocaust and the future of Zionism.

In addition to linking the memories of the dead to a future in Palestine, this call to prayer also placed the Shoah in the cycles of Jewish history. The banner headline of the poster read, "Remember what Amalek did to you!" This suggested that Hitler and the Nazis were a reincarnation of the biblical enemy Amalek, who had reappeared in other moments of Jewish history, such as the destruction of the Temple in Jerusalem and the expulsion from Spain. Orthodox DP publications elaborated this understanding of the Holocaust as a familiar form of calamity (*hurban*). They emphasized that after each destruction the Jewish people had been renewed. In the post-Holocaust era that renewal was to be the return to the Land of Israel and the creation of a Jewish state. The lesson of the Holocaust was to be that the state and the Torah were intrinsically intertwined. As one scholar has noted, "The urge for *aliyyah* [*sic*] was inseparable in the Orthodox mind from going to the only place where Torah could be properly and purely advanced and where the people could be filled with its living source. Only in the Holy Land could that pattern of assimilation which catalyzed God's release of Amalek be decisively ended. For the Orthodox survivors, Torah and state were inseparable."[33] The Shoah was understood as belonging to the flow of history in its similarity to earlier destructions but as unique in providing the opportunity to break the cycle. Orthodoxy and Zionism were reconciled in the call for a Jewish state based on the Torah.

Within the DP camps, Agudath Israel, which in the prewar period had eschewed cooperation with secular Jewish parties, began to work with Zionist leaders, even encouraging some followers to join pluralistic DP kibbutzim before founding their own religious kibbutzim. At the Second Congress of Agudath Israel in Germany in September 1946, leaders of the party addressed three concerns: the Land of Israel, education of youths, and unity of Orthodox Jews. Jicchok Zemba, president of the organization in Germany, proclaimed that his party "felt itself to be an integral part of the builders of the Land of Israel" and offered a blessing to the fighting Jewish Yishuv because "you fight for truth and righteousness."[34] In addition to this unprecedented support for the Zionists in Palestine, these Orthodox survivors proclaimed their unequivocal desire for aliyah. "We have declared to world Agudath Israel that the Agudists of the She'erit Hapletah [Surviving Remnant] see for themselves nothing other than the Land of Israel and we continue to hold that position."[35] Frustration with the American Agudath Israel's emphasis on bringing DP Agudists to the United States was evident, as was a meeting of the minds with Poale Agudath Israel in Palestine. In the interests of unity, however, DP Agudists chose to keep their identification with Agudath Israel. DP Orthodox thinkers now viewed aliyah as facilitating the redemption of the Jewish people and the arrival of the messiah.[36]

On the question of youth education, the leaders noted the important work of their kibbutzim and decided to approach Mizrahi, the religious Zionist party, about creating a joint educational program. The conference noted that the party had a voice in DP politics and had won the confidence of other political parties. The willingness to cooperate with secular parties marked a radical change in Agudist politics. Reflecting the general desire for unity among the survivors and their almost universal quest for a Jewish homeland, Agudath Israel in Germany's political agenda became more like that of Mizrahi. The lesson drawn from the Shoah was that Jewish life was no longer possible in the Diaspora. Only a Jewish homeland could secure the future of the Jewish people and the Torah. The commemoration of victims of the Shoah reinforced that lesson, serving to link the past, present, and future of the Jewish people with a Zionist bent. It also served the immediate religious and psychological needs of the survivors.

Jewish liturgy provided the survivors with regular opportunities to remember deceased parents and close relatives. Yizkor, "based on the firm belief that the living, by acts of piety and goodness, can redeem the dead,"[37] was recited on four major holidays: Yom Kippur, Passover, Shavuot, and Sukkot. DP camp religious offices made certain to notify DPs of these dates. Recitation of the memorial prayer played a major role in many survivors' experience. Bertha Ferderber-Salz admits, "In the synagogue I can visualize the unforgettable figures who were cruelly torn from me, especially during the memorial prayer (*Yizkor*), when they appear before me as clearly and tangibly as if they had come back to life and followed me to the house of prayer. I admit that I go to synagogue, not to pray or listen to the cantor's devotions, but solely in order to meet my dear ones once more. Only there can I bring them to mind as they were in their lifetimes."[38] For Ferderber-Salz, the synagogue became a place not so much of worship but of reunion with her murdered family. Yizkor provided a link between the living and the dead. It served to connect the survivor with the prewar world.

For some the connection to the past was unbearably painful. One survivor reported that on Jewish holidays she was devastatingly reminded of her lost loved ones. "It was more than I could stand. For a long time I couldn't practice Judaism again as I previously had. But I forced myself to go to the synagogue for *Yizkor,* the service for the dead, three times a year and at the high holy days and that helped me gradually to resume practicing Judaism again almost as I had previously."[39] Here, the ritual obligation to remember the dead helped facilitate a survivor's reconciliation to her religious heritage; her decline in religious observance was temporary. Even those whose faith had been shaken by their wartime experiences sought to honor the dead as they would have wished it. As we will see below, parents' values and religious observance influenced many survivors in their continuing performance of Jewish ritual after the Shoah.

Other dates for commemorating the dead were more difficult to determine. The primary purpose of Yahrzeit was to commemorate the date of a parent's death, although it could be observed for any relative or friend. It was observed with the lighting of a memorial candle and with the recitation of Kaddish at the synagogue. With families torn apart by Nazi persecution and with the fate of so many unknown, it was impossible for many survivors to determine the exact dates of their parents' deaths. Rabbinic texts permitted those unable to remember or to determine the date of a parent's death to choose the date of the Yahrzeit.[40] Some chose the date of their parents' deportation to the concentration camps as the date of death. Others commemorated their deceased parents on Tisha b'Av, the day for commemorating the destruction of the Temple in Jerusalem. This day was a traditional one for visiting family graves, and as the saddest date in the Hebrew calendar, it seemed fitting. Later the State of Israel created a state holiday, Yom HaShoah, that in essence is a community Yahrzeit and is now observed by Jewish communities around the world in recognition that there are families for whom no survivors remain to remember them.[41]

A more secular commemoration event occurred in the mourning academies (*troyer akademyen*) organized by survivors. These events helped establish community among DPs of different social backgrounds and wartime experiences. Announced in posters and in newspapers, these gatherings brought together survivors of particular regions or cities on the dates of major Nazi actions and ghetto liquidations.[42] One such academy was held in the Landsberg DP camp on October 29, 1946, marking the fifth Yahrzeit of the October Action in the Kovno Ghetto, which coincided with the liquidation of Lithuanian Jewry. All Lithuanian Jews in the American zone were invited to "participate in the academy with memories and creative presentations about the Jewish tragedy in Lithuania."[43] The remembrance of Lithuanian Jewry began with a memorial service at the mass graves in Dachau, where many survivors of the Kovno Ghetto perished. It was followed by the mourning academy in the Landsberg DP camp at which survivors spoke about life in the Lithuanian ghettos and about the liquidation.[44] Survivors who had been separated from their families, either by flight into the Soviet Union or through going into hiding, could thus learn about the conditions they had faced and about their deaths. Through this sharing of memories, the survivors formed a collective memory of the Shoah and found ways to narrate their experiences and integrate them into their personal and communal histories.

Mourning academies created a venue in which the survivors could express their loss and find comfort with others whose families had shared a similar fate. Despite the overwhelming sense that all Jews had undergone the same trials and that unity of the Jewish community should prevail, there seemed to be a greater level of comfort among people of the same national or regional origin. They could reminisce about the neighborhoods of their youth and discover friends in common. Mourning academies created community. They also provided a forum in which those who had survived the war years in the Soviet Union and who had arrived later in the DP camps could share their grief with others from their hometown and become integrated into the preexisting DP society. In the mourning academies the shared loss of home and family could unite survivors of differing wartime experiences and shape a common DP identity.

Ritual observances for the dead had both personal and social significance for the survivors. The presence of deceased family members was especially felt during Yizkor, and the ritual of commemorating the dead helped revive the survivors' commitment to Jewish traditions. Memorial services forged community out of grieving individuals, providing opportunities to participate in common rituals and prayers, to share memories of prewar and wartime experiences, and to create a social memory of the Holocaust that informed DP identity. Reburials on German soil forced the participation of Germans in honoring the dead and helped survivors feel that the dead were being vindicated.

MARRIAGE UNDER THE CANOPY

Even as they honored the dead, Jewish DPs began new lives and new families. Most of them chose to create Jewish marriages and homes. Even secular Jews wanted a religious wedding ceremony as a means of forming links with the past and to ensure family continuity.[45] Erna Rubinstein's sister had lost her faith during the war, but as she prepared to marry she told Rubinstein that "although it was sometimes difficult to believe in God after all we had been through, she and Dolek [her fiancé] felt very strongly that they must forever continue the Jewish tradition that the Nazis had tried to destroy. Pola said that to celebrate her marriage without our parents and without our little brother was very sad, but she and Dolek felt they had to go on, to hold onto their Jewish heritage and to build a better future for themselves and for their children."[46] The urgency for rebuilding Jewish life and transmitting it to the next generation was great, if only to rob the Nazis of a belated victory. The legacy of their prewar upbringings continued to influence the DPs even as they struggled with questions of faith raised by the Shoah. While their faith in God may have been shaken, they retained their Jewish identity and their prewar level of adherence to the performance of Jewish ritual.

Marriage and sexual relations raised the issue of family purity laws. While in some Orthodox communities men may have had the custom of visiting the *mikvah* (ritual bath) on Friday afternoon before the Sabbath and before the start of holidays, the *mikvah* was expressly the legal obligation of married women. Observant married Jewish women were required to ritually purify themselves in the *mikvah* after menstruation before marital relations could take place. The importance of the *mikvah* was such that Jewish law requires that a new community build one before constructing the synagogue. Since no functioning *mikvah* had survived Nazi rule, the building of the *mikvah* was a top priority for religious DPs. The efforts undertaken in communities to construct a *mikvah* were also a sign of community regeneration.[47]

Determined Orthodox DPs were successful in enlisting the aid of Jewish chaplains and relief workers in obtaining the property and materials necessary for the construction of ritual baths. According to Isaac Levy, one of two Jewish military chaplains in the British zone of occupied Germany, "The expressed desire for marriage grew in such alarming proportions that the Chassidic Rabbi, one of the five dispatched to us, felt compelled to contact the authorities and even succeeded in obtaining the help of the Royal Engineers to build a *mikvah* for the use of potential brides."[48] Secular leaders questioned the priorities of this rabbi, since the wood used for the *mikvah* construction could have served as heating fuel in the bitter winter of 1945–46.[49] By Passover 1946, the Föhrenwald DP camp had a *mikvah* that was open daily for women's ritual purification and for men on mornings before the Sabbath and the beginning of holidays.[50] At Landsberg, DPs hired German laborers to dig the *mikvah*.[51] The satisfaction, the sense of retribution, that Jewish DPs felt at ordering Germans to do manual labor so that Jewish family life could flourish is easy to imagine.

With sexual activity on the rise, the religious leaders sought to educate young couples in proper Jewish relations. Despite the severe paper shortage, a rabbi in the Föhrenwald DP camp managed to publish a volume on Jewish marital law, instructing women and men about such things as the proper timing of marital relations and use of the *mikvah* after menstruation. Exhorting young couples to observe the traditions, the author pulled no punches: "Whoever does not observe them puts his health in danger and corrupts the Jewish youth, the remainder that is left to us after the bloody deluge, the seed from which the Jewish future will sprout, the roots from which the Jewish people will branch out. . . . Whoever honors and values his parents—and who among us is not filled with reverence for our martyrs—will observe

　　　　　　　　　　　　　　　　　Margarete Myers Feinstein

completely the Jewish marital laws."[52] The Feldafing-based Agudath Israel used similar language in an appeal to Jewish wives and mothers: "Do not break the Jewish future! Sacred is the memory of your parents! Should the above words show you the path to your people, the attached booklet [on Jewish marital law] shall be your guide for how to build a pure, Jewish life."[53] In addition to using the stick of guilt, one group of American Hassidic Jews provided the lure of a dowry to impoverished women who agreed to wear a wig after marriage in a traditional act of modesty.[54] These heavy-handed attempts to persuade Jewish DPs, the women in particular, to follow religious law indicated the religious leaders' concern that young survivors were ignorant of the traditions and not particularly interested in learning about them. But it was not only secular Jews who ignored the directives of the religious authorities. Even more traditional Jews occasionally found it difficult to abide by the policies of Orthodox rabbis.

In the absence of a *mikvah*, traditional women could use a river for the purpose of immersion so that marriages could take place. At the Bergen-Belsen DP camp the initial absence of a *mikvah* led to a minirevolt against rabbinic authority. A couple engaged before the war found themselves reunited as DPs. A British rabbi had agreed to officiate at the Sunday wedding in June 1945. On Friday afternoon, however, the rabbi informed a camp leader, Dr. Hadassah Bimko (later Rosensaft), that the marriage could not take place because there was no *mikvah* available for the bride. Bimko, a widow of Orthodox upbringing, informed the rabbi that Jewish law permitted any Jew to perform a marriage ceremony and that the wedding would go on with or without him. In the end the rabbi presided over the nuptials. Bimko recalled that "it turned out to be an anti-mikvah wedding that took place on Freedom Square in Belsen, under a blue sky. It was the beginning of life."[55] The difficult material conditions of the early months following liberation required religiously observant survivors to make compromises and innovations in their adherence to Jewish law and tradition. As Bimko correctly observed, it is possible to follow Jewish law and tradition even without a presiding rabbi. The DPs' determination to marry and create Jewish families often overrode obedience to rabbinic decisions. It also points to the loss of rabbinic authority brought about by the dissolution of established communities and the wartime struggle for survival that often forced individuals to rely on their own judgments.

The resolve of DPs to marry and the sympathy of Jewish chaplains meant that rules were often bent. Approached by young couples seeking to wed, Rabbi Levy wrote to the London Beth Din (religious court) for guidance. The response, "No marriages may be solemnised until a complete list of survivors is obtained," was out of touch with the reality of the situation. As Levy states, "To [the Beth Din's decision] my reaction was 'How long, O Lord, how long' would we have to wait for this to be achieved. It was obvious to us that those who wished to marry or, what was more probable, to cohabit, would not wait indefinitely."[56] While the Beth Din undoubtedly had wanted to verify the status of purported widows and widowers before authorizing a second marriage, a complete list of survivors would not be compiled within any reasonable amount of time. Many Jewish chaplains responded kindly to the urgency of DP couples.

Problems arose for those DPs who could not prove the death of a spouse before remarriage. Since the Nazis did not issue death certificates for the vast majority of their victims in the ghettos and concentration camps, many widows and widowers had to rely on eyewitness accounts and rumors for information on the fate of their spouses. When rabbis demanded further proof before solemnizing a second marriage, survivors searched for authorities who were willing to accept their testimony as proof. Frequently non-Orthodox Jewish military chaplains would take pity on these people. Some survivors in postwar Europe would not examine too closely the credentials of a man claiming to be a rabbi if he consented to officiate the wedding.[57] The inability of DPs to procure official documents combined with their drive to create new families led them to disregard the strictures of rabbis. This resulted in ceremonies of questionable validity in Jewish law and in conflict between various rabbinic movements.[58] If no accommodating rabbi were to be found, some DPs would proclaim their intent to marry before witnesses and enter into a common-law marriage.[59] Other DPs chose to live with their new partners without the benefit of marriage while they awaited further evidence of their spouses' fates.[60]

Rabbis had established the strict standards for proof of death for a reason, especially in the instance of a previously married woman. Without sufficient evidence of a husband's death, a woman was traditionally considered abandoned and ineligible for remarriage. The standards of proof were less stringent for men since the consequences of their remarriage were not as severe. The rabbis wanted to avoid the possibility of sanctioning a bigamous relationship: if a previous husband should in fact be alive, not only would there be emotional distress to the various spouses, but the children of the second marriage would be deemed *mamzerim* (illegitimate children born of a forbidden relationship). This would mean that although the children were legally Jewish, they would not be allowed to marry Jews unless they themselves were also *mamzerim*.[61] In turn, offspring from a *mamzer* couple would continue to be *mamzer*. After the Holocaust "there were

Margarete Myers Feinstein

thousands of cases of *agunot* [abandoned wives], and the importance of marriage to the Jew can be seen in the fact that many of the world's most famous and prominent rabbis dedicated most of their time to finding legal ways through which such women could be freed for marriage again."[62]

This question of *agunot* was such an important issue that one of the first acts of the DP rabbinate in the American zone was to send a request for guidance on the issue to Palestine.[63] In August 1946 the Rabbinic Council created a committee dedicated to the problem of *agunot*. It resolved that only a rabbi who was part of a *bet din* of three rabbis or a rabbi appointed by the *agunot* committee could hear evidence in such cases.[64] Trying to accommodate DP demands, camp religious offices published lists of engaged couples with the request that anyone with a reason to oppose the marriage inform the office.[65] In 1948 a rabbinic responsum from Palestine, recognizing the unusual circumstances of the Shoah, eased the requirements of proof in order to allow more remarriages. On the question of whether to accept testimony from witnesses who may be repeating rumor or may have profaned the Sabbath, Rabbi Shlomo David Kahana wrote, "But in our time, a time of general annihilation, a time when many of the martyrs submitted to death for the sanctification of God's name[,] . . . we should not worry about such suspicions."[66] Despite the care of the rabbis, the system was not infallible. One survivor reported a case in which DP newlyweds were faced with the return of a surviving husband. Both the first and second marriages were dissolved by religious divorce, and the survivors were then allowed to choose who to marry.[67] Traditionally, both former spouses would have been prohibited to the adulteress.

Like all weddings, DP weddings were emotional occasions, but unlike most, DP weddings were always accompanied by sorrow. In 1946 dozens of weddings took place on Lag B'Omer in the Bergen-Belsen DP camp.[68] As one Orthodox woman recalls, "The souls of parents who had not survived to lead their children beneath the wedding canopy hovered in the air of the camp. . . . After the ceremony each couple went to their own corner, to commune with their sorrow, and there was no sound of rejoicing, singing or dancing, as is customary."[69] A similar mood prevailed at Sam Halpern's wedding to Gladys Landau. "Although we were not officially in mourning, our mood of loss remained with us. . . . We celebrated this enormously important moment in our lives with a small meal and no music."[70] The usual joy surrounding the ceremony was marred by the absence of parents and extended family, and yet it was in this setting that past generations were remembered and a future generation was anticipated. The bridal

Cards in honor of the wedding of Rivka Oksenhendler and Moshe Jakubowicz
(June 12, 1946) from their friends in Kibbutz Betar al shem Ze'ev Jabotinsky.
(Courtesy of Regina [Oksenhendler] Jacobs and Fred Jacobs [Moshe Jakubowicz])

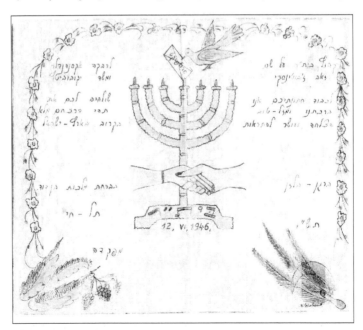

party and assembled guests created community and enacted the continuity of Jewish life.

Marriages were an important step in re-creating the family life that had been destroyed by Nazi persecution. Jewish ceremonies indicated the survivors' determination to continue their traditions. That these rituals necessitated building *mikvaot* (ritual baths) on German soil, sometimes with German labor, highlighted the significance of survival and Jewish marital relations as a defeat of Nazism. The memories of the dead were vivid at these occasions that linked past and present and held the promise of future offspring. The tensions between DPs and rabbis over family purity laws reflected a loss of rabbinic authority but also the creativity of the survivors in adapting religious ritual and law to their unusual circumstances.

ENTERING THE COVENANT: CIRCUMCISIONS AND BNAI MITZVAH

Other than easing loneliness and reassuring the newlyweds that they now belonged to someone once again, marriage did not immediately alter their lives. Housing in most DP camps was so limited that couples shared living quarters with other DPs. Eventually, however, women DPs in particular found their lives shaped by the consequence of sexual relations and marriage: motherhood. Despite the hardships of DP camp life and the uncertainty of the future, many Jewish women DPs consciously chose to become mothers. DPs viewed children as essential to the revival of the Jewish people; thus, children were more than the products of private relationships. Births were celebrated by the parents, their immediate circle of friends, and the entire camp population. Strangers would visit new parents to offer their congratulations and to witness the miracle of a Jewish child. Reproduction became a civic responsibility for the survivors. As one DP recollected, "The young adults who survived . . . had great hopes of building a new and better world. To accomplish this goal they had to produce a new generation, and so having children was one of their immediate goals."[71] Jewish births were a sign of the survivors' vitality and their triumph over their oppressors.

According to DP artist Samuel Bak, "Men were looking for women and women for men. Giving birth to a Jewish child was a form of retaliation against the brutal cruelty of the recent past."[72] The birth of a new Jewish generation in the land of Nazism served as what Atina Grossmann has called "biological revenge."[73] As one woman DP recalls, "We all wanted to have families again. The feeling inside us was to show the Germans that they had not eliminated us all."[74] A parade of Jewish mothers pushing baby carriages down a German street clearly demonstrated Jewish triumph and Nazi defeat. At the same time, memories of deceased parents and of murdered children aroused bitterness and even fear. The absence of older women to guide the young mothers through pregnancy and child rearing was keenly felt.

The increasing numbers of young families benefited the Zionist leadership by helping to keep pressure on the Allies to solve the DP problem. The Zionist leadership insisted that unrestricted immigration to Palestine was the only option for the Jewish survivors. The Central Committee of Liberated Jews in the American zone and the Bergen-Belsen camp committee in the British zone of occupied Germany both successfully opposed relief workers' attempts to resettle Jewish orphans to places other than Palestine. They insisted that the survivors were the ones responsible for the children's future and that their future would be in Palestine.[75] Children and young families could promote the image of Jewish DPs as a healthy community unjustly confined to the land of their persecutors.

As the guarantors of the Jewish people's survival, DP children also aroused the interest of the religious leadership. Some religious authorities, such as the religious committee of Eschwege DP camp, required that all births be registered at their office.[76] In the late summer of 1946 UNRRA clerks at the Landsberg DP hospital were kept busy reporting births to the religious office.[77] This was part of the rabbis' efforts to regulate who belonged to the Jewish community. In 1947 the Central Rabbinate of the British zone reaffirmed matrilineal descent (that is, the inclusion of only children of Jewish mothers in the Jewish community) and reserved for itself the right to decide whether or not Jewish children introduced to another faith could be considered members of the Jewish community. This question was of concern for children who had spent the war years passing as gentiles as well as those of mixed marriages, which included many surviving German Jews. In the same document the Central Rabbinate mandated that camp committees and communal organizations forward to the rabbinate the names of all uncircumcised Jewish children.[78]

Just as with officiation at weddings, the rabbis found themselves in conflict with maverick DPs and German Jews over circumcision (Brith Milah). Jewish male infants are circumcised as evidence of God's covenant with Abraham, marking their membership in the Jewish community on their bodies. Some DPs may have chosen not to circumcise their sons in order to increase their chances of passing as a gentile should anti-Semitic violence once again become a threat.[79] Intermarried DPs and German Jews also may have decided against circumcision as part of a resolution not to rear their children as Jews.

Margarete Myers Feinstein

The rabbinate would want to know which families were no longer to be included on Jewish membership lists; however, the Central Rabbinate was also concerned about unauthorized circumcisions. In guarding rabbinic prerogative and stemming the tide of assimilation, the Central Rabbinate decreed that circumcisions performed by unauthorized individuals were not religiously valid and called for the "strongest measures" to be taken against the offender.[80] Given the low numbers of qualified religious leaders, these rabbinic orders must have seemed unrealistic and controlling to DPs and German Jews who were content to have lay leaders perform the ritual. Even as the divisions between Jews over levels of observance reemerged among the DPs, parents affirmed their commitment to Jewish tradition by circumcising their sons. The gathering of friends and dignitaries to witness the ceremony and to celebrate the entry of a new Jewish male into the covenant forged social bonds of community and signified Jewish renewal.

As with other life cycle events, the absence of the older generation was intensely felt upon the birth of a child. The parents of the first Jewish boy born in Belsen after liberation kept the assembled friends and UNRRA dignitaries waiting at the circumcision because they did not know what to name the boy. Tradition was to name the first born male

An American official holds the baby during a circumcision ceremony in the Schlachtensee DP camp. (United States Holocaust Memorial Museum, courtesy of Mayer and Rachel Abramowitz)

Mourning, Marriage, and Birth Rituals among DPs in Germany   277

after the mother's father, but only if he were deceased. The couple finally decided that since they did not know for certain the grandfather's fate, they would choose another name.[81] As time passed other couples gave up hope of their parents' survival and gave their names to the newborn generation.[82] Despite the devastation of the Holocaust, Jewish couples strove to continue their family traditions and enter their children into the covenant. Marking their Jewish identity on the bodies of their sons, the survivors embraced the heritage that the Nazis had attempted to eradicate and proclaimed their determination to build a Jewish future.

At thirteen years of age Jewish boys marked their assumption of adult religious responsibility with their first public reading of the Torah, known as bar mitzvah. The DP camps closed before the baby boys born there were old enough for bar mitzvah. Among those survivors liberated from the concentration camps there were very few children younger than sixteen years of age. The arrival of families who had survived the war in the Soviet Union increased the number of children, and both secular and religious schools flourished in the DP camps. By October 1945 the Rabbinic Council of the U.S. zone had established yeshivas (academies for Talmudic study) in the Foehrenwald, Landsberg, and other DP camps. From the Feldafing DP camp, Rabbi Yekusiel Halberstam, founder of the Klausenberg Hasidic dynasty, established eight yeshivas. The American Orthodox organization Vaad Hatzala founded religious schools, including Talmud Torahs (Jewish primary schools for boys) and yeshivas in thirty-four DP camps in the U.S. zone, reaching more than 3,000 students. At the high point, Vaad Hatzala maintained approximately fourteen yeshivas and fifty-nine Talmud Torahs for boys and seven Beth Jacob schools for girls.[83] In May 1948 the American Jewish Joint Distribution Committee provided support to sixty-two Talmud Torahs and twelve yeshivas serving 4,170 students in the American zone.[84] These schools provided traditional religious education to male youths and prepared them for their bnai mitzvah. Even secular Jews viewed bar mitzvah as a social necessity for Jewish male adulthood and engaged religious tutors for their sons.[85] This rite of passage reassured the community that the next generation was secured. Jewish communal life would continue.

CONCLUSION

Among scholars there has been an assumption that religion played a small role in the survivors' lives. Most DPs were non-Orthodox, and some appeared to have lost at least part of their faith in the ghettos and concentration camps. In his study of Holocaust survivors living in Israel, Reeve Brenner measured the survivors' level of observance by the number and type of rituals they practiced. His statistics demonstrated that a total of 55 percent of survivors had been at least moderately observant prior to the war. In his sample, 25 percent of survivors had been ultra-Orthodox before the war, another 16 percent had been highly observant, and another 14 percent had been moderately observant. The remaining 45 percent Brenner defined as unobservant, although this category includes those who practiced a limited number of Jewish traditions as well as those who observed none at all. In the immediate postwar period 66 percent of survivors could be characterized under Brenner's schema as nonobservant, an increase of 21 percent over the prewar era. Only 34 percent of survivors were identified as observant in the immediate postwar period, although by the time of his study in the 1970s observant survivors had risen to 43 percent.[86] Thus, in the aftermath of the Shoah many survivors had restricted, at least temporarily, their observance of Jewish ritual. However, a closer look at Brenner's argument and at DP sources cautions us not to dismiss the importance of religion and ritual in the DP communities.

By defining "observant" as the fulfillment of more than five ritual acts, Brenner seeks to distinguish the somewhat regular synagogue attendees and observers of Sabbath rest from those Jews who appeared at synagogue only for Yom Kippur, lit Chanukah candles, and celebrated Passover but were otherwise disengaged from religious practice. Thus, Brenner's category of nonobservant included those who occasionally practiced Jewish ritual and those who never participated in such acts. It is important to remember that the survivor who went to synagogue only to commemorate the anniversary of a parent's death and perhaps observed the dietary laws but otherwise refrained from religious acts would be considered nonobservant in Brenner's study. Nonobservance, therefore, should not be interpreted as a rejection of Jewish identity or peoplehood or as evidence of atheism.

Ritual practice and faith can be treated as two distinct categories. Orthodox Jews may be motivated by their belief in God and/or by their family heritage to fulfill religious rituals, but secular Jews may also perform religious observances for reasons of ethnic identity.[87] Brenner found that some survivors retained their faith after the Shoah but restricted their ritual observance because they had gotten out of the habit, and it was too difficult to return to their previously intense level of observance.[88] In the DP camps the lack of ritual objects, such as *mikvaot* and *tefillin,* as well as difficulties procuring kosher food made religious observance difficult. The decline in immediate postwar observance that Brenner documented may have as much to do with such obstacles to practice as with lack of desire.

On the question of faith, Alexander Groth's survey of survivors in North America and Israel discovered that 56 percent had faith in God. The remaining 44 percent described themselves as nonbelievers or doubters.[89] This split is remarkably similar to Brenner's findings of prewar observant and nonobservant Jews. Groth further notes that those from religious and nonassimilated prewar homes were more likely to be believers, and those from assimilated nonreligious backgrounds were significantly less likely to be believers. Groth concludes: "What the surviving remnant 'learned' [from the Holocaust] was substantially conditioned by the legacy of their past. There were dramatic crossovers, but most of the religious kept their faith; most of the secular Jews remained within the realm of their earlier agnosticism or atheism."[90] The continuity of faith, or lack thereof, from the prewar era to the postliberation period is striking. Brenner also found that 68 percent of his respondents "retained unwaveringly the religious or irreligious conviction of their childhood and youth."[91] Family upbringing and religious education influenced the survivors more than their Holocaust experiences.

This stability of religious belief and practice is consistent with Elizabeth Weiss Ozorak's study of American adolescents:

> Parents' affiliation and their faith in that affiliation act as cognitive anchors from which the child's beliefs evolve over time. Family cohesion seems to limit modification of religious practices but exerts less pressure on beliefs, which become increasingly individual with maturation. Parents differ, as do faiths, in the amount and direction of variation that is tolerated, but the child has little difficulty learning the specific limits acceptable within a particular family.[92]

Good family relations encouraged adolescents to respect the limits that their parents had put on deviation in religious practice but did not preclude the development of differences in belief. Most survivors were adolescents during the war years, and as we have seen, they continued the rituals of their family homes even as some struggled with religious doubt.

The changes in observance that Brenner identified may have had more to do with prewar trends toward secularization than with the Holocaust experience itself. Secularization had been a trend among East European Jews prior to the Shoah. Children of Orthodox parents had been joining secular Zionist youth movements, attending public schools, migrating to cities, and moving away from their families' traditional observances in the interwar period. In one case an Orthodox family moved from their shtetl to a city, and contact with secular and liberal Jews along with the attractions of Yiddish theater facilitated change in the religious and social lives of the younger generation.[93] In families with strained relations between parents and children, this secularizing trend could be viewed as rebellion against parental values, but by the same token, the willingness of parents to tolerate experimentation and questioning could allow adolescents with strong family ties to move away from the practices of their childhood home. One survivor recalls his childhood wearing *payas* (earlocks) and growing up surrounded by ultra-Orthodox relatives, while his parents befriended Christians and occasionally ate nonkosher foods: "And so the days and years passed, torn between my family's secretive tries to break away from tradition and their need to still get along with my ultra-Orthodox relatives, all living under the same roof."[94] In such a case, the seeds of secularization were sown by the parents.

Since the Holocaust was an extended traumatic event, it is natural that young survivors would attribute changes in their religious beliefs and practices to their wartime experiences. That many of the survivors were adolescents during the war, however, may offer another interpretation of their religious change. Ozorak found that "existential questioning may be a *result* of change, not a cause."[95] The DPs who experienced religious change may have already been on that path, regardless of the war. The Holocaust gave their questioning a particular character, but it may not have caused it. Thus, while Brenner's statistics certainly indicate that a significant minority of the DP population became less observant, we need to be careful not to attribute the change solely to the Holocaust. Moreover, these statistics also do not tell us the role that religious ritual played in creating social bonds between the survivors or in shaping their identity.

DPs strove to re-create a sense of normalcy in their lives. Asserting their values and rebuilding Jewish community was part of that process, and religious ritual played an important role. The priority that DPs gave to burying the dead and to commemorating them through prayer speaks to the power of prewar values. No longer at the mercy of their Nazi tormentors, survivors demanded respectable treatment for the Jewish dead. In addition to asserting their agency with Allied officials and Germans, these efforts led to some of the earliest Jewish social organizations in postwar Germany as survivors founded burial societies.

Commemoration of the dead also created opportunities for social interaction and for identity construction. Mourning assemblies allowed all who had lost loved ones to join together and to share a common DP experience regardless of how and where they had survived the war years. Funerals and memorial services opened spaces for contemplating the legacy of those who had died and its lesson for the living. Rabbis encouraged DPs to honor the dead by leading religiously observant lives, and virtually all leaders urged DPs to embrace the Zionist cause as a means of vindicating the dead.

Weddings, births, and circumcisions provided DPs with other opportunities to affirm their commitment to Jewish tradition. Even secular Jews dreamed of standing beneath the marriage canopy, passing on their deceased parents' names to a new generation, circumcising their sons, and seeing their sons become bnai mitzvah. While the rituals had different meanings for observant and secular Jews, most embraced them as signs of continuity with the world they had lost and as the heart of the new Jewish community they were creating. Regardless of their motivation, Jewish DPs participated in rituals that affirmed Jewish community and values.[96] Where Orthodox DPs found spiritual meaning, secular Jews sought to maintain an ethnic identity. These differences occasionally led to tensions such as in the case of circumcisions performed by unauthorized *mohalim* (ritual circumcisers). Yet ritual can also create solidarity even among those of differing beliefs and rationalizations.

By engaging in Jewish ritual practices, the DPs were performing Jewish community.[97] David Kertzer's observation that "solidarity is produced by people acting together, not by people thinking together,"[98] is instructive here. The power of ritual lies in its ability to form community out of autonomous individuals. The performance of Jewish funeral rites, weddings, and circumcisions facilitated the creation of community and solidarity despite differences over levels of observance and questions about God. This unity was channeled into the political arena with the emphasis on Jewish nationhood and Zionist politics. Secular and religious Jews alike embraced a common DP identity and shared the goal of a Jewish homeland.

NOTES

1. Gershon Greenberg, "From *Hurban* to Redemption: Orthodox Jewish Thought in the Munich Area, 1945–1948," *Simon Wiesenthal Center Annual* 6 (1989): 81–112, and "Yehudah Leb Gerst's Religious 'Ascent' through the Holocaust," *Holocaust and Genocide Studies* 13:1 (Spring 1999): 62–89. Judith Tydor Baumel, "The Politics of Spiritual Rehabilitation in the DP Camps," *Simon Wiesenthal Center Annual* 6 (1989): 58–79.
2. Ernest Landau, "The First Days of Freedom," in *After the Holocaust: Rebuilding Jewish Lives in Postwar Germany,* edited by Michael Brenner,

translated by Barbara Harshav (Princeton, NJ: Princeton University Press, 1997), 82.

3. According to tradition, only those in mourning or commemorating the Yahrzeit (anniversary of death) for an immediate family member stand for the Kaddish, a prayer in praise of God that does not mention death, reaffirms the faith of the living, and provides a sense of continuity between the ages. Kaddish "transfers, subliminally, the fixed, inner gaze of the mourner from the departed to the living, from crisis to peace, from despair to hope, from isolation to community." Maurice Lamm, *The Jewish Way in Death and Mourning* (New York: Jonathan David, 1969), 154-55.

4. Landau, "The First Days of Freedom," 82.

5. Although today the Reform and Conservative movements permit women to be counted toward the minyan, the DPs would not have done so in the 1940s.

6. In traditional Judaism, women are not obligated to recite the Kaddish since it would interfere with their household duties.

7. Elie Wiesel, *All Rivers Run to the Sea: Memoirs* (New York: Knopf, 1995), 96.

8. Rivkah Horowitz, quoted in Pearl Benisch, *To Vanquish the Dragon* (New York: Feldheim, 1991), 417.

9. Benisch, *To Vanquish the Dragon*, 417.

10. Lamm, *The Jewish Way in Death and Mourning*, 239.

11. Only Jews are to handle the casket, and Jewish law prohibits the use of anonymous gravediggers. See Lamm, *The Jewish Way in Death and Mourning*, 59.

12. Benisch, *To Vanquish the Dragon*, 407.

13. "Kurzer Bericht über den Werdegang der Jüdischen Gemeinde Neunburg v. Wald vom Tage der Befreiung am 23. 4. 1945," undated, Record group (hereafter RG) M1, folder P-65, Yad Vashem Archives (hereafter YVA).

14. Landau, "The First Days of Freedom," 84.

15. "Council Meeting of Jews in Bavaria [Yiddish]," *Unzer Weg*, October 19, 1945, p. 4.

16. Norbert Wollheim, "Jewish Autonomy in the British Zone," in *After the Holocaust*, 96.

17. Wolf Weil, "A Schindler Jew in the Bavarian Province," in *After the Holocaust*, 155-56.

18. Captain Cav. George J. Ganer to Captain Hoar, "Exhumation of KZ victims," August 22, 1945, RG 260, 390/47/2−3/6−1, box 955, folder 22, United States National Archives.

19. Joseph Sher, interview with John Menszer, http://www.holocaustsurvivors.org, accessed July 11, 2006.

20. Lilli Marx, "The Renewal of the German-Jewish Press," in *After the Holocaust*, 126.

21. The following description is based on Alfred Slomnicki, "Bericht über

die Beerdigung von 39 Juden am 20. 8. 1946 in Floss," August 25, 1946, RG M1, folder P-74, YVA.

22. Ray Mariels (nephew of Lyle Mariels), interview by the author, April 26, 2006.

23. According to Jewish law, once the body is exhumed, it is to be treated with the same respect as was due on the day of death. See Lamm, *The Jewish Way in Death and Mourning*, 71–74.

24. See Irving J. Rosenbaum, *The Holocaust and Halakhah* (New York: KTAV, 1976), 144; Rabbi Shimon Efrati, responsum on the status of the mass graves and execution sites, quoted in Robert Kirschner, ed., *Rabbinic Responsa of the Holocaust Era* (New York: Schocken, 1985), 151 and 161n6.

25. Michael Asheri, *Living Jewish: The Lore and Law of the Practicing Jew* (New York: Everest House, 1978), 110.

26. Lamm, *The Jewish Way in Death and Mourning*, 75.

27. Slomnicki, "Bericht über die Beerdigung von 39 Juden am 20. 8. 1946 in Floss," YVA.

28. DPs delighted in disproving anti-Semitic attitudes concerning Jewish criminality, and the DP police played a role in this endeavor. In another memorial procession, DP organizers remarked with pride that Jewish DP police had maintained order along the parade route without assistance from American or German police. See Chaim Diamand, "Bericht über die Trauer-Akademie am 28. April 1946 in der Gemeinde Eggenfelden," May 5, 1946, RG 294.2, microfilm MK 483.63, folder 888, frame 466, Archives of the YIVO Institute for Jewish Research (hereafter YIVO).

29. Josef Kohs, "Rede des 2. Vorsitzenden des Jüdischen Komitees Tirschenreuth Josef Kohs Gehalten anläßlich der Bestattung von 39 KZ-Häftlingen in Floß," August 20, 1946, RG M1, folder P-74, YVA.

30. Ibid.

31. Zeev Mankowitz, *Life between Memory and Hope: The Survivors of the Holocaust in Occupied Germany* (Cambridge: Cambridge University Press, 2002), 69.

32. Bergen-Belsen Rabbinate, "Remember What Amalek Did to You [Yiddish]," Intermediary days of Passover 5708 [April 1948], RG O70, folder 29, YVA.

33. Greenberg, "From *Hurban* to Redemption," 102.

34. Mosze Fridenzon, "2-te landes-konferenc fun Agudas-Jisroel in Dajczland," *Landsberger Lager Cajtung*, September 25, 1946, n.p.

35. Ibid.

36. Greenberg, "From *Hurban* to Redemption," 103–5.

37. Lamm, *The Jewish Way in Death and Mourning*, 196.

38. Bertha Ferderber-Salz, *And the Sun Kept Shining* (New York: Holocaust Library, 1980), 229.

39. Anonymous Polish female survivor, quoted in Reeve Robert Brenner, *The Faith and Doubt of Holocaust Survivors* (New York: Free Press,

1980), 61.

40. Rabbi Katriel Tchorsh, responsum on whether all Jews are obliged to recite Kaddish for the Holocaust Victims, quoted in Kirschner, *Rabbinic Responsa of the Holocaust Era,* 172 and 176n8.

41. Ibid., 165–76.

42. See, for example, *Unzer Weg,* August 30, 1946, p. 7, and *Unzer Weg,* November 15, 1946, p. 12, reel 64-y-471, YIVO.

43. Organizer Komitet, "Achtung Jidn Fun Lite!!!" October 22, 1946, RG M1, folder P-10 II, YVA. The October Action referred to the murder of ninety-two hundred Jews from Kovno at the Ninth Fort by the Germans and their accomplices on October 29, 1941.

44. "Yizkor for Lithuanian Jewry [Yiddish]," *Unzer Weg,* November 15, 1946, p. 6.

45. Hagit Lavsky, *New Beginnings: Holocaust Survivors in Bergen-Belsen and the British Zone in Germany, 1945–1950* (Detroit: Wayne State University Press, 2002), 149.

46. Erna Rubinstein, *After the Holocaust: The Long Road to Freedom* (North Haven, CT: Archon Books, 1995), 98.

47. On the purpose of the *mikvah,* see Asheri, *Living Jewish,* 90–93.

48. Isaac Levy, "Belsen Testimonies," in *Belsen in History and Memory,* edited by Jo Reilly, Tony Kushner, and Colin Richmond (London: Frank Cass, 1997), 240.

49. Lavsky, *New Beginnings,* 114.

50. Rabinat in Fernwald, "Ojfruf cu Pejsach," 1946, RG M1, folder P-121, YVA.

51. Irving Heymont, *Among the Survivor of the Holocaust, 1945: The Landsberg DP Camp Letters of Major Irving Heymont, United States Army* (Cincinnati: Hebrew Union College Press, 1982), 83.

52. N. Z. Friedmann, *Taharat Hamischpacha: Von di jidische Ehe-Gesetze,* Föhrenwald, Germany, 1945–46, RG M1, folder P-65, YVA.

53. Agudath Israel, "Jewish Wife! Jewish Mother!" [Yiddish], RG M1, folder P-65, YVA.

54. Jacob Biber, *Risen from the Ashes: A Story of the Jewish Displaced Persons in the Aftermath of World War II* (San Bernardino, CA: Borgo, 1990), 34.

55. Hadassah Rosensaft, *Yesterday: My Story* (Washington, DC: United States Holocaust Memorial Museum, 2004), 79.

56. Levy, "Belsen Testimonies," 239–40. See also Rabbi Yehezkel Abramski, responsum on permission for marriage (in Bergen-Belsen DP Camp), whether assignment in the direction of the crematoria is sufficient proof of death, and whether ghetto expediency marriages are valid, in Kirschner, *Rabbinic Responsa of the Holocaust Era,* 137–38.

57. Ferderber-Salz, *And the Sun Kept Shining,* 213.

58. Yehuda Bauer, *Out of the Ashes: The Impact of American Jews on Post-Holocaust European Jewry* (New York: Pergamon, 1989), 96.

59. Levy, "Belsen Testimonies," 240.

60. Rosensaft, *Yesterday,* 109.

61. Asheri, *Living Jewish,* 71.

62. Ibid., 72.

63. "Council Meeting of Jews in Bavaria," *Unzer Weg,* October 19, 1946, p. 4.

64. Alex Grobman, *Battling for Souls: The Vaad Hatzala Rescue Committee in Post-War Europe* (Jersey City, NJ: KTAV, 2004), 168.

65. See, for example, Landsberg Religjezer Amt, "Meldung fun Religjezn Amt," September 6, 1946, RG M1, folder P-65, YVA; Eschwege Religjezer-Amt, "Meldung," August 1, 1946 (a second such document is undated), RG M1, folder P-65, YVA.

66. Rabbi Shlomo David Kahana, responsum on permission for *agunot* to remarry (after the war), in Kirschner, *Rabbinic Responsa of the Holocaust Era,* 139–47, esp. 144-45.

67. Hannah Modenstein, interview by the author, tape recording, July 18, 1995.

68. During the seven weeks between Passover and Shavuot, traditional Jews observe a period of semimourning. No marriages are performed during this time except on Lag B'Omer, which occurs on the thirty-third day of this period. Many couples wanting a spring wedding will choose this date.

69. Ferderber-Salz, *And the Sun Kept Shining,* 226.

70. Sam Halpern, *Darkness and Hope* (New York: Shengold, 1996), 176–77.

71. Rubinstein, *After the Holocaust,* 61.

72. Samuel Bak, "Landsberg Revisited," *Dimensions* 13 (1999): 33.

73. Atina Grossmann, "Trauma, Memory and Motherhood: Germans and Jewish Displaced Persons in Post-Nazi Germany, 1945–1949," *Archiv für Sozialgeschichte* 38 (1998): 215–39.

74. Modenstein interview.

75. Koppel S. Pinson, "Jewish Life in Liberated Germany: A Study of the Jewish DP's," *Jewish Social Studies* 9, no. 2 (1947): 116–17; Mankowitz, *Life between Memory and Hope,* 103–5.

76. Eschwege Religious Committee, "Meldung," undated, RG M1, folder P-65, YVA.

77. M. Fratkin, multiple memos from Landsberg DP Hospital to Religious Office, August–September 1946, RG M1, folder P-73, YVA.

78. "Resolution of the Central Rabbinate to the 2nd Congress of the She'erit Hapletah in the British Zone," July 22, 1947, RG O70, folder 29, YVA.

79. One mother claimed that had her child been a boy, she would have run away to prevent his circumcision "because this is why my brothers were killed." See Lynn Rapaport, *Jews in Germany after the Holocaust: Memory, Identity, and Jewish-German Relations* (Cambridge: Cambridge University Press, 1997), 92.

80. Rat der Rabbiner in der Britschen Zone Deutschlands, letter to Zentralkomitee der Befreiten Juden in der Britischen Zone, August 10, 1948, RG O70, folder 29, YVA.

81. Muriel Knox Doherty, Letter 6/14, December 1945, in *Letters from Belsen*

1945: An Australian nurse's experiences with the survivors of war, edited by Judith Cornell and R. Lynette Russell (St. Leonards, New South Wales: Allen & Unwin, 2000), 199.

82. Rachela Walshaw and Sam Walshaw, *From Out of the Firestorm: A Memoir of the Holocaust* (New York: Shapolsky, 1991), 139.

83. The number of schools supported by Vaad Hatzala is approximate due to the organization's irregular accounting practices and disagreements among yeshiva directors as to which organization provided their essential needs. Grobman, *Battling for Souls,* 163–64 and 250–52; Solomon Goldman, "Education among Jewish Displaced Persons: The Sheerit Hapletah in Germany, 1945–1950" (PhD dissertation, Dropsie University, 1978), 105.

84. Some of the schools supported by the American Jewish Joint Distribution Committee also received some minimal aid from Vaad Hatzala and may have been included in their statistics. Goldman, "Education among Jewish Displaced Persons," 104.

85. Bak, "Landsberg Revisited," 36.

86. Brenner, *The Faith and Doubt of Holocaust Survivors,* 37.

87. A study of contemporary Jews in Israel found that traditional (nonaffiliated) and Orthodox Jews participated in rituals primarily for motives concerning religion and continuity with past family practices. Secular Jews also performed rituals but were motivated by ethnic feelings and desire for family gatherings. See Aryeh Lazar, Shlomo Kravetz, and Peri Frederich-Kedem, "The Multidimensionality of Motivation for Jewish Religious Behavior: Content, Structure, and Relationship to Religious Identity," *Journal for the Scientific Study of Religion* 41, no. 3 (2002): 509–19.

88. Brenner, *The Faith and Doubt of Holocaust Survivors,* 78–80.

89. Alexander J. Groth, *Holocaust Voices: An Attitudinal Survey of Survivors* (Amherst, NY: Humanity Books, 2003), 94.

90. Ibid.

91. Brenner, *The Faith and Doubt of Holocaust Survivors,* 122.

92. The study included Catholic, Protestant, and Jewish adolescents. The author noted that Jewish adolescents were least likely to exhibit change. Since none of these subjects had experienced anything remotely comparable to the Holocaust, it is not possible to ascertain how such a traumatic event might have influenced the results. Still, the findings are consistent with those of Brenner in *The Faith and Doubt of Holocaust Survivors,* Groth in *Holocaust Voices,* and this work. It is interesting to consider how age and developmental factors affected the DPs. See Elizabeth Weiss Ozorak, "Social and Cognitive Influences on the Development of Religious Beliefs and Commitment in Adolescence," *Journal for the Scientific Study of Religion* 28 (December 1989): 460 and 461.

93. Nathan Katz, *Teach Us to Count Our Days: A Story of Survival, Sacrifice and Success* (Cranbury, NJ: Cornwall Books, 1999), 41–43. In postwar St. Louis, Katz joined an Orthodox synagogue but observed conserva-

tive practices in his home unless his more observant father was visiting (180).

94. Thomas Toivi Blatt, *From the Ashes of Sobibor: A Story of Survival* (Evanston, IL: Northwestern University Press, 1997), 9.

95. Ozorak, "Social and Cognitive Influences on the Development of Religions Beliefs and Commitment in Adolescence," 461.

96. Rapaport, *Jews in Germany*, 106, notes that in the predominantly secular postwar Frankfurt Jewish community, religious ritual benefits "the maintenance of Jewish identity and the vitality of the community." High Holy Day observance establishes and reinforces group solidarity and serves as a sign of ethnic identity, a public demonstration of Jewishness as opposed to Germanness.

97. For an interesting empirical study of the relationship between ritual and social bonds, see Richard Sosis and Bradley J. Ruffle, "Religious Ritual and Cooperation: Testing for a Relationship on Israeli Religious and Secular Kibbutzim," *Current Anthropology* 44, no. 5 (2003), 713–21.

98. David I. Kertzer, *Ritual, Politics & Power* (New Haven, CT: Yale University Press, 1988), 76.

"We Long for a Home"

*Songs and Survival among
Jewish Displaced Persons*

SHIRLI GILBERT

INTRODUCTION

While much has been written about the extraordinary renewal of
Jewish life in the camps for displaced persons (DPs) in postwar Europe—the marriages, the baby boom, the vibrant and autonomous
political life—as yet little has been written about the remarkably
heterogeneous musical activities that flourished in these transitional
spaces. Songs from the prewar period and from the wartime ghettos
and camps were widely sung. Visiting performances were given by
renowned artists including Yehudi Menuhin, Benjamin Britten, and
Leonard Bernstein. Zionist songs featured prominently in children's
education as well as in communal events. In addition, a good deal
of new music was created by the DPs themselves: homegrown ensembles were established that toured the camps, and new songs were
created recounting the horrors of the war years, chronicling mourning
and loss, and relating illegal immigration to Palestine, among other
contemporary responses.

This chapter offers a preliminary overview of the diverse musical
life that thrived among Jewish DPs. It represents the beginnings of
an ongoing research project and draws on a portion of the extant archival evidence; as such, it is intended as a contribution toward filling

a significant gap in the literature. In addition to documenting some important activities and events, this chapter proposes that musical life provides a valuable lens through which to explore an issue of wider historical significance: how surviving victims shaped their understanding of what had happened to them and their relationship to the individual and collective future. The immediate postwar years were a formative transitional moment in Jewish history and witnessed the "first sustained public attempt to grapple with both the implications of the Shoah and some of the major questions of post-Holocaust Jewish life."[1] As a historical source, music can offer distinctive insight into our understanding of this transition, in particular by providing a glimpse into the inner life of these temporary communities and the ways in which they went about negotiating the shift toward postwar life.

Although the literature relating to Jewish DPs is extensive, research on the subject of music is sparse.[2] One factor that might explain this dearth is the sizable number of camps and refugee centers in Western and Central Europe that would fall within the scope of an inclusive study.[3] In addition, emphasis has been focused overwhelmingly on music during the Holocaust period despite the fact that archival materials relating to the postwar period are plentiful. A substantial number of DP publications survive, including songbooks and newspapers that provide information about specific events. In addition, numerous former DPs (musicians as well as nonmusicians) have published accounts of their experiences, as have musicians who visited DP centers. Perhaps most valuable as sources are several song collection projects that were carried out in 1946–47, in particular the transcribed songs collected by Shmerke Katsherginski primarily in Lithuania and Poland; the recordings gathered by the Central Jewish Historical Commission in Munich; and the interview project carried out by the psychologist David Boder in France, Italy, Germany, and Switzerland. Although these collection projects were conceived as broad efforts to document and preserve in the aftermath of the destruction, rather than as specifically musical initiatives, in all three cases extensive amounts of musical material were accumulated.[4] This rich variety of sources makes music among Jewish DPs a subject ripe for further discussion and research.

MUSICAL PERFORMANCES

Perhaps the most prominent and public element of musical life among Jewish DPs was the performances given by visiting artists, primarily from Britain and the United States. In July 1945 the violinist Yehudi

Menuhin and the British composer and pianist Benjamin Britten traveled to Germany to perform "in the saddest ruins of the Third Reich," including two concerts at Bergen-Belsen. They played a range of works from the standard violin repertoire, including pieces by Beethoven, Mendelssohn, Debussy, and Bach.[5] Between April and October 1946 the American singer Emma Lazaroff Schaver performed a packed schedule of concerts for Jewish DPs, offering a repertoire made up primarily of prewar and wartime Jewish songs. In April and May, Schaver appeared as an official representative of the Cultural Mission of the World Jewish Congress together with the poet H. Leivick and the author Israel Efros; several weeks after the completion of the mission, Schaver returned to Europe alone to continue with her performing and outreach work.[6] In August 1947 the Yiddish entertainer Herman Yablokoff traveled from the United States to Bergen-Belsen, offering performances of folk songs, theater songs, and dramatic excerpts, and in May 1949 the American conductor and composer Leonard Bernstein performed with the St. Ottilien Orchestra. Numerous additional concerts were given by visiting soloists, symphony orchestras, and chamber groups from the United States, Europe, and Palestine.[7]

These guest performances were largely intended to help restore morale among Jewish DPs, both by showing that the world had not forgotten them and by representing a move toward the normalization of cultural life. In his autobiography, Menuhin describes his concert tour as being motivated by his desire "to offer the living victims the sorrow, the repentance, the solidarity of the unharmed."[8] A nurse present at one of his concerts recalled that "it was inspiring to see these two compassionate men, clad simply in shirt and shorts, creating glorious melody and moving among the people in the crowded hut who were difficult to rouse from a deadly mental lethargy as a result of the horrors and privations they had suffered. They were successful in some cases in wooing them back to life and hope and commence [sic] the healing of the mind and body."[9] Many of the performers also felt it their personal duty as Jews to bring what comfort and pleasure they could to the Jewish DPs and to show their solidarity. Yablokoff, for example, refused payment for his performances, which he hoped would provide at least momentary distraction to the survivors. In his autobiographical account he affirms his sense of duty to his fellow Jews in despair and assures them that "the Jewish communities in the free world have not forsaken you, and never will!"[10] In her published account of the World Jewish Congress mission, Emma Schaver wrote frequently of the sense of responsibility she felt toward her people:

I wanted at least to pay my debt to the people [folks-khoyv], to give these unfortunate people joy, pleasure, spiritual enjoyment. To bring to life for them again the almost forgotten Yiddish and Hebrew songs, to bring to them through sound the fragrance of Eretz-Yisrael to which they aspired with all their being. To refresh for them the songs that they heard in their childhood from their mothers. . . . And the more I sang and saw the light in their eyes, and heard their drawn breath, the more I felt that I owed it to them.[11]

In addition to performances by visiting artists, a wide range of musical activities were organized by the DPs themselves. In informal settings and at formal events, DPs sang prewar Yiddish folk songs, songs from the wartime ghettos and camps, Yiddish theater songs, excerpts from operas and operettas, and other preexisting repertoire. Several performing groups were also established that regularly traveled to other camps and refugee centers. The earliest musical group was almost certainly the orchestra led by Michael Hofmekler together with eight other former members of the Kovno Ghetto orchestra at St. Ottilien, a monastery that was used as a Jewish hospital and DP camp from April 1945 until November 1948. Originally named the St. Ottilien Orchestra, later the Ex-Concentration Camp Orchestra, and finally the Representative Orchestra of the She'erit Hapletah, the group performed at the Liberation Concert, the first official gathering of Jewish survivors held on May 27, 1945, at St. Ottilien. The event was supported by the American Jewish Joint Distribution Committee (JDC)—the JDC backed a range of cultural and educational activities among DPs, including organizing guest appearances by visiting artists[12]—and performed classical repertoire and Jewish music at DP centers across Bavaria as well as at high-profile events in Germany.[13] Numerous theater groups were also established by Jewish DPs, some of which incorporated music in their performances. Föhrenwald, in the American zone, was home to several theater and music ensembles.[14] In Bergen-Belsen, the former inmate Samy Feder organized a thirty-member theater troupe named the Kazet-Teater (Concentration Camp Theater) that performed Yiddish plays and songs, first in Belsen and later traveling to other camps and hospitals in Germany as well as to France and Belgium. Feder also published a small songbook, *Zamlung fun katset un geto lider* (Collection of Camp and Ghetto Songs), in 1946.[15] Bergen-Belsen was also home to the Workers' Theatre, under the auspices of the left-wing Zionist movement Poale Zion, which staged several successful shows.[16] A popular band led by Chaim (Henry) Baigelman and called The Happy Boys, made up of eight surviving musicians from Łódź, traveled to DP camps across the

American zone between 1945 and 1949 performing a variety of instrumental and vocal music from Jewish folk songs to operetta and jazz.[17]

As was the case with Feder, the St. Ottilien Orchestra, and the
Happy Boys, Jewish musicians who had been active in music making
before and during the war years often continued their work as DPs.
Diana Blumenfeld, for example, a well-known singer in the Warsaw
Ghetto, worked with her husband, the actor Yonas Turkov, toward the
reestablishment of Polish Jewish cultural life in the immediate postwar
period. The first cultural event organized by the Association of Jewish
Writers, Journalists and Actors, of which Turkov was the chairman,
was a concert in Lublin in December 1944 at which Blumenfeld performed Yiddish songs; she also toured DP camps in Germany, giving
concerts for other survivors.[18] Henny Durmashkin, who sang in the
Vilna Ghetto, performed extensively with the St. Ottilien Orchestra in
DP centers across Germany.[19] The cellist Anita Lasker-Wallfisch, who
along with fellow members of the women's orchestra in Auschwitz

Portrait of Henia Durmashkin at
the St. Ottilien DP hospital, 1945.
(United States Holocaust Memorial Museum, Photo no. 30647,
courtesy of Henny Durmashkin
Gurko)

Songs and Survival among Jewish DPs

Members of the Jewish Ex-Concentration Camp Orchestra perform on stage in Nuremberg, 1946. (United States Holocaust Memorial Museum, Photo no. 29734, courtesy of David Granat)

Group portrait of The Happy Boys. *Left to right:* Sam Spaismacher, Henry Eisenman, Abraham Mutzman, Chaim (Henry) Baigelman, Elek Silberstein, Itchak Lewin, Abraham Lewin, and Josel Lewin. (United States Holocaust Memorial Museum, Photo no. 10324A, courtesy of Henry Baigelman)

was transported to Bergen-Belsen in the final months of the war, also performed in the DP camp that was subsequently established there as well as in other camps.[20]

NEWLY CREATED SONGS

Although Jewish DPs drew largely on preexisting musical repertoire, a not insignificant contemporaneous repertoire also began to emerge at this time, made up primarily of songs. The songs tackled a range of topical issues from loss, displacement, and loneliness to the longing for Palestine and the perils of illegal immigration. They also offered defiant affirmations of Jewish existence as well as satirical jabs at aid agencies such as the JDC, the Organization for Rehabilitation through Training, and the United Nations Relief and Rehabilitation Administration.

As suggested in the introduction, songs of this kind are valuable sources that can enrich our understanding of this historical period. In particular, as texts produced by the DPs themselves, they offer a significant internal perspective on individual and community responses. Songs were a forum through which surviving victims could not only record experiences but also bear witness on behalf of those who had not survived. They reveal something of victims' interpretations of the realities they confronted and the kinds of attitudes they espoused and advocated. Moreover, while songs frequently functioned as a medium for expressing desperation and continued suffering, they were also a forum for raising morale, encouraging affirmative responses, and imagining possible futures.

Many songs created by Jewish DPs unsurprisingly addressed the emotional difficulties faced in the immediate aftermath of the war as survivors struggled both to come to terms with what they had experienced and to begin the process of recovery. One example is a song titled "Dort in dem lager" (There in the Camp), collected by David Boder in September 1946:

> Dort in dem lager in a vinkele bay nakht
> Shteyt zikh a yidele, farzinken, fartrakht
> Er trakht vegn takhles, un er zingt zikh azoy tsi
> A shod yeder arbayt, a shod yeder mi
> Tatenyu in himl
> Vi lang nokh es doyert?
> Ale mitlen hob ikh shoyn probirt
> Ikh hob shoyn mer keyn koyekh
> Un yetst bin ikh alayn do

Un trakht vegn mayn umgliklikhe sho
Hob shoyn rakhmones
Tatenyu.

There in the camp in a corner at night
Stands a Jew sunken, absorbed in thought
He thinks about serious matters, and he sings softly to himself
Any work is pointless, any effort is a waste
Dear father in heaven
How much more to endure?
I've already tried all means
I have no more strength
And now I am alone here
Thinking of my unfortunate fate
Have pity
Dear father.[21]

The song's remaining verses chronicle loneliness, suffering, and especially the loss of family. The composer and lyricist are unknown, and it is unclear whether the song in fact originated after the war or at an earlier point. Nonetheless, the narrative seems unmistakably to reflect on what has already happened and on wrestling with the aftereffects: the difficulty of being isolated from the world and confronting this "unfortunate fate."

Although many songs similarly express the pain of coming to terms with the past and the despair of the present, few are as unremittingly bleak as "Dort in dem lager." The song "Es benkt zikh nokh a haym" (We Long for a Home), for example, written by Happy Boys leader Chaim Baigelman, describes the "bad dream" of the Nazi era but also reveals a cautious readiness to long for a better future even if this seems only a distant possibility:

Es benkt zikh nokh a haym, vi gefint men zi af der velt?
Es benkt zikh nokh a haym, yeder veg iz far undz farshtelt.
Hofn darf men dokh, es ken nisht andersh zayn,
Damols ken dos lebn zayn shayn mit khayn, un gliklekh zayn.

We long for a home, where can one find such a place in the world?
We long for a home, every road is blocked to us.
Yet one must keep hoping, it can't be otherwise,
Then life can be full of beauty, charm, and happiness.[22]

The varying attitudes and emphases that emerge from these songs

ES BENGT ZICH NUCH A HAJM

Musik: Stranski   Text: H. Beigelman

A szlechter chulym iz dus besztimt gewejn
Jejder zejt erszt ject wus es iz geszejn
Dus beste iz awek, es iz a grojl a szrek, a szrek!
Wi men gejt un sztejt wen es zol niszt zajn
Umetum hert zich dus zelbige gewajn
Jejder ajner filt dem tifen szmerc wus ich, wajl . . .

REFREIN

Es bengt zich nuch a Hajm
wi ge'int, men zi ojf der welt?
Es bengt zich nuch a Hajm
jejder wejg iz far unc fersztelt
Hofen darf men doch, es ken niszt andersz zajn
Damuls ken dus leben erszt zajn szajn
mit chajn, und gliklich zajn!
Es bengt zich nuch a Hajm
A wareme Hajm wi a muhl
Es bengt zich nuch a Hajm
Unzer aw!e muz wejren becuhlt
Es iz gewejzen szlecht
Ojf gut hot zich doch gehajt
Ject darf men lejben
Wajl es iz di cajt! !

Song sheet for "Es benkt zikh nokh a haym" (We Long for Home), performed by the Happy Boys. (United States Holocaust Memorial Museum, Photo no. No3182, courtesy of Henry Baigelman)

doubtless stem in part from the context of their creation and performance. Many were presumably written by individuals reflecting on their personal circumstances, and those songs that resonated with the experiences of the larger group or appealed to a general sentiment might have circulated more widely. In the case of groups such as the unambiguously named Happy Boys, whose primary function was to provide entertainment for DPs, the unsurprising intent seems to have been to raise morale and encourage a positive outlook even while honestly acknowledging the reality of the circumstances.

In addition to confronting the survivors' present difficulties, many of the newly created songs express the longing for Palestine and lament the obstacles to immigration. While the strength of Zionist sentiment among Jewish DPs has been well documented, there has been much debate as to its nature: to what extent it was a natural, "almost intuitive"[23] response to the Holocaust as opposed to a response to pressure from and manipulation by emissaries from the Yishuv. Avinoam

Patt has argued that neither extreme in isolation offers a suitable explanation and attributes much of the movement's popularity to the therapeutic and practical functions that it served for young DPs, in particular "by providing a secure environment for vocational and agricultural training, education, rehabilitation and a surrogate family that could ultimately restore their belief in humanity."[24] The extant musical evidence affirms, along Patt's line, that while efforts were certainly directed at DPs from the Yishuv, there was also a strong and genuine internal impetus toward Zionism. Zionist songs featured prominently in DP camp cultural activities, particularly in children's and youth education. Surviving songbooks and recordings reveal that a fairly wide repertoire was in circulation[25] and suggest either the presence of Zionist emissaries or at least the direct provision of educational materials from the Yishuv.[26] At the same time, songs created by DPs themselves seem to reveal a heartfelt Zionist sentiment based in large part on the need for community and belonging. Bret Werb explains that the popular song "Vu ahin zol ikh geyn" (Where Should I Go), for example—written by a person by the name of Korntayer in the Warsaw Ghetto and adapted by Sigmunt Berland from a prewar melody—was frequently modified in its postwar performance so that the title question "Where should I go?" was answered "keyn tsion!" (to Zion!). In addition, beneath the singer's final note in Berland's arrangement were the unmistakable opening strains of "Hatikvah" in the piano accompaniment.[27] The song "S'vet geshen" (It Will Happen), written by Shmerke Katsherginski and composed by Sigmunt Berland, was dedicated to the illegal immigrants of the ship *Exodus:*

Fray shvimen shifn oyf yamen
Di mastn flatern tsum blo
Nor ikh mit mayn oremer mamen
Bahaltn muz ikh afn dno.
Di shif muz in ergets antrinen
Es zol undz keyner nit gefinen.
O shturm vind, o derbreng mame, kind
Gikh tsum breg dem gegartn . . .
Genug shoyn gevart!
   S'vet geshen, s'vet geshen
   Un mir ale veln vider zayn tsuzamen
   Ir vet zen, ir vet zen
   Oykh undzer shif vet shvimen fray af ale yamen.
   Undzer heyliker farlang
   Umtsukern zikh in land fun di neviim
   Vet mekuyem vern, kh'her shoyn di gezangn

                                                    Shirli Gilbert

Vi men bentsht undz brukhim-habo'im.
Der natsi fun shtub undz fartribn
Mir muzn alts bay im nor zayn
Yesoymim mir zaynen geblibn
O ver vet zikh merakhem zaym?
Land yedes folk hot bakumen
Farvoglte mir muzn shtumen.
O brider zogt, ven vet kumen der tog
Undzer tog der gegarter?
Genug shoyn gevart!

Ships float freely on the seas
The masts flutter in the blue
But my poor mother and I
Must hide down below.
The ship must disappear somewhere
Where nobody will find us.
Oh stormy wind, carry mother and child
Quickly to the shore that we long for . . .
We've waited enough already!
   It will happen, it will happen
   And we will all be together again
   You will see, you will see
   Our ship, too, will sail freely on all the seas.
   Our sacred desire
   To return to the land of the prophets
   Will be fulfilled, I already hear the singing
   That is blessing our welcome.
The Nazis drove us from our homes
We are all tied to them
We were left orphans
Oh who will take pity on us?
Every nation received their land
We, homeless, must be silent.
Oh brothers say, when will the day come
The day that we long for?
We've waited enough already![28]

Several contemporary songs focus similarly on illegal immigration. From the Kibbutz Hakhshara Tradate in Italy, Boder collected in September 1946 a song titled "Di shif Seder" (The Ship Seder), which describes the all-too-common fate of an illegal immigrant ship intercepted by the British.[29] In "Ikh bin a yidisher DP" (I Am a Jewish DP), a visitor to the DP camps, the poet H. Leivick, portrayed a similar scenario of survivors betrayed by the British and abandoned by the world:

Ikh bin a yidisher di-pi
A yid fun eybikn nit hi.
Mayn veg keyn erets halt farshlosn
John Bull blokadet shif oyf shif.
Mayn zun, der oyle, ligt dershosn
Oyf same breg fun tel aviv.

I am a Jewish DP
A Jew from eternal nowhere.
My path to Palestine remains barred
John Bull blockades ship after ship.
My son, the immigrant, lies shot
On the very shores of Tel Aviv.[30]

Katsherginski's representation in "S'vet geshen" is perhaps distinctive among these songs in the balance that it strikes between hope and acknowledgment. On one level, the tenor of the song is unmistakably affirmative and defiant, particularly as reflected in the chorus and most explicitly the title. This is at the same time infused with a forthright acknowledgment of continued Jewish suffering: the consequences of the Nazi onslaught and the ongoing dangers of and obstacles to immigration. The song is neither an uncomplicatedly optimistic account nor a relentlessly despairing one but rather a poignant affirmation of Jewish endurance grounded in the knowledge that the longed-for moment may yet be some time in coming.

Songs such as "S'vet geshen" and "Es benkt zikh nokh a haym" exemplify a trend revealed more broadly in DP musical life: a complex engagement with the reality that frankly acknowledges its despairs and challenges and simultaneously recognizes the need to imagine the future and develop affirmative responses. Some of the songs, to be sure, are persistently bleak in outlook and suggest little possibility of redemption. Others use humor and satire in a way that masks the seriousness of the situation they portray, such as survivors' grievances against aid agencies.[31] On the whole, however, musical activities among Jewish DPs—both those organized by outsiders and those motivated by the survivors themselves—seem consciously to be centered around the need for comfort, strength, and regeneration at this critical transitional moment and to recognize the constructive role that music could play in that process.

Thus far this chapter has explored music's significance at the level of performances and compositions. As this final section will elaborate, there is a further dimension in which music can add to our understanding of this period: namely, at the level of discourse. Put briefly, this refers to the ways in which people perceived that songs might contribute to the process of documenting and remembering the genocide. In distinguishing between the music itself and its surrounding discourse, this chapter thus argues for two layers of music's significance. On one level, as previously discussed, songs provide a glimpse into survivors' perspectives on the past and its consequences. On another level, the discourse that emerged at this time relating to songs also offers revealing and perhaps even more explicit insight into how survivors imagined the events might be memorialized.

Of the many issues being negotiated by Jewish DPs during this period, one of the most important and highly charged was memory.[32] How were such devastating events to be recorded, and how were their victims to be remembered? In the immediate aftermath of the war, numerous independent Jewish initiatives were launched to document the Nazi era and to preserve the memory of the victims. Although those involved in these initiatives placed their primary emphasis on testimonies, many also consistently expressed their interest in songs, stories, jokes, and other cultural remnants of the communities they sought to memorialize. Songs were seen to play an integral role both as historical sources that would enable future researchers to reconstruct what had happened and as artifacts that could perhaps preserve the voices, and thereby the memory, of the victims. A distinction was seldom made between documenting on the one hand and preserving memory on the other, since these activities were seen as practically synonymous. As Laura Jockusch argues in chapter 2 of this volume, many collectors conceived of documentation itself as a means of commemorating the dead: a call to survivors in the U.S. zone of occupation, for example, urged that "every document, picture, song, legend is the only gravestone which we can place on the unknown graves of our parents, siblings, and children!"[33]

Music featured prominently in several documentation initiatives, including the work of Shmerke Katsherginski and the Central Jewish Historical Commission mentioned earlier. Themselves survivors, Katsherginski and the directors of the commission made explicit observations about how the songs they collected might help to memorialize the events. Songs were perceived as illuminating a specific dimension of history: not how the victims were acted upon as passive objects but rather the ways in which they, as historical subjects with agency, lived under the Nazi occupation and actively responded to what was happening. Referring to the paucity of documents relating to the inner life of Jews under Nazi rule, commission director Moyshe Feigenbaum urged that it was the duty of survivors to record whatever they could in order to lay the foundation for writing a comprehensive history of the catastrophe. The documents being amassed in anticipation of the Nuremberg Trials, he wrote,

> are just a fragment of our tragedy. They show only how the murderers behaved toward us, how they treated us and what they did with us. Do our lives in those nightmarish days consist only of such fragments? On what basis will the historian be able to create an image of what happened in the ghettos? How will one be able to depict our suffering- and pain-filled lives? From where will one be able to know about our heroic deeds and how will one determine our attitudes toward our oppressors? . . . We, the she'erit hapletah, the surviving witnesses, must create for the historian the foundation, represent to him the sources, from which he will be able to create a clear image of what happened to us and between us. Therefore each testimony of a saved Jew, every song from the Nazi era, every proverb, every anecdote and joke, every photograph is for us of tremendous value.[34]

Like Feigenbaum, Katsherginski emphasized the light that songs could shed on the inner lives of Jewish communities under internment. His comments similarly reveal a desire to give the victims' voices agency: How did Jews respond to the Nazi onslaught? How did they live before they died? Katsherginski emphasized that the picture that the songs painted was not a uniformly rosy one: they documented not only Nazi crimes but also internecine community struggles, corrupt Jewish officials, and other less savory aspects of everyday life. But these elements, too, were crucial to enabling historians to document what had happened:

> Few documents were preserved that would allow even a partial picture of the practical, official existence and the way of life of Jews in the occupied territories. Therefore, I think that the songs that Jews from ghettos, death camps and partisans sang from their sad hearts will be a great contribution to the history of Jewish martyrdom and struggle. . . . The daily Jewish life in the ghetto with all its accompanying phenomena, like arrests,

death, work, Gestapo, Jewish power-mongers, internal way of life, etc.—are reflected in precisely this bloody folklore. It will help future history-writers and researchers as well as readers to fathom the soul of our people.[35]

Like Katsherginski, other collectors made frequent reference to the value that historians, researchers, and future generations would glean from the songs, an aspect of their commentary that is particularly revealing. In a narrow sense, their observations about music are significant for what they suggest about the potential role of songs in memorializing the genocide. Over and above this, they reveal some prevalent conceptions about what, in a larger sense, survivors considered important to remember and which aspects of the wartime experience they considered essential for historians to understand and record. Rather than merely chronicling "how the murderers behaved toward us, how they treated us and what they did with us," their emphasis falls unambiguously on the victims' internal life and responses, from the banal to the heroic and everything in between. As they articulated it, songs—taken alongside other documents such as testimonies and photographs—have the potential to open a distinctive window onto this larger historical picture.

CONCLUSION

Much work remains to be done to uncover recordings, songbooks, musical transcriptions, interviews, testimonies, and other sources that would contribute toward a fuller study of the subject of music among Jewish DPs. Considerable published material is available, and substantial untapped sources undoubtedly exist in archives across Europe, Israel, and the United States.

As a preliminary overview, this chapter has been intended primarily to draw attention to the wide-ranging sources relating to musical life among Jewish DPs and the interpretive value that these sources can offer to the history of the period. Music broadly construed as source material—performances, traveling groups, educational activities, and the musical objects themselves as well as conceptions about music—has much to contribute to our understanding of this formative transitional moment, particularly by providing an internal perspective into the survivors' understanding of and responses to their experiences. As one means through which the DPs negotiated individual and collective identity in the aftermath of the catastrophe, music offers a helpful focus for restoring their historical agency rather than portraying them as passive victims—a pervasive image both at the time and in subsequent historiography—or casting them simply as outsiders viewed them. A growing body of research is focusing on the inner history of Jewish DPs, although much work remains to be done. The implications of exploring musical life among Jewish survivors thus extend beyond a specialized music-historical interest, offering to add another dimension to our understanding of DP life and to deepen our knowledge more broadly of how Jewish identity and memory were negotiated at this decisive juncture in Jewish history.

NOTES

Research for this chapter was supported by the Center for Advanced Holocaust Studies at the United States Holocaust Memorial Museum (USHMM) and the Michigan Society of Fellows. Thanks in particular to Bret Werb, music archivist at the USHMM, for sharing his knowledge on this subject and for ongoing help in locating archival material and to Khayele Beer for her advice on translations from Yiddish.

1. Zeev W. Mankowitz, *Life between Memory and Hope: The Survivors of the Holocaust in Occupied Germany* (Cambridge: Cambridge University Press, 2002), 4.

2. Published sources relating specifically to music are few. See Sophie Fetthauer, Peter Petersen, Bahne Sievers, and Silke Wenzel, "Musik in DP-Camps: Bericht über ein laufendes Projekt der Arbeitsgruppe Exilmusik," in *Form Follows Function: Zwischen Musik, Form und Funktion: Beiträge zum 18. internationalen studentischen Symposium des DVSM (Dachverband der Studierenden der Musikwissenschaft) in Hamburg, 2003,* edited by T. Knipper, M. Kranz, T. Kühnrich, and C. Neubauer, 187-215 (Hamburg: von Bockel, 2005); for more on this ongoing project, see http://www1.uni-hamburg.de/musik//exil/texte/dp-camps.html. See also Bret Werb, "Vu ahin zol ikh geyn? Music of Jewish Displaced Persons," unpublished lecture delivered at the National Yiddish Book Center, Amherst, Massachusetts, June 4, 2000. Scattered references to music appear in several general accounts of life among Jewish DPs. See, for example, Angelika Königseder and Juliane Wetzel, *Waiting for Hope: Jewish Displaced Persons in Post–World War II Germany* (Evanston, IL: Northwestern University Press, 2001), 80, 103, 118–22, 155; Mankowitz, *Life between Memory and Hope,* 30–31, 197–98, 219; Michael Brenner, *After the Holocaust: Rebuilding Jewish Lives in Postwar Germany* (Princeton, NJ: Princeton University Press, 1997), 29; Ruth Gay, *Safe among the Germans: Liberated Jews after World War II* (New Haven, CT: Yale University Press, 2002), 56–59. Jacqueline Giere, "We're on Our Way, but We're Not in the Wilderness," in *The Holocaust and History: The Known, the Unknown, the Disputed and the Reexamined,* edited by M. Berenbaum and A. J. Peck, 699–715 (Bloomington: Indiana University Press, 1998), examines the ways in which cultural life—specifi-

cally newspapers, theater, and education—helped Jewish survivors to "recover from their past and prepare for their future" (703), although music does not feature significantly in her analysis.

3. Werb, "Vu ahin zol ikh geyn?"

4. The songs collected by Katsherginski were published in his monumental work, edited with H. Leivick, *Lider fun di Getos un Lagern* (New York: Alveltlekher Yidisher Kultur-Kongres, 1948), which remains the largest and most important collection of Yiddish songs from the Holocaust period. Katsherginski also recorded several of these songs for the Jewish Historical Commission in 1946. The Tsentrale historishe komisye (Central Historical Commission), created under the auspices of the Central Committee of Liberated Jews in Munich in December 1945, urged survivors to record the songs that they remembered and managed to collect hundreds, some of which it published in its newspaper *Fun letstn khurbn: Tsaytshrift far geshikhte fun yidishn lebn beysn natsi rezhim;* the recordings are held at the National Sound Archive in Jerusalem. David Boder traveled to DP and refugee centers in France, Italy, Switzerland, and Germany between late July and early October 1946 and recorded several individual and group performances in the course of his interviews with survivors; the recordings are held at the USHMM Archive (hereafter USHMM) and at the Library of Congress. For more on these collection projects and their implications, see Shirli Gilbert, "Buried Monuments: Yiddish Songs and Holocaust Memory," *History Workshop Journal* 66 (2008): 107–28.

5. Yehudi Menuhin, *Unfinished Journey* (London: Pimlico, 2001), 185–86; Anita Lasker-Wallfisch, *Inherit the Truth, 1939–1945* (London: Giles de la Mare, 1996), 120; Fetthauer, Petersen, Sievers, and Wenzel, "Musik in DP-Camps," 204–7; file HA6A-3/8, Wiener Library Institute of Contemporary History, London.

6. Emma Schaver, *Mir zaynen do! Ayndrukn un batrakhtungen fun a bazukh bay der sheyres ha-pleytah* (Detroit: Yitshak un Hendele Foundeyshon, 1948); see also various materials, in particular boxes 3, 14, 15, 16 and miscellaneous photographs and albums, contained in the Emma Lazaroff-Schaver Archive, located at the Michigan Jewish Institute, 25401 Coolidge Highway, Oak Park, MI.

7. Herman Yablokoff, *Der Payatz: Around the World with Yiddish Theater* (Silver Spring, MD: Bartleby, 1995), 353–58; Königseder and Wetzel, *Waiting for Hope,* 73, 190; Fetthauer, Petersen, Sievers, and Wenzel, "Musik in DP-Camps," 197–98; Molly Picon and Jean Bergantini Grillo, *Molly!* (New York: Simon & Schuster, 1980).

8. Menuhin, *Unfinished Journey,* 185.

9. Cited in Fetthauer, Petersen, Sievers, and Wenzel, "Musik in DP-Camps," 205.

10. Yablokoff, *Der Payatz,* 357; Königseder and Wetzel, *Waiting for Hope,* 190.

11. Schaver, *Mir zaynen do,* 11.

12. For more on the JDC's assistance to Jewish DPs, including in the realm of culture, see Königseder and Wetzel, *Waiting for Hope*, 55–77, 154–55.

13. Henny Durmashkin-Gurko, "Songs to Remember," in *Anthology on Armed Jewish Resistance, 1939–1945,* Vol. 3, edited by I. Kowalski, 629–30 (New York: Jewish Combatants Publishers House, 1986); Königseder and Wetzel, *Waiting for Hope,* 80–81; Mankowitz, *Life between Memory and Hope,* 30–31. See also Robert L. Hilliard's recollection of the initial concert in "The Liberation Concert," *Boston Jewish Times,* October 1989.

14. Königseder and Wetzel, *Waiting for Hope,* 118–22.

15. Samy Feder, *Zamlung fun Katset un Geto Lider* (Bergen-Belsen: Central Jewish Committee in Bergen-Belsen, 1946).

16. Samy Feder, "The Yiddish Theater of Belsen," in *Theatrical Performance during the Holocaust: Texts, Documents, Memoirs,* edited by R. Rovit and A. Goldfarb, 156–58 (Baltimore: Johns Hopkins University Press, 1999); Königseder and Wetzel, *Waiting for Hope,* 188–89.

17. Concert programs and other ephemera relating to Happy Boys, file 1996.A.0403, USHMM; Photo archives N03182, N03183, and N03184, USHMM; Gay, *Safe among the Germans,* 56–59. Chaim was the only surviving member of the musical Baigelman family from Łódź, which included the well-known composer and conductor Dovid.

18. Nathan Cohen, "The Renewed Association of Yiddish Writers and Journalists in Poland, 1945–48," *Mendele Review* 9, no. 4 (March 15 2005), http://www2.trincoll.edu/~mendele/tmr/tmr09004.htm.

19. Durmashkin-Gurko, "Songs to Remember," 629–30.

20. Lasker-Wallfisch, *Inherit the Truth,* 110–13, 119.

21. Transcription from recording of "Dort in dem lager," Boder Collection, file RVA-0492, Tradate, September 1, 1946, USHMM.

22. Transcription from recording of "Es benkt zikh nokh a haym," performed by Adrienne Cooper and Zalmen Mlotek at *L'Chaim—To Life! A Musical Tribute Dedicated to our Parents,* concert at the conference Life Reborn: Jewish Displaced Persons, 1945–1951, United States Holocaust Memorial Museum, Washington, D.C., January 16, 2000; see also accompanying concert program, *Life Reborn: Jewish Displaced Persons 1945-1951: L'chaim—To life!: A Musical Tribute Dedicated to our Parents: International Conference, January 14-17, 2000, Washington, D.C.* (Washington, DC: United States Holocaust Memorial Museum & American Jewish Joint Distribution Committee, 2000).

23. Mankowitz, *Life between Memory and Hope,* 69.

24. Avinoam J. Patt, *Finding Home and Homeland: Jewish Youth and Zionism in the Aftermath of the Holocaust* (Detroit: Wayne State University Press, 2009).

25. See, for example, Record group 19.051, USHMM; Photo archive N04770, USHMM.

26. For recordings of survivors singing Zionist songs, see, for example, Boder Collection, file RVA-0509, Paris, September 7–8, 1946, USHMM; Boder Collection, file RVA-0492, Tradate, September 1,

1946, USHMM. Education was one of the She'erit Hapletah's earliest priorities, and the teaching of Hebrew and Zionism was central to curricula. Many teachers were brought from Palestine to work with the survivors, and educational materials were also provided; see Mankowitz, *Life between Memory and Hope*, 137.

27. Werb, "Vu ahin zol ikh geyn?"
28. Transcription from recording of "S'vet geshen" by Shmerke Katsherginski, Jewish Historical Commission recordings (1946), National Sound Archive, Jerusalem.
29. Boder Collection, file RVA-0492, Tradate, September 1, 1946, USHMM.
30. Transcription from recording of "Ikh bin a yidisher DP," performed by Frieda Enoch and ensemble at *L'Chaim—To Life!*; see also accompanying concert program, *Life Reborn*.
31. Henny Durmashkin, for example, who survived the war in the Vilna Ghetto and elsewhere, recorded in her memoir this snippet from a song that she wrote while in the DP camp in Furstenfeldbruck:

> UNNRA, JOINT and ORT
> Hand us tiny crumbs,
> and butter their own bread
> with tidy sums.

Durmashkin-Gurko, "Songs to Remember," 631. See also Miriam Hoffman songbook from DP camp Hindenburg Kaserne, Archives of the YIVO Institute for Jewish Research.

32. For more on this complex and highly charged issue, see Mankowitz, *Life between Memory and Hope*, chap. 9.
33. See chapter 2, this volume, note 25.
34. Moyshe Feigenbaum, "Tsu vos historishe komisyes?" *Fun Letsten Hurbn* 1 (August 1946): 2.
35. Katsherginski and Leivick, *Lider fun di Getos un Lagern*, xv, xviii.

Dangling Roots?

*Yiddish Language and Culture
in the German Diaspora*

Tamar Lewinsky

The emergence of a multifaceted Yiddish press and literature has often been cited as strong evidence for the agency of displaced persons (DPs); it has also been understood and described as a continuation of East European cultural traditions. Ruth Gay referred to this emergence in a recent work detailing Jewish life in postwar Germany: "In time, the displaced persons camps became little villages, a continuation of the old Jewish world, a last evocation in microcosm of the prewar Eastern European Jewish Culture. . . . In the camp newspapers and other periodicals we find the last spontaneous expression of prewar Jewish life, with old debates carried on as if they had only just been interrupted."[1] At first glance, this almost romanticized perception of the She'erit Hapletah (Surviving Remnant) as the bearer of "an epilogue of prewar East European Yiddish culture in miniature,"[2] and the claims for it as evidence of a continuity of Eastern European cultural heritage in Jewish DP camps seem to be convincing, especially in the realm of the printed word: between 1945 and 1950 almost 150 mostly Yiddish newspapers were published in Germany. A thriving party press represented all major Zionist parties ranging from the Left Poale Zion to the right-wing Revisionists. Literary journals, a magazine, books by DP writers (prose and poetry books as well as literary

criticism), reprints of religious books, historical research, world literature in translation, and other miscellaneous publications complete the
picture.[3] Munich, Landsberg, Regensburg, and Bergen-Belsen were
the new printing centers. Together they created, one might argue, a
new cultural landscape in Yiddish, a landscape in which the DP camps
replaced the East European small towns.

However, this view, which portrays DPs as the saving remnant of
the shtetl Jew living in extraterritorial units, needs still to be proven,
as does the claim for a direct cultural continuity built on the ruins of a
vanished world. This chapter seeks to follow up the DP writers' claims
of cultural self-assurance as well as of cultural reintegration into the
international Yiddish-speaking world and the emerging State of Israel.
It aims to discuss the question of a cultural continuity and disconti-
nuity in the realm of press and literature. In this context, the shifting
perceptions and self-perceptions of the Jewish DPs as well as current
debates over survivors' agency and the paramount importance of accurate periodization of the transient Jewish community in the wake of
the Holocaust need to be addressed.

As small as the group of writers might appear—it never exceeded
fifty members—its impact should not be underestimated. Already in
Eastern Europe before the war, Yiddish writers did not restrict themselves to the narrow field of literary production; they were primarily
journalists, editors, teachers, historians, publishers, and politicians.
The same was true for the literary community in postwar Germany.
Although small in quantity, this group was one of the most consistent and active elements in the demographically fluid society of the
She'erit Hapletah. They were among the first who engaged in the
plight for autonomy and self-governance and were among the last to
leave Germany in the early 1950s. In addition, this self-reflexive group
was diverse not only in background and experience but also in political orientation. As a productive social body, which at the same time
reflected and evaluated its own creativity, the literary and journalis-
tic circles, officially represented by the Writers' Union, document the
shifting self-conceptions and ideologies of the Jewish DPs.

THE NEED FOR PERIODIZATION AND PERSPECTIVE
IN DP HISTORIOGRAPHY

The majority of the early accounts, be it by visiting intellectuals, relief
workers, or leading figures of the She'erit Hapletah, depict the DPs as
broken Holocaust survivors who were excessively occupied with their
past and saw their future nowhere else but in the State of Israel. In a
report dating from April 1946, Koppel S. Pinson, a sociologist who

was appointed director of education and culture to the American Jewish Joint Distribution Committee (JDC) in Germany, stated:

> One of the most tragic aspects of the Jewish catastrophe in Europe has been the almost complete annihilation of the Jewish intelligenzia [sic]. Very few of our poets, writers, artists, musicians and scientists remain. All talent of this kind must be sought out, nurtured and given full encouragement. Very often these gifted people are shy and shun the market places of the DP camp. They have to be unearthed and discovered. Most of the time they are extreme individuals either disgusted with the seamy side of mass culture and mass mores or else so wrapped up in their own creative work. That [sic] they have little or no social responsibility. These things must not be held against them. We must be more patient and more tolerant with such individuals than with others. Every poet, painter, musician, scholar or scientist salvaged from the wrecks of European Jewry is a treasure that must be carefully protected and brought to a position where they can begin once again to release their creative energies for the good of the Jewish people and mankind.[4]

After his return to the United States, Pinson published a sociological study based on the observations he made while working for the JDC during the previous year.[5] However, as must be kept in mind when studying the time period, every month matters when it comes to the formation of the She'erit Hapletah. Pinson had visited Germany when the demographic structure had begun to change dramatically through the influx of Polish Jews repatriated from the Soviet Union. The small number of intellectuals had increased, unions were founded, the United Zionist Party was thrown apart through the growing political diversification, and writers and journalists had taken on responsibility for the education of the masses. At the time when Pinson's oft-cited study went to press, the She'erit Hapletah was a highly politicized and demographically complex entity. Its publication was therefore met with criticism among Jewish DPs. The immediate response to Pinson's study was a satirical feuilleton that denied the researcher's right to make generalizations and overall judgments about the Jews in Germany: "[If a professor] says a word, it is said, and when he diagnoses someone with something, it is unimpeachable . . . and if you are a 'Joint-professor' it is top-notch anyway. And because there is a vast interest across the ocean to know what kind of mass the She'erit Hapletah is, there was not much hesitation and a professor was sent . . . in order to explain to the world what is meant by the expression *sheyres-hapleytenik*."[6] This critical reply remained unheard outside Germany. Research until recently either has followed outsider's accounts, often unaware of the incessantly changing outlook of the She'erit Hapletah, or has relied on official utterances made by leading figures of the Central Committee of Liberated Jews in Germany, utterances that better reflect the common ground between the leading parties than give an overall account of the different ideologies in circulation. Yet among the bulk of still unexplored source material, the variety of Yiddish publications in Germany reveals a much more differentiated and steadily changing self-perception of the DPs from the emergence of the She'erit Hapletah until its eventual dissolution. This high degree of self-awareness and self-criticism is especially evident in the realm of artistic creativity and writing. The literature of the She'erit Hapletah was seen as a product of historical circumstances—with technical and financial shortages at its core—and was perceived as shaped by them.

OF ALL PLACES: YIDDISH PUBLISHING IN GERMANY

Under the title *Tkhies hameysim* (The Resurrection of the Dead), the first handwritten newspaper appeared only three weeks after the liberation of the Buchenwald concentration camp on May 4, 1945, as a "first attempt of a Yiddish . . . survivors' press."[7] Five months later, three major weekly (later biweekly) editions were distributed in the American zone, with circulations numbering as high as twenty thousand, in addition to dozens of local and regional newspapers that were printed under the most difficult conditions in all major DP camps. This surviving remnant desperately longed for reading material after years of intellectual deprivation. However, the newspapers could only partially meet the need for reading material because limited printing facilities and short supplies only allowed for a small number of pages and because licenses issued by the American military authorities restricted the allocation to one newspaper per five readers.[8] Although the licensing policies for all DPs were identical, the Central Committee of Liberated Jews in the American zone stated that the demographic situation of the Jewish DPs, which differed dramatically from other DP nationalities, had to be taken into consideration:

> The circle of readers of other nationalities is the unit of the family . . . but our reading unit is [a] single person. The number of children among other nationalities is one third; our number of children is without importance. This is one reason for the fact that it is impossible to count with the average num-

bers, in our case. We would like to add besides this point that we had nothing to read for 6 years. For that reason the hunger for something to read is greater today compared with the situation of other nationalities where the newspaper has not this cultural task, because of the permanent publishing of books.[9]

There are only very contradictory accounts of the licensing policies, but it seems that restrictions were handled laxly, which allowed for a flowering of the DP press in Germany during the months following liberation. Since camp newspapers did not require any licensing, almost every camp began to run its own publication, often subpar in outlook and quality. The postwar circumstances also led to an unprecedented episode in the history of Yiddish printing with the use of Latin characters instead of Hebrew type. Initially, with the exception of *Undzer veg* (Our Way), the official newspaper of the Central Committee, all newspapers handled the lack of appropriate characters by printing Lithuanian Yiddish in Latin characters using Polish orthography. From its first issue on, *Undzer veg* was printed entirely in Hebrew characters.[10]

The cultural department of the JDC tried to bypass the lack of reading material through the establishment of camp libraries and, to a lesser extent, through its own printing enterprise. The JDC, however, focused on primers, textbooks, and religious books, and the libraries remained badly equipped. Although Pinson succeeded in removing several thousand books from the Offenbach Archival Depot, the selection could only include nonvaluable items. After his demission, the painstaking work of choosing the appropriate books was continued by the young JDC field worker Lucy Schildkret (later to become acclaimed historian Lucy Dawidowicz). Donated books from Jewish organizations such as the World Jewish Congress and, after 1948, the Jewish Labor Committee in New York could not fill the gaps on the library shelves. For the writers, who were searching for inspiration, this situation was especially painful. Literary critic Yitskhok Goldkorn was compelled to ask the poet Shmerke Katsherginski in Paris for books: "I am in dire need of a series of books by writers who encourage me to write. We do have here a certain number of books though, but few— and not appropriately selected."[11]

Goldkorn had arrived in Munich in late 1946 after years in Siberia and Soviet Central Asia and at the front line of Leningrad.[12] He came to Germany when the population of the She'erit Hapletah had reached its peak. Approximately 150,000 Jews now lived in the American zone. Among them were many families with children. Under these circumstances, when books were intended to cover the elemen-

The staff of the DP newspaper *Unterwegs* [The Transient] at work in their office in the Zeilsheim DP camp. (United States Holocaust Memorial Museum, Photo no. 89559, courtesy of Alice Lev)

tary need for reading material for a broad audience with an emphasis on textbooks for the developing school system in the camps, there was very little space for belles lettres. However, literature was made accessible through newspapers. Almost every issue dedicated space to poetry, short stories, and even literary criticism in an effort not only to compensate for the blatant lack of reading material but also to serve as an educational measure with the goal of schooling the DPs to make for better readers and a better understanding of Yiddish lore and literature.[13] Since all major American Yiddish newspapers were distributed in the camps, the DPs were also informed about the contemporary Yiddish literature abroad.[14]

Yet another change that took place with the growth of the DP population was that the strongly politicized community advanced the establishment of a thriving party press. After the abolishment of a united Zionist party in February 1947, all major protagonists on the Zionist scene edited their own central weekly newspapers. Since the quality of these newly established papers exceeded that of the existing press, they found their readers not only among party members. Partly as a result, the local and regional Yiddish press was eventually terminated in October 1947. This abolishment had a multiple impact on the development of the press as a whole. On one hand, it put an end to Yiddish newspaper publications in Latin characters; on the other hand, all printing enterprises—except for the *Jidisze cajtung* (Jewish Newspaper) in Landsberg—now shifted to Munich.

It was during this chapter of the She'erit Hapletah that literature began to flower. Every newspaper devoted at least one weekly page to literary and cultural issues. Yet an even more important achievement of the party press in the field of literature may have been their involvement in editing books. Although the Sochnut (Jewish Agency for Palestine), the Central Committee, and the JDC had founded a JDC board for education and culture in February 1947 in order to combine their efforts, its achievements in the sector of publication never went further than the publishing of textbooks. The establishment of a publishing house, planned in the early days of the board, was not realized. Instead, it was the party press that began to promote Yiddish literature. What began as an enterprise for the printing and dissemination of political literature—for example, works of the Zionist theoreticians Ber Borokhov, Yaakov Zerubavel, and Nachman Sirkin—was after a short time span to include original publications by DP writers.

It should not come as a surprise that the Left Poale Zion participated in this new chapter in the history of Yiddish DP literature. Ideologically still indebted to its founder Ber Borokhov, the party traditionally pursued pro–Yiddish-language politics. Especially in interwar Poland the Left Poale Zion was, next to the Bund, the leading force behind the secular Yiddish school system, and many historians of the *yunger historiker* (young historian) group were its members.[15] Since 1934 the Left Poale Zion had edited its Yiddish newspaper *Nayvelt* (New World) in Palestine. Yet the Poale Zion-Hitakhdut and the Poale Zion (Socialist Zionists) also subsidized the publication of several books. And even the Tsiyonim Klali'im (General Zionists) supported Yiddish printing to some extent with a one-time literary journal named *Velt: Umophengiker zhurnal far politik, literatur un sport* (World: Independent Journal for Politics, Literature and Sports) that was published in December 1947 by a joint editorial board of Ruven Rubinshteyn, the editor of the Central Committee's official newspaper *Undzer veg;* Mordkhe Libhaber of *Ibergang* (Transition), which was the weekly publication of the Landsmanshaft of Polish Jews in Germany; and Ovadya Feld of the Tsiyonim Klali'im.

The publishing of Yiddish literary works by DP writers reached its peak starting in late 1947 and during 1948 and came to an end with the subsequent liquidation of the camps and cultural enterprises of the She'erit Hapletah. The pace of publishing slowed down dramatically with the monetary reform in the summer of 1948. When in late 1949 the majority of the Zionist parties celebrated the exodus

Tamar Lewinsky

A Jewish DP reads the announcements posted on the newspaper kiosk at the Neu Freimann DP camp. (United States Holocaust Memorial Museum, Photo no. 96437, courtesy of Jack Sutin)

from Germany (*yetsies germaniya*) and ceased to edit their newspapers, hopes for the final dissolution of the press were expressed especially by those opposing the reestablishment of Jewish communal life in Germany. Yet these hopes were soon to be disappointed. The number of Jews still remaining in the American zone at that time was more than thirty thousand.[16] *Undzer veg* was eventually closed down in 1949 after Rubinshteyn's aliyah but, since the emigration process dragged on longer than expected, resumed its publication with its ultimate goal to "help the She'erit Hapletah to reach its long awaited wish—its complete dissolution."[17]

THE WRITERS' UNION AND THE GOLDEN CHAIN

With the influx of repatriated Jews from the Soviet Union, the small literary scene in Germany was joined by writers and journalists of some prewar reputation who had survived serving in the Red Army, deportation to Siberia, or exile in Kazakhstan and Uzbekistan. In 1946 the Writers' Union was eventually founded in order to fight for the economic interests of its members and to establish contact with the literary Yiddish circles outside Germany.

As Rubinshteyn, the doyen of the Yiddish press in Germany, declared on the second conference of the Writers' Union in 1947, this group had to take on the grievous responsibility of assuming the literary legacy of East European Jewry.[18] During the initial phase of the She'erit Hapletah at least there was very little writers could do in order to promote their adopted identity as the legitimate heirs of classic Yiddish fiction on a broader basis. Visitors were disillusioned with the intellectual agency of the She'erit Hapletah. This was especially true for those familiar with the thriving literary centers in Warsaw and Vilnius in the interwar period. Was this group of writers and journalists then, as it were, only an anecdotal footnote to the historiography of the Jewish DPs? When the Writers' Union hosted its first literary soiree in the autumn of 1946, Lucy Schildkret must have thought so:

> This afternoon I was invited to attend a literary meeting. . . .
> I suppose this is sooner "cultural" than "recreational." It was
> the first public meeting of the Jewish Writers Union, recently
> organized in Munich and was devoted to a reading from the
> work of S. Berlinski, a young writer who had won some measure of recognition in pre-war Poland. The meeting was held
> in one of the rooms of Kultur Amt, unheated because today is
> Saturday, with a total of about 18 people, including Berlinski,
> the chairman, and the author's wife. . . . Israel Kaplan, editor of
> the journal of the Central Historical Commission, presented
> an analysis of the work of Berlinski. Kaplan, a pre-war Yiddish
> journalist from Kovno, of some repute, is a very nearsighted
> guy, practically blind, with very piercing and ironic humor—
> about everything. He started out by speaking about the black
> market . . . ; how everything has exchange value, including a

yortsayt [anniversary of death] date which will be sold to any-one interested (e.g. Historical Commission) and that Berlin-ski, though talented, does not seem to have exchange value, ergo the small audience. Then he spoke about his work. Ber-linski read some excerpts from a novel and a couple of stories, one of which was a gem, except for a few very minor flaws [but] since the place was freezing, I left. Berlinski, I am told, is the only writer here who has [a] pre-war reputation and the only one of undisputed ability. Certainly it would seem so. The bad lighting, the cold, the small audience, the general depress-ing character of the meeting made me feel very sad. Especially when I make comparisons with what I know used to be in Warsaw and Vilna.[19]

The Yiddish writers and journalists in Germany were very much aware of the lack of artistic and organizational possibilities. The reso-lutions taken at the first meeting of the Writers' Union had therefore envisioned financial support—especially for the newly arriving writ-ers from Poland—but also a workshop for young talents and the pub-lication of a literary journal that aimed to gather the whole spectrum of literati in the She'erit Hapletah. The journal was especially intended to reintegrate the DP writers into the international Yiddish literary discourse, the center of which had shifted, by default one might argue, to New York.

The plan of editing this literary journal under the name of *Shriftn* was only implemented in 1948, though. Neither the Central Commit-tee nor the JDC had shown interest in supporting its publication in a time when the She'erit Hapletah still struggled for basic allocations. Its eventual publication was made possible thanks to the sponsor-ship of an American reform community.[20] The dependence on the goodwill of the JDC and the Central Committee was felt even more strongly in 1948 when the board for education decided to edit a liter-ary journal named *Hemshekh* (Continuation) as a presentable result of its cultural work and asked the Writers' Union for its collaboration.[21] The writers felt betrayed. They had struggled for the publication of *Shriftn* (Writings) for almost three years, and now a subsidized sec-ond journal was going to be published after some months of editorial work.[22] A memo sent to the JDC headquarters in Paris justifies the writers' skepticism. As S. Lewis Gaber described it enthusiastically, "The Hemshekh story—a joint (also Joint) venture." Several subse-quent letters also suggest that the JDC had in mind to use the journal primarily for publicity and, to some extent, in order to cover the lack of reading material in the She'erit Hapletah.[23]

Whereas this professional reintegration was meant to cover the need of the individual writer and journalist, the Writers' Union also supervised the raising and dissemination of knowledge about Jewish literature, culture, history, and traditions among the wider DP population. Rubinshteyn stressed that persons engaged in the cultural sector had not only a profession but also a cultural mission to accomplish.[24] Besides the publication and dissemination of their own texts, the writers therefore assumed responsibility for the schooling of the She'erit Hapletah in the literary traditions that their society was presumably built upon. The literary sections of the newspapers thus provided the readers with information about literature and famous personalities of Jewish history and the Zionist movement; commemorations were held in honor of Sholem Yankev Abramovitsh (Mendele Moykher Sforim) and other Yiddish and bilingual Hebrew-Yiddish writers.[25] Commemorative services dedicated to the Warsaw Ghetto Uprising and mass demonstrations targeted at current political developments shared the same purpose: They were intended to provide the She'erit Hapletah with a sense of a usable past, a continuity of cultural and political traditions that should extend into the present.

These commemorative services, which were likely to attract a broad audience, were increasingly important in 1947, when it became apparent that hopes for a speedy emigration were shattered and the morale of the She'erit Hapletah steadily dropped. Although improvements in allocation, housing, schooling, and recreation had seemingly ameliorated the DPs' situation, the dangling cultural roots of this temporary society had started to whither. Samuel Gringauz attested to an immense gap in the cultural continuity of thousands of years of Jewish cultural history. "Nowadays, it is difficult to reach the people of the She'erit Hapletah with dry ideas. Libraries are empty, lectures are not being attended, and people's universities open their doors in order to close them again the day after. Courses are created and die shortly after from interest-tuberculosis. There was a time, when . . . Jewish cultural life roared and pulsated in Eastern Europe. That was before the war."[26]

Among the journalists and writers, two major trends of addressing the problem of cultural uprootedness began to crystallize. Hershl Vaynroykh, the only Soviet writer among the She'erit Hapletah, had dissociated himself from the modernist literary movements of the interwar period. He called up his colleagues to fulfill their national duty by returning to a traditional understanding of literature. According to the former communist writer Vaynroykh, the cosmopolitan aspirations in the literary trends on the eve of the Holocaust had led to error. He pleaded for a canon built on the classical writing of Sholem

Aleykhem Abramovitsh, Yitskhok Leybush Peretz, and Hayyim Nachman Bialik, extending their national visions into the present.[27]

> We have to call up the Jews to fight for their homeland[;] . . . we
> have to start in the times of King David, Bar Kochba, the Mac-
> cabees and show that the nation hasn't ceased to fight for its
> soil. We have to show the "golden chain" of the Jewish people,
> festive Jews [shabesyontevdik] . . . , the traditional religious Jew,
> the Jew of the concentration camp, of the Ghetto, partisans,
> soldiers and officers in the allied armies, the fighting Jewish
> woman, the Jews in Erets-Israel who fight for their brethren,
> Jews in the German Diaspora, in the Polish and Russian Dias-
> poras, Jews of the She'erit Hapletah who heroically board little
> ships . . . and reach for their home, their homeland.[28]

A second group didn't call for the abolition of trends that had emerged before the war. Mordkhe Libhaber asked for a more pragmatic approach. In spite of his ex post facto critique of the acculturation process in Poland, he delineated the difference between the appropriation of foreign cultures and the loss of any cultural foundation: "The assimilationist trends before the war were wrong and fatal . . . , but it was a road to culture. Our youth from Poland today travels a road to a lack of culture [kulturlozikayt]." His critique was directed toward the Zionist parties that he asked to resume the prewar involvement in cultural education and offer lectures on classic Yiddish fiction, Hassidism, and Hebrew and Yiddish literature during the war.[29]

While Vaynroykh and Libhaber envisioned different models, both agreed on the parties' responsibility to educate the masses. Moreover, they argued, East European cultural traditions were at the core of any national and Zionist education. Hebrew literature had to be merged with Yiddish literature, and the Hebrew language had to become "Yiddishized," because "the elements of Yiddish are closer to the contemporary Jewish psyche. The precise and sharp expression of Yiddish is closer to the Jew than the metaphorical biblical Hebrew."[30]

Similar rhetoric was used to describe the cultural identity of the She'erit Hapletah in the tradition of famous Jewish Diaspora communities. However, it was not the Golden Age of Sephardic Jewry but rather the Marrano community in Amsterdam after the expulsion from Spain that served as a viable pattern of identification and impetus for extraordinary creativity.[31] Yet, at the same time, another discourse sprang into life: The scattered seeds of European Jewry were assembled in the DP camps and formed a kibuts galuyot (ingathering of the exiles) par excellence.[32] The imposition of this historically

Front page of the Yiddish monthly *Yidishe bilder,* May 1948. (Bayerische Staatsbibliothek Munich)

loaded concept on the She'erit Hapletah supported the self-image of the DPs as "citizens of the Jewish states on the move."[33] It is this bias of simultaneous glorification of the Diaspora and its clear rejection that characterizes the discourse on cultural identity.

CULTURE OF CONGRESSES AND A POCKET-SIZED LANGUAGE WAR

The reactions to the plan to organize the Congress for Jewish Culture (CJC) in New York demonstrates that put into practice, the writers' approach to the preservation and continuation of linguistic and cultural traditions was much more unsentimental and pragmatic. The preparations for the CJC, which was eventually established in the autumn of 1948, were accompanied by discussions in the Jewish press in Europe,

Israel, and the United States on the role of Jewish and especially Yiddish culture after the Holocaust.[34] The Poale Zion in Germany called to attention the fact that Yiddish culture was vanishing due to assimilation in the United States, the Holocaust in Europe, and restrictive cultural politics in the Soviet Union. Linguistic assimilation, the loss of the Yiddish mother tongue, was, in the minds of the Poale Zion members, the biggest threat to national identity: "[Jews] in the so-called 'Diaspora' who cease to speak Yiddish, will not do so in favor of Hebrew, but adopt the national language." This argument was directed against the critics of the CJC who blamed it for being anti-Zionist. According to the Poale Zion, the attempt to foster Yiddish language and culture wasn't in any way identical to a deliberate minimizing of the national and cultural significance of Hebrew. Only "blind fools" could negate the natural connection between Yiddish and Hebrew for the national enterprise.[35] The aims of the CJC were also discussed during the second yearly assembly of the Writers' Union in 1947. The literary critic Mordkhe Kroshnits pointed out in his address that the political struggle for a Jewish state could not be fought independently from the struggle for the preservation of Jewish culture. The declared aim was thus the transplantation of the culture of the Jewish Diaspora into Palestine.[36]

Yitskhok Goldkorn considered the Congress an intellectual tour de force with no real-life implication. He commented on one of the CJC's resolutions that called for moral and cultural support of the Jews in Germany. Although Goldkorn agreed on this appeal, he also raised the question of whether it was rather American Jewry who was in need of cultural support.[37] Natural growth of national cultures and national languages could only be achieved if they were rooted in all spheres of society. It could not be substituted by a "culture of congresses."[38] Samuel Gringauz, one of the leading personalities in the initial organization of the survivors, also commented on the CJC—from his new home in the United States—that the Jewish culture under scrutiny, an all-embracing culture, had ceased to exist and that its remnants found themselves in a geographical and cultural transitory condition. Only Israel could therefore represent a new territorial base for a continuation of East European Jewish culture.[39] The writers and journalists in the She'erit Hapletah, despite their different political affiliations, hence tended to favor Hebrew as the national language of the Jewish state but strongly adhered to the use of Yiddish in the Diaspora and its cultural continuity in Israel. For the present time, official decisions on the use of language had to be pragmatic.

This pragmatism had become evident already a year prior to the establishment of the CJC. In February 1947 the newly founded Board for Education and Culture (also known as the Board for Education) started to reorganize the school system. In order to work out a standardized syllabus and because teachers were brought from the Yishuv, the decision was made to accept Hebrew as the language of instruction. While there was a general agreement between the Zionist parties that Hebrew had to be taught in schools, there was no consensus about which part was assigned to what language. A small paragraph in the procedures of the Board for Education provoked a miniature language war:

> The basic language of the school is Hebrew. This is according to the wishes of the most part of the parents, to the general principles of the pedagogical philosophy of the Board for Education and to the actual situation that the destination of almost all the children is Eretz Israel. . . . The principal attitude of the Board for Education is to teach the children in Hebrew but not to fight against Yiddish. Yiddish is the Language in which educational and cultural *stuff* [is] to be delivered to the Jewish masses of the Shaarith Haplatah. Yiddish is the language of the meetings of the Board for Education. Both Yiddish and Hebrew are the official languages for the correspondence of the Board, for the office work and the dealing with the customers.[40]

Even though this statement didn't reject Yiddish but instead promoted a bilingualism that favored Hebrew for educational purposes, it alerted Jewish journalists in the United States and France, who began to call it "a ban against Yiddish." The president of the Jewish Labor Committee in New York, Yankev Patt, declared in the *Yiddish Daily Forward* that the Zionist authorities in the She'erit Hapletah were robbing the surviving Jewish youths of their mother tongue.[41] The Yiddish press in Germany dealt with the matter according to party lines. The Poale Zion rejected the reproach and suspected a confederacy between Bund and the Jewish Labor Committee,[42] while the Left Poale Zion argued that any language war had lost its purpose after the destruction of Jewish Eastern Europe:

> It is useless to confront a nation with an absurd principle by creating dualistic theories like unconditional "renewal" and thereby negating the basis of the national life of generations. No child can become a good Jew if he is taken away artificially from the root, the past, the popular things [*di folkishe zakhn*]. For a generation alienated from Sholem Aleykhem, Peretz

and Sholem Ash, also Bialik, will be unintelligible. Life remains dry and shattered for people who do not know their parents and grandparents. . . . The Jewish child and the Jewish youth who escaped from the camps, those deprived from the very center of Jewish identity, need without fail to become acquainted with the glorious past, with the culture and language of a people burnt alive.[43]

This argumentation, which highlights the central position of classic Yiddish fiction for the Yiddish tradition and the connection between past and future, was in line with the claims of the Writers' Union and paralleled the arguments that were presented in the course of the discussion preceding the establishment of the CJC.

There is no clear answer to the question of whether the Board for Education or the Central Committee worked a politics that was anti-Yiddish language. Official as well as private communications convey a contradictory image.[44] However, the ideological weapons that were used reflect a continuity of decades of language war between Hebrew and Yiddish. At the climax of the conflict, the small Bundist party in Germany had one of its rare public appearances. In its one-time publication of the Paris-based newspaper *Veker* (Alarm) in Germany, the party not only supported Patt's accusation but also took advantage of the publicity in order to protest against the discrimination of Bund members in DP camps and their exclusion from camp committees.[45] Moyshe Lestni turned these accusations down. He argued that the fact that the Bundists needed to revive the old language war between Yiddish and Hebrew only attested to the immense ideological disorganization among its remaining members. He claimed that the camps in Germany had achieved the goals that the Bund and all other adherents of Yiddish had never been able to accomplish in the interwar period in Poland:

> The press is Yiddish, the theater is Yiddish, libraries—Yiddish meetings, lectures, discussions—are held in Yiddish. The official language of the offices is Yiddish, slogans and captions scream down to you from all walls: Speak Yiddish and learn Hebrew. Also the school system is partly Yiddish and partly Hebrew. . . . Thousands of Jews stemming from Poland, Russia, Romania, Hungary, Greece, Czechoslovakia etc. and were illiterate in the Hebrew alphabet, speak today [only] Yiddish, write Yiddish, hear Yiddish.[46]

Put under pressure, the Central Committee sent a declaration to the

World Jewish Congress in which it negated any form of discrimination against the Yiddish language in the She'erit Hapletah.[47] The Writers' Union declared in its second conference that no such ban existed. Rubinshteyn, a member of the Tsiyonim Klali'im, highlighted the close continuity of East European cultural identity before the Holocaust. He corroborated the argument contrasting the situation in the She'erit Hapletah with the linguistic situation in the United States, where books and newspapers were still produced but no new readers were educated. He fiercely rejected the boycott and accused American Jewry of being responsible for the ruin of Yiddish in the States.[48] Reproaches concerning the ban against Yiddish in the camps were leveled against the American Yiddish educational system. The poet Yitskhok Goldkorn assessed that New York, with its newspapers, printing houses, and institutions, had become the center of Yiddish culture, a *"yerusholayim d'amerike,"* after the destruction of East European Jewry. However, in his words, it was doomed due to its failure to promote new talents: "To tell the truth, for one of our Eastern-European Jews, the *yidishkayt* [Jewishness] of business-driven America has always given the impression of a marinated *yidishkayt* of prosperity-aged parvenus."[49] The source of rejuvenation had been the creativity of East European Yiddish culture. The Writers' Union saw itself, as it were, as the addressee for the reimbursement, as an actor on the contemporary Yiddish literary scene, and not merely as a group of financially dependent survivors.

Scattered Seeds and Shattered Hopes

The experience of the Holocaust and the witnessing of the extinction of East European Yiddish culture had advanced a Zionist fervor among the writers and journalists of the She'erit Hapletah, but it had also brought them to the conviction that the remnants of this vanishing culture—in all spheres of public life—was an act of remembrance and sanctification of the victims. The decision to stand up for the Yiddish language was no longer bound to ideological affiliation. Now, forty years after the 1908 Czernovitz Language Conference, even ardent Yiddishists would not make any claims for Yiddish as the official language in Israel. But who among the writers would have thought that the Jewish state would continue its Hebraist stance in the face of the loss of the majority of the world's Yiddish speakers? After the establishment of the State of Israel, when the DPs' hope for a country of their own was finally realized, this future was suddenly palpable, and the writers in Germany grew more sensitive to the status of Yiddish in Israel. The attacks against the language were not as hostile as they had been before the Holocaust, but in the official discourse there was little change.[50]

After the proclamation of the existence of the State of Israel, when open immigration had finally turned into reality, writers and journalists took a pragmatic approach; the mystification of the Zionist dream was under scrutiny. Levi Shalit, a prewar revisionist and one of the founders of the Yiddish press in Germany, wrote a concerned article about the status of Yiddish in Israel upon his return from a visit to Israel and several encounters with Yiddish writers in Tel Aviv. Shalit raised the question of whether or not there was a "ban against Yiddish in Israel"; he was well aware of the turmoil that his rhetoric was likely to produce in the She'erit Hapletah.[51] One of the writers he interviewed on his trip was Mendel Mann, who had made aliyah in 1948 and was working for the only literary Yiddish journal in Israel, *Di goldene keyt* (The Golden Chain). At that time Mann was relatively content about his situation, but just three years later his initial enthusiasm was gone. In a 1952 letter to his colleague Meylekh Tshemni, who was still in Munich, Mann sorrowfully wrote about the lack of integration of the Yiddish writers, which had caused "apathy, malice, brokenness and, most tragically, unproductiveness" among them.[52] One year later, a letter to Tshemni, who had in the meantime immigrated to Brazil, reads: "The case of Yiddish is sad, bitter and catastrophic. . . . You can't find Yiddish books here, nobody wants to touch them."[53]

But it was the poet Yitskhok Perlov, of all people, who complained most bitterly about the threat to the Yiddish language and Yiddish literature. Perlov was a hero for many DPs in Germany. Together with his wife, the Yiddish actress Lola Polman, he was aboard the *Exodus 1947* and wrote about this historical journey.[54] He warned that Yiddish in Israel was not only endangered but was also officially oppressed. What he experienced was the banishment of Yiddish culture from public life.[55] "No one can suspect the Yiddish writers in Israel of hatred of Zion [*sin'at tsion*] . . . but they came here in order to create in their language and not in order to fight against the police." He adds that "it is not only about the writers and artists, but about thousands and thousands of immigrants who are doomed to mute-deaf illiteracy. With their disdained 'Diaspora-language' and 'Diaspora-psychology' they are put into a position here that makes them feel as if in the Diaspora."[56]

At the same time, the situation in Germany wasn't any better. The subsequent consolidation and liquidation of the DP camps, the anti-Semitism in German society, and financial shortages after the monetary reform had left the writers in a hopeless situation. Since 1948, when camp closures began on a larger scale, the rift between the different wings of the Zionist enterprise had aggravated. The closing of the Board for Education and Culture and the subsequent disbanding of unions, cultural institutions and libraries in the camps months prior to the emigration of its inhabitants was viewed with particular concern. Rumors about the involvement of leading party members in black market activities were made public, and the increased pressure put on persons who were unwilling to immigrate to Israel was met with criticism. It was only a matter of time until a group of anonymous writers published a satirical newspaper. It touched on the most ardent issues of the day and accused the Tsiyonim Klali'im and the Central Committee of having sold camp libraries to German printing plants as wastepaper. Some months later, one of the editors of the *Naye yidishe tsaytung* (New Jewish Newspaper), a Yiddish newspaper founded in Munich in 1950, asked, "Who could have imagined that Jews . . . would sell Jewish books, creations of the Jewish mind, as wastepaper to Jewish printers? Can a Jewish heart understand . . . that Jews, smitten by Hitler, would hire Germans to burn Jewish books . . . ? Yes, Germans have again set fire . . . to Jewish books . . . , but this time with the approval of the Jews themselves." It was not astonishing though, the article argues, that Jewish books ended up in "Germany's garbage cans" because the Jewish population was doomed to intellectual impoverishment after the closing of cultural institutions prior to the liquidation of the camps.[57]

The consolidation and closure of the camps had already started when the administration was transferred to the International Refugee Organization. Now, during the last chapter of the history of the She'erit Hapletah, the remaining camps were closed one after the other, and the camp population was moved up to four times. Many DPs chose to settle in nearby cities in order to wait until their visas were issued.[58] Jewish communities in German cities and towns did not just come into being at that moment, however. Almost one-third of the overall Jewish DP population in the American zone, including most members of the Writers' Union, chose to settle outside the closed social systems of the camps.[59] After the regional and local presses were closed and the party press took over, the majority of contributors settled in the former "Hauptstadt der Bewegung" (Capital of the Movement, referring to Munich) in search of employment.[60] The unnatural closeness of the literary circles that developed would later lead to stormy debates and rivalries. This closeness also explains why the Zionist press was still working when most other cultural enterprises had ceased to exist. Munich, being the administrative center of the DP institutions, witnessed a strong cultural activity even after most of the local committees had closed down and DP camps had been liquidated.

Less than a year before, relief workers and visitors had described with amazement the shtetl-like infrastructure and outlook of the camps with all its social institutions. The Yiddish poet Shmerke Katshergin-ski, who visited camp Pocking near Waldstadt from Paris, commented that it was a Jewish shtetl from twenty or thirty years back, "but here it is even more Jewish, really a piece of Jewish life taken out from a book, as if in a fantasy."[61] Now, during the disintegration of the DP camps, this fantasy was re-created through satires and parodies. Using the language and imagery of classic Yiddish fiction, the writers created a parallel Jewish geography layered on German landscapes. A street in Stuttgart where the majority of the local Jewish population lived was called the "Jewish Pale of Settlement."[62] Meylekh Tshemni's ad-vice for readers who wanted to understand what Sholem-Aleykhem or Mendele had in mind when they portrayed their fictional small towns Kasrilevke and Yehupets was to visit Föhrenwald on a rainy day: "Föhr-enwald is a 'modern' Jewish shtetl, as 'modern' as Jewish life in Ger-many is nowadays."[63] The most extraordinary examples are the satires by Baruch Graubard who, adopting Abramovitsh's style, documented every aspect of Jewish daily life in Munich during the liquidation pe-riod.[64]

As critically as these parodies talked about the present, such views are filtered through an almost nostalgic view of the She'erit Hapletah. Writers were interested in both the positive and the negative aspects of Jewish life in the DP camps. Baruch Graubard, for example, was convinced that only a society that also displayed negative characteris-tics moved in the direction of normalcy: "[L]ike the resurrection [gilgul] of a vanished world a new life was interwoven with reality, grotesque, black-grayish pettiness that connected with its negative sides pathos and reality and brought it back into the sphere of normal humane-ness. The deep stream of pathos carried along slime and waste, and little big-mouthed fish. . . . And it had to be like that, in order that the stream could flow into the sea—that is called life."[65]

As much as the postwar German Diaspora was rejected, it had inspired the DPs with a temporary sense of home and belonging. Here they had established families, worked, and studied. Here they had established a temporary Yiddish-speaking cultural home that was unlikely to have a continuation in the United States or in Israel.

Notwithstanding the low social and cultural status of Yiddish in Israel, a high percentage of the writers and journalists chose to settle there. The rest left Germany with different destinations in North and South America and South Africa. Wherever they went, however, there was only a remainder of their language and culture. Although they had finally found a new home, the cultural and linguistic displacement was stronger than ever before. Ironically, then, their displacement in Germany had in this respect provided them with a temporary sense of continuity. However, to consider it a kind of epilogue to East European Jewish cultural life does not do justice to the She'erit Hapletah.

CONCLUSION: NEGATION OF EXILE OR NEGATION OF THE GERMAN DIASPORA?

In studies about refugees, DPs have often been described as, to quote Michael Marrus, "torn loose from their culture."[66] If we consider the linguistic dimensions of a culture, the case of the Jewish DPs in Germany is very distinctive. Yiddish as a transnational language hadn't ceased to exist. As a cohesive group as well as on a personal level, the writers and journalists in the She'erit Hapletah tried to reintegrate themselves into the contemporary international literary discourse. Although diverse in age, in their experience of the Holocaust, in their political affiliation, and in their professional experience, these writers defined themselves as the heirs of East European Yiddish cultural tradition and claimed a distinctive identity vis-à-vis American Yiddish writing. The She'erit Hapletah, the remnant of East European Jewry, was displaced and uprooted but not deracinated.

Doomed to physical inertia in the German Diaspora as refugees with an uncertain future, DPs nevertheless built a dense network of cultural and social institutions, institutions that were financially supported by international relief organizations and Jewish nonprofit organizations. Since 1947 the press of this strongly Zionist community was almost entirely a party press that borrowed exhaustively from the publications in the Yishuv. The pages devoted to cultural issues, however, differed from Yishuv newspapers: they were created and edited by DP journalists and writers. And the newspapers were not the only cultural outlets for DPs. DP actors of some prewar stardom staged plays in the camps, DP historians trained in European universities before the war collected documentation on the catastrophe, and DP journalists trained in the Yiddish press of interwar Poland formed the editorial boards of the Yiddish press in Germany. With such backgrounds, do the main proponents of DP camp cultural life support subsequent claims that DP culture was a revival of the shtetl?

The notion of the shtetl—synonymously understood to encompass all the vanished *lebenswelten* (life world)—serves as a good image if the political dimensions of the cultural expressions found in the She'erit Hapletah are also taken into account. The negation of exile (*shlilat ha-golah*), which in the Yishuv and later in Israel embraced not

Tamar Lewinsky

only the territoriality of the Diaspora but also its language and culture, had a different meaning among the writers and journalists of the She'erit Hapletah in Germany.[67] In the DP camps, the negation of exile could not signify a complete denial of diasporic culture. On the one hand, as self-declared heirs of a literary and cultural tradition, they showed an affirmative approach to Yiddish culture. On the other hand, the schooling of the masses, the fight against demoralization, could only be carried out in the language spoken by the majority of the DPs. The real threat to a Jewish and Zionist consciousness, as perceived by the writers and journalists, was not the golden chain of a century-old tradition but rather its loss. This loss produced a gap that would be filled, as they put it, by default by foreign and hostile cultural practices. The negation of exile did not concern the cultural realm but instead had a purely territorial basis. The negation of the unloved German Diaspora (*shlilat galut germaniyah*) and its dissolution was the ultimate goal of the writers and journalists of the She'erit Hapletah.

NOTES

1. Ruth Gay, *Safe among the Germans: Liberated Jews after World War II* (New Haven, CT: Yale University Press, 2002), 65–66.
2. Michael Brenner, *After the Holocaust: Rebuilding Jewish Lives in Postwar Germany* (Princeton, NJ: Princeton University Press, 1997), 18.
3. Two fundamental studies, both written by former DP journalists, are Tsemach M. Tsamriyon, *Ha-itonut shel she'erit ha-pleta be-germaniya ke-bitui le-be'ayoteha* (Tel Aviv: Irgun she'erit ha-pleta me-ha-ezor ha-briti [Bergen-Belsen] ve-ha-makhanot, 1970); and Yosef Gar, "Bafrayte yidn," in *Fun noentn over*, Vol. 3, 150–77 (New York: Alveltlekher yidisher kultur-kongres, 1957). The topic was only rediscovered in the 1990s; see Jacqueline Giere, "'Wir sind unterwegs, aber nicht in der Wüste': Erziehung und Kultur in den jüdischen Displaced Persons Lagern der amerikanischen Zone im Nachkriegsdeutschland, 1945–1949" (PhD dissertation, University of Frankfurt, 1993); and Tamar Lewinsky, *Displaced Poets: Jiddische Schriftsteller im Nachkriegsdeutschland, 1945–1951* (Göttingen, Vandenhoeck & Ruprecht, 2008). Recently some case studies on individual newspapers have been presented. See Ayelet Kuper Margalioth, "Yiddish Periodicals Published by Displaced Persons, 1946–1949" (PhD dissertation, Magdalen College, Oxford, UK, 1997); Ela Avital-Florsheim, "Hantsakha be-emtsa'ut ti'ud ve-yetsirah—ha-iton 'undzer shtime' be-makhane ha-ikurim Bergen-Belsen, 1945–1947" (Master's thesis, Hebrew University, Jerusalem, 2003); and Philipp Grammes "'Ein Beweis, dass wir da sind': Die Jiddische Wochenzeitung 'Undzer Vort'; Kommunikationsstrukturen und-Interesse von Displaced Persons" (Master's thesis, University of Munich, 2004). Parts of the local newspaper are available as reprints with some introductory remarks;

see Dieter E. Kesper, ed., *Unsere Hoffnung: Das Schicksal Überlebender des Holocaust im Spiegel einer Lagerzeitung von 1946* (Eschwege: Kluthe, 1996); Walter Fürnrohr and Felix Muschialik, *Überleben und Neubeginn: DP-Hospital Gauting ab 1945; Mit Faksimileabdruck der Patientenzeitung "Unser Leben" von 1947–1948* (München: Kirchheim, 2005); Hildegard Harck, *Unzer Sztyme: Jiddische Quellen zur Geschichte der jüdischen Gemeinden in der Britischen Zone, 1945–1947* (Kiel: Landeszentrale für politische Bildung, 2004). The Yiddish DP press was almost completely made available on microfilm through YIVO; see Zachary M. Baker, ed., *Jewish Displaced Persons Periodicals from the Collections of the YIVO Institute* (Bethesda: University Publications of America, 1990). Bibliographies of DP books and newspapers were already published among the She'erit Hapletah; see Ben-Tsien Feldshu, *Sh[eyres]-h[apleyte]-bibliografye* (Stuttgart: American Jewish Joint Distribution Committee, 1948); Ben-Tsien Kosowski, *Bibliografye fun di yidishe oysgabes in der britisher zone fun Daytshland* (Bergen-Belsen: Central Committee of Liberated Jews, British Zone, 1950); Mordkhe Kroshnits, "Bibliografishe notitsn," *Hemshekh* 2 (1949); G-R [Yosef Gar], "Bibliografishe notitsn," *Undzer vort*, January 1, 1947; Shulik, "Bibliografishe notitsn," *Undzer veg*, May 1, 1947. The literary creativity of the She'erit Hapletah was for the first time acknowledged outside Germany by Philip Friedman, "Dos gedrukte vort ba der sheyres hapleyte in Daytshland/Dos kultur lebn fun der sheyres hapleyte in Daytshland in ir eygenem shpigl," *Tsukunft* 151 (1949): 151–55.

4. Koppel S. Pinson, General directive for educational program JDC in Germany and Austria, April 25, 1946, Record group (hereafter RG) 294.1, folder 10, Archives of the YIVO Institute for Jewish Research (hereafter YIVO).

5. Koppel S. Pinson, "Jewish Life in Liberated Germany," *Jewish Social Studies* 9, no. 1 (1947): 101–26. This study is widely cited and has served—without a discussion of its genesis—as an influential text about the ideology of the Jewish DPs. See, for example, Cilly Kugelmann, "The Identity and Ideology of Jewish Displaced Persons," in *Jews, Germans, Memory: Reconstructions of Jewish Life in Germany*, edited by Y. Michal Bodemann, 65–76 (Ann Arbor: University of Michigan Press, 1996).

6. J. Szaw, "A modner profesor (feljeton)," *Ibergang*, June 26, 1947.

7. "Farvos a tsaytung?," *Tkhies hameysim*, May 4, 1945. On the genesis of *Tkhies hameysim*, see Yechiel Szeintuch, "'Tekhiyat ha-metim'—ha-iton ha-rishon shel she'erit ha-pleta ve-orkho," *Khulyot* 10 (2006): 191–218.

8. United States Forces, European Theater, directive, "Displaced Persons Publishing Activities," September 9, 1946, RG 294.1, folder 396, frames 0971–73, YIVO.

9. Central Committee of Liberated Jews to Joslow, Culture Officer, Munich, August 5, 1946, RG 294.1, folder 396, frame 0989, YIVO.

10. Literally Hebrew, since the only full set of letters they could obtain in 1945 was Hebrew and not Yiddish. The typesetters spent days scratch-

ing off the Hebrew diacritics, and at some point they ran out of the letter "ayin," a letter frequently used in Yiddish but not in Hebrew. See Avrom Krasniovski, "Vi azoy mir zetsn a tsaytung," *Undzer veg*, May 22, 1946.

11. Goldkorn to Katsherginski, January 15, 1948, RG P18-9, Yad Vashem Archives, Jerusalem.

12. Yitskhok Goldkorn, RG 294.2, folder 1345, YIVO; Shmuel Niger and Yankev Shatski, eds., *Leksikon fun der nayer yidisher literature*, Vol. 2 (New York: Congress for Yiddish Culture, 1958), 89-90.

13. The important role of the press in the dissemination of literary texts was no novelty in the history of Yiddish literature; it had existed ever since the publication of the first Yiddish newspapers in modern times in the 1860s, which featured Sholem Yankev Abramovitsh (Mendele Moykher Sforim), *Dos kleyne mentshele*, as a sequel. The readers of Yiddish literature in the She'erit Hapletah were therefore accustomed to this system.

14. Melvin S. Goldstein to JDC Munich, Subscriptions to forward, Day and journal, April 2, 1947, RG 294.1, folder 396, frame 1012, YIVO; Charles Malamuth to JDC Munich, Yiddish newspapers published outside Germany, August 25, 1947, frame 1018, YIVO; "Khronik: Kultur-amt bam ts.k.; Shrayber-farband," *Hemshekh* 2 (1949): 62.

15. Samuel D. Kassow, "The Left Poale Zion in Inter-War Poland," in *Yiddish and the Left*, edited by Gennady Estraikh and Mikhail Krutikov, 109–28 (Oxford, UK: European Humanities Research Centre, 2001).

16. Boris Sapir, "Central Europe," *American Jewish Year Book* 51 (1950): 315.

17. Editors of *Undzer veg* to Volpe, January 1, 1950, RG 4-1683, letter 349, Jewish National and University Library Archives, Jerusalem (hereafter JNUL).

18. Ruven Rubinshteyn, "Der shrayber in der sheyres-hapleyte," *Undzer veg*, November 11, 1947.

19. Lucy Schildkret Dawidowicz (1915–1990) Papers 1938–90, RG P-675, box 55, folder 3, Munich, November 17, 1946, American Jewish Historical Society, Newton Centre, Massachusetts, and New York, New York.

20. lange nun, "A zhurnal aza (nit keyn retsenzye)," *Dos vort*, February 6, 1948.

21. Minutes of the Writers' Union, September 19, 1947, RG 294.2, folder 1343, YIVO.

22. Ben-Tsien Hibel and Philip Friedman, eds., *Shriftn far literatur, kunst un gezelshaftlekhe fragn* (Kassel: Hessische Nachrichten, 1948); Yosef Gar, Baruch Graubard, Dovid Volpe, and Philip Friedman, eds., *Hemshekh: Shriftn far literatur, kunst, kritik un kultur-gezelshaftlekhe frages*, Vols. 1 and 2 (Munich: Direktorium far dertsiung un kultur un shrayber-farband fun der sheyres-hapleyte, 1948–49).

23. S. Lewis Gaber to Samuel Haber, September 26, 1948, RG 294.2, folder 400, frame 1279, YIVO.

24. Moyshe Fridenzon, "Yerlekhe konferents fun yid: Shrayber, zhurnalistn un kinstler," *Jidisze cajtung*, November 14, 1947.

25. Program "Fun der fayerlekher 'Mendele-Akademye,' gevidmet dem 30tn yortsayt funem 'zeydn' fun undzer moderner literatur, dinstik dem 30tn detsember 1947" ["Solemn 'Mendele-Akademye,' in honor of the 30th anniversary of the death of the grandfather of our modern literature, Tuesday, December 30, 1947"], RG 294.2, folder 1560, YIVO.

26. Samuel Gringauz, "'Yidishe bilder'—REDIVIVUS!," *Yidishe bilder* 1 (1947): 1.

27. Hershl Vaynroykh, "Jidisze Literatur Problemen (Diskusje Artikl)," *Ibergang*, December 20, 1946.

28. Ibid.

29. Mordkhe Libhaber, "Der kern fun asimilacje un kulturlozigkajt," *Ibergang*, February 2, 1947. A similar rhetoric is also used in Meyer Ushpiz, "Kultur-oyfgabn in der sh[eyres]-h[apleyte]," *Dos vort*, May 5, 1947.

30. Baruch Graubard, "Literatur-problemen in der sheyres-hapleyte," *Bafrayung*, December 31, 1948.

31. Mordkhe Kroshnits, "Tsum problem fun a yidishn kultur-kongres (oystsugn fun a referat gehaltn af der konferents fun shrayber-farband)," *Bafrayung*, November 14, 1947.

32. Baruch Graubard, "Vegn a sheyres-hapleyte-almanakh," *Bafrayung*, November 19, 1948.

33. M. Verstaendig, "Refleksn iber jeusz un trejst," *Ibergang*, January 26, 1947.

34. Although it was called the International Congress for Jewish Culture, the congress represented only a fraction of the contemporary Jewish world. The congress was organized by members of Poale Zion, Bundists, and several nonpartisan groups and personalities. Moreover, communist countries boycotted the congress.

35. L. Sinal, "Undzer yidish kultur-lebn," *Dos vort*, January 23, 1948. In a similar vein, see also Levi Shalit, "Nokhn kultur-kongres," *Jidisze cajtung*, August 16, 1948.

36. Mordkhe Kroshnits, "Tsum problem fun a yidishn kultur-kongres (oystsugn fun a referat gehaltn af der konferents fun shrayber-farband)," *Bafrayung*, November 14, 1947.

37. Yitskhok Goldkorn, "Far an alveltlekhn yidishn kultur-kongres," *Nayvelt*, November 9, 1947.

38. Yitshok Goldkorn, "A kultur fun kongresn," *Bafrayung*, July 16, 1948.

39. Samuel Gringauz, "Ein Kongress für uns," *Neue Welt*, October 12, 1948.

40. Board for Education and Culture, RG 294.1, folder 407, frame 0290, YIVO. My emphasis.

41. Yankev Patt, "A kheyrem af yidish in di lagern," *Forverts*, March 2, 1947.

42. F. Inster, "Yankev Patt—un der 'kheyrem af yidish' in di lagern in Daytshland," *Bafrayung*, May 11, 1947. As regards the critical stance of Poale Zion in this matter, see M. Tshinshtork, "Tsvishn di shures," *Bafrayung*, June 27, 1947.

43. A. Krigel, "Efsher yo a kheyrem?," *Nayvelt*, November 9, 1947.

44. Lucy Dawidowicz, for example, knew of no such discrimination, where-

as the DP writers Mendel Mann and Hershl Vaynroykh attested to it. Vaynroykh to Rivlin, Geltendorf, May 1947, RG 701, folder 459, YIVO; Cable, Gerovitsh to Patt, April 5, 1947, RG 7015, microfilm MK 90, box 33, folder 19, Tamiment Library & Robert F. Wagner Labor Archives, New York (hereafter Tamiment); Cable, Leyvik/Novick to Schildkret, May 3, 1947, RG 7015, microfilm MK 90, box 33, folder 19, Tamiment.

45. In Bad Reichenhall, for instance, a leaflet dating from 1947 contains slogans such as "Jews, remember the past, don't let the *Bund* lead you back into the ghettos, to the crematoria!" Leaflet, Wagner 232, box 5, folder 95, Tamiment. See also Gerovitsh to Patt, April 28, 1947, Wagner 232, box 5, folder 95, Tamiment; Letter Labor Committee, [1947], Wagner 232, box 5, folder 95, Tamiment; Patt to Sobel, April 26, 1947, file GI/21B/S-1104, Joint Distribution Committee Archives, Jerusalem.

46. Mosze Lestni, "Di ofensiwe fun 'Bund' un zajne sibes," *Jidisze cajtung*, June 6, 1947.

47. "Keyn shum boykot af yidish in di lagern," *Bafrayung*, May 18, 1947.

48. Fridenzon, "Yerlekhe konferents fun yid."

49. Yitskhok Goldkorn, "Yidish—in Amerike," *Bafrayung*, July 25, 1947.

50. For the situation of Yiddish in the Yishuv, see Arye Leyb Pilovski, *Tsvishn yo un neyn: Yidish un yidish-literatur in Erets-Yisroel, 1907–1948* (Tel Aviv: World Council for Yiddish and Yiddish Culture, 1986), 227–50; and Tom Segev, *One Palestine, Complete* (New York: Holt, 2000), 263–69.

51. Levi Shalit, "Naye trit af alte vegn (mikoyekh yidish loshn in yidishn land)," *Der morgn*, May 20, 1949. Since the revisionist newspaper *Undzer velt*, of which Shalit was a regular contributor, refused the publication of this article, he chose to publish it in the *Mapam* newspaper in Germany.

52. Mendel Mann to Meylekh Tshemni, September 6, 1952, Archive Tshemni, JNUL.

53. Mendel Mann to Meylekh Tshemni, August 9, 1953, Archive Tshemni, JNUL.

54. Yitskhok Perlov, *"Ekzodus 1947": Poeme un andere lider* (Munich: Bafrayung, 1948); idem, *Di mentshn fun ekzodus: Roman* (Buenos Aires: Tsentral-farband fun poylishe yidn in Argentine, 1949).

55. On the language question during the first years of statehood, see Rachel Rojanski, "The Status of Yiddish in Israel, 1948–1951: An Overview," in *Yiddish after the Holocaust*, edited by Joseph Sherman, 46–59 (Oxford, UK: Boulevard Books, 2004), 46–59.

56. Yitskhok Perlov, "Eyner fun di zekhtsik alarmirt," *Der veker*, August 1951. Mendel Mann settled in Paris after a decade in Israel, and Levi Shalit went to Johannesburg after a short stay in Tel Aviv.

57. Moyshe Lestni, "Natsionale profanatsye," *Naye yidishe tsaytung*, December 1, 1950. See also *Grupe jidisze kultur-tuer in Minchen*, October 30, 1950, Mordechai Bernstein Collection, box 5, folder 8, Yeshiva University Archives, New York.

58. Bund-Archives, RG ME-18, box 1270, folder 173, *naye faktn vegn der "likvidatsye" fun di yidishe di-pi-lagern in Daytshland,* file 1400, YIVO.

59. In 1948 only eight out of thirty-five members did not live in Munich. Mitglieder fun Schreiber, Journalistn-un Kinstler-farband fun Scheirith Hapleita in Deitschland (American zone) [1948], RG 7015, microfilm MK 253, box 86, folder 15, Tamiment.

60. In fact, it seems that some of the writers did not publish according to party lines but instead took advantage of any possibility to get on the payroll of an editorial board.

61. Shmerke Katsherginski, *Shmerke Katsherginski ondenk-bukh* (Buenos Aires: Aroysgegebn fun a komitet, 1955), 425.

62. Y. B. Alterman, "Tsvey konferentsn," *Dos vort,* March 7, 1947.

63. Meylekh Tshemni, "Di 'khasene' in Fernvald . . . ," *Naye yidishe tsaytung,* December 15, 1950.

64. Baruch Graubard, *Geven a sheyres-hapleyte: Notitsbukh fun Moyshe Yoslen* (München: Farlag Moyshe Yosl, 1949). The satires previously appeared in the Poale Zionist newspaper *Bafrayung.*

65. Baruch Graubard, "Der 'sheyres-hapleyte'-etap in yidishn teater," *Hemshekh* 2 (1949): 25.

66. Michael Marrus, *The Unwanted: European Refugees in the Twentieth Century* (New York: Oxford University Press, 1985), 8.

67. Anita Shapira, "Whatever Became of 'Negating Exile'?," in *Israeli Identity in Transition,* edited by Anita Shapira (Westport, CT: Praeger, 2004), 70.

Glossary of Hebrew and Yiddish Terms

aliyah	Ascent. Jewish immigration to the land of Israel.
Amoleykim	Amalekites.
asefa	Assembly.
bochers	Boys.
Bricha	Flight. The movement to lead Holocaust survivors out of Europe to Palestine.
chalutz(im)	Pioneer(s). Agricultural laborers in Palestine.
chuppah	Wedding canopy.
Eretz Israel	The Land of Israel.
Goldene Medinah	Literally, the Golden Land. A synonym for the United States of America.
Ha'apalah	Upward struggle. Clandestine immigration to Palestine.
hakhsharah	Preparation. Agricultural training in preparation for aliyah.
halutziut	The pioneering way.
judenrein	Cleansed of Jews.
katsetler	Concentration camp inmate.
kehillot	Religious communities.
kibbutz(im)	The term used to refer to collective groups organized by Zionist youth movements in postwar Europe. Also used to refer to agricultural settlements in Palestine.
kibuts galuyot	Ingathering of the exiles.
kippot	Religious head coverings.
kordinazia	Coordinated organization.
Kristallnacht	The Night of Broken Glass.
landsmanschaftn	Hometown social groups.
lebenswelten	Life world.

madrich (pl. *madrichim*)	Leader. Title applied to instructors in Zionist youth groups.
mamzerim	Illegitimate children born of a forbidden relationship.
mezuzah	Parchment inscribed with specific verses from the Torah and affixed to the doorframe of a Jewish home.
mikvah (pl., *mikvaot*)	Ritual bath.
mir zaynen doh	Yiddish phrase meaning "we are here."
mishpocha	Family.
mohalim	Ritual circumcisers.
musselmen	Older concentration camp inmate who were the weakest and least likely to survive.
oneg shabbes	Enjoying the Sabbath.
Ostjuden	Eastern Jews.
payas	Earlocks.
protokolant	Protocol writer.
seforim	Hebrew-language books for learning Torah, ritual, and religious law.
shaliach (f., *shlichah*; pl., *shlichim*)	Emissary. Representative from the Yishuv assigned to promote aliyah from the Diaspora.
She'erit Hapletah	Surviving Remnant. The term used to refer to the community of Jewish Holocaust survivors in Europe.
shituf	Sharing.
shlichim	Emissaries.
shlilat galut germaniyah	Negation of the unloved German Diaspora.
shlilat ha-golah	Negation of exile.
simcha	Festive or joyous occasion.
Shoah	Holocaust.
tales (pl., *taleisim*)	Prayer shawl.
tefillin	Prayer phylacteries.
Verfluchte deutsche Erde	Accursed German soil.
Yishuv	Settlement. The term used to refer to the Jewish community in Palestine.

CONTRIBUTORS

MICHAEL BERKOWITZ is professor of modern Jewish history in the Department of Hebrew and Jewish Studies at University College London and was president of the British Association of Jewish Studies in 2007. He is author of *The Crime of My Very Existence: Nazism and the Myth of Jewish Criminality, The Jewish Self-Image, Western Jewry and the Zionist Project*, and *Zionist Culture and West European Jewry before the First World War*. He has also co-edited (with Ruti Ungar) *Fighting Back? Jewish and Black Boxers in Britain;* edited *Nationalism, Zionism, and the Ethnic Mobilization of the Jews;* and co-edited (with Susan Tananbaum and Sam Bloom) *Forging Modern Jewish Identities*.

SUZANNE BROWN-FLEMING is senior program officer in the University Programs Division of the United States Holocaust Memorial Museum's Center for Advanced Holocaust Studies (CAHS) and a former Center Fellow (2000). Her book, *The Holocaust and Catholic Conscience: Cardinal Aloisius Muench and the Guilt Question in Germany*, was among the 2006 University Press Books Selected for Public and Secondary School Libraries by the American Association of University Presses (Category of Religion). Dr. Brown-Fleming's current research project, "The Vatican-German Relationship Re-Examined, 1922–1939," is a study of the Vatican nunciature in Munich and Berlin during the Weimar Republic (1918–33) and the period of Eugenio Pacelli's tenure as Secretary of State (1930–39).

BETH B. COHEN teaches at California State University, Northridge. In 2004–5, she was a "Life Reborn" Fellow at the U.S. Holocaust Memorial Museum's Center for Advanced Holocaust Studies. Her first book, *Case Closed: Holocaust Survivors in America*, challenges the prevailing optimistic perception of the lives of Holocaust survivors in postwar America by scrutinizing their first years through the eyes of those who lived it. She is the recipient of numerous prestigious awards and fellowships and is the former director of education at the Rhode Island Holocaust Memorial Museum.

BOAZ COHEN is the head of the Holocaust studies program of the Western Galilee College in Acco, Israel. He is also a researcher in Bar-Ilan University's "Voices of Child Survivors: Children's Holocaust Testimonies" project and is the author of an essay titled "The Children's Voice: Postwar Collection of Testimonies from Child Survivors of the Holocaust" in *Holocaust and Genocide Studies*. His dissertation, "Holocaust Research in Israel 1945–1980: Characteristics, Trends, Developments," traces the way the research and academic study of the Holocaust developed in Israel. He is now researching early Holocaust testimonies, especially those taken from children in the immediate aftermath of the Holocaust.

MARGARETE MYERS FEINSTEIN holds a Ph.D. in modern European history from the University of California at Davis. Interested in questions of identity and legacies of the Nazi regime, her research has focused on postwar German national identity and Jewish displaced persons. She is the author of *State Symbols: The Quest for Legitimacy in the Federal Republic of Germany and the German Democratic Republic, 1949–1959* as well as numerous articles. Her latest book, *Holocaust Survivors in Postwar Germany, 1945–1957*, will be released in 2010 by Cambridge University Press.

SHIRLI GILBERT is Karten Lecturer in Jewish/non-Jewish relations at the University of Southampton. She obtained her D.Phil. in modern history at the University of Oxford. Her research is currently focused in two principal areas: cultural life among Jewish displaced persons (1945–48), and Holocaust memory in apartheid and post-apartheid South Africa. Her book *Music in the Holocaust: Confronting Life in the Nazi Ghettos and Camps* was a finalist for the 2005 National Jewish Book Award.

ATINA GROSSMANN teaches modern European and German history and women's and gender studies at The Cooper Union in New York City. Her publications include *Reforming Sex: The German Movement for Birth Control and Abortion Reform 1920–1950;* co-edited collections *When Biology Became Destiny: Women in Weimar and Nazi Germany* and *Crimes of War: Guilt and Denial in the Twentieth Century;* and numerous articles on gender, modernity, war and genocide, and German and Jewish memory in twentieth-century Germany. Her most recent book, *Jews, Germans, and Allies: Close Encounters in Occupied Germany*, won the Fraenkel Prize in Contemporary History from the Wiener Library, London.

LAURA J. HILTON is an associate professor of history at Muskingum College in New Concord, Ohio, where she teaches courses in modern European and world history. She has recently published an article on Polish and Latvian displaced persons and cultural nationalism in *The Historian*. She is working on a monograph that examines the interaction of Jewish, Polish, and Latvian DPs with occupation authorities, the German population, and staff from intergovernmental and voluntary agencies from 1945–52 in the American Zone in Germany.

LAURA JOCKUSCH is currently a post-doctoral fellow at the International Institute for Holocaust Research at Yad Vashem, Jerusalem, and at the Department of Jewish History at Ben-Gurion University of the Negev, Beer Sheva, Israel, where she teaches modern Jewish history. She received her Ph.D. in modern Jewish history at New York University, where her dissertation examined the beginnings of Holocaust research in the immediate aftermath of the Second World War. Her publications in English include "*Khurbn Forshung*—Jewish Historical Commissions in Europe, 1943–1949" in the *Simon Dubnow Institute Yearbook* and "Chroniclers of Catastrophe: History Writing as a Jewish Response to Persecution before and after the Holocaust" in *Holocaust Historiography in Context.*

HAGIT LAVSKY is the Samuel L. and Perry Haber Chair in Post-Holocaust Studies at the Institute of Contemporary Jewry at the Department of Jewish History at Hebrew University in Jerusalem. She is the author, editor, and co-editor of six books including *New Beginnings: Holocaust Survivors in Bergen-Belsen and the British Zone* and *Before Catastrophe: The Distinctive Path of German Zionism, 1918–1932,* which won the Arnold Wiznitzer Prize for best book of the year in the field of Jewish history. Prof. Lavsky has held visiting professorships at Harvard University, Brandeis University, New York University, UCLA, and was a 2004–5 Matthew Family Fellow at the Center for Advanced Holocaust Studies of the USHMM.

TAMAR LEWINSKY is a lecturer for Yiddish language in the Department of Jewish History at the University of Munich. She received her Ph.D. in history at the Ludwig-Maximilian University of Munich, where her thesis focused on Yiddish literature and culture among Jewish DPs in Germany. She also serves as coordinator and co-author of the fifth volume of *German-Jewish History in Modern Times.* She is the author of *Displaced Poets: Jiddische Schriftsteller im Nachkriegsdeutschland, 1945–1951* and has published various articles on German-Jewish postwar history.

AVINOAM J. PATT is the Philip D. Feltman Professor of Modern Jewish History at the Maurice Greenberg Center for Judaic Studies at the University of Hartford, where he is also director of the Sherman Museum of Jewish Civilization. He previously worked as the Miles Lerman Applied Research Scholar for Jewish Life and Culture at the United States Holocaust Memorial Museum (USHMM). His first book, *Finding Home and Homeland: Jewish Youth and Zionism in the Aftermath of the Holocaust* (Wayne State University Press, 2009) examines young survivors in Europe after the Holocaust and their role in the creation of the state of Israel. He is currently writing an archival document collection titled *Jewish Responses to Persecution,* which will be published by the USHMM for use by university professors and scholars.

Index

Page numbers in italics refer to illustrations

211; DP conflict with German police, 181; DP contact with former Nazis and SS, 56, 180–81; DP recruitment of Germans for sports teams, 25n7; German association of Jews with communism, 175; German blame for anti-Semitism on Jews, 177; German evasion of responsibility for DPs' situation, 178; German negative stereotypes of Jewish DPs, 8, 168–78, 185; German perceptions of DPs as criminals, 167–85; German perceptions of privileged or powerful Jewish DPs, 169; German refusal to sell food or clothing to Jews, 184; Germans as workers in Jewish DP camps, 16, 18, 19; Germans' sexuality-related fears of Jews, 174; interactions in everyday life, 15–17, 21–22; Jewish aggression and defiance of authority, 179–80; Jewish men, sex with and marriage to German women, 18–19; and reversed power dynamic, 16, 179; violent confrontations, 17

German women: employment as nurses and domestic servants for Jewish DPS, 18, 19; fraternization with American GIs, 174; sex with Jewish men, 18–19

Germany: *See* American Zone of occupation; British Zone of occupation; German Jews; Germans, relations with Jewish DPs

Gestapo, 181

ghettos: Kovno Ghetto, 80–82, 83, 85, 268; Łódź Ghetto, 81; Podhajce Ghetto, 88; Theresienstadt Ghetto, 205; Vilna Ghetto, 120, 134n67, 307n31; Warsaw Ghetto Uprising, 119–20, 318

Glassgold, Abraham, *110*

Glik, Hirsch, 3, 216n1

Gnadenwald DP camp, 182

Goldberg, Markus, 171

Goldene Keyt, di (The Golden Chain newspaper) (325)

Goldene Medinah, 8

Goldkorn, Yitskhok, 312, 321, 324

Gordoniah youth movement, 108, 130n38

Gottlieb, Hayim-Meir, 1

Gräfenberg, Richard, 57

Grammes, Phillip, 25n7

Graubard, Baruch, 242, 268, 269, 327

Great Britain: Mandate in Palestine, 138, 247; White Paper of 1939, 138, 254n48. *See also* British Jewish community; British zone of occupation

Greek Jews, 102

Greenberg, Gershon, 257

Greenleigh, Arthur (Executive Director, USNA), 142

Grilihes (Grillechs), Ela, 84

Grinberg, Zalman, 123, 129n34

Gringauz, Samuel, 108, 109, 123, 129n34, 318, 321

Grossmann, Atina, 275

Groth, Alexander J.: *Holocaust Voices*, 280, 287nn89, 92

Grüber, Heinrich, 167

Gruenbaum, Eliyahu, 105

Guy, Trevor, 210–11

Ha'apala, 42

Haber, William, 220n38

Haganah, 124n5

hakhsharah (training farms), 109–14; confirmed necessity of immigration to Palestine, *112;* defined, 124n3; growth of in American zone, *112*

Ha-Kibbutz Ha-Me'uhad (United Kibbutz Movement), 130n38

Halberstam, Yekusiel, 278

Halpern, Sam, 273

halutziut, 119

Hamburg, 228

Hano'ar Hazioni, 83

Hapo'el Hamizrahi (religious Zionists), 239

The Happy Boys, 292–93, *294,* 296, 297

Harrison, Earl, 105, 128n26, 128n27, 137, 186n6, 200, 230; head of Citizens Committee for Displaced Persons, 219n33; recommendation for immigration to Palestine, 239

Harrison Report, 109, 126n14, 137, 176, 186n6, 195, 199; and DP housing, 211; focus of attention on resettlement and Palestine, 200; resulted in German Jews being

youths as unsuitable for agricultural labor, 111; and educational system at Bergen-Belsen, 243; and surviving children, 74

Jewish Brigade, 102, 105, 198; in British Zone, 237; and educational system at Bergen-Belsen, 243; first postwar contact with Jews, 218n23; and Zeilsheim DPs, 212

Jewish Committee for Relief Abroad (JCRA), 234

Jewish DP tribunals (*Ehrengerichte*), 19

Jewish Family and Children's Services (JFCS), Boston: art therapy programs, 154; strategies for refugee children, 153–56

Jewish Family and Children's Services (JFCS), Denver, Colorado, 137, 142, 143

Jewish Historical Commission, Belsen, *Undzer khurbn in bild*, 52

Jewish Historical Commission, Göttingen, 52, 55, 57

Jewish Historical Commission, Leipheim, 42

Jewish Historical Commission, Lower-Saxonia, 33

Jewish Historical Commissions, in DP camps of Germany, Austria, and Italy, 31–73; broad concept of historical sources, 50–51, 53; call to Jews for accurate account of Jewish suffering, 38–39; collection of eyewitness testimonies from survivors and Nazi data, 31; concern that DP obsession with past would harm historical work, 40; conflicts with German Jewish survivors, 56–58; contact with Jewish research institutions in Palestine, 58; difficulty in motivating survivors, 40–42, 43, 60; display of material in exhibitions, 46; distrust of accounts of non-Jewish Germans, 39, 54–58; editing of testimonies, 52; foundation of, 32–35; goal of bringing perpetrators to justice in Austria, 34; historical documentation as holy work, 35; impact on Holocaust documentation, 58–60; interaction with larger public of She'erit Hapletah, 39–49; motivations

behind, 35–39; pace in collecting testimonies, 42–43; preparation for historical writing, 53; propaganda posters (*propagande plakatn*), 44–46; propaganda work, 43–49; and psychological burden of recording past, 41; questionnaires, 51; relations with YIVO and other American Jewish institutions, 58–60; research methods, 50–54; transmission of material to Israel, 59; use of nonprofessional *zamlers*, 49, 53

Jewish Historical Documentation in Vienna, 49

Jewish Labor Committee, New York, 312, 322

Jewish Relief Unit (JRU), 234–35, 243, 247–48

Jewish welfare organizations, 232–36; aid from British Jewry, 233, 234–35; aid from Palestine, 233; and British policy, 232–33; cooperation between Zionists and non-Zionists, 235–36; headquartered in American zone, 232

Jidisze cajtung, 314

Jockusch, Laura, 301

kaddish, 258, 259, 264, 265, 267, 268, 283n6

Kaganowicz, Moyshe, 34, 52, 64n21

Kahana, Rabbi Shlomo David, 273

Kaplan, Israel, 8, 33, 41, 46, 51–52, 53; biography, 63; and collection of children's testimonies, 75, 76–80; *In der tog-teglekher historisher arbet*, 52; *Dos folks-moyl in natsi klem*, 52; editor of *Fun Letsten Hurbn*, 76; immigration to Israel, 59; relationship with son, 78–80; with son Shalom, *80, 81*

Kaplan, Shalom (Shalom Eilati), 79, *80, 81*

Kaplan, Yosef, 120, 133n55

katsetler, 45

Katsherginski, Shmerke, 290, 300, 301, 302–3, 312; *Lider fun di Getos un Lagern* (with H., Leivick), 305n4; on Shtetl-like structure of DP camps, 327

Katz, Karl, 239

Katz, Nathan, 287n93

Kazet-Teater (Concentration Camp Theater), 292
Kertzer, David, 282
kever Yisrael, 260
Kibbutz Atid, 83
Kibbutz Buchenwald, 105–7; diary of, 1; dual function of, 106; immigration of original members to Palestine, 109; success in improving DP morale preparing for future, 109–10, 131n46
Kibbutz Ha-Arzi (National Kibbutz movement), 130n38
Kibbutz Hakhshara Tradate, Italy, 299
kibbutzim: appeal to young Jewish survivors, 8; Jewish displaced youths and Zionism in, 98–124; occupied by youths from Poland or Soviet Union, 114; postwar meaning of, 124n3; psychological support for displaced youths, 116–17
Kibbutz Lochamei HaGetaot al shem Tosia Altman, 114–23; celebrations of Jewish and Zionist holidays, 117–18; contact with Germans, 120; daily structure, 117; diary, *115;* education and cultural activities, 117; growth of Zionist enthusiasm, 116, 117; immigration to Palestine, 116, 121–23; *madrichim,* 114, 118; nature activities, 118–19; *oneg shabbes,* 117–18
Kibbutz Mishmar HaEmek, Palestine, 119
kibbutz movements, Palestine, 130n38
Kibbutz Nili, 98–99, 110, 114, 121; members of carrying rakes and hoes, *122*
Kibbutz Shmuel Breslaw, 122
Kibbutz Tosia Altman. *See* Kibbutz Lochamei HaGetaot al shem Tosia Altman
Kibbutz Yosef Kaplan, 118–19
kibuts galuyot, 319–20
Kielce pogrom, 231
kippot, 258
Klausenberg Hasidic dynasty, 278
Klausner, Abraham, 79, 103, 104, 105, *110,* 127n19
Kliger, Ruth, 127n22
Klinger, Chaya, 120
Kloster-Indersdorf displaced children's

center, 174, 179
Korczak, Janusz, 118
kordinazia, 74
Korzcak, Ruzhka, 120
kosher food, difficulty of procuring in camps, 279
Kovner, Abba, 120, 134n67
Kovno Ghetto, 80–82, 83, 85; October Action, 268
Kovno Ghetto orchestra, 292
Krecht, Otto, 171
Kristallnacht (Night of the Broken Glass), 206
Kubowitzki, Leon, 207
Kvintman, Yitzkhok, 42
KZ (Konzentratzionslager)Jews
KZ Yiddish theater, 239

Labor Federation (Histadrut), 130n36
Lag B'Omer, 273, 286n68
Lagerausweise, 16
Landau, Ernst, 258
Landau, Gladys, 273
Landau, Jonas, 180
Landkreis Dachau, 174
Land of Israel studies, 237
Landsberg, 309
Landsberg DP camp, 108, 170, 187n15, 231; Ben-Gurion's visit to, 109; camp newspaper, 98–99; kibbutz, 114, 117; *mikvah,* 270; mourning academy (*troyer akademyen*), 268; registration of births, 276; riots, 181
landsmanschaftn, 140
language war, between Hebrew and Yiddish, 319, 322–28, 329
Lasker-Wallfisch, Anita, 293, 295
Laufer, Berl Dov, 239
La Vista, Vincent: *The Modern Wandering Jew* (La Vista), 175–77
Lazaroff Schaver, Emma, 291–92
League for Labor Palestine, 133n57
Left Po'ale Tsion, 2, 314, 322–23
Leib, M., 211
Leipheim DP camp 118, 117, 170
Leivick, H., 291
Lemberg, 183
Lestni, Moyshe, 323
Levinthal, Louis, 220n38
Levy, Isaac, 14, 271–72
Lewin, Abraham, *294*

Lewin, Itchak, *294*
Lewin, Jacob, 83–84
Lewin, Josel, *294*
Lewin, Kurt, 233
Lewinsky, Tamar, 30n30
Liberation Concert, 292
Libhaber, Mordkhe, 314, 319
Lichtenau-bei-Kessel (Hesse), 183
Lichtenstern, Oscar, 183
Limburg, 171
Lindenfels DP camp, 83
Linz, 56
literary journals, 308
Lithuanian Jewry, remembrance of, 268
Łódź Ghetto, 81
Lopatin, 183
Lowenthal, E. G., 235
Lower Saxony, 228
Lüneburg trials, 239
Lustiger, Arno, 179–80, 198, 219n30

madrichim, 114
Mainz, 177
mamzerim, 272
Mankowitz, Zeev, 100, 219n28, 265
Mann, Mendel, 325, 333n44
Mapam newspapers, 334n51
Marcus, Robert, 208
Margolis, Dora, 154
Mariels, Lyle, 262, 263
Marrano community, Amsterdam, 319
marriages, Jewish DPs, 269–75;
    accompanied by sorrow, 273–75;
    bending of rules for, 271–72; cards
    in honor of, *274;* common-law
    marriage, 272; difficulty in proving
    death of a spouse before remarriage,
    272–73; and family purity laws,
    270–71; instruction in Jewish marital
    relations, 270–71
Marrus, Michael, 328
martyrdom, 302
Marx, Karl, 261
mass graves, 259, 261, 263, 264, 268
matrilineal descent, 276
Mauthausen, 84
McCloy, John J., 207
McNarney, General Joseph, 168, 172,
    189n31
memory: collective, 242, 268, 269; and
    music, 301–3

Menuhim, Yehudi, 290–91
Mercedes Benz, 169
Michigan Society of Fellows, 304
mikvah, 270–71, 275, 279
Milch, Arieh, 78, 82–83, 91
military chaplains, 102–3, 204, 208,
    220n38, 258, 271–72
Mintzer, Oscar, 202, 209, 212–13, 213
minyan, 258, 260, 283n5
mir zaynen doh ("we are here"), 3, *21,*
    195, 216
Mishmar Hanegev children's home,
    Ludwikowo, 83
Mizrahi, 266–67
mohalim, 282
Möhlstrasse, 16
Morgan, Frederick, 176
mourning academies (*troyer akademyen*),
    268–69. *See also* commemoration of
    dead, Jewish DPs
mourning assemblies, 281–82
Muench, Bishop Aloisius, 171, 172, 174,
    177, 188n27
Munich: cultural activity after liquidation
    of DP camps, 326; as printing center,
    309
music, among Jewish DPs, 289–
    304; expression of longing for
    Palestine, 297–300; and memory,
    301–3; musical performance by
    visiting artists, 290–92; musical
    performances by DPs, 292–95;
    newly created songs by DPs, 295–
    300
Mutzman, Abraham, *294*

Nadich, Rabbi Judah, 128n26, 131n46,
    204, 220n38, 253n31
National Catholic Welfare Conference,
    177
National Council of Jewish Women's
    Service to Foreign Born, 138
National Jewish Hospital, Denver,
    142–43
National Refugee Service, 138
National Socialism, 177
National Sound Archive, Jerusalem,
    305n4
Naye yidishe tsaytung (New Jewish
    Newspaper), 326
Nayvelt (New World), 314

of kibbutz groups, 116–17; and collection of children's testimonies, 78; East European DPs from, 66n61, 102, 195, 201, 231
police, DP, 171, 179, 284n28
policy, regarding Jewish DPs: and classification as "Jewish," 126n14, 194, 198; effect on three key policy decisions, 194–95; inclusion in local decision making, 194
Polish Hasidim, 232
Polman, Lola, 325
population, Jewish DPs: in Bavaria in 1946, 128n22; in continental Europe in 1947, 3; from Eastern Europe, 24, 169; in Europe in 1948, 170; in Federal Republic in 1959, 170; in Germany, Austria, and Italy in 1945 and 1946, 169, 187n11; in Germany after liberation, 1, 9, 102–5; in Germany in 1947, 170, 231; higher Jewish birth rate than any world population in 1946–47, 14; from Hungary and Romania, 126n16; immigration to Israel, 170; immigration to U.S., 5, 170; Jewish population of Germany, 1933 and 1946–47, 14; as percentage of all European DPs, 169
Posnansky, Arthur, 105
post-traumatic stress disorder (PTSD), 150
Potsdam Agreement, 169
Purim, 118

questionnaires, Jewish Historical Commissions, 51, 68n87

Rabbinic authority: and *agunot*, 272, 273; and marriages, 271–72; and *mikvah*, 270, 271; and reburial of victims, 263
Rabbinic Council of U.S. zone: establishment of yeshivas, 278; and problem of DP *agunot*, 273
rabbis, DP, 270
Regensburg, 309
Reifsmeier, Sister, 174–75
Reik, Chaviva, 133n55
Reilly, Joanne: *Belsen: The Liberation of a Concentration Camp*, 254n48
religious belief and practice, 9–10,

279–82; adolescents, pre-and post-Holocaust, 280–81; legacy of prewar upbringing, 269–70; Orthodox Jews, 279, 282, 287n87; secular Jews, 279, 282, 287n87. *See also* childbirth, among Jewish DPs; commemoration of dead, Jewish DPs; marriages, Jewish DPs
repatriation, Jewish rejection of, 195, 197, 198–99
Representative Orchestra of the She'erit Hapletah, 292
resilience, 221n49
Revisionist Zionist Movement, 62n5, 308
Richter, Josef (Tzunik), 121
Rifkind, Simon, 128n26, 200, 220n38, 253n31
Rimalt, Elimelech, 124n8
Ringelblum, Emmanuel, 37
Ringelblum archive, 93
ritual: and maintenance of ethnic identity for secular Jews, 279, 282, 287n87; power of, 282. *See also* childbirth, among Jewish DPs; commemoration of dead; marriages, Jewish DPs
Romanian Jews, 102
Roosevelt, Eleanor, 225n102
Rosenberg, Edwin (President, USNA), 141, 149
Rosenberg, Yossel, 236
Rosensaft, Yossel, 239
Rosenthal, David, 32, 62n5, 237, 239
Ross, Ralph, 143
Rozen, Hadasa, 83
Rubenstein, Richard L.: *After Auschwitz: Radical Theology and Contemporary Judaism*, 167
Rubin, Hannah, 145
Rubinshetyn, Ruven, 314, 315, 316, 318, 324
Rubinstein, Erna, 269
Ruhr region, 228
Rupp, Father, 174
Russian DPs, 178, 187n16

Saar region, 228
Sabras, 125n9
Salomon, Emil (Executive Director, Tulsa Jewish Federation), 141

Sandelowski, Amalie, 158
Sayonne, Bernie, 158
Schlachtensee DP camp, circumcision
  ceremony, *277*
Schleswig-Holstein, 228
Schmidt, Samuel, 208, 209, 213–14
Scholars' Workshop on Jewish DPs,
  United States Holocaust Museum,
  30n30
Schwalb, Nathan, 106, 128n24
secondary anti-Semitism, 168
Second Congress of the Liberated Jews
  in the British Zone, *248*
Second Congress of the She'erit
  Hapletah, 240, 241
secular Jews, maintenance of ethnic
  identity through ritual, 279, 282,
  287n87
Segalman, Ralph, 203
Selig, Fannie Stern, 184
Sender, Sadie, 210, 214
Serkess, Leonard, 153, 154
sex, Jewish DP men and German
  women, 18–19
Shalit, Levi, 325, 334n51
Shalom Eilati. *See* Kaplan, Shalom
Shaltiel, David, 127n22
Shapira, Aryeh, 83
Shavuot, 267
She'erit Hapletah (Surviving Remnant),
  14, 21, 22, 195; changing outlook of,
  310–11; commitment to Zionism
  and Jewish identity, 24, 248; early
  political leadership, 106–7; Eastern
  European Jewry as numerical
  core of, 23; education as priority,
  307n26; as exterritorial immigrant
  population, 246; functional Zionism,
  246; invention of in DP camps,
  24–25; means of addressing cultural
  uprootedness, 318–20; *mir zaynen
  doh,* 216; nostalgic view of, 308, 327;
  origin of term, 216n1; and question
  of Yiddish in, 323–24; Representative
  Orchestra of the She'erit Hapletah,
  292; as represented in Bergen-Belsen
  DP camp, 246–50; Second Congress
  of, 240, 241; Third Congress of, 124;
  in U.S. zone of Germany, 38–39;
  youthful demographic makeup, 101.
  See also survivors

Shenhavi, Mordechai, 59
Shochet, 213
Shriftn (Writings), 317
Shuldnreyn, P., 45
Shurz, Genia, 80, 84–85, 87, 88–89,
  90–92
Shushan, Zelig, 119
Shuster, Joseph, 82, 84, 85, 86–87, 90
Shvarts, Pinchas, 45
Silberstein, Elek, *294*
silence, conspiracy of, 150, 158
simcha, 6
Sinka, Ehrling, 178
Sirkin, Nachman, 314
Sittl, Anton Rupert, 169
Sivan, Emmanuel, 125n9
Sochnut (Jewish Agency for Palestine),
  314
social memory, 268, 269
Solomon, Robert, 235
songs: created by DPs, 295–300; as
  historical sources and artifacts,
  301–4; Yiddish folk and theater
  songs, 292
Sosnowiec, 116
South Africa, settlement of Yiddish
  writers and journalists in, 327
South America: escape of former Nazis
  to, 176; settlement of writers and
  journalists in, 327
Soviet Union, postwar Jewish migration
  from, 5, 22–23
Spaismacher, Sam, *294*
SS *General Black,* 136
St. Ottilien Orchestra, 292, 293
statelessness, concept of, 7, 197
State of Israel: declaration of
  independence, 100; foundation
  of, 59, 168, 170, 324; and German
  anti-Semitism, 168; proclamation of
  existence, 325; status of Yiddish in,
  324; and Zionism of DPs, 99–100
Sterling, Simon, 183–84
Stohr, Bishop Albert, 177
Stolpce, 180
Streicher, Julius, 98
Stuttgart, 181, 231, 327
Sukkot, 267
Supreme Headquarters Allied
  Expeditionary Force (SHAEF), 207
survivors: identification of Jewish

displaced persons (DPs) as, 195; preoccupation with recent past, 39–40. *See also* She'erit Hapletah (Surviving Remnant)
survivor testimonies published in *Fun Letsten Hurbn, 1946–1949*, 74–94
"S'vet geshen" (song), 298–99, 300
Szurowicz, 183

Talmud Torah, 278
Tanner, Paul, 177
Tartakower, Arieh, 204
Tarthun, 178
tefillin, 279
Tennenbaum, Benjamin, 93
theater groups, of Jewish DPs, 292
Theresienstadt, 204, 206, 221n58, 232
Theresienstadt Ghetto, 205
Third Congress of the She'erit Hapletah, 46
Third Reich, 167, 171, 181
Tichauer, Erwin, 174, 182
Tirschenreuth Jewish Committee, 262, 263, 264–65
Tisha b'Av, 267
Tkhies hameysim (The Resurrection of the Dead), 311
trauma, 150, 154, 155
Trepman, Paul, 32, 62n5, 237, 239
Truman, Harry S., 105, 136, 138, 186n6, 189n31, 199–200, 230
Truman Directive, 170
Trumpeldor (Josef), 118
Tshemni, Meylekh, 325, 327
Tsiyonim Klali'im (General Zionists), 314, 324, 326
Tu Be-Shevat, 119
Tulas Jewish Federation, 141
Tulipan, Philip, 208, 209, 223n81
Turkov, Yonas, 293
Tydor, Yechezkel, 105, 106

Ukrainian-Jewish DPs, 172
Ulm, 183, 231
Umterwegs (The Transient), *313*
Undzer veg (Our Way), 312, 314, 315
Undzer velt, 334n51
United Nations: Relief and Rehabilitation Administration (UNRRA), 7, 16, 78, 104, 169, 176, 187n12, 195, 228, 262; Special

Committee on Palestine, 123; vote for partition of Palestine, 123
United Partisans Organization, 120, 134n67
United Service for New Americans (USNA): affidavit-granting status, 138–39; depersonalization of Jewish immigrants, 141–42; negotiations with U.S. communities to take in DPs, 140; progressive and humanitarian immigrant care, 149; representative greeting new arrivals, *139*
United States: advocated sending Jewish DPs to Palestine, 138; nativist sentiment, 139; postwar anti-Semitism, 139; restrictive immigration laws, 137
United States Army: commodities given to DPs by soldiers, 183; failure to prioritize needs of Jewish DPs, 211; failure to understand German treatment of DPs, 203–4; lawlessness of soldiers, 184; military chaplains, 102–3, 204, 208, 220n38, 258, 271–72; negative perception of Jews, 195
United States Forces, European Theater (USFET), 168, 211
United Zionist Organization (UZO), 107, 129n34, 130n36
UNRRA (United Nations Relief and Rehabilitation Administration), 104; and exclusion of German Jews from support in British zone, 233; limited sympathy for Jews who rejected repatriation, 195; perceptions of Jewish DPs, 202; support for agricultural training farms, 110–11
Unzer Sztyme (periodical), 32, 62n5, 242; editors, 239; first issue of, 237; official organ of Central Committee of British zone, 244

Vaad Hatzala, 208, 213, 278, 287n83
Van Dam, Henryk, 235
Vaynroykh, Hershl, 318–19, 319, 333n44
Vaysbrod, Avrom: *Ez shtarbt a shetetl,* 52
Veker (Alarm), 323
Velt: Umophengiker zhurnal far politik, literatur un sport Velt, 314
Vendig, Malcolm, 174, 177–78